WOMEN
I'VE
UNDRESSED

WOMEN
I'VE
UNDRESSED

ORRY-KELLY

ALLEN&UNWIN

CONTENTS

Bette Davis
Now, Voyager

FOREWORD

CATHERINE MARTIN

ORRY-KELLY HAD AN inexhaustible appetite for life and experience. He was a romantic at heart, who as a child defied the xenophobia of Australian small-town life by building worlds beyond its borders using only a toy theatre and his red 'Lady's Companion', containing spools of coloured silk, as vehicles for escape.

Orry-Kelly's imagination and capacity to transcend his own provincial experience gave him the skills to create costumes that would support some of the most extraordinary and demanding actresses of his day. This underlying sensitivity to life and all of its complexities would give him the ability to translate story into clothes.

That is not to say he denied his country roots; as a child he was able to sustain his rich imaginary life and his invisible companion Bijou, while also being completely aware that there was no Santa Claus. This ability to call a spade a spade won him many admirers in the dressing room. Actresses felt secure in the notion that the romance of his personality was always combined with the sharpness of his eye to ensure they always looked their best.

One of Orry-Kelly's most enduring collaborations was with the indomitable Bette Davis. As a child I religiously watched the black-and-white Saturday matinee films. My favourites always included films starring Bette Davis. In reacquainting myself with Orry-Kelly's vast career, I was struck by the costumes he designed for Bette's portrayal of Charlotte Vale, the heroine of *Now, Voyager*. The parallels between Nicole Kidman's blue-and-white travelling suit and matching white fedora from the film *Australia* are only too evident. Charlotte Vale's heroic female journey left a lasting psychological imprint on me, and I am sure Orry-Kelly's character-illuminating costumes were an intrinsic part of this imprinting.

Orry-Kelly had an appreciation for high and low culture. He had the dexterity of personality that allowed him to mingle, party and work with the gangland toughs of Prohibition-era New York and, in contrast, both real European and faux Hollywood royalty. Orry-Kelly drew on these multiple friendships in his work, allowing him to dress everyone from the working girl to the most aristocratic of ladies.

Orry-Kelly loved people, both their good and bad points, and drew upon this extraordinary landscape of human character to find indelible inspiration for film. As a designer he always took his work seriously, but never himself. He had a wicked sense of humour and saw the funny side of almost every situation. This self-deprecating humour is well illustrated in the joke he plays on himself in his own memoir when failing to mention his three Oscar wins – not even in passing.

I find it incredibly meaningful and touching that at his funeral his pallbearers included an amazing cast of Hollywood luminaries – Tony Curtis, Cary Grant, Billy Wilder and George Cukor. His eulogy was read by Jack Warner and his three little gold men went to Jack's wife, Ann, Orry's long-time friend and confidante.

He had touched them, not only with the breadth of his work, but also as a friend and as a miraculous character who was able to reach the hearts of so many with his personality, rambunctious spirit and love of the romance of the creative world that could always be just a little bit better than reality.

My favourite films as a child always starred Bette Davis, and Orry-Kelly's designs for Bette in Now, Voyager clearly inspired me when I was designing Nicole Kidman's wardrobe for Australia.

If there's no such thing as Santa, I'll have the red Lady's Companion.

I WAS SIX YEARS OLD the Christmas my mother took me to Major's Emporium in the tiny town of Kiama on the south coast of Australia. In her no-nonsense British manner she said, 'You're a big boy. It's time to know there's no such thing as Santa Claus. How about that set of carpenter's tools?'

Upon a hand-painted card, in the middle of the window, were printed the words: 'A Lady's Companion'. Underneath were two plush boxes – one red, one green – containing many spools of coloured silks. Mother caught me eyeing them and moved me towards a football. But I backed away and announced, 'If there's no such thing as Santa Claus, I'll have the red Lady's Companion.'

From then on my needle was threaded.

'And it's been threaded ever since,' Fanny Brice told me one afternoon as we sat discussing this book. 'When you write about me,' she continued, 'I want you to tell the truth. Don't hedge around, be brutally frank. I've never done anything in my life I'm ashamed of' – she paused, and gave a sly wink – 'but go easy on me, kid!'

'When it comes to me,' I told her, 'I don't know how anyone's going to get a straight storyline.'

She laughed. 'Wasn't it Gracie Allen – of all people – who christened you "Circles Kelly"?'

It was. But Fanny herself would say, when I'd start telling a story, 'Hang on to your hats, kids, here we go again, Orry's talking in circles'.

How right dear Fanny was. My life, like my mind, has never been organised. I run on different currents: my mind AC and my tongue DC. I have never learned to think before I speak. Most Australians are exceedingly thrifty with words, relying more on inflection, but in my youth I found it difficult to soften the H when I was told I must say 'an hotel', and yet I didn't want to drop my H's like the cockney 'help'.

I am not particularly literary. The biggest dunce in my class, there was no one worse in English. At arithmetic I was 'less worse', but I shone in art.

During my life I've been split up by agents in more ways than one, so a split infinitive at this stage of the game isn't going to hurt. I find punctuation complicated. It's full of commas, parentheses, dots and dashes. Who cares if I put a dash instead of a full stop. I put a dash in my name when Warner Brothers engaged me. Mr William Koenig, head of production, said, 'Kelly is too common a name. How do you spell it in French?' I told him Koenigs, Cohens and Kellys remain as is.

Koenig said, 'Fancy it up.'

I hyphenated it.

Through the years, I've received hundreds of letters asking about the hyphen in my name. I've even been asked, 'Are you one or are you two?'

This book is not meant as a complete autobiography, but the prospect of writing even part of my life seems formidable.

Up until a week before she died, Miss Ethel Barrymore read and re-read chapter after chapter. She insisted I write myself; there must be no ghosts. When I told her I felt I needed professional help with the form, she replied, 'You create your own form when you design a dress, don't you, Kelly? Then form your own pattern with the book.' And so I have. I'd like to write simply, without any frills, for my dressmaking world has had enough of those – but then again, certain cities remind me of dresses.

In my fitting room the conversation is not always so fitting. It's full of naked emotions. I see the pretty, not-so-pretty and the 'ugs'. It's those ugly ones with crepe-paper armpits, shrivelled elbows like boiled chicken wings, and knotty knees that spray the fitting room with 'spite-wick'. Disappointed and disillusioned with their careers and their husbands' impotencies, they fuss with ribbons and bows, while thinking of their young beaux-on-the-side.

The fitter rips, pins and pin-pricks. There's much 'oohing' and 'aahing'. Then re-fitting, unzipping and stripping.

Red necked and bottomed, stripped of everything, the 'ugs' rip into the seamy side. Often they have asked me, 'Is that blonde with the multiple top and sway-back bottom really a blonde? Now tell me the naked truth, Orry.'

But Hollywood dislikes naked truths. Truth is rarely served at their dinner parties. When it is, it's so sugar-coated it belongs with the dessert that lacks the squeeze of lemon – that slight tart taste my mother said belonged to any well-prepared sweet. Seldom does Hollywood dish out a wholesome straightforward truth along with the bloody rare roast beef.

This book deals with famous people I have known and dressed. And some I've undressed, draping them in the sheerest chiffon, a fabric the French call *ninon*. It's when these beauties face the three-way mirror in my fitting room, 'ninon over none-on', unmasked, that they let their hair down!

It's their story I want to tell.

When I mentioned that I was writing my life story to writer and producer Sid Skolsky, the man who in a 1934 column gave the nickname 'Oscar' to Katharine Hepburn's first Academy Award. Sid said: 'Don't call it *Women I've Dressed* – make it *Women I've Undressed*.' And so it is.

I sat fascinated at a world I'd never known existed.

MY MOTHER TOLD ME that when I was young that everyone and everything was just a thing, I was forever talking about 'Bijou'. My parents paid little attention. There was a Bijou Theatre they went to, and they thought perhaps that was what I had in mind. But as I grew older, being an only child, I would wander off by myself down to the beach and scuff the water with flat stones. It was then I knew that Bijou was my dog, my friend and my invisible companion. He's been with me ever since.

As I grew older I learned to make the stones skip far out into the Pacific – then I'd whisper, 'Look, Bijou, that one went all the way to America.'

Bijou was a great comfort to me when my father's voice awakened me at night; I could hear it plainly upstairs in my bed. Then I'd hear Mother say, 'If you would drink like a Purdue you would drink like a gent, but you drink like a Kelly.'

My father would shout again, 'What's wrong with the Kellys? My grandfather was architect to the Duke of Atholl . . .' And on and on it went, far into the night.

Orry was my given name. I was born in 1897. My father was a Manxman, from the Isle of Man, and I was named for a Danish king who had conquered the island centuries ago.

In the seaport town of Kiama, where I lived, I was considered 'bush' – the term used for those born in the country. I didn't have a poor childhood. I had a nurse. Socially, we didn't belong in the top drawer of the highboy with the dress shirts, but neither did we fit in with the socks in the lower drawer; we belonged somewhere in the middle, for we were in 'trade'. The sign over my father's shop read: 'WILLIAM KELLY, Merchant Tailor', and at home I remember much talk of importing worsteds, flannels, serges and tweeds.

My mother was a Purdue, and for this reason I was allowed to attend Miss Ingall's private school, where little boys and girls were taught manners, given lessons in ballroom etiquette and shown the steps of the polka. In dancing class I liked best the shiny dancing pumps with their flat bows.

Among my earliest recollections, I remember running home from school, bawling my eyes out, my classmates shouting after me: 'You're bankrupt, you're bankrupt, your old man's bankrupt!' I didn't know what the word meant, but I was sure it was something awful. And my mother thought so too. With the help of her brother-in-law, a contractor, Mother was able to build some income property on her Purdue-owned land. To economise, I was sent to a publicly supported school. It took years, but eventually Mother paid off every penny of my father's debts.

My father didn't drink so much after the bankruptcy, but he retreated from the annoyances of life by immersing himself in the culture of carnations. He won many blue ribbons at the horticultural shows with his unique 'Ringer' – a hybrid he developed – a white carnation, its petals edged with violet. He also hybridised another prize carnation – a shocker in shocking pink, which he named 'Orry Kelly'.

When I was seven, my mother took me to Her Majesty's Theatre in Sydney to my first pantomime, *Dick Whittington and His Cat*. The part of Dick was played by a beautiful lady with a long quill in her cap. She wore a leather jerkin, high-laced suede boots, and carried a swag across her shoulder. At her side was a black cat. There was a demon king, and a devil who came up from a trapdoor with a flash of lightning. I liked best the transformation scene: Beginning with an exterior of the palace, a series of scrims lighted up. The audience was taken through a series of long corridors, finally reaching the Throne Room. When the panto ended and the house lights went up, I sat as in a dream. Mother had trouble making me budge.

The following Christmas I got a miniature stage set. Not liking the scenery, I set about designing my own. Between the proscenium arch I glued two curtains – one red, the other gold. I made reflectors for the footlights out of tinfoil from cigarette boxes. From the same boxes I collected coloured photos of London's famed musical comedy performers, the Gaiety Girls.

Our rambling two-storey house had extra rooms built on downstairs, and there was a small section with no roof where wonderful ferns were planted. We had a huge garden, which took up about three house plots; among the flowerbeds were many fruit trees, a grape arbour and a small fish pond.

Dressed to impress in the front row (second from right) at the Kiama Church of England Sunday School concert in 1905.

I played with my toy theatre-land in the pigeon loft of a two-storey building behind the house. Saturdays I spent most of the day making additional figures out of cardboard. I dressed the Queen in a long red robe made out of some velvet scraps I'd nicked from Mother's sewing room, but I found coloured crinkled paper much more to my liking because, with a little glue, the costumes could be fastened more easily to the painted cut-outs. My Lady's Companion wasn't much use since the scissors wouldn't cut, and I couldn't thread the needles, but the coloured silk was useful. I used tiny candles to light up the stage windows in the transformation scene.

One Saturday, right after lunch, I had almost finished the transformation scene when along came Father in his striped pants and swallow-tail coat. He had been gardening. He said something to me about a boy, seven years old, playing with dolls. He broke the cardboard figures and kicked the Lady's Companion to smithereens. Taking me outside, he put a huge wheelbarrow in my hands and ordered me to go to the Point and fetch manure for his garden.

About five miles outside Kiama lived the wealthy Fuller family. Early settlers, their huge tracts of land included their own railway station. The oldest son, George, had been sent home to Oxford to finish his education. He was one of Sydney's leading barristers.

I knew that on Saturdays the Fuller family drove to Kiama in their phaetons and broughams, and played tennis at a private court that was located on the point jutting out from our house. The coachman usually drove the young daughters, who went to my dancing class, in their dog cart. By the tennis courts was a section where horses grazed, and it was to this pasture my father had ordered me. I was afraid the girls would see me with my wheelbarrow full of manure.

It took most of the afternoon to load up. The trip home was long. I kept dodging behind trees, hiding from people driving in their traps and sulkies. I was almost home when I caught sight of the Fuller girls approaching in their dog cart. In my excitement, pushing my heavy load on the run towards a nearby fig tree, my wheelbarrow overturned. And so did I. I heard shrieks of laughter from the girls as they passed. I rolled over, away from the roadside, and cried with humiliation. When I arrived home I looked terrible, and smelled worse.

At the far end of the Point, below the lighthouse, my father had built wonderful natural swimming baths surrounded by irregular lava rock. It was named for him. This was my favourite playground.

My father was a great diver and champion plunger, and was once given a gold medal for diving into the shark-infested harbour to plug a hole in a cargo ship. One summer I had saved a boy who was caught in a rip-tide, and for this was presented a bronze medal. In no time at all the medallion turned dark brown, much like an Australian penny. The engraved inscription meant nothing to me, so I threw it away. I thought they should have given me a gold one like my father's.

After my first taste of the theatre at seven years old, I was hooked.
When the house lights went up, I sat as if in a dream.

After incidents such as that, my cobbers would decide I was fair dinkum or a good sport. Other times I would let my mates down on a Saturday afternoon by going off to paint a seascape with my teacher, Walter Cocks. Again, I was the odd one.

The poorer kids earned sixpence by riding the mail to Jamberoo, about five miles away. I had no pony. I offered to carry the heavy leather bag of mail for nothing. They often were short of saddles at the livery stables, but no matter, I'd ride bareback; cantering over the hills was great fun – until the cheeky kids beat me up for scabbing.

I was really the last hope on the football team. Although I had no strength in my arms, I could run with the best of them. I also played cricket, until a cricket ball broke my nose.

Mother made me study piano. I could play the melody but had little control over my left hand. After rapping my knuckles for six years Mother said, 'You'll never get anywhere in life without bass.' That ended the piano lessons. At the age of twelve I started to study painting professionally. Endless years of school followed.

When I turned seventeen and still couldn't pass my exams, Mother decided to send me to Sydney for additional studies. She said, 'You must matriculate – pass your banker's exams. You will mix with gentler people and, who knows, one day you may end up as Manager.' I realised that Mother was not without a bit of snobbery in her make-up.

With my schoolmates' farewells and shouts of 'coo-wee' ringing in my ears, I was sent to live with my Aunt Em in Parramatta, my mother's birthplace, about three-quarters of an hour's train ride to the technical college in Sydney.

The Grand Opera House was close by the Sydney railway station. The pantomime had been running for several months, and I found myself hanging around the stage door. With this new pastime I was increasingly late getting home to Aunt Em.

One night, just about dusk, while I was watching the show people entering the stage door, a beautiful red-headed girl passed me on the street. She turned and smiled. I decided she must be an actress, for it was obvious she hadn't been able to remove all the make-up around her eyes. This was my chance to meet and talk to a *real* Sydney actress! I followed her. At the corner she crossed the street and walked towards Surry Hills, a cheap section of town. She waited for me by an alley and seemed rather vague when I asked her about the theatre. Before I knew it, we were in a dark doorway. There was some talk of money. I was physically excited. Luckily I had bought a season train ticket, because she took four shillings – all I had in my pocket. She also took my virginity.

She took four shillings . . .
She also took my virginity.

Somehow, I got through my school examinations and went to work in the Bank of New South Wales. But my mind was never on my desk. I loved the theatre. During lunch hour I would dash uptown to audition for shows going into rehearsal.

When I turned eighteen, I desperately wanted to enlist, but the Army accepted no one under twenty-one without parents' consent. But within a year the war ended. Lloyd George assured us there would be a just and honest peace, a phrase which became very popular. There was dancing in the streets of Sydney.

We were launched on a decade of frivolity. Tango Teas were given at the Tivoli Theatre on off-matinee days, and the rich racy set paid top prices for the privilege of dancing on the stage while tea was served in the mezzanine. Jazz bands and wailing saxophones encouraged the younger set to throw away their iron girdles when they danced the foxtrot. Overnight, music became barbaric, its call: freedom of movement. The restricting underpinnings gave way to simple slips, camisoles and lace panties.

During the war the Aussies fraternised with the 'mademoiselles from Armentières', as the song said. They returned home to find the girls they left behind wearing flesh-coloured hosiery – before they left, only black lisle, mouse grey, white and pale pink stockings were worn.

The Haymarket branch of the Bank of New South Wales was near the railway station. For over a year I simply went by train to work and returned to my aunt's in Parramatta. I saw little of Sydney. Then, one day, my audition paid off. I was engaged as a straight man with one line in the bawdy revue *Stiffy and Moe*.

Thanking my aunt for her kindness, I packed up and moved to Sydney. I found diggings on Hunter Street, in the moist heart of the city with four pubs to every block. I was growing up – I added a couple of years to my age. Sydney took on a new look and so did I.

In my imagination it seemed that Sydney as a whole wore a large over-stuffed Victorian dress. Like most cities, the railway station, the introduction to the traveller, was surrounded by slums. Sydney had one square squalid mile.

Stately Macquarie Street, dignified Potts Point, and other fashionable harbour frontages that were built later, had an Edwardian look. Like their owners, the buildings had a feeling of quality. There was none of the gingerbread and folderol. The people who lived in them wore their clothes well and stood erect, their proud heads held high, with a surety of tilt to their chins. Descendants of the early settlers, they sought adventure in the New World of 'Down Under'.

Macquarie Street was Sydney's Mayfair; the lines of the houses were as clean and simple as the lines of the Georgian silver used in the fashionable town flats above the shining offices of professional men whose offices were on the ground floors. Here were located doctors, barristers and solicitors, pioneers' sons who had been sent home to Oxford and Cambridge for their degrees.

But the hard core of Sydney, the details of its arcades and gingerbread buildings, resembled the heavy Battenburg laces and passementerie trimmings of Good Old Queen Victoria.

Extending from its huge leg-o'-mutton sleeves, like bent elbows, were narrow crooked streets named Bourke, Palmer and Leichhardt. From its frayed skirt and dusty petticoats, other streets, like bandy legs, stretched out to toe the foot of Woolloomooloo. Sitting in the lap of this over-decorated creation was the shining harbour.

The city might have been overdressed, but it had a respectable heart – right in the middle of the shopping district was a park with a kiosk where shoppers lunched and children played. On its left stood Queen's Square, and to the right stood the huge St Mary's Cathedral, a block

Overnight, music became barbaric, its call: freedom of movement.
Restricting underpinnings gave way to slips, camisoles and lace panties . . .

long. Through the iron gates was the Domain, a spreading park covered with a patchwork quilt of flowerbeds. Below the cathedral was Sydney's toughest section – Woolloomooloo.

Just above the Loo were a series of clay-faced houses, their black sooty chimneys handcuffed together, pointing to the sky. They were built by parolees, the defiant ones. Themselves doomed, they seemed to have purposely planned a way out for their children. At night the streets ended in shadows, making it impossible for the law to track down criminals who darted through a maze of passageways and alleys.

By full moon there was a certain charm, but when the morning sun undressed this voluptuous creature and exposed her tattered and frayed underpinnings, you found this section of Sydney wore dirty drawers. This was the violent part of the town where people lived violently. This was the home of the Sydney underworld.

It was in this section, on Bourke Street, that Alice O'Grady ran her sly grog, a place one could drink on the sly, no matter the time of day. Australian law called for pubs to open at 6 am and close at 6 pm.

I had made the acquaintance of another actor, named Ralph, slightly older than I, and it was to Alice O'Grady's he suggested we go for a beer, or a 'pig's ear', as he called it. I was excited the moment we got on the tram. Passing Macquarie Street, Ralph, pointing to the streetwalkers strolling in and out of the shadows, said, 'There go the Two-Guinea Girls, you'll be seeing them at Alice's after midnight.' I wanted to ask what he meant by 'two-guinea', but I was afraid he'd think me 'bush'.

The tram rattled and bumped down to the foot of the Loo. I saw figures in doorways darkened by verandahs laced with iron grill work. About halfway up to Kings Cross we got off at Bourke Street. Ralph said we had a two-block walk up the incline to the sly grog.

In the first block, a man darted out through a hole in a tin fence and disappeared up an alley. In the second block, tired-looking prostitutes stood in every other doorway, with one foot on the pavement and the other foot on the stoop behind them. One such trull called out to us: 'Hello, ducks, 'ows about comin' in for a go?' We hurried past. Ralph explained that by British law, which still governed Australia at the time, the girls were

protected and could not be prosecuted if they kept one foot on their own property. I looked on either side of the street: The sallow-faced houses in this slum looked all alike, except now and then a china or iron cat chained to the doorway indicated that the establishment was a 'cathouse'. The yellowy moon made the painted china cats look just as bilious as the flabby, bulbous-busted prostitutes. I was greatly relieved when Ralph and I were let into the quiet-looking house by big, wholesome Alice O'Grady herself.

She didn't look as though she belonged in this smoky atmosphere, for she wore no paint and her skin had the sheen of respectability in contrast to the ladies of the 'ensemble' in her front parlour.

We sat down, Ralph ordered a brandy and I had beer. Certain things in one's past are crystal clear, others hazy. The midnight faces at Alice O'Grady's seem like ghosts of my past.

The gas wall-brackets cast a yellow glow on the women's sensuous faces, making them look like papier-mâché masks. Ralph nodded towards some men, their faces like visors, with slits for eyes and cruel sagging mouths. 'They are the Two-Guinea Girls' bludgers.' He saw me frown. 'They are also known as pimps.'

By half past midnight there was no place to sit; the so-called Gaiety Girls had arrived. They swept back and forth, laughing, hugging, kissing their bludgers. Bottoms were patted by some and kicked by others, for there were those whose passion was to be beaten. They all had one thing in common – all of them would give their men their earnings, or it would be taken from them.

After a while Alice came by and said a few words to Ralph, who followed her up the stairs. He stopped long enough to tell me there was no charge for our drinks. A flashily dressed little man with a yellow diamond stickpin in his tie and another diamond on his pinkie was taking some bets. He was chewing on a cigar bigger than himself. His eyes followed Ralph and Alice going up the stairway. He mumbled out of the side of his mouth, 'Alice's got it bad for the young actor.' Then I put two and two together.

I looked around the small room: heavy burgundy drapes were drawn over the windows, partially hiding starched white lace curtains held back by two large velvet butterflies. Little Tich played the pianola. Named after the famous English music hall star, Little Tich, who had six fingers on each hand, this Little Tich had six toes on each

The gas lights at Alice O'Grady's sly grog cast a yellow glow on the women's sensuous faces, making them look like papier-mâché masks.

foot, Ralph told me. With the white and black keys of the pianola jumping up and down, blue cigarette smoke curling slowly to the ceiling and the raucous laughter of the painted hussies, jockeys and bludgers, who took turns shouting for the house – all this gave me the feeling of a three-ring circus.

I sat fascinated at a world I'd never known existed.

That night, as I watched the strange figures in the smoky room, I heard names like Rosie Boot, Lena the Fox, The Odd One, Spanish Nell, Port Wine Pansy, The Cameo, Minna the Toad, Terrible Tilly, Rose Rooney and Gentleman George.

My actor friend came downstairs. He said Big Alice O'Grady wasn't feeling too good. He had called a cab. As we went out, the famous Rosie Boot went in.

In the country, when I was seventeen, I had to be home by 10 pm on the few nights I was allowed out.

When I got back to town we bought cold pork sandwiches at one of the few late spots and went to Ralph's apartment. With more beers, I asked questions until daybreak. Ralph, of course, knew all the lowdown. He told me: Alice's husband, Tibby O'Grady, had been Sydney's best known pickpocket until he left for the Old Country and the Wembley Exhibition, with its bigger crowds and purses to be snatched.

Rosie Boot had the melancholy blood of a third-generation whore. Her mumma had followed an officer of an old-line British regiment to India and, as Rosie herself often said, 'Between the heat and one thing and another, I came along.' Rosie was only sixteen when her mumma told her the way of life and put her on the town – it was as simple as that. As far as Rosie was concerned, that's what was expected of her. The name Rose was taken from an English scent, 'Old Rose'. Rosie used to brag that the family name went back three generations; Grandma Rose was now called 'very Old Rose', Mumma was 'Old Rose', and when Rosie took the boat for Sydney she decided to take the name of her favourite Gaiety Girl, Rosie Boote. She didn't think she was doing anything wrong and, besides, she felt it was so far away, no one would know the difference. Still, she gave her last name the boot and kicked off the E, spelling it 'Boot'.

Rose pink was Rosie's favourite colour. Her hats, clothes, umbrellas and bags were pink, even to the uppers of her black patent leather shoes. When Rosie first landed in Sydney, in 1903, her face had a wonderful rosy glow. At the end of the First World War, her bloom no longer blooming, Rosie Boot 'hit the pave'. She conceived the idea of using stately Macquarie Street as her beat. This lady of ideas decided to organise a club; she got hold of Minna the Toad.

Minna was a fetcher and carrier, a doormat for the madams, or anyone, where there was a quid to be made. She met all the boats arriving at Circular Quay. 'The Toad' was always on the lookout for a pretty new face among the trulls who hoped the hot weather of Sydney would be much more to their liking than the hot water they had gotten into back home. Rosie and Minna gathered the prettiest English hussies for their club, which they called The Gaiety Girls.

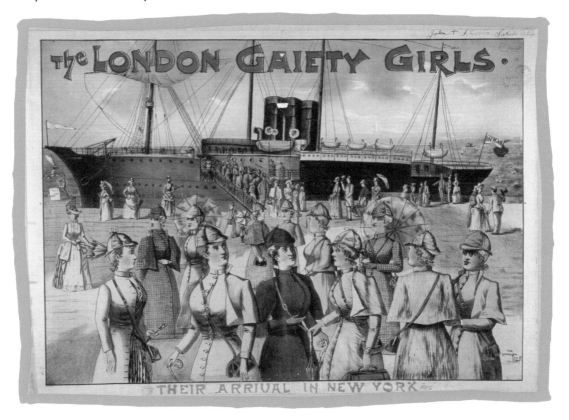

The girls realised that it paid Rosie well to pose as a Gaiety Girl who had grown tired of the theatre. Following suit, they too took the names of famous Gaiety Girls. One blonde impertinently took the name of lovely Gertie Millar. Another called herself after the beautiful Miss Lily Elsie. Two look-alikes were known as Phyllis and Zena Dare. Others called themselves Miss Gabrielle Ray, Marie Lloyd and Connie Ediss.

A pee-pot elegant puss became known as The Duchess of Teck, after the Dowager Queen Mary. And, to add the royal touch, she wore an ermine choker and muff.

This put them in the two-guinea class, for Macquarie Street's professional men started their fees at two guineas. Hence the girls became known as the Two-Guinea Girls.

Macquarie Street was usually deserted by five o'clock in the afternoon. At dusk the street had a calm, relaxed air of seclusion – that is, until the lights were lit and a succession of hansom cabs carrying the laced-mutton ladies of the evening somewhat altered the serenity of the scene. With a slight stretch of the imagination, when not ruffled and on their best behaviour, they could well have been ladies of the ensemble of Mr Cochran's chorus at the Gaiety Theatre in London's West End.

The boys from the bush had heard fantastic tales of the Macquarie Street girls. The moment they hit the city, their first purchase was often a piece of the much-talked-of two-guinea 'Gaiety Girls'. Sydney's fanciest floozies played up the fact that they were imports, but the two guineas were only the starting point, a down payment.

A black satin dress was the basic part of the black-and-white ensemble which Rosie had decreed. Their hats were varied – some wore swathed turbans that veiled their eyebrows, others had white aigrettes or pale bird-of-paradise feathers jutting up from the crown and white fox furs slung over one shoulder, the head always biting the tail. They wore enormous corsages of white camellias, white double violets, and bouvardia backed with maidenhair fern. It was an age of elegance and even the prostitutes were elegant. They looked like Aubrey Beardsley drawings. Apart from the beaded bags they swung, the short black kid gloves, they usually wore a tiny black cross on a fine gold chain around their necks. Yet none were on good terms with their Maker. Their motto was 'The Lord helps those who help themselves,' and they had many keepers. Profoundly honest Rosie, unlike the other girls, never wore a cross.

It was an eerie effect when a motor car or a passing taxi flashed and lit up their dead white faces plastered with Java rice powder. Others needed little light to make their Gaiety Blue-shaded belladonna eyes gleam – belladonna was a dangerous substance used to dilate and make the pupils flash – as their bloodthirsty lips parted with professional smiles.

There would be a low whistle from the cop on Rosie's payroll when a small theatre party came out from their town flat onto the street to hail a hansom cab. The trulls, looking like black-and-white abstractions, would fade and disappear into iron and charcoal recesses, forming weird shadows. The proud street would revert to its calm and dignified look, as if out of respect or reverence for the proximity of Government House and His Majesty's representative.

The moment the cab turned the corner, the cop would give the all-clear signal and, just as a theatre scrim is lighted from behind, stately Macquarie Street became alive. From the dark recesses, like black-and-white frogs, with sexual abandon the painted lizzies leaped out at their prey. The whole street buzzed with activity; men of all types appeared, usually in the thirty-to-fifty bracket. They had whiskers, pot bellies and wore bowler hats. Sheer black stockings were adjusted, garters snapped and white thighs were exposed. Imitation diamond earrings, bracelets, brooches and shoe buckles sparkled and shone.

This section of the city wore dirty drawers.
This was the home of Sydney's underworld.

There was a stretch in the pavement where new pipes had been installed and irregular streaks of still-wet tar dribbled and ran over the sidewalks, giving a Rouault lead-glass effect. The streetlights beat down on the black-and-white harlots, the oily surface reflecting their voluptuous bodies as they sucked in their stomachs, while their navel buttons beat out a rhythm to their shimmying nipples.

Hacks were called. The girls and their tired businessmen bundled in and started jogging towards the Loo. I am not so sure how pleased His Excellency Lachlan Macquarie Esquire, Captain General and Governor-in-Chief of His Majesty's Territory of New South Wales and its Dependencies, etcetera, would have been had he lived to see what happened to his beautiful street.

Yet you couldn't blame Rosie Boot for choosing his street. Directly opposite their beat was Government House; there were no walls surrounding the apple-green lawns and its floral sash of flowerbeds. The perfume of the night-blooming flowers and honeysuckle that drifted across the way gave momentary relief from the soiled shirts, dirty dickies, stale singlets and stinking socks of their quick trips and tricks to the foot of Darlinghurst and the Loo, where the animalism of the older Adams with the younger Eves often went far beyond the normal sexual habit.

Miss Boot had decided the girls would hit the pavement about eight o'clock in the evening. As she said: 'A businessman should have time to let his dinner settle before taking his pleasure with the ladies of the evening.' The girls worked four hours – until midnight – and they drank and played until four in the morning.

Midnight, Macquarie Street, facing Queen's Square, was deserted. The average businessman, by now about to fall apart, made his weary way home after a long day at the office and a longer night on Macquarie Street. Climbing their steep stairs, taking off everything but their earrings half a dozen times, the Gaiety Girls, too, had just about fallen apart.

By early morning, the heavy enamel they plastered on their faces had been clogged and caked with sporadic pattings of Java rice powder. They looked like wild mysterious plumed birds of the Australian bush, standing under the lamp posts, tossing their tall feathered hats back and forth, impatiently waiting for a hansom cab to take them to Alice O'Grady's sly grog, where they would meet and turn over their earnings to their bludgers.

I was wide awake by now. I asked about others I had seen. Ralph, who had been drinking brandy, seemed just as fascinated telling me all about them:

Lena the Fox, then in her sixties, didn't need the late hours to give her face the effect of a crinkling and crackling mask. She had grey-green skin, and several of her chins were hiked up with the aid of a couple of wide dog collars. Her shifty, tiny blackcurrant eyes were set far back into her skull, and perched on top of her badly dyed hair was a veiled grey crown-like toque, trimmed with Parma violets. In fact, she copied every detail of the Dowager Queen Mary's dress, even to the unbecoming two-tone shoes and conventional grey gloves. Her grey coat was a work of art, particularly the sleeves; anything could, and did, disappear into them, from a piece of jewellery to an ermine tippet. Even the grey fur which bordered the short cape on her grey coat had that British elegant lived-with look. Had I known earlier in the evening that Lena was Australia's number one shoplifter, I would have been more appreciative of her dress.

The Odd One, like Rosie Boot, was third generation and born into her profession. While she knew what was expected of her, she loathed it. Her grandma's experiences, the terrible evils of transportation to Botany Bay, were forever fresh in her mind. There was no fancy man in her life. Usually she sat alone in Alice's sly grog. Although her moods were strange and unpredictable, the other girls paid little attention, because there was something hopelessly pathetic about her.

From the dark recesses of Macquarie Street, the painted lizzies
leaped out at their prey . . . black stockings were adjusted,
garters snapped and white thighs exposed.

Spanish Nell acquired this name after she had lost her looks. In her youth the dark-complexioned Nell had been likened to a blood-red dahlia. When this once wonderful skin became a mass of purple veins, forming rivers and tributaries all over her face, she was anything but attractive. She became an abortionist. Nell was a nightly patron at the sly grog. When Alice would cry out, 'Nell, it's for you!' she'd run to the phone, listen a moment, hang up, grab her banjo case filled with Epsom salts, permanganate of potash and other appurtenances, and away she'd fly on a 'case'. It was this instant response to the call of duty that had won her the full title: 'Spanish Nell, the Flying Angel'.

Terrible Tilly was the most notorious and ruthless cockney that ever sailed through Sydney Heads. And she slashed many a head with the old-fashioned razor she carried in her black patent leather bag. In fact, it was for slashing an innocent victim's throat that Tilly was deported back to London. But she got back to Australia. How? No one knows!

She was about twenty-six years old. Beneath her floppy horsehair hat the horsy Tilly glued a peroxide cowlick on her puce-pink cheeks. Her mouth was a scarlet gash. It was obvious she wore nothing underneath her sheer skin-coloured sleeveless beaded dresses. Her powerful arms shone with three or four ornate diamond bracelets. Being a southpaw, Tilly wore an expanding green-eyed diamond lizard around the muscle of her left arm. Black patent spike-heeled shoes completed her 'night and day' ensemble. Her get-up was as bold as herself. Tilly lived far away from Bourke Street in another slum section called Surry Hills, adjoining the railway station. Big Alice O'Grady was one of the few who defied Tilly.

Tilly was not a prostitute – the prostitutes had bludgers. She turned the tables. Two punch-drunk ex-pugs robbed and helped her rob; and she, in turn, gave them pin money for *her* favours.

She allowed no strumpets in her territory. Tilly used the entire square block of Anthony Hordern's department store near the railway station as her beat. Approaching a rich squatter or wool buyer, fresh from the train, she would pretend to be a prostitute. 'I've got me own car,' she'd say, nodding to the big convertible parked at the kerb. One of her fancy men would be dressed as a chauffeur, the other hidden in the back. The moment her 'customer' got in, he was blackjacked, robbed, taken on a short trip to Surry Hills and dumped in an alley. Then Tilly and her fancy men went back for another 'prospect'. She became rich, and her many exploits were often common gossip in Sydney's underworld and in the pages of *Truth*.

Rose Rooney was known as the 'Queen of Diamonds' and was a sort of henna-haired edition of Mae West. She shone from head to foot; in fact, even the heels of her shoes were solidly studded with real diamonds. She wore two diamond combs in her hair and dazzling, dangling earrings which almost reached the elaborate necklace at her throat. Her arms were covered with bracelets and her fingers sported diamonds of all shapes and sizes – marquise, pear-shaped, clusters and double clusters – some a little yellow, but still the real McCoy.

Terrible Tilly slashed many a head with the old-fashioned razor she carried in her black patent leather bag.

At the beginning of the twenties, the newspaper used few photographs, but Sydney's *Truth* never missed printing a shot of Rose Rooney on Cup Day at the races. The Governor-General and his Lady always appeared in their box just before the second race. When the band struck up 'God Save the Queen', that was Rose's cue to parade directly in front of the Governor-General's box, in some outrageous creation. Rose was usually accompanied by two of her barmaids – nobody else would accompany her. She was ablaze with diamonds. Her huge black velvet hat with white aigrettes swept high in the air; the black velvet dress slashed to the knee to show off her real diamond garter. Her train spread out and trailed behind her on the lawn as her white-gloved hand clutched a Tosca diamond-studded staff.

Port Wine Pansy was the best and the richest of the peddlers. She was a flower vendor who sold 'seconds'. In fact, her flowers wilted before her customers could get out of the theatre. It was rumoured she owned half a block of slum houses. In her sixties, she had never changed the Victorian style of her dress: Her large hat had once featured a tulle butterfly, but now only the wide frame remained and some rain-soaked tulle hung down like cobwebs, partially hiding her face. The threadbare patches and rags of her cloak – her outer prop – trailed along in the dust, almost hiding her spotless white cotton stockings and broken-down elastic-sided boots.

At her side was a pale urchin of a girl, Cammie, dressed like Eliza Doolittle, who sold flowers from Pansy's basket. Next to port wine, Pansy liked the theatre and sat in her usual

Like Port Wine Pansy, I spent many magic hours at Her Majesty's Theatre, decked out in all her finery here for a visit by the Prince of Wales.

front row centre seat way up in 'the gods', as we Aussies called the top balcony. Shaw's *Pygmalion* was her favourite play. She was an avid first-nighter and a walking theatrical encyclopedia.

Occasionally, when she dropped by Alice's sly grog for a port, hanging up her hat and discarding her mass of threadbare rags, she looked like Whistler's Mother. The clothes under her props were immaculate and she had a well-scrubbed look about her. In a quiet voice, touched with a good English accent, she told tales of early players. She went as far back as Italy's leading actress, Madame Ristori, who opened in *Medea*. Pansy told of the seething crowd that burst through when Bernhardt – 'Sinuous Sarah', as she termed her – opened in *Camille* in 1891. After she had seen American stage actress Mrs Brown-Potter she referred to her as 'Minor Bernhardt'.

After prosperity descended on Australia with the gold rush, as Pansy put it, 'in the full flush of inflation, Robert Brough, Dion Boucicault and Irene Vanbrugh arrived from Britain with their companies.'

Woolloomooloo-born comic opera star Miss Nellie Stewart had more farewell appearances as Sweet Nell of Old Drury than Dame Nellie Melba. 'But at least,' said Pansy, 'Nellie Stewart showed up for hers – Melba was always refunding money.'

She told of English comedic and light-opera star Marie Tempest and her husband, the actor Graham Brown, and Australia's own golden-voiced Gladys Moncrieff. Another Australian, Miss Minnie Everett, formed ballets and trained choruses, out of which came such stars as Madge Elliott and Cyril Ritchard. Patronisingly, Pansy said, 'In between there were cheapjacks, often Americans with their variety shows.'

The London Gaiety Company made the longest journey in theatrical history, all around the Cape of Good Hope, to give the world premiere of *Cinder Ellen* in Melbourne. Pansy went home to Melbourne for this event, which proved to be the biggest thrill of her life. She said that Fred Leslie, Nellie Farron and Sylvia Grey had rehearsed the show on the long voyage. 'The Aussies went mad,' continued Pansy, 'and Leslie was sued for five hundred pounds when he punched an Aussie for making a disparaging remark about King Edward VII.'

The Cameo, like Topsy, just sprang up. She was brought up by an aunt who lived at The Rocks. When Cammie asked what her surname was, her aunt said, 'Your name is Cammie, just think of a cameo – that's you.' And she was a cameo, even in the boy's knickers and checked cap she usually wore. Cammie earned money by running messages, buying sweepstake tickets for the harlots, and at times 'calling cops' for Alice O'Grady.

Minnie the Toad, with her 'never-ending nether-end', was a disagreeable, sallow-faced, hawk-nosed procurer. Her business was putting her nose in other people's business, providing they were important. Her magenta heart-attack mouth sagged with the disappointments of life – particularly in her love life. But there were those who said that Minna was kind. 'Anyone who has such a big, angry fuselage as The Toad ought to be kind' was a favourite remark of Gentleman George.

There were so many throat slashings that Darlinghurst became known as Razorhurst.

Gentleman George was Sydney's number one pickpocket, a title he'd held since Alice O'Grady's husband, Tibby, had left her for the Old Country and a bigger purse.

He cut quite a figure in his too-light grey suit, white silk shirt with a two-inch rounded unattached collar, gold pin under the knot of his black tie, black patent leather shoes with grey suede uppers and mother-of-pearl buttons, and his ever-present field glasses which he slung over his shoulder. In the spring he always sported a large bachelor's button in his lapel. He had an enormous amount of reserve strength across the back of his neck and shoulders from his many street brawls. To top it all, he was a double for Wallace Reid, the silent movie star.

His principal weapons were dash and daring. He was tricky, cunning and brutally frank. There was no end to his chicanery if it meant getting what he wanted. Of course, all these qualities were below the surface, for he looked, behaved and spoke like a gentleman.

The underworld knew this well-dressed pickpocket as Gee Gee – an Australian term used for racehorses. When he wasn't at the gee-gees, he was usually busy at the tram stop at Darlinghurst, an intersection known as Kings Cross. Some called it 'Kings Bloody Cross'. In fact, there were so many throat slashings in that area that Darlinghurst was referred to as 'Razorhurst'. Another favourite tram stop was Bathurst Street corner, known to the pros as 'The Street of Great Expectations'. There was a Dickensian flavour about the old curiosity shoppes, pawn brokers and Mrs Woolf's second-hand clothing store. Standing around, hamming it up, old stock actors used the phrase: 'Here comes a sheep in Mrs Woolf's clothing!'

Gee Gee actually had little interest in this local colour, or in the small German band playing on the corner. It was the wool man, the rich squatter or anyone sporting a gold chain across his vest that caught his undivided attention.

Gee Gee had a certain humour along with his stealing. So quick and expert was he that he could clip a gold watch from a man's chain, duck into a pawn shop, return and attach the pawn ticket back on the chain, without being detected. The bland, almost childlike expression in his big blue eyes made him the last person anyone would suspect of thievery – but these same blissfully serene eyes could also ice up the moment he spotted the law.

Another trick he used for disposing of his stolen watches was to take them around to a pub, or public house keeper, or anyone who might be on the lookout for a bargain. He might accept five pounds for a twenty-pound timepiece, while he casually suggested that since the watch was 'hot' it should be hidden for six months. The watch would then be put away under the flooring, or in some other safe place, but when the buyer retrieved the stolen property, it would often be verdigris green – Gee Gee, at the last moment, had switched a brass watch for the expensive one!

Gentleman George, unlike the other bludgers who went to Alice's at midnight to collect from their tarts, had not only one, but three girls – a blonde, a brunette and a redhead – who gave him their earnings, out of which they got their expenses and pin money. This was the reason some other trulls referred to him as The Stallion.

It was eight o'clock when I left Ralph. I then did what I was often to do in my youth: I went to a barber, was shaved, with hot towels and then ice-cold ones. And, after a shower and change of clothes, I was ready for another twenty-four hours of fun . . .

CHAPTER TWO

It was as if I had suddenly broken off my leash.

I'D HAD MY FIRST taste of Sydney's underworld life that night at Alice O'Grady's sly grog. You would have thought my first trip, treading on the dangerous quicksand of the underworld, would have sufficed. But no, it was as if I had suddenly broken off my leash. Fascinated with the Loo and with Bourke Street's Fauvism, I went panting back for more. With these new, strange acquaintances I began hearing a brand new lingo: Hows-yer-doin' matie orright? Good-o, then you can shout me to a beer. Ye won't, eh? Then yer a stinkeroo, abso-bloody-lutely. Yer may be smart orright, yer not as smart as yer think yer are, but . . .

The King's English may have stumped me at school, but these new expressions were a cinch.

Meanwhile, the theatre world of Sydney was flourishing and our revue was a hit. Sydneysiders were flocking to see Charlie Chaplin in *The Kid* and Mary Pickford in *Pollyanna*. Irish tenor John McCormack had concluded successful concerts at the Town Hall, and musical comedy star Maude Fane was playing nightly in a long run of *A Night Out*. Every night, after the show, she was seeing a great deal of young Robert Peel – in fact, too much, for her husband had been in South Africa for the past year, producing shows. As Maude's show progressed she added a small muff to her ensemble and began to carry it throughout the play. As the months increased, so did the size of the

The theatre world of Sydney was flourishing and our revue was a hit.

muffs, and by the time she had to quit the show the muffs were gargantuan. At this time Bobby Peel was called home; his father was dying. He became Sir Robert Peel.

Maude's baby arrived not long after her husband's return. They were divorced. A little later, Sir Robert Peel made the actress and comedienne Beatrice Lillie Lady Peel.

'Didya read what Johnny Norton said in *Truth*?' That phrase rang in my ears the first time I heard it, and forty years later I can still hear it.

Although Norton had been dead four years when I became a Sydneysider, no one spoke of it. John Norton ran a weekly yellow rag, the first of the tabloids, called *Truth*. It appealed to the Larrikin, the rowdy – or, for that matter, all the fun-loving, pugnacious youth who mimicked his alliterations and Nortonese manner of speech. Gentleman George's hero was Johnny Norton. He kept clippings about Norton in his wallet. Gee Gee copied Norton's way of using alliterations, and sprinkled his speech with such phrases as: 'the bulbous-breasted, broad-buttocked, bare-legged bouncing beauties'.

Like the conceited, cocky, concupiscent young curs I began running around with, I couldn't wait for the Sunday edition.

Adultery, according to British law, being the only means of divorce, all the details and positions of the prone bodies were minutely described. Many *nice* families also couldn't wait for *Truth* to come out each Sunday; but instead of having it delivered on the lawn with *The Sydney Morning Herald* and *The Sun*, it was dropped by the back door.

Wanting to get all of the bush out of my system, I began talking Nortonese.

By then I knew and was on good terms with Rosie Boot. I began meeting others – a newspaper reporter, brother of a famous Australian athlete, who often dropped by Alice O'Grady's sly grog for beers and a laugh. This particular evening, as I was sitting drinking with Rosie and the newspaperman, the Gaiety Girls had trooped in and were just settling down to their drinks. We heard a sharp knock on the door. Now, all Alice's customers knocked with a code; this loud rap meant trouble – and it was!

Cautiously, Alice listened, then, recognising the voice, opened up. In bounced Miss Gertie Millar, her half-unbuttoned blouse showing her bosoms bouncing like a couple of jellies capsized out of a mould. She eventually quietened down long enough to tell

Alice that Cammie had told her the cops were in the next block with their Black Maria. I thought, this is it! I wanted excitement and I was about to get it.

Gertie said the tough police sergeant, whom they all feared and hated, had been tipped off that Lena the Fox was carrying cocaine, and he was now on his way here to get her. As soon as Gertie finished her spiel, all camaraderie ceased and everyone sprang into action: Bottles were slipped into hand-knitted woollen jackets, which the girls had kindly made and given to Alice for just such occasions. These jackets protected the Scotch and brandy bottles from breaking when they descended, via a miniature chute, into the backyard of the respectable Irish family next door. A secret panel covered the chute, and over the panel was hung a framed petit point, with cross-stitched Old English lettering: 'There's No Place Like Home'. Directly above this bit of sentimentality was an old framed broadside of a verse from an early Botany Bay song, which read:

> *You lecherous whore-masters, who practice vile arts,*
> *To ruin young virgins and break parents' hearts,*
> *Or from the fond husband the wife leads astray,*
> *Let such debauch'd stallions be sent to Botany Bay.*

Just as everything was put to rights, we heard a screech of tyres and then a loud rap on the door. Little Tich sat down at the pianola and played 'Bill'. Ginger beer was put on the tables. Miss Gabrielle Ray started telling Lily Elsie's fortune. The Duchess of Teck nervously toyed with her ermine tibbet. Alice opened the door.

'Good evening, sergeant,' she said warmly.

A plump trollop who had taken the name of Marie Lloyd stood by the pianola and started to sing the chorus of 'Bill'.

> *For 'e loves me. Yes, I'm certain that 'e loves me*
> *With a friendly clout 'e lays me out, and if I 'e still 'as any doubt*
> *That 'e loves me, in the gutter then 'e shoves me*
> *But what's the use of tears and sighs,*
> *Of tales of woe, when they're all lies*
> *Why, I'd rather toddle 'ome with two black eyes*
> *Knowin' that my Bill still loves me*

The sergeant looked angrily at the calm, almost sedate, scene before him. 'All right! Quiet! Enough of that singin'!' he shouted.

It was an age of elegance and even the prostitutes were elegant.

The pianola stopped. You could hear a pin drop as Lena said in an off-hand manner, 'Oh, I'm out of cigarettes, who's got one?' She casually tossed her Capstan cigarette box onto the floor at the sergeant's feet.

'All right, Lena, into the back room with you, and I'll need you too, Alice, while I frisk her,' he said.

They made their way through the shotgun hallway to a back room where Lena was thoroughly frisked.

The sergeant's men, with only a few bottles of ginger beer and lemonade in sight, shifted uncomfortably about. Finally the trio returned and you could tell by the angry flashing eyes of the sergeant, and the smug look on Lena's face, that nothing had been found. Furiously, the sergeant, whose cheeks blushed with Johnnie Walker, turned:

'Since when did the whole bunch of you turn wowsers?'

The police stamped out angrily. A few moments later we heard the Black Maria pull away from the kerb. The scene inside reverted to the chaos of an hour before. The moment the door closed, Lena leaped for the cigarette box. It was full of cocaine! She took a couple of good sniffs up her nostrils. This was the first time I, as well as a few others, knew for sure that Lena had given up shoplifting and turned to dope peddling.

Drinks were ordered and Lena was toasted: 'Here's to Foxy Lena, she can still outfox 'em!' Rosie had a melancholy glow on – she was feeling her nips. The reporter ordered a shout. The pianola was playing Rosie's favourite tune. Tilting a chair on its two back legs and leaning against the wall, the gas jets highlighting her pale enamelled face and her half-closed heavily mascara'd eyelashes, Rosie sang along with the pianola:

> Smile my honey dear
> While I wipe away each tear,
> Or else you will be melancholy too.

The notoriously sentimental Rosie began to reminisce:

'I was just sixteen when I pointed the toe of me rosy boot, coming down the gangway at Sydney's Circular Quay. The wharf was loaded down with passengers, bundles, satchels and tin boxes of all kinds. I went straight to The Rocks and rented meself lodgins on Vinegar Lane. I unpacked me portmanteau and put on a nice fresh shirtwaist and 'ad a go at lookin' the town over. Right back of St George's Church was a two-up school; they flipped coins there in the air and bet on 'eads or tails. Passing the church I runs into a man whose pockets and two hands were full of sovereigns. 'E stopped me and said, "Would a nice young lidy like you mind 'elpin' me put some of this gold in me pockets?" It wasn't long' – Rosie laughed – 'before 'e was 'elpin' me undo me corset and 'e 'elped 'imself, and I 'elped meself to 'is golden sovereigns. That was me Sydney debut!

'With the golden sovereigns I started playin' pak-a-pu at a Chinese lottery, right near the two-up school. There were four banks a day, includin' Sunday, and they started payin' off at noon. If all ten numbers were marked, ye could win seven 'undred and fifty pounds, but that was pretty 'ard to do.

'I learned plenty when I got me first job as barmaid, pullin' the tap and tappin' the till at the old Crimson Cow. I'd 'eard 'em tell tales of men bein' put in jail for stealin' a few tomatoes and put in parliament for stealin' a whole tract of land!' She sighed. 'And men singin' in church on Sundays and beatin' the 'ell out of their wives durin' the week. Parliament 'ouse in Macquarie Street was called the "Beer Garden", and Johnny Norton made a "water closet" out of the refreshment room.

'At first I told people I'd come to Sydney to search for me father who'd left twenty years before for the Australian gold rush. It was later, when I got all dressed up in me big pink feathered 'ats and boas, that I started tellin' men I was a Gaiety Girl. Every Saterdee night I'd 'ave one of me Johns take me to the Joseph Banks big razzle-dazzle Pleasure Ground; twenty-five acres it was, and sometimes ten thousand people would mill around the concessions on a weekend. The ballroom 'ad one strict rule, and big bruisers to see it was obeyed: No two ladies were allowed to dance together, and no two gentlemen were allowed to dance together. 'Ow does that strike ya, ducks?'

We ordered another shout. Filled with a rosy glow, Rosie went on:

'Me first friend was Port Wine Pansy. She always used a ragamuffin little flower girl and a decoy. And Pansy was clever, she bought some tenements, there's no upkeep on them. When I first met 'er, that 'at she wears was new and the butterfly bow was crisp as a piece of celery. She wears the same 'at today, only now ther ain't nothin' left except the milliner's wire frame and a bit of cobwebby tulle.' Rosie smiled; her face softened. 'Pansy was kind to me. I ain't ever forgot 'er.'

There was a long pause. She raised her brandy glass. Clicking our glasses, Rosie said, 'Let's drink to me motto: The best is good enough for me.' Getting up from the table, throwing her white fox around her shoulders, Rosie sighed, 'It's gettin' late.'

'It's getting very late,' Big Alice chimed in. 'All right, ladies and gents, pack up your troubles, I'm closing up!'

The newspaperman at my table indicated that he was tired and wanted to leave. As I lived near him, we decided to walk home together. We paid our tabs and stepped rather unsteadily into the street. He called goodnight to Jimmy Clabby, an American fighter who was walking in the opposite direction with one of the girls.

In the early morning light the putty-coloured monotonous-faced houses were all in darkness. One or two doors were still open, with the gas jets left burning in the dark hallways. A woman, with cheeks like fallen dumplings, pressed her face against an attic windowpane; a drunk lay halfway over the worn doorstep, saliva dribbling from his mouth. A stray dog limped by some fallen bricks. Even the cabbies had all gone home to bed. There were strange night sounds. Every now and then, from out of a dark alley, a hissing black cat bounded out directly in front of us.

The columnist complained of feeling wobbly – it was no wonder, after the amount of brandy he had put away! Travelling things, manmade things, fire hydrants – all seemed to be spinning like tops. Finally we came to a 'hole in the wall'. It was just that, big enough for a small man and a tiny handcart behind a cut-out in the wall. He sold vile wieners, tepid tea and evil pastry. Standing up in the street, we ate the bad food, but it sobered us up.

Leaving Bourke and William Streets and the Loo behind us, we walked towards the Domain. We gazed at the downy blue monotone of the irregular shoreline of the harbour. The shimmering moon in the dark sky was the same weary moon that had looked down on the transports *Neptune*, *Scarborough* and *Surprize*, which had limped into Botany Bay carrying convicts on the Second Fleet 160 years ago. But now, the cliffs across the bay were tiered with thousands of terracotta rooftops which shone like rows of English china, reflecting all the colours from pink to bronze.

As we walked, the moon took on a chartreuse glow. A cock crowed, and muted bird whistles pierced the early morning air. We were nearing Queen's Square. I looked up at good old Queen Vic standing erect in the middle of Queen's Square, loved and revered by everyone except the pigeons – and Johnny Norton. I looked over at Prince Albert's statue nearby. The newspaperman broke his long silence: 'Johnny Norton thought old Albert's statue over there was offensive.' He laughed. 'Johnny used to say that Queen Vic up here keeps one eye on the Mint while the other eye ogles the ugly statue of the father of her

Minnie's magenta heart-attack mouth sagged with the
disappointments of life – particularly in her love life.

children.' Turning from the statue, he said, 'He was a wowser.'

'Wowser?' I asked, struck with still another unfamiliar word I had heard twice that night.

He smiled. 'The word *wowser* was Johnny's invention, a term he applied to any branch of society – those leaning too close to the clergy, a Wesleyan, or more specifically, a hypocrite or a bluenose. The first time Johnny used it was when he applied it to Alderman Waterhouse, whom he referred to as "a white, woolly, weary, watery, word-wasting wowser from Waverley". But Johnny was the wildest wowser of them all!'

It was just before dawn. The reporter held his hand in the air and, flicking his fingers, he said, 'Feel that cool breeze flowing in from the cove.' I told him I learned at school that Sydney was built on water. He laughed. 'If it was, water never became their favourite drink. One hundred years after the first convict ships arrived, this sprawling city had a population of two hundred and eighty-eight thousand, and there were three thousand one hundred and sixty seven pubs to take care of its inhabitants' unquenchable thirst. But, you are right, it was built on water. On January 21st, 1788, Captain Phillip's First Fleet of eleven ships and one thousand souls, consisting of convicts, crew, soldiers and officials, arrived at Port Jackson. In a little cove, among the craggy rocks, he found a stream contaminated by the salt water of the ocean. Governor Phillip's first dispatch was headed "Sydney Cove", naming it after Lord Sydney of the Home Office. After the crew had made a clearing in the bush, one day they stepped ashore and took the name with them. They named it Sydney Town. And something else I bet you didn't know, young cobber, until the War of Independence, England had shipped her political prisoners and those convicted under the rigid laws of the time to her American colonies. When America broke away and England could no longer do this, her own jails became so overcrowded she decided to dump her convicts in Australia, by forming a penal colony at Botany.'

The more I heard from this man, the more I wanted to know. I was learning things that weren't in the copybooks at school in Kiama. But it was late, or I should say, early morning. We were approaching Macquarie Street, with its scale, proportion and correct placements. Within a few hours the city would be moving into another day; men with pigskin briefcases, pinpoint leather doctor's bags, would be entering and exiting.

I lived on Phillip Street, directly below Macquarie. We stood for a while on the corner and talked about the many things we'd seen and heard, unobserved in daylight. I thanked him for teaching me more in one evening that I ever learned at school. Then I walked through the old carriage entrance to my room, and to bed.

Clicking our glasses, Rosie said,
Let's drink to me motto: The best is good enough for me.

About a week later I was going home in the tram from the races. I was quite surprised when Gentleman George gave me a friendly greeting – at the sly grog he had always ignored me. I wondered why he jostled me clear into the middle of the crowded tram, then abruptly stopped me, put his hand on my shoulder, and said, 'This will do.' He soon had me laughing with his lively rhyming slang. At a curve in the tramlines he almost fell on top of me, and as he lurched me forward I bumped into another man. When he got off the tram he called out, 'See you around Alice's!'

I had just about decided to give the sly grog the go-by – after all, there were pubs on every corner and some in the middle of each block. I could do my drinking in the daytime. Besides, I'd heard if you wanted to know when, where, why or what was doing, you went to a Sydney bar. If you stood in good enough you could get it straight from the barmaid's mouth, for she often had a good hot tip. There was much rivalry between these ladies who tapped the draught beer; often they were able to tap the owner and get the dope if his horse was really trying.

A few days after the tram ride with Gee Gee I went to the pictures to see Rudolph Valentino in *The Four Horsemen of the Apocalypse*, co-starring beautiful Alice Terry. Afterwards I dropped into the lavishly decorated Marble Bar. Many painted nudes looked down from the high ceiling and walls; everywhere you looked, the mirrors tripled the number of nude paintings. The floor, the pillars and sections of the walls were marble. The place was beautiful, but draughty.

A snooty barmaid, almost marbelised from the cold bar room, looked down her paper-thin nose at me and said, 'What's your pleasure, ducks?' While making my mind up I couldn't help noticing how incongruous her pompadour and black velvet Degas ribbon at her throat looked along with her English tweed suit and sweater. 'Come on, ducks, whata you want, 'alf and 'alf?'

Thinking I'd show her a thing or two, I said, 'Absinthe drip.'

'Make that two!' I heard a familiar voice behind me. Turning around, I looked into the handsome face of Gentleman George. When the barmaid returned with our absinthe, Gee Gee pushed my money aside and placed a gold sovereign on the bar counter.

Eyeing the bar to see if anyone was looking, the barmaid, who by now was just about over the hill, leaned over and, giving Gee Gee a very knowing look, said, 'I've got an idea, the drinks are on me.'

Gee Gee pushed the sovereign across the counter and said, 'I've got a better idea, you keep the change.' Then he flipped another golden sovereign at me and said, 'You brought me luck, bumping into you on the tram that day. If you stick around and bring me more luck, the shout will always be on me.'

As my stage salary was only three sovereigns a week, I said, 'Good-ho,' and started following him around like a cocker spaniel.

Gee Gee kept me well supplied with racetrack tickets, and even an odd tip now and again. He seldom went to the track with me, but always arranged to meet me 'under the clock' after the last race. Usually he would say, rather grimly, 'Come on, let's get crackin'.' And I would know he'd had a bad day.

We would board the overcrowded tram, which always looked like a huge roast turkey, with people – like dressing – dribbling out over the sides. At first I wondered why he always pushed and bumped his way to the middle, but later I found out it was because he had spotted an out-of-towner who'd won a bundle at the track.

Gee Gee knew every rough spot in the road on that thirty-minute drive back to town, and just before the tram lurched, he'd start kidding some odd-looking bloke. He was very witty; spotting a chap with a large nose, he'd call out to divert attention: 'Git the "I suppose" (nose) on the bloke with the check waistcoat.' As the passengers would turn and smile at him, Gee Gee's left hand would jar me, and I, in turn, would bump into the bloke, allowing Gee Gee to slip his hand into the inside breast pocket and lift the wallet.

Upon reaching town we would stop at one of the three top pubs: the Australia, the Ushers, or the Carlton. We'd wash up before going into the bar, where Gee Gee always stood the shout. Sometimes I would notice his wallet bulging with banknotes, yellowed newspaper clippings and women's addresses. Being as young as I was and still somewhat bush, I didn't realise that with the jostling of the bloke on the tram I'd become a 'straight

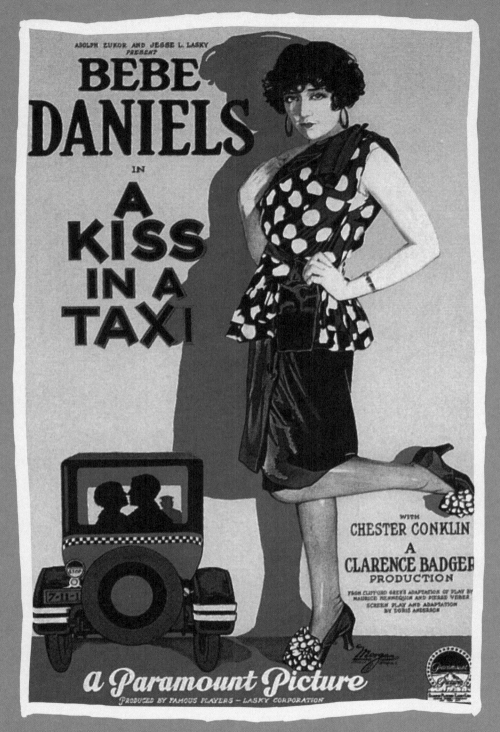

If anyone had told me that eight years later I would be dressing Miss Bebe Daniels at the First National Studios in Burbank I would have flipped.

man' for Gee Gee. In fact, I felt quite cocky when I heard people say, 'There goes Gentleman George's straight man.'

One evening, after the show, I was nearing Alice's place when Spanish Nell came dashing out on an 'errand of mercy'. She paused just long enough to tell me that Gee Gee had been picked up by the police. Even now, one of his wailing sheilas was inside singing 'After You've Gone and Left Me Sighing', to the accompaniment of Little Tich's playing.

Within the week I received a letter from Gee Gee, sent in care of Alice. He was in jail in Rushcutters Bay. He asked me to bring ten pounds in an envelope addressed to him and present it at the desk at eight o'clock the following morning. He added cryptically that he had to be out of the joint before the end of the month because, if he came up before a certain judge, he would be sentenced and they'd more than likely throw away the key. He added a postscript, bidding me to tell no one and to stay away from Alice O'Grady's. I duly presented the envelope at the jail and waited. Half an hour later a very subdued Gee Gee appeared, adjusting his silk collar. We took the tram to town but got off at the first Itie's for steak, eggs and beer. Gee Gee said very little about his predicament, only that he had to go into 'smoke' for a while.

Since he had to lay low during the day, I left him at the pictures, where a new Bebe Daniels film was playing. She was his favourite actress and he always called her *Babe* Daniels. If anyone had told me that eight years later I would be dressing Miss Daniels at the First National Studios in Burbank, California, I would have flipped.

Gee Gee had asked me to make arrangements with my landlady so that he could hide out at my diggings for ten days. He planned to sleep the rest of that day in the theatre, then, at dusk, go to Macquarie Street to collect the money his three tabbies had earned during the fortnight he was in jail.

That evening, when I came home after the revue, Gee Gee was standing in the shadows of the old carriage entrance. Under one arm he had a bundle of fish and chips wrapped in newspaper, and under the other arm a bottle of champagne and some Guinness stout. He looked my diggings over. The double bed took up most of the floor space; there was a high wardrobe, a washstand with a commode below, a dressing table over which we spread our supper.

Gee Gee threw three separate wads of money on the dressing table and got himself comfortable. He opened a bottle of stout, poured the dark liquid into two glasses, topped it with champagne, and said, 'Tonight we're living on velvet.' That was my introduction to Black Velvets.

After filling ourselves with cold fish and chips, we chewed the rag about Alice's sly grog, and then we turned in for the night. When the lights were out, Gee Gee murmured groggily, 'You know something? Your eyes remind me of Bebe Daniels'. From now on I'm going to call you Babe.'

The next morning, when Gee Gee learned the breakfast which went with my room was only tea, toast and marmalade, he shouted, 'I'll need more than tea and toast to take care of my three sheilas. I'll go to the Itie's for steak and eggs.' Then he added, 'This is going to be a laugh, each one of my tabbies it going to swear to the other two that I stayed with her last night!'

'You know something? Your eyes remind me of Bebe Daniels.
From now on I'm going to call you Babe.'

The following night he brought home a suitcase and a bottle of whiskey. As we began to feel our nips, I noticed he had only a trace of Aussie accent; in fact, his speech was similar to my cousin's who had been educated at King's School. When I asked him about his schooling, he wanted to know if I'd heard of a well-known Melbourne college. He had gone there! Mentioning the name of a famous person, he said, 'She's my aunt.' Then suddenly he confided, 'I came home from college one day and this aunt was in my mother's bedroom, sitting on the Crown Derby commode. Yes, even the pot had to be royal. They had been drinking too much and I heard my aunt say, "Sure we are all bastards, we come from a long line of bastards, but the Crown takes care of us. After all, he was the king, but you had to have a child by a no-good gambler".'

Gee Gee continued grimly, 'I knew where Mum had some money hidden. I took all of it and ran away. When the money ran out I got a cabin job on a boat working up and down the coast. Finally I landed here in Sydney. I've never been back home. I hate my mother. I hate all women.' He paused and smiled wryly. 'But I'll use 'em for all they've got' – he winked – 'for I've got plenty . . .'

I took another sip of the drink, watching him finger the gold medallion he always wore on his watch fob.

'Did I ever show you this?' he asked suddenly.

'That's Napoleon, isn't it?'

'The old boy himself. Here, take a look, you might say it's my good luck piece.' I turned the charm around in my hand; the bold bas-relief of the emperor in profile caught the light. 'It was once owned by Johnny Norton,' Gee Gee said, nodding his head and smiling.

'Now, there was a character,' he continued. 'Although I knew he was two ends of a scoundrel, I always looked up to him. It doesn't seem possible that he's been dead five years. He hated Queen Victoria, you know, and used to attack her regularly in print. In fact, I think I have a clipping somewhere . . .'

He fished for a moment in his pocket and came up with a brand new wallet. From a secret compartment he took out a yellowed piece of newspaper. Looking up with a half-smile, he said, 'Listen to what Johnny said in *Truth*:

> *William IV, Queen Victoria's uncle, was a cross between a wild and mad bull. By a Mrs Jordan, whom he afterwards cast off in a most callous fashion, this scoundrel had sixteen bastards, all of whom were foisted on the state.*

'He called George IV "the biggest blasphemer, the greatest liar, the foulest adulterer, the most infamous swindler and welsher that the world has ever seen". And listen to what he said about Victoria:

> *The Queen, while amassing a fabulous private fortune and drawing enormous state allowances, without performing the duties for which they were granted, has literally swamped the Court with German Princelings.*'

'My God,' I said, 'how did Norton get away with that?'

Gee Gee laughed. 'That's not the best part – listen':

> *Her chief claim to the remembrance of posterity will be that she has been the means of afflicting the English people with a most prolific brood . . . Among them is her eldest son, the Prince of Wales. This future King of England is one of the most unmitigated scoundrels and foul-living rascals. He is the chum of card-sharps and horse jockeys; the consort of ballet girls and the houses of the demi-monde.*

'Talk about libel!' I said. 'It's a wonder Norton wasn't drawn and quartered.'

'Well,' Gee Gee said, 'he almost was. In '87 he was tried for sedition. My aunt used to talk about the scandal when I was a lad. He was charged with trying to incite discontent among Her Majesty's subjects and causing the old girl to be held up in public ridicule.'

'How could he get away with such disloyalty?' I asked.

'Well, you see, Babe, few people in those days cared what they said about monarchy. They knew of the British Government's contempt for colonial policy.' Gee Gee continued heatedly, 'Johnny appealed to the man in the street, the Labor Party, but mainly to the Aussie who had a fondness for toppling the bloke on top.'

The booze was working on me; I was hearing things about early Sydney that excited me. 'Was he sent to jail?' I asked.

'I can see you know little about Johnny. He was a born barrister, and could outwit anyone at the Bar. A diminutive Hercules – barely five feet tall – he was three times alderman and four times a member of parliament. He had the finest library of Napoleona and was a great historian as well.' Gee Gee took a sip of the drink. 'He showed up at the trial loaded down with enormous books out of which he picked other seditious excerpts to read to the court. Remember, Babe, in those days anti-German fervour ran high. Victoria had shown Germany all kinds of favours and turned thumbs down on similar appeals from us Aussies. She virtually turned her back on the colonies. Disraeli referred to Australia as a "millstone around her neck". Naturally Norton played up this sentiment in court. The jury was locked up all night. Norton pointed out that the judge himself was of German origin, and not even a naturalised subject! The case was, posthaste, discontinued by the Crown. Norton was a free man and even gained added popularity by the acquittal.'

'But Rosie told me he was a drunkard,' I said.

'True,' said Gee Gee grimly, 'and Norton, with all his brilliance, ended badly. After the turn of the century he started on a pub crawl which lasted ten years. Norton and I' – he sighed – 'had a lot in common – we were both bastards. In fact, once Norton said, "I'm the bastard son of a parson – a child of pure love, like Napoleon and all other bloody men with brains. We have it on the authority of Shakespeare that bastards are very capable men; bastardy means genius, goodness and greatness".'

The Scotch had done its work. Gentleman George was fast asleep. I sat there for a long time, thinking over what Gee Gee had told me. It all seemed impossible, and I wondered if it was true.

CHAPTER THREE

'You should only be ashamed of bein' ashamed.'

IT WAS A BEAUTIFUL spring morning. There was a blithe spirit in the air. Gee Gee had already left. It had been two weeks since he had gone to the races; I supposed he'd gone to the track. Gee Gee had the trained eye of a thoroughbred racehorse; he was able to see both sides and straight ahead at the same time.

Bridget, the maid, rapped loudly on the door and called out, 'Breakfast!' I opened the door. Her face, which looked like a very old new potato, came through the doorway, along with the breakfast tray. She looked at the empty bed and exclaimed, 'Oh, for a moment I thought yer friend 'adn't stayed the night, but I sees both pillows 'as been used.'

Turning my back, I set the tray on the dressing table, then reached for a dressing gown, but Bridget had no intention of leaving.

'E's sure a natty dresser, 'e is. I saw 'im leavin' 'ere yestiddy mornin' and I could've sworn 'e was Wally Reid of the pictures.'

Finally I got rid of her and ate my breakfast. I had a date with Lena the Fox to help make arrangements for a tea party for her niece, Leonora, who was coming at the end of the week for a visit. Lena wanted to make sure that everything should be first rate and had chosen the Wintergarden at the Hotel Australia for the party.

I'd turned the corner of Palmer Street, where Lena lived. It was just a few blocks from Alice O'Grady's sly grog. A fat Irish mama was sitting on her stoop, shelling peas. Her stiffly starched sanctimonious bodice was buttoned up to the nape of her neck and her mannish cranky-looking black straw hat matched the disapproval on her face as she looked at the prostitute next door. The Two-Shilling Girl was standing with one foot on the pavement and the other foot on her doorstep. Her cheap, gaudy wrapover exposed the half moons of her irregular sagging breasts and emphasised the large button of her navel. She wore broken-down faded turquoise satin shoes with diamond buckles, and rolled stockings. A drunk approached; she called out, "Ello, dearie, 'ow 's about comin' in fer a good time?' He paused for a moment, then shrugged his shoulders and staggered away.

Walking along, I saw passageways lined with faded, torn wallpaper damp with kalsomine. From the doorways oozed a potpourri of foul odours. The reactions of people who lived in this section were mixed; many took it for granted that a fancy lady lived next door, but the more religious Irish objected.

Now and again you could see through the open door of a respectable family. Inside, on the hall stand, was some wax fruit and Dad's cap on the rack above a vase of dead flowers. The working families' time-worn, pock-marked doorsteps were freshly pipe-clayed, reflecting the shining honesty of the immigrants who lived over their threshold. The wives of these hard-working men wore freshly ironed cotton dresses in direct contrast to the pink, purple or orange china silk wrapovers of their two-shilling neighbours. Bounding in and out of side fences were dozens of scrawny alley cats.

Suddenly a large convertible screeched around the corner with almost Keystone Comedy madness, and out jumped Terrible Tilly. Hurriedly I knocked at Lena's door and was let in. We peered through the starched lace curtains. Lena hated Tilly with a vengeance.

Every trollop, grandma, mother and daughter fled to slam doors and windows. We heard Tilly holler, 'I'm going to tear this firkin street inside firkin out!' A firkin is an old-fashioned implement used for measuring churned butter, but I don't think Tilly had this in mind, although she certainly churned up the entire street!

Tilly crossed the street to the house where Connie Ediss lived. Lena and I held our breath. Lena said, 'I warned Connie, but she wouldn't listen to me.' She'd been working Tilly's territory. Tilly approached Connie's stoop, reached down, removed one shoe, and with an enraged wallop knocked out the windowpanes of Connie's house. Then she shouted for the whole street to hear, 'If I ever catch you near my beat again, I'll slash your bloody throat, abso-bloody-lutely!'

Bewildered, Connie appeared in the doorway, all done up in a spring print of blood-red poppies on a field of green. She was adjusting her high military black straw hat with scarlet cock feathers. 'What yer doin'?' screamed Connie. 'An' who the 'ell do ya think y'are?'

'I'll tell you who the 'ell I think I am,' Tilly shouted back, 'and I'll show you who I am!'

Like a red bantam rooster, Connie leaped onto the footpath in front of Tilly. She, too, placed her hands on her hips. They glared at each other with fire in their eyes.

Lena nudged me. 'She shouldn't have done that. Tilly'll make mincemeat out of her.' And she did.

Tilly gave Connie an uppercut, a smack to the chin with her southpaw. Then, pushing her against the house with her powerful arms, she began grinding her diamond lizard over Connie's face. Blood gushed out of her nose, mouth and all over her poppy print until she looked like Flanders Fields. At last Connie lay still. Tilly called to one of her fancy men: 'Bring me that bottle of mixed pickles, it's in the bag with the tinned meat.' She stomped one of her spiked heels in Connie's ribs, reached down and snatched the hat off her head. Handing it to the bruiser, she took the lid off the pickles and doused them all over Connie's face.

Strutting triumphantly to her car, Tilly called out for all to hear, 'Mincemeat with sauce, anybody?'

She jumped into the front seat, between her two fancy men, and the big car backfired and roared its way down Palmer Street. No sooner had the car sped away than the whole street became alive. The girls left their doorsteps and gathered in groups, protesting:

'Something must be done about Tilly.'

'It's a disgrace to allow a cockney like that in the country.'

'She's ruining a nice neighbourhood.'

Little Cammie came running around the corner calling out, 'Cops!' Hastily everyone left the middle of the street. The fat respectable mama sent her child out to collect the peas she had dropped in her hurry. A rags-bags-and-bottle cart went by, the driver calling out for rubbish. An old douche bag was hurled out an open window and landed on top of the discards in the cart.

Most of the Two-Shilling Girls took up their positions with one foot on their property, and the mamas went back to peeling potatoes and shelling peas. One of the girls went inside and started playing her pianola and singing a local favourite:

> She's me Lou, Lou, Lou from Woolloomooloo,
> She's just the little tabby I adore.
> I takes her for a walk and I show her round the shops.
> And if she gives me any cheek, I slap her on the chops,
> Because she's mine, mine all the time.
> She is, so help me Bob, and strike me blue.
> Though she's not exactly what you call a lady
> She's me Lou, Lou, Lou from Woolloomooloo.

By the time the cop with his swinging stick rounded the corner, the scene was just one happy family. However, Lena took no chances; she handed Cammie threepence, telling her to get a hansom cab.

Lena had covered her badly dyed hair and was sporting a handsome grey transformation. She wore pince-nez and, with her conservative dress and toque, her face took on the innocence of a dove. Her disguise was complete; no one would recognise the shoplifter turned dope peddler. She decided we should take a ride through the Domain; she wanted to get away from Bourke Street and the memory of Terrible Tilly.

To calm her nerves, she opened her Capstan cigarette box and, pulling out a little capsule, quickly took out the powdered substance and gave a strong sniff up each nostril. Between sniffs she inhaled a deep breath. 'My, that salt sea breeze coming in from Sydney Cove is invigorating.' She told me it was snuff that her grandmother used – she forgot I was at Alice's that night.

As we jogged along the jumbled streets of Woolloomooloo she reminisced:

'It was right here in the Loo that I was born, and I've remained a Sydneysider ever since.' Pointing to a long row of barnacled stone houses sandwiched together, Lena told me that's where the Sydney Coves – convicts who had served their sentences – hung out before they left for San Francisco to establish criminal gangs and teach the Yanks a thing or two.

Turning a sharp corner, Lena began to peel back the years; she pointed to a row of tiny houses. 'Right on the pavement, under the dimly lit cribs in the alleys of these blood-clotted slums, the lowest of all human flesh carried their own small mattresses while their lecherous whore-masters drank up their earnings. But the girls paying rent in the cribs were not without revenge, for a large iron kettle of water was kept simmering, and when a mattress was thrown outside the windows, the man no sooner had his pants half down when the scalding water was poured over him.' Lena laughed loudly. 'I'd like a quid for every burnt arse I've seen as some poor bugger ran away, unable to pull up the back of his pants!'

A Greek, selling live fish, passed by with his cart, calling out, 'Live fish-os!' Another cart carried a row of skinned pink rabbits, looking like trapeze aerialists hanging by their toes; the cart owner called out, '*Live* rabbit-os!'

Lena said, 'There was much more activity around here in my day. Old Mother Five-Bob carried a box of fruit on her head; wearing her kelly-green dress and feathered hat, she was more Irish than old Patty O'Brien with hat in hand, singing "Irish Eyes Are Smiling", ever was! And a little man playing a concertina sang "Gentle Annie"' – Lena winked slyly – 'and they called him Gentle Annie.' Worldly Lena's smile disappeared when she recalled Paddy the Ram, who used to roam the streets of the Loo – when mad drunk he'd ram anyone in sight with his head.

'Paddy always reminded me of the delinquents, or Larrikins, as we used to call them,' Lena said. 'The Larrikins went around in "pushes", or packs, and many young blokes stayed with their push even after marrying.' For years these pushes went unchecked. Each push had a name and was identified by the way they dressed: the Darlos came from Darlington; the Bristley's Mob from York and Kent Streets; the Bay Street Crowd from Glebe; the Loo Rat Pack from Woolloomooloo. Others were the Golden Dragons and the Forty Thieves. The most evil push was known as The Rocks and came from The Rocks at Millers Point.

It was the day of shirts with unattached collars, and none of the gang members wore collars, leaving the top button opened. They bloused their shirts at the waist over skin-tight pants moulded to the calves. The pants jutted out into bell-bottoms which almost hid the high-cut heels of their shoes; these heels added height and gave them a stilted Navy-like walk. They leaped out of doorways, knocking the hats off startled passersby. Frequenting the gods of the theatres they'd often corner unsuspecting patrons, whom they'd bounce back and forth like ping-pong balls.

Lena said it took the return of the lash and finally the World War in 1914 to put an end to Larrikinism.

We drove through the beautiful Domain, the gardens looking like Jacob's coat of many colours. Towering above everything else, the pious bulk of St Mary's Cathedral shone in the sunlight. It was an awe-inspiring sight and must have put Lena in a generous mood, for between the view and the 'nose candy', Lena the Fox gave the head waiter at the Wintergarden an oversized tip.

The arrangements for Leonora's proper tea party made, I put Lena in a cab and walked the couple of blocks to my diggings.

The next day, after being patched up, Connie signed a complaint charging Terrible Tilly with Assault and Battery and Theft of Hat. A trial date was set a fortnight away.

The case rocked the underworld like an earthquake. The courtroom was packed with everyone from Bourke Street to Tilly's own stamping grounds, Surry Hills. Macquarie Street's Gaiety Girls outdid themselves in the most elegant fashions. Even Lena the Fox and Spanish Nell couldn't resist an opportunity to flaunt themselves before the whole Sydney detective force. Alice O'Grady, my actor friend Ralph, myself and Gee Gee made up another party. Gee Gee never made public appearances with any of his three girls.

The court was patterned after the English courts, as was almost everything else in

DARLINGHURST NIGHTS

BY
KENNETH SLESSOR
&
VIRGIL REILLY

Australia. The judge wore a long black robe and ill-fitting white curled wig. Outside the little wooden gate of the courtroom two officers of the law were stationed. It was the custom that no one could be arrested for any other offence while still inside these gates of the court.

Tilly was decked out in Connie's scarlet-feathered hat and a skin-coloured georgette beaded evening gown; the sunlight beaming through the window made it obvious she wore no undergarments. She was called to plead her case. The charge of Assault and Battery and Theft of Hat was made, and the witness called. Connie told the judge what happened, leaving out, of course, the part about her cruising on Tilly's beat, ending with, 'Why, Your Honour, she 'as me very own 'at on 'er 'ead this very moment!'

'Take the bloody thing, it doesn't suit me any'ow!' Tilly yelled as she tore off the hat and threw it at Connie.

Rapping the bench, the judge called, 'Order in court!' Then, speaking directly to Tilly, he said, 'The court finds you guilty of Assault and Battery. Ten guineas and costs.'

Furious, Terrible Tilly stalked up to the judge with her back to the spectators. She threw her beaded dress high above her waist and yelled, 'Kiss me, judge!' There were stunned ohs, ahs and raucous laughter.

The judge rapped on the bench. 'Order in the court!'

The moment Tilly stepped through the gates the judge called out, 'Arrest that woman!' The two policemen, putting their hands on either shoulder, led Tilly back through the gates and up to the judge, who sternly announced, 'I fine you twenty guineas.' Up went Tilly's skirt in the air as she repeated her performance. Just as she got through the gates again, the judge roared, 'Arrest that woman!'

She upped her skirt that day until the fine was upped to sixty guineas. Finally Tilly gave up, muttering as she left the courtroom, 'Oh hell, what's the use!'

Truth published the complete case in detail the following Sunday, and Terrible Tilly was more famous than ever.

Along with all the Easter visitors for the Sydney Cup, Lena the Fox's niece, her schooling at a convent completed, arrived for her visit with Auntie.

Before going to Lena's tea party we all met at Alice's. Gentleman George took over. He had seen snapshots of Lena's niece and was already shook on her. Knowing she was a good girl, he wanted no one to look out of place; hats, dresses, shoes and gloves were looked over – some were changed, others were rejected. He told some of the girls to tone down their make-up. Never had there been a more sedate group than the one who met the beautiful girl, just down from Sister Kenny's country.

As the party progressed, Lena's face became leaden. She sensed the 'chemical something' was happening between Gee Gee and her relative, and when she heard him inviting her to the races the next day, Lena ended the party abruptly.

Leaving the hotel she ushered her niece into a waiting hansom cab. Smiling sweetly at Gee Gee, she said, 'So you're taking her to the races tomorrow?' Still smiling, but gritting her bottom gold-capped teeth, she softly hissed, 'Over my flowered basket!'

That evening Lena and Rosie went to the station, and as the Melbourne Express pulled out, they waved goodbye to Lena's sweet young niece. Hurrying away from the station, which was usually a hotbed of detectives, Lena smugly announced, 'That's one time I outfoxed the Stallion. He'll not befoul, befuddle and betray my Leonora!'

One evening, several months later, The Odd One's shrieking voice stabbed the night – she was crushed to death by a passing truck, at the foot of the Loo. No one knew whether she had done it deliberately or whether it had been an accident.

The girls had paid little attention to her strange moods, but their grief at her death was genuine. Funeral arrangements were made by Rosie Boot. At her instigation, all the Gaiety Girls agreed that out of respect for The Odd One, no one would work Macquarie Street the night of the funeral. Besides, as Gertie Millar aptly put it, 'We can all do with a rest.'

There was great excitement and much preparation. Except at funerals, only older women wore black. The regular streetwalker often has a child's mind. It was as though they were little girls playing house. The ingenious Macquarie Street girls bought the most elegant, but certainly inappropriate, draped French models and had them dyed black. In fact, there wasn't an inch of nun's veiling left in the Sydney stores. The girls fashioned their mourning weeds with long flying black squares bordered with three-inch mourning crepe.

The brocaded Poiret fashions and extreme afternoon dresses made them look like trailing tarantulas, collars jutted straight up, covering chins but allowing the cardinal red lips to show. Some of the girls even carried huge muffs of black fox. Their caterpillar trains outdid all of the atrocious Hollywood creations of the silent screen vamps such as Olga Petrova and

Theda Bara. The Gaiety Girls looked like black vampires.

Rosie Boot didn't attend the services. The day of the funeral she paid a visit to the little Catholic church where she supplied wherewithal for children's picnics. Then she made arrangements for high tea at Alice O'Grady's, following the funeral. Few of the fancy men were invited. But I told Rosie this was one tea party I didn't want to miss. She also decided a collection should be taken for a suitable tombstone.

After the services all the Gaiety Girls met in the front parlour at Alice's, where Rosie *received* them. They were a strange vision, all in deep black, except Rosie, who was a scarlet Jezebel from the red glazed ostrich feather that shot up from her turban to the ruby buckles on her red satin slippers. With the girls grouped around her, she looked like a flaming torch in a black abstraction.

Rosie shouted for the house, and after a few more shouts the girls began to speak of the things most personal to them. Rosie expounded her philosophy of life: 'You should only be ashamed of bein' ashamed. We all belong to the world's oldest profession. I've saved me money for the day when I've outlived me usefulness.' Rosie contended that a woman – whether a great beauty of the stage, the screen or the pavement – when she'd outlived her usefulness, she'd outlived her life.

In her scarlet outfit, Rosie Boot had really taken centre stage – and some of the girls were a little put out at her. Once she got the floor, even Gertie Millar couldn't budge her. She was full of tricks; there were certain stock phrases she used to hold her audience so that no one could cut in as she gulped down a beer, her voice giving a jolt on the opening line of a new sentence. She'd say, 'But let me tell you . . .', 'You know what I mean . . .', 'Don't you know . . .', and she had a vile case of the 'and-ers'. She would say, 'My body belongs to me, I do as I please with it. An-der, thank Gawd the nice women like to remain passive as they call it, because if they were to pick and choose just as freely as the men do, why our profession would be shot to hell.'

Lena the Fox agreed: 'If you ask me, the only reason the society ladies *don't* is they're afraid of being looked down on.'

The Duchess of Teck said she knew a girl who came right out of London's Limehouse District; she started by pointing her toe in the Gaiety and penetrated some of England's finest drawing rooms, including that of a duchess.

'I'll bet she pointed more than her toe,' laughed Alice O'Grady.

'And I've known some,' continued the Duchess, 'who have gone from pot-carrying to train-carrying, and with three white ostrich tips on the top of their heads!'

Some talked of saving enough and 'going 'ome to Mum'. But most of them never wanted to leave Australia and its climate. Others spoke of getting married or 'settling down'. That was the cue for Connie Ediss to burst forth into the song which her counterpart was singing at Her Majesty's Theatre in Sydney. J.C. Williamson had put on *So Long, Letty*, starring Australian actress and singer Dorothy Brunton, and the real Connie Ediss stopped the show every night, singing, 'Here Come the Married Men'. Connie finished the wartime song:

> *If every married man,*
> *Throughout his married life,*
> *Were so true to his country*
> *As he was to his wife –*
> *Heaven help the country then!*

It was the wise old owl, Lena the Fox, who went on 'next to closing'. No one knew exactly how old Lena was, but she was getting to an age when she had begun straightening things out, going over her books, as it were, and checking the ledger. With a slightly world-weary voice she began to advise these lost travellers.

'Look at Rosie,' she said. 'She has no man.'

'No man sez you. Well, I like that!' It was Connie Ediss talking again. She had just flopped back into the big armchair with the broken springs. She came up from behind her stomach as she said, 'What about 'er Bill?'

We all knew that Mondays and Thursdays were Bill Darcy's days on Bourke Street. He sold strictly fresh eggs and poultry. Bill was as rugged as the Australian coastline, but no relation to Les Darcy, Australia's champion heavyweight. He was lean and sunburned; his skin was seared in the same way that heat dried the inland plains. Big, brash and brutally frank, and at times brutal, he was also good to look at in a sort of Newfoundland dog way. Twice a week Bill's cart could be seen at Rosie's place. Some of the cheap two-bob hussies would call out to each other: 'Rosie's givin' Bill a bit on the 'ouse. She makes the toffs pay 'er two guineas, but . . .'

'As I was saying, before I was rudely interrupted,' said Lena, 'Rosie has no bludger. Why don't you girls wake up! The Duchess of Teck is right – start looking for a man, any good, honest working man; it's a known fact that whores make the best wives once they quit the business. First of all, start stuffing your stocking; a bludger won't take care of you when you are old, cold and hungry.'

Alice always kept a full larder, but this day her table was weighted down with the finest delicacies. The Gaiety Girls drank Australian sparkling hock and stuffed themselves with sandwiches, trifle and Sargents tarts.

Rosie Boot took up the collection for the tombstone. Some wanted an angel, others a flaming torch, but Rosie said it should be a simple stone – maybe with two lines out of The Odd One's favourite song:

> Some day hating will cease,
> Some day there will be peace.

All agreed it was perfect. They were deeply moved. These melancholy babes might gossip, fight, hate and beat each other, but in a pinch they were capable of loving, befriending, even nursing each other. And, when there was a funeral, such as this one, the town florists were completely bought out.

Alice called out, 'Last round!'

It had been a long day. I went back to my diggings, a little more thoughtful than before.

Rosie Boot had her own ideas about religion. She would drop in at church at odd times when the mood struck her. She would walk up Bourke Street to the top of Oxford Street, over and down to Surry Hills, where she was unknown. For these journeys she always wore the same nondescript coat and hat, with no make-up. In this guise she fitted easily into the neighbourhood.

Over the years, Rosie, as plain Mrs Boot, had contributed sums of money to the convent so that the slum kids could have a picnic and be taken up the harbour in a ferry boat. She liked to think of the food her money bought: many sandwiches, dozens of meat pies, sausage rolls and Sargents tarts. Her eyes would get quite misty when she thought of the joy she was bringing to the underprivileged kids. But this was not her only charity – she had sent groceries when the father of one of the ragamuffins had been in an accident; and sometimes she would send baby clothes to a new mother. These things she always did anonymously.

Once a small boy pointed her out to the Monsignor as the benefactress who had given money for medicine for his mother.

Rosie dropped by the church one day for a visit. She knelt in her usual place in the back pew. Later she walked over the top of Oxford Street and made her way downhill to her Bourke Street block. Her mind was far off. Looking up, she saw a priest rounding the corner and coming towards her. Horrified, she realised it was the Monsignor from her church. What in the devil was he doing way across town? And on Bourke Street of all places! She tried to sweep past him, but he recognised her and called, 'Mrs Boot, Mrs Boot.' Rosie turned – she could hardly pretend she was deaf. She looked up innocently into the Monsignor's face.

A Two-Bob Girl, standing in her doorway with one foot stretched out on the pavement, called out, 'How are you doin', Rosie, orright?' Then, pulling her sleazy housecoat over her half-exposed breast, she cried out, 'And 'ow's the Bible-banging business doin', Father, orright?'

Rosie looked away. The priest's face reddened. 'Mrs Boot,' he said, ignoring the woman in the doorway, 'I personally want to thank you for your kind contributions to the convent. You don't know how the children appreciate –'

But he got no further, for the loose woman screamed, '*Mrs Boot!* Mrs Boot yer calls 'er! Well, I like that! She's the notorious *Rosie* Boot, and the only dif'rence between me and 'er is she gits two pounds two shillin's fur turnin' a trick, 'n' I ony gits two shillin's, but.' Her spiel over, the Two-Bob Girl folded her arms, using her breast as a shelf, and triumphantly stared at both of them.

Stunned, the Monsignor looked at Rosie, and Rosie glared at the Two-Bob Girl. 'Father, I didn't think I was doin' wrong givin' you money for the kids. When I was young I never went on an outin'. In fact,' Rose finished wistfully, 'I never was young – Mumma saw to that.'

The Monsignor shook his head; his strange predicament was apparent in his furrowed brow. Obviously he could not condone this woman's conduct. On the other hand, if he refused the money, the children . . .

He said aloud, 'I'm sorry, Mrs Boot, I cannot accept more money from you if this woman speaks the truth.'

'It's the truth!' shouted the Two-Bob Girl. 'Why, Gawd's truth, you and the Sisters aughta be ashamed of yerselves acceptin' 'er tainted quids! You aughta see 'er walkin' down

Macquarie Street in the evenin', flauntin' 'er fancy clothes and white fox furs!'

The priest turned and stared at the woman. 'That will be enough, Miss!'

The girl's eyes flashed. She turned on her heels and went indoors.

'Mrs Boot,' the Monsignor said, not unkindly, 'remember, the church is always open. If we cannot accept your money, we can always accept your repentance. Good day.' And he tipped his hat to this woman who had given so many happy outings to his charges.

The moment he had gone, the Two-Bob Girl came out on the stoop and resumed her old position. Her front gold tooth, which matched the yellow stained bottom teeth, flashed as she cried out to Rosie, 'It won't be long now, Rosie dear, before you're doin' doorstep trade same as me. After all, dearie, you've been turnin' tricks since the turn of the century.'

The rags-bags-and-bottle cart was dragging along, the owner calling out, 'Any rags, bags, bottles?'

Rosie took off her drab grey coat and threw it on the cart. Under the coat she wore a scarlet bias-cut dress. She threw her black hat up in the air and it, too, landed on the junk. Then fluffing out her hair, she took a pot of rouge and lipstick from her purse and, standing in the middle of the pavement, one hip thrown out provocatively, she made up her face. Shrugging her shoulders at the other woman, snapping her purse, she began swinging her beaded bag.

By now all Bourke Street was on its front steps. Upstairs windows shot up – yawning trollops leaned over their windowsills.

Prostitutes love to dramatise, in their melancholy way. Feeling all eyes on her, Rosie Boot – Sydney's best-dressed laced-mutton lady – started to sing in her husky contralto.

A trull called down from her window, 'Good Old Rosie got a dirty deal, but.'

Little Cammie dashed round the corner, calling, 'Cops!' Suddenly doors bolted like thunder. Windows slammed tight as a tick. When the cop appeared everyone had skedaddled except an Irish grandma sitting on her white-washed steps, wearing a faded challis housedress. In her lap was an ancient prayer book; the corners of its worn leather cover had been thumbed back. She was fingering a string of timeworn wooden rosary beads. As the cop passed he bid her good day.

'And a good day to you, too,' she greeted Officer O'Toole – between beads.

Dolores del Rio
In Caliente

CHAPTER FOUR

She slipped me fivers under the table just to go dancing.

I HAD LEFT THE revue and gone into the chorus of *Irene*. After six months in Sydney and a similar run in Melbourne, we played New Zealand, where I had the good fortune to meet Miss Marie Tempest, star of comedy and light opera.

Glad to be away from my Sydney Coves and their crim con, I resolved on my return to have no part of them or their con.

Returning to Sydney, everyone was doing the Bunny Hug and the Turkey Trot. I teamed up with a beautiful girl with raven black hair and violet eyes, and did a ballroom dancing act. Mrs McLaughlin, who staged tea dances at her Wentworth Hotel, engaged us. I was soon in demand with the rich, racy set – bookmakers' wives with lots of time on their hands and money to slip under the table when the check arrived.

I knew a buyer who was the same size as myself. I had him order Bond Street clothes for me.

The wife of Sydney's biggest tobacconist was on the loose; she slipped me fivers under the table just to go dancing. Then, I met an extremely wealthy widow ten years older than I. She wasn't so good looking as she was chic. Her jewels were beautiful. She had chauffeur-driven imported cars, and she loved dancing and cocaine. I was given handsome cufflinks, watches and studs. A chauffeur in a dubonnet uniform, matching the Fiat car, began picking me up when I got through dancing. I was now living at the Australia Hotel. My room and meals cost double my salary. There was talk.

Ten years later, the same rich widow met another Aussie just down from New Guinea named Errol Flynn.

Occasionally I would run into Gee Gee either in a bar or on the street. I would notice him looking me over in my English-cut clothes, no longer bush in appearance. Gee Gee now pestered me to go to the track with him, but I always had an alibi – tea dances were held on Wednesdays and Saturdays. I also told him I stayed with relatives in Parramatta. I was no longer fascinated by his rhyming slang and, besides, my rich widow called him a racetrack tout.

Then, one day it happened. I had a win on the last race and had just collected when I came face to face with Gee Gee. He was in a foul mood. Every filly had run out on him. He started talking in his slang language. He was hearts of oak (broke). Leaving the racecourse we went out into the field of wheat (the street), and around the Johnnie Horner (corner) he shuffled me into the bread and jam (the tram), which was very crowded. Standing up, I could see Gee Gee looking at a pot and pan (man) and trying to ascertain how much bee and honey (money) he had in his sky rocket (pocket). I knew what was on Gee Gee's mind but could do nothing about it. The well-dressed man sported a Simple Simon (a diamond) stick pin on his tie. Gee Gee jostled me as we hit a bump in the tracks and I, in turn, hit the man, who lunged forward slightly. I could smell the gay and frisky (whiskey) on his breath. In that split second, I saw Gee Gee's hand snatch at the man's wallet, which fell at my feet. I could see that the man's Chevy Chase (face) was untroubled – he didn't even know his sky rocket had been touched.

I looked quickly at Gee Gee, unruffled as ever; only his Nelly Blyes (eyes) had a hard glitter as he indicated I should stoop down and pick up the billfold. Tensely I mouthed the word 'no'. Glancing at the man, my heart stood still when he put his hand into his breast pocket, then he felt all his pockets, frantically looking for his wallet. Finally he found the billfold at my feet. Gee Gee was furious. His whole face tensed, his mouth tightened, his jawbones cracked, his teeth gritted, but his cold steel eyes, flashing like lightning, never left mine during the remaining fifteen minutes' ride. When we got to town, as he got off one side of the tram, I quickly turned and jumped off the other side, into a waiting taxi. That evening, scared of Gee Gee and afraid to go near my diggings, I took a cheap room down by The Rocks.

For the first time I thought like an adult. My mind went back to my bush days when my world was soft and gentle, my chums kind, and Bijou my constant companion. But I wanted to be different. I got out of the bush world. Now I was a Sydneysider. It had suited me all to pieces to be around the flashy Gee Gee with his idle ways. He had short brushes with the law. I always kidded myself that he was on the level, but all the time I knew he was on the cross. I also liked the mysterious flavour of sensuality surrounding Bourke and Palmer Streets, in fact, all of Kings Bloody Cross.

What a rum thing I'd made of myself, changing names as often as the shows I'd been in. I'd used up four outrageous monikers; and Babe, the one Gee Gee had tacked on to me, made five. At the rate I was going – accepting under-the-table money from women twice my age – I'd end up a lounge lizard.

She had chauffeur-driven imported cars,
and she loved dancing and cocaine.

Now I'd run out of names and excuses for becoming part of this riff-raff. Frightened, disgusted and disillusioned, I called my mother. When I told her I wanted to go to America she said, 'I know, son, all the Purdues were rovers. You know, one branch went to Australia and the other to America. From the time you learned to scuff the water you were forever saying, "Look, Bijou, that one went all the way to America."' Mother came up from the country.

Being a friend of the Fuller family, and with Sir George Fuller now Premier of New South Wales, a hurried visitor's visa was arranged for me so that I could sail on *The Sonora*, which was leaving in a few days.

I called an American girl I knew, Grace Cornell. She was a wiseacre, and when I told her I was going to the United States, she said, 'Well, when you get to Honolulu, don't buy a ukulele, and when you get to New York, don't look up.'

Cup Week was Sydney's biggest event, and sailing day was Cup Day at the races. I arranged to sit in the Members' Stand with some of my mother's friends, where I would be out of the sight of my charming Macquarie Street companions. I could see them very well, but they couldn't see me.

Just as the second race was starting, the Governor-General and his Lady entered the Royal Box. The band struck up 'God Save the King'. Simultaneously with the music, Rose Rooney – Queen of Diamonds – started to parade in a fabulous Paris gown, sparkling with diamonds, on the beautiful green lawn directly in front of the Governor-General's box. I'm afraid few people took the time to look at the bonafide Governor-General's Lady in her dowdy ashes-of-roses lace dress. Apart from Rose, parading below were madams of the five seaport cities, haughtily showing off the French imports of Vionnet, Patou and Poiret. And in the midst of this tossed salad were Gee Gee and all the other racy characters.

I left with my friends, who always skipped the last race, and we motored into town. I was already packed. Only my mother and several relatives were going to see me off.

That evening, as *The Sonora* slowly moved down the long pier, I saw a pair of boots with grey suede uppers, bounding along, keeping distance with the ship. It was Gee Gee calling out aloud: 'Coo-wee, Coo-wee.' Tipping his hat he shouted at the top of his lungs, 'I'll never find another straight man like you!'

I heard the soft strains of the customary farewell song:

> *Goodbye Sydney Town,*
> *Sydney Town goodbye.*
> *I am leaving you today,*
> *For a country far away.*

I was in my early twenties and a whole new world waited for me over the horizon. Everything – the pier, the faces – turned to mist as I found myself singing the last verse of the song:

> *Though today I'm stony broke,*
> *Without a single crown,*
> *When I make my fortune*
> *I'll come back and spend it in*
> *Dear old Sydney Town.*

The Sonora pulled out to sea . . .

I didn't buy the uke in Honolulu – our route was via Tahiti. I'd remembered what Grace Cornell had said, but coming out from the 34th Street Penn Station, I looked up at the tall New York skyscrapers in amazement. When I looked down, a man had my bags.

'What hotel, sir?'

'The Coolidge.'

'Well now, isn't that a coincidence, I just happen to be a Coolidge man.'

He led me down a long line of taxis – at the very end stood a solitary open Victoria. He threw my baggage onto one seat and, taking my elbow, heaved me onto the opposite seat. Like a flash he leaped up front. With a crack of his whip we were off and on our way before I could change my mind. It was a very hot July day, and between the heat and the traffic, we slowed down to a trot.

I wore a grey cross-bar suit, which was an exact copy of what the Prince of Wales (later the Duke of Windsor) was wearing; I even duplicated his light grey homburg. In the old broken-down open carriage I must have been an odd sight. People on the street stared and giggled, and when we drove by the Palace Theatre, they laughed out loud. I must say, I found them just as amusing.

In 1923 American men had not yet caught on to the casual style of English clothing. In fact, many wore high-crowned hats or caps with bills. Coats were pinched in at the waist, with an angry slit way up the back which flapped in the breeze; they wore skin-tight pants, and fancy two-tone shoes.

By the time we reached the Hotel Coolidge on 47th Street, I knew there was nothing presidential about my future home.

My sitting room, bedroom and bath was third floor front. In the adjoining apartment lived a cute young Irish lass named Gracie. Larry Reilly, an Irish actor with a green moustache who should have done a single – a solo show – had just broken in an act with her, but he made the mistake of billing it: Larry Reilly and Company. *Variety*, reviewing the act, said, 'We don't know who the *and company* is, but she's mighty snappy company.' A young man named Nate Burns must have thought so too, for soon he was breaking in an act with the same Irish lass. Their billing was: Burns and Allen.

Gracie's room-mate was Mary Kelly, of Kelly and Swift. She sang, 'It Was Mary, Mary, Long Before the Fashions Changed' – and she changed boyfriends every other night. One night she would go out with a young vaudevillian who lived down the street at the

Somerset Hotel. He had big blue eyes, played the fiddle and was twenty-nine years old. The next night she would see Ray Myers, a booker for Keith's Metropolitan Vaudeville Theatre. She must have thought the booker the best bet, for instead of meeting Jack Benny she married Ray. How lucky for the other Mary – Mary Livingstone, that is, whom Benny would later wed.

Living directly above me was a young Southern boy named Gene Austin. One evening Gene stopped by with a bottle of gin; he wanted to celebrate having just sold his first song outright for fifty dollars. But if Gene Austin only got fifty for 'How Come You Do Me Like You Do?', he made up for it later with 'My Blue Heaven'.

It was on this same street that the wonderful vaudeville actor Polly Moran, who would later become a silent movie star, did her funniest act. She'd rush up to some tired-looking gal with blonde curls and say, 'Please, Miss Pickford, may I have your autograph?' She'd wait for this to sink in and then continue: 'Now come, come Mary, I know the camera makes you look a lot younger.' When she had the old gal in her palm, she'd turn to us and let out a string of naughty words. The little old blonde lady, shocked beyond belief, would leap and bound down to Broadway.

Here, too, were vaudeville's Wilton Sisters with their long-bearded little men who would, at the first sprinkle of rain, dash up from the dark basements with their arms loaded down with antique umbrellas which they'd sell for a dollar a piece.

Writer Damon Runyon tabbed 47th Street 'Dream Street', because so many actors lolled around, dreaming of how, if only given the chance, they would fracture them at the Palace.

On this street I saw actress Trixie Friganza, toy balloons, babies, balls and Babe Ruth; strippers who dressed up between strips; girls who rehearsed more in bed than on the boards; male and female prostitutes; the bums and the bandits of Broadway; the lost, the strangers, the unwanted – for whom this street had no dreams.

Mary Kelly went on the road, and another friend of Gracie's, Rena Arnold, moved in with her. This girl took herself very seriously and was super-sensitive. She did a single called *Pills* on the subway circuit – the 'legitimate theatres', as they were known, which were close to subway stops and where shows played before going on tour. When she returned home in the evenings, Nate Burns always asked her, 'How did you do this evening, Rena?'

Her answer was always the same: 'I took three *legitimate* bows.'

One evening, gathered around my rented piano, Burns – as always – had Jack Benny in hysterics. We had all put in money for gin and supper. Rena made what she called her 'Rena Arnold Sandwiches'; I guess we neglected to praise her enough, because she left. We were having so much fun, nobody missed Rena. Burns impersonated the female impersonator The Creole Fashion Plate. Singing 'Where the Lazy Daisies Grow', pointing his toe and daintily holding up one trouser leg like a skirt, he alternated between foggy bass and high soprano.

When the party broke up and Nate kissed Gracie goodnight at her door, there was a muffled knock from inside. With too many nips and not enough attention, Rena had coyly hidden in her trunk, thinking, of course, that we'd all go looking for her. Accidentally the trunk had snapped shut! She was locked in!

During the endless rounds of agents, I ran into many small-time acts, and many small-time people. Most actors practically lived in their trunks, and I was told, 'There are only two trunks that'll gain you respect – a Hartmann or an H & M.' The closest to Broadway the old ham who gave me this piece of information ever got was Proctor's 28th Street Theatre! In Australia we called trunks *boxes*, and I couldn't seem to refer to them as anything else. Actors often had handsome covers tailored for their trunks, while actresses put colourful chintz covers over their boxes. I saw some that were bigger than the iceboxes Betty Furness advertised on television.

Unable to find work, and my Australian pound a dollar less than the English pound, I pawned all my suits, with the exception of the cross-bar tweed and my grey homburg, which I couldn't bear to part with. Gracie and Nate had gone on the road for six months as Burns and Allen. I had been alone for a long time when I ran into Grace Cornell – the American girl who had warned me about the ukulele. She was living over a speakeasy on 48th Street. As my funds were getting low, she arranged for a room for me at her brownstone, for twelve dollars a week. I'd been paying twenty-seven at the Coolidge.

Never being able to remember names, places or people, I'd often get mixed up and refer to a speakeasy as a *talk-softly*, which would send Grace into hysterics.

My new neighbour in New York was a cute young Irish lass named
Gracie who was breaking in an act with a young man called Nate,
later to become George. Their billing was: Burns and Allen.

During the long summer of 1924, I trudged in and out of agents' offices and up and down producers' stairs. I got nothing but a look. By midsummer, even the look soured. The receptionist of Rhome & Richards, in the Strand Theatre Building, took an instant dislike to me. It was mutual. I'd no sooner come in when her head would rise from her desk to the level of my knees, not looking further up, and she'd bark, 'Nothing for you.'

'But,' I would say, 'you don't know who I am.'

'Oh yes, I do,' she'd reply, still pounding the typewriter. 'You're from Australia. Play juveniles. You dance. Not bad looking. Black hair with a grey streak. English accent. Bond Street clothes. Buyer friend exactly your size used to order them for you. Coat has no button. No vent in the back. Pants have pleats, and if I weren't so busy, I'd look up to still find you wearing that same silly hat.'

One day I was leaving this office when Jolly Marie and her daughter, Dainty Jolly Marie, entered. I had worked for Mama Marie in small-time suburban vaudeville units in Australia. Jolly Marie had a circus background, and quite a front. She was a contortionist and a dancer, and had taken some hard knocks, and her face showed it. I'd heard she'd soaked her daughter in olive oil from the cradle. The secretary had long since banished her. I noticed Dainty Jolly Marie's legs were blue with the cold. Mama had dressed her – snow or no snow – in nothing but a diamanté-studded leotard.

Just at that moment Mr Richards, whom neither of us had ever met before, brought in some papers to the secretary. Like a flash, Mama Marie whipped off her daughter's snow-covered wool coat and stocking cap. Dainty Jolly Marie, in her dazzling leotard and skullcap, started kicking front, sideways and backwards; she then sprang into the air and landed in a split from which she recovered sufficiently to roll herself into a figure eight with her head between her thighs.

Mr Richards opened the door to his office, saying, 'Please bring in the girl.' But Dainty Marie, still rolled up like a diamond-studded ball, rolled herself into his office ahead of him. It was no time at all before a five-hundred-dollar-a-week contract was signed. Later, I dressed her in a Shubert revue.

I paid daily visits to another agent. The office was located up a long flight of stairs in the Loew's State Theatre and always featured a waiting line. I remember the little owl-like face of the receptionist. I was told he had been a chorus boy back in the high-button-shoe days; dressed as a bird, he swung far out over the audience.

It was the same every day: The top half of the door would open and the little bird-man would rest his elbows on the ledge, then, clutching both cheeks with his hands and with his head moving back and forth, like a cuckoo clock, he would repeat exactly four words as we filed by:

'Nothing' – 'Not a thing.'

'Nothing' – 'Not a thing.'

I used to bet with the person in front of me whether I would be a 'Nothing' or a 'Not a thing'. We never got beyond 'Minnie the Bird Girl', as someone called him.

Bryant Park was located on Sixth Avenue, and opposite was Bryant Hall, where many vaudeville acts auditioned and rehearsed. In fact, I practically lived there during my first six months in New York. I had only worked a few last halves. The acts were all bad and, I guess, I was worse, for invariably I was closed before the three days were up.

One day I was called to Bryant Hall to audition with a comedian in a two-act. After looking me over and listening to my slight Down Under twang, the old ham decided we'd switch parts.

'Why, with your English accent,' he said, 'and my dialogue and jokes, and that get-up you're wearing, we'd be a riot.'

I told him I was a straight man and I had never been funny.

'That's what you think!' He laughed.

We opened a matinee at Boonton, New Jersey, where Gracie and Nate had broken in their act. The moment I got on stage I froze . . . nothing would come out. The audience roared – my partner went grey – and I walked off stage. He sang a number and wasn't much better than I. The manager came back and told us both to get the hell out of the theatre. I may have lacked talent, but I did have nerve.

At the Century Theatre I auditioned for the Harry Fender singing-and-dancing role in the road company of *The Lady in Ermine*. Walter Woolf and Wilda Bennett were the stars. The Shuberts liked my voice and my reading, and after rehearsing for a week, I began the dance routines. One number finished with the ingenue leaping from a table into my outstretched arms. In fact, I was supposed not only to catch her, but waltz casually off into the wings. She leaped! We collided! I collapsed! Her chin hit the stage! Not waiting to apologise, I got up, dashed down five flights of stairs and headed towards the nearest speakeasy!

Later I dressed this same ingenue in a Shubert revue.

That same season, done up as an Apache, I did a small dance with Miss Estelle Winwood in her play *The Red Poppy*. It was Bela Lugosi's first appearance in America, and my last. We broke in out of town for a week, but didn't last even that long at the Greenwich Village Theatre. The backers dropped out – but not before I had literally dropped Miss Winwood!

I felt I had dropped enough people and it was time I dropped the theatre. I guess it was a mutual parting. Let's just say, the theatre left me.

My pay cheque was going to the landlord for arrears but bounced before we got to the bank. On the way to get it cashed I ran into Grace Cornell, also a *Red Poppy* alumnus, who'd found out the backer had no funds.

My landlord said he needed my room, but his wife, who had a soft spot in her heart for show people, put a cot in a broom closet on a tiny landing six steps above the top floor. As there was only a skylight, I painted my first trompe-l'oeil, a window complete with geranium boxes and a superb view of the Hudson. The door had to be left open permanently as my short cot didn't quite fit into the broom closet, leaving my feet protruding six inches onto the landing – I spent my first New York winter with my feet outside my roomette!

Living on the landing had other complications: The bathroom, which always seemed to be in use, was six steps and two floors below. On the fourth floor there were three or four male singers from the chorus of the Met. One in particular would sing 'Ciribiribin' in the john for half an hour each morning, then call out something in Italian – a signal to his friends, no doubt, that he was almost through. By the time I'd bolt down my six steps and trot down to the third floor, another one would be closing the bathroom door. That winter I learned the power of self-control, but it was a bit awkward in more ways than one.

One evening Rosalie Stewart, the Broadway agent, paid a visit to our 'speak'. Among others, Rosalie discovered the dancer Gilda Gray, who was the creator of the Shimmy, and she unearthed the hidden talent of an Australian named Pearl Regay. Pearl, the daughter of a circus man, migrated to New Orleans, where she learned the backbends for which she became famous.

But it was in *Rose-Marie*, with the aid of a huge feather fan, that she back-bent and kicked her way to fame. Having little schooling, Pearl was a natural Miss Malaprop. Once she opened Rosalie Stewart's office door to discover Rosalie in conference with George Kelly, the writer. Pearl let out with, 'Pardon me, was I protruding?' And she used to say, 'I've just given my hair a henna wrench.' The most quoted was when she opened in the Orpheum Circuit, after her great Broadway hit in *Rose-Marie*. Followed by a coloured maid, loaded down with hat boxes, Pearl dressed to the teeth swept up to the desk of the hotel and registered: 'Pearl Regay and Made'.

I may have lacked talent, but I did have nerve.

A rash of bad taste in decoration accompanied the bad booze of the twenties; everything was extremely moderne. A great deal of black and gold was used, along with some questionable Chinese Ming. But, as Bert Lahr was saying to Fanny Brice in a Louis XIV skit, 'Madame, remember your period.' Fanny, with a sweep of her fan, was answering, 'Vat's a period to a questionable woman?'

Nate Burns, at Gracie's suggestion, became George Burns. His family home in Brooklyn was too far away from Gracie, so he had taken an apartment on 46th Street and, not wanting to be out of style, had painted the walls, floors and furniture black. He put in an emergency call to me: 'Would you come over and paint some gold dragons? It's awfully dark in here.'

I put in a call to bootlegger Manny Manishore to deliver three for five (gin, that is), and by the time I'd completed the gold dragons, we had drained one fifth. I was painting the red tongues on the dragons when something slipped. It was me! A stream of scarlet crept into the middle of George's living room. The Burns panatela cigar jolted from his jaw. Before the startled-eyed George could close his mouth, I had painted a long angry red tongue right up the leg of the chair and into the gold dragon's mouth. George's eyes popped.

'That's fine,' he cracked, 'but what if someone moves the chair?'

'They won't,' I told him.

George mumbled, 'That'll be just dandy.'

Then, overconfident with my trompe-l'oeil nightmare – or maybe over-nipped, I've forgotten which – I dropped the tube of red paint. Another tongue swirled and swayed to the top of his black table. Another gold dragon's mouth, and we were in business. George took another nip and began to see the possibilities of a mad, mad room. Soon he was directing me.

For a quarter of a century, George Burns told this story. On each occasion the tongues became larger and larger, until he had me painting red tongues into the hall, down the stairs, out onto 46th Street and all the way up 47th.

My main means of support at that time was painting good likenesses of bad drunks. Still, this enabled me to get some of my clothes out of hock. Grace Cornell, who was no better off than I, dug up the jobs, collected the ten dollars and we split fifty-fifty. One cold early morning, Grace frantically awakened me: An Arab acrobatic troupe – The Seven Blue Demons – were whooping it up on coffee grappa downstairs. They had given her twenty dollars for a painting of themselves. Untying the cashmere sports coat which was wrapped around my protruding feet, I followed her down to the warm kitchen at the back of the speakeasy. By four o'clock I had finished the group portrait. But, in my haze, I'd painted only *six* demons; they must have been in a heavier daze, because they didn't notice the difference.

Spring came and my feet began to thaw, with the help of coffee grappa, for which I'd begun to acquire a taste.

Julian Johnson – later a story editor for 20th Century Fox – was impressed with the King Tut dados I'd painted around the walls of the speakeasy. He hired me at seventy-five dollars a week to do illustrative titles – symbolic charcoal sketches for silent films. Gagmen thought up such corny ideas as: A miser's hand counting his gold. A candle flickering out, or a moth being devoured by a flame. And, for a lapse of time, through a window I sketched peach blossoms, then falling leaves, and finally falling snow. In the evenings I painted rather bad but lifelike portraits of any customers Grace could dig up.

For some time I had secretly been experimenting with a process of hand-blocking fabrics. There were two things I had to overcome: I didn't want the paint to stiffen the material, and I wanted the fabrics to be washable. After a while I hit on the process and began painting shawls. Everyone who saw the shawls swore they were French hand-blocked prints. Hundreds were sold. We painted them in a loft uptown where I supervised

My favourite comic star and dear friend Fanny Brice, offering her
own unique take on the fan dance in The Great Ziegfeld.

the work of about twenty women – my head woman was Roscoe 'Fatty' Arbuckle's sister-in-law. Mr Weiner, a smart young promoter, was behind the whole idea. He paid me the sum of seventy-five dollars a week, and promised me a bonus. I received neither credit nor bonus.

Weiner advertised the shawls as imports from Le Touquet, France. The first lot was actually re-shipped from Le Touquet to New York. It was a great thrill for me to walk down Fifth Avenue and see my creations in half a dozen top stores, even though I didn't get credit. It had been a hard pull.

Then, one morning, a cable arrived from Mother. My father was very ill. She asked me to come home immediately. After much haggling, I managed to get a small bonus from the crafty Weiner – certainly very little money for the hundreds of shawls I had made, but enough to get me home.

I arrived in San Francisco and waited for the boat. Then began the long twenty-three-day voyage back to Australia. Our route was by way of Pago Pago, in American Samoa. I had seen the floral profusion of the pink and crimson sunset of Tahiti, but entering the narrow opening which forms the harbour of Pago Pago, the sunrise was much more breathtaking. Pago Pago wore a below-the-bust strapless tappa cloth dress, many beads, no shoes and carried an umbrella.

Pago Pago's mountainous slopes of lush exotic greens, blues and violets sweep horizontally into the vaporous sky as moist clouds dampen the brilliant colours, turning them into misty blues and greys. Suddenly, and without warning, while the sun still shines, the island is drenched in rain. Magically the tropical sun dries you before the next torrent, which seems to switch on and off every fifteen minutes.

Two of my bridge partners, an American couple, were on the way to play the Tivoli Vaudeville Circuit. We became friendly. The night before our arrival at Pago Pago, I suggested we all retire early as we were due in about seven in the morning. I wanted them to see the beauty of this tropical isle which was once the home of Robert Louis Stevenson.

We met early the next morning. But, just as we were to go ashore, a strange foreboding sensation came over me. Disturbed, I excused myself and wandered around to the deserted side of the ship. I was alone. As I gazed out to sea, my eyes and thoughts turned towards Australia. I found myself pacing the deck and looking out towards Home. I stretched out on a deck chair, searching my mind for an explanation of this disquiet which had settled over me. I thought of the Great Empire of Silence – the Kingdom of Death. We come into this world on our backs and we go out on our backs. What are we here for? From whence did we come? Where do we go, if anywhere? Half awake, I lay there realising my friends were waiting. I let them go ashore without me; somehow, I couldn't join them.

Five hours later we started on the last seven days of the journey through Suva to Auckland, New Zealand, and then on to Sydney. As soon as we were out to sea I cabled my mother of my homecoming. Finally we entered Sydney Heads, which is always choppy, and on down through the beautiful harbour.

A distant aunt dressed in black, even to her lisle stockings, met me at the pier. My father, she said, had passed away the previous week. I asked the purser the time difference between Sydney and Pago Pago. My father had died at the exact hour we entered the harbour of Pago Pago. This was the first of many psychic happenings.

Arriving at Kiama, I found our old two-storey house had been converted into four flats, and Mother living in a small cottage on the property. She thought this more practical because my father had been in such poor health. His wonderful garden, with over a hundred varieties of carnations, was no more. The Ringer, the violet-edged camellia-like hybrid that he had created, died with him, but the shocker, the serrated-edged shocking pink Orry-Kelly was in full bloom.

I moved Mother to Parramatta, just outside Sydney, where I felt she would be more comfortable. Some of her sisters still resided there, and it was her birthplace.

It's strange how the past is always catching up with you. Passing the Tivoli Theatre one matinee day, I heard a voice calling, 'Hey you! You owe us one Blue Demon!' I looked back . . . Yes, the Seven Blue Demons I had painted that early morning in New York! They all started to chase me, but, knowing the pubs better than they, I ducked in a door, scrambled though a couple of bars and lost them in another side street. It wasn't a matter of not wanting to paint the missing Blue Demon for them, I simply had no time as I was due to sail for America.

Kay Francis
Mandalay

CHAPTER FIVE

Parties, like chocolates, should be well mixed and well assorted.

LATE IN 1926, I returned to New York and found Gracie Allen had now become Mrs George Burns. *Lamb Chops*, the act Al Boasberg had written for them, had made the big time, but they still hadn't played the Palace.

Broadway was wearing its gaudiest dress, cloche hats, beaded sheaths, rolled stockings and flasks.

Gracie realised she had graduated from her Coolidge apartment and Dream Street, and she wanted no part of George's Angry Red Tongues on 46th Street. They moved to the Forrest Hotel, where Damon Runyon had made the lobby his club and finally went to roost in the wee small hours of the morning.

As his friend the journalist Walter Winchell would say, 'the gentry of the main artery' grouped about Damon Runyon in his natty Nat Lewis haberdashery. Many were colourful characters: Mike Jacobs, who ran the ticket agency across the street; 'Butch' Towers, one-time actor and now a betting commissioner; a sprinkling of fighters and managers such as Joe Benjamin, Jack Sharkey, Charley Cooke, Champ Segal, Joe Jacobs, Jack Kearns; Jack Conway, the sports writer; Lou Smith, the big boss of Rockingham Racetrack; Bill Fallon, the attorney; and Morgan – not Helen or J.P. but Swifty – Broadway's ambassador at large without portfolio.

Jack Benny had left Dream Street and moved to the Old Claridge on Broadway. Soon after he opened at the Palace. I remember so well the Monday matinee . . . Handsome, prematurely grey, Benny walked onto the Palace stage, violin in hand, and said to the orchestra leader, 'How's the show been? Great? Well, I'll put a stop to that!' He stopped the show cold.

Shawls were no longer fashionable. Anyway, they took up too much space. I wanted something I could do in my own studio. I came up with the idea of making hand-blocked ties and soon was doing well enough to take a large studio at 10 Commerce Street in Greenwich Village. It was just around the corner from the Cherry Lane Theatre, where I had slipped and landed on the floor with Miss Estelle Winwood. Number 10 was sandwiched in the middle of a row of three-storey buildings, all of indefinite proportions – some wide, some narrow. The tiniest one of all joined mine and in it lived the poetess Miss Edna St. Vincent Millay. From the street, black iron gates opened into our communal courtyard.

One winter evening, through these same black iron gates walked Archie Leach – later better known as Cary Grant. He was carrying a little two-foot-square shiny black tin box which held all his worldly possessions, and he was wearing a much shinier black suit. He had been locked out of his hall bedroom.

I took him in.

Every morning he would press the shine out of his black suit, get on the subway at 12th Street and go uptown to the National Vaudeville Association – known as the NVA – hoping to hear about a job. This was a club where the working vaudevillians hung out. But Archie hung outside, where the actors lied to each other about the size of their salaries and what a riot they were on the well-known Pantages Circuit, when in actual fact most of them worked the Gus Sun Time, one of the smallest circuits of the time.

Around the corner on Eighth Avenue was a cheap lunch counter called Ye Eat Shoppe, selling sixty-five-cent and forty-five-cent meals, and run by an ex-pro. Here Archie's good looks and charm often gained him an extra piece of pie on the house from a young waitress called Dixie.

When he returned at dinnertime, tired and disillusioned, he would tell of his daily doings. After all the agents were checked, he would usually join another group in the afternoon for coffee. He spoke of names such as playwright and screenwriter Moss Hart and producer Oscar Serlin – just names at that time. Summer arrived and Archibald was still wearing his basic black, only by now the sheen refused to dim.

One winter evening a young man named Archie Leach turned up,
carrying a black tin box with all his worldly possessions. I took him in.

When Archie first moved in he was not in good health; in fact, for almost the first six months he was under the doctor's care. He began wearing my hand-blocked neckties to the doctor's, and his physician, Dr Berson, who went on to become a famous plastic surgeon – only in those days he wasn't fixing up faces – became my best customer. The democratic doctor put in a range of my neckwear, for he had everyone from prize fighters to politicians dropping in for treatment. The doctor's orders came in by the dozen, and I gave Archie a commission. So, although my ties were much too expensive for Archie's out-of-work friends around the NVA, he did quite well.

One evening, in a particularly dejected mood, he spoke of his early life: He was born in Bristol, England. His mother had been very ill when he was a child. His father was a tailor – we had something in common there. When he was a young kid, every evening at sundown his job was to make the rounds of the city, turning on the streetlights with a long pole, hooked at one end. He hated that job. At the age of fifteen he ran away from home and joined a stilt-walking act called The Pender Troupe. They played the Continent and were later brought to New York for a Dillingham show at The Globe. The stilts were too high, or Mr Dillingham's proscenium was too low, for the faces of the two tallest stilt walkers were completely hidden, but actually it didn't matter much as they all wore masks anyway. Archie felt that, mask or no mask, the audience should see him.

Dillingham sold the act to the Hippodrome, which had a huge stage where they were seen to better advantage. Now, six years later, he was still on stilts, working odd weekends at Coney Island as a shill. His face wasn't covered up, but he was so high up in the air that no one noticed his good looks. Archie and I had another thing in common – the theatre. I wanted to design scenery and never set foot on a stage again. Archie, on the other hand, was longing to get off his stilts and put his feet down on the stage.

On another occasion Archie told me he used to sketch at school, and offered to go to work pounding out the stencils for my ties, while I did the delicate filigree and handwork. We did so well that I offered him a fifty-fifty split if he could keep his mind off his blondes and the NVA, and not mess up too many ties. We signed the ties Kelly-Leach. This way Archie could work from dinnertime until the early hours of the morning, and still have his days free for auditions and his blondes. He was no longer on the sick list.

Shortly after the Kelly-Leach ties began to flourish, Archie came bouncing in with a suit box under his arm. Breaking open the box and slipping into the jacket of the new suit, he announced, 'I walked up one flight and saved ten dollars.' Directly opposite the Palace on Broadway, at the top of a long flight of stairs, a huge sign announced:

'Walk Up One Flight And Save Ten Dollars'.

And the people you saw walking down, looked it! I told him he should have either waited or paid more for a better suit. He didn't agree. This was the first of our many arguments. We were both very opinionated.

Much later, this man, who took his place among the best-dressed men in the world, returned from England wearing a plum-coloured suit the likes of which I'd only seen on cockney vaudevillians in Australia. When I told him the purple plum shade made him look bilious, he dashed right out and bought a sun lamp – a habit he kept up for years.

Whenever Archie had any money, he'd go to the movies to study technique.

Shortly after Archie moved in on me, looking in the mirror, and said, 'There's no division between my jawbone and my neck.' Only a little past his twenty-first birthday, he began a daily exercise: jutting his chin first to the left, sharply pulling it back, then out front and back, then to the right and back again. This kept his neck and face in such good shape that decades later when he was nearing 60 he looked more like 40.

Whenever Archie had any spare money or time, he'd go to the movies to study technique. He saw all of the English comic Stanley Lupino's films. He also liked that little guy, Stan Laurel, and he learned many tricks from vaudeville and silent-movie comedian Harry Langdon. That startled look, the veering to one side, all came in handy in later years when he became the greatest of the light comedians.

One day he was called to replace a friend in an act owned by the actor Sam Liebert called *Toplisky Sez*. Excitedly he dashed off for the interview. At last his dream was coming true; he was going to walk on stage on his own two feet! When he returned home, his enthusiasm was greatly dampened. In complete dejection he threw a pair of sweaty old red-dyed underwear on his bed, along with a red stocking with slits for eyes and mouth. He was to play the Devil! Again the audience wouldn't see his face. The act got odd – very odd – jobs for months to come.

Two things were much more on his mind than the ties we painted: footlights, and his love life. He fell in and out of love with many blondes, all beautiful. Only one turned him down, and she turned his stomach. Barbara was a Ziegfeld Girl, with beautiful legs. One evening, during dinner, I unfolded the newspaper; an advertisement carried a huge picture of Barbara modelling stockings. Archie took one look, dashed to the bathroom and chucked up his dinner. Barbara's mother had been the cause of the breakup. She wanted someone better than an actor for her daughter. I wonder how Mama felt about that later?

Gradually Archie's taste was improving; his straw hats weren't too high, nor were the collars on his shirts. He was meeting people in homes instead of outside the NVA; and instead of walking on stilts he was a walking ad for a tie business. In fact, Tony Cancino, the champion featherweight fighter, whom we met through Dr Berson, wanted to finance us. But Archie's mind was on the theatre.

Sometimes, when we worked far into the night filling a large order, Archie would make mistakes and I'd yell, 'Why don't you get your mind off that NVA and think about what you're doing?' The battle would be on. But then we were just two young enthusiastic Britishers, over-anxious to get somewhere in life.

Now and then Archie played the Devil in his red underwear on the Fish and Crab Circuit. He was determined to act. As a breather from the ties, I'd design ideas for scenery, what we called *open changes*, with the scene being changed before the eyes of the

Queen of the Nightclubs in Prohibition era New York, Texas Guinan, greeted each newcomer with 'Hello, sucker!' and was raided so often she wore a necklace of padlocks.

audience. In those days it was very revolutionary. My pantomime transformation scenes were starting to pay off. There is nothing new under the sun – I did the same things differently, giving them a new twist.

Archie teamed up with a guy and a girl; their act was known as Robinson, Janis and Leach. He began to get more work. And so did I.

After peddling my ideas up and down Broadway, I got my first chance through Big Jim Timony who, among other things, was Mae West's attorney and manager.

I was signed to do three sets of scenery and costumes for *Padlocks of 1927*. My contract called for me to dress Mary Louise Cecilia Guinan from Waco, Texas – better known as Texas Guinan. With a brief screen career as a two-gun cowgirl behind her, Texas became a hostess at the Beaux Arts Cafe, and she made her first dent in the Great White Way at Larry Fay's El Fey Club. Broadway producer Nils T. Granlund had recommended her to Fay, who also operated the million-dollar El Fey Taxi Company. After only a few weeks, she became the rage of New York's nightlife. When the mayor and his committees finished welcoming visiting celebrities, they all ended up at the El Fey, where Texas knocked them on the head with a clapper as she greeted them with, 'Hello, sucker!'

After the El Fey, Texas never worked for Larry Fay again, although she remained on good terms with him. In fact, she even bought his armoured car later on. She then worked for a nightclub company which had something like ten different places, among them, the Rendezvous, the Club Intime, the Argonaut, and the Salon Royale.

She was raided so often, she wore a necklace made of padlocks. Once, when they carted her off to the wagon, she blew loudly on her own gold whistle, which was a copy of a policeman's whistle, except hers was attached to an oversized diamond bracelet.

Another time, introducing a pretty little tap dancer, Ruby Keeler, she got as far as, 'Give this little girl a great big –' when a federal agent jumped up and yelled 'Handcuff!' as he snapped the bracelets on Texas. She went off to the wagon, as always, in the best of spirits.

So crowded was the floor of her club that when all the dancing girls appeared at once, they seemed to be kicking over the customers' shoulders. But her crowded club floor had nothing on the crowded sitting room of her house, downtown. The locality is vague to me; I think it was somewhere around 12th Street.

Timony told me to be at Tex's house early one day. A maid opened the door and I stepped into a room which looked like Elmo's Flea Market, with furniture of every size, shape and period. I was informed that Miss Guinan was finishing breakfast and would join me soon. Looking around, I finally sat on something Empire. She appeared shortly.

From the moment I met this lovable, dynamic character, I knew I liked her. I don't remember what she wore, but there seemed to be a lot of lace on her negligee and too many rings for breakfast. And I've never seen so many marcelled waves on anyone except, later on, when I met the headline-grabbing evangelist Aimee Semple McPherson. Writer Mark Hellinger described Tex best as 'a paradoxical creature with the nimble brain of Wilson Mizner, and the child-like heart of Shirley Temple.'

She was brief and to the point about her own costumes. She also told me to create something stunning for the blonde girl who did the Shimmy in the production. I remember this girl had an exquisite body. She was Tex's favourite.

After much rehearsing, costume fitting and scenery painting, we broke in *Padlocks* at Newark. Most of my scenery was done for the people down front – I hadn't yet learned to be broad for those in the gallery. It wasn't a good job.

When the girls finished the last four bars of the opening number, Texas, dressed as a cowgirl in white suede and rhinestones, was supposed to enter on a white charger. On opening night the chorines, with their squeaky voices, sang Billie Rose's lyrics:

> *Fifty million lovers,*
> *Fight to pay the covers,*
> *You're Broadway's sweetheart now.*

And pointed offstage. No Texas. Again the chorines sang and pointed. No Texas. Again they sang. No Texas – the horse refused to get on the treadmill. Perhaps it was opening-night nerves, or the noise, or the lights, but whatever it was, horse manure flew in all directions! The wind from the moving treadmill blew the stuff onstage! Texas gave the horse one hell of a dig with her white suede boots, and finally the animal leaped on the treadmill. Once on stage, it reared on its hind legs, and as its front legs went up in the air, so did Texas's upper plate! A very splattered and slit-mouthed Miss Guinan finally galloped madly across the stage as the girls, on the eighth try, finished:

> *Fifty million lovers,*
> *Fight to pay the covers,*
> *You're Broadway's sweetheart now.*

Texas being escorted to the police wagon, again. One day she surprised
even them by blowing loudly on her own gold police whistle,
attached to an oversized diamond bracelet.

In the second act Texas did a dramatic sketch, which she shouldn't have! Many people did not wait for this unfortunate bit. And, thirty years later, I was still waiting for my money. But Timmy didn't live here anymore. Neither did wonderful Texas, who never lost her balance, whether shaking the hand of society or slapping the hand of the underworld.

She was made to make the world laugh. She lived for fun and she made it fun to be alive. Like all sentimentalists who scoff at sentiment, she herself was a sucker for any sob story. Dead at forty-nine, after earning as much as $4000 a week, Texas left only $28,000. On her deathbed, this truly sentimental gal said, referring to the funeral parlor known for its memorial services for the stars, 'Send me back to Broadway. Put me on view at Campbell's. I want to give all the suckers a last look at me, without a cover charge.'

Grace Cornell, who had been a Mack Sennett Bathing Beauty, knew many of the silent stars. Sydney Chaplin, Charlie's brother, had come into prominence; he'd made *Charley's Aunt* and other box office hit movies and had become almost as popular as his brother. Grace took me to meet Minnie, his wife. Minnie was blonde – too blonde – with a prop laugh. On her left hand she wore a huge twentieth-century-cut diamond tinged with yellow, and there were clips and bracelets scattered about her person. She was very nice, very easy to know, and very cockney. Liking younger women seemed to run in the Chaplin family, for Sydney and Minnie sort of went their own way, as Minnie was no spring chicken. There was another drawback: she'd had a bad nose job – something had happened to one side. Back then, plastic surgery wasn't so efficient. She looked a bit like a pecked-at parakeet.

I told Minnie about Archie being from Bristol and arranged for her to come down to the studio. One look at Archie and Minnie said, 'Gawd's truth, but you're 'andsome!' After a few gins, Minnie had ideas about Archie. But the idea which interested him most was the screen test that she promised to arrange with Warner's New York office.

The Kelly-Leach ties were going better. Archie's act was laying off and he was back at 10 Commerce Street. George and Gracie, having played all over the Orpheum Circuit, had finally made the Palace. In fact, George made many sales for us backstage, running up and down to dressing rooms with Archie following with pad and pencil. Block and Sully, Blossom Seeley, Benny Fields and everyone on the bill bought our ties. We started to monogram them – something new at that time. Pepe de Albrew and his wife, Wilda Bennett, who were on the bill with George and Gracie, practically bought us out during their New York appearance. Wilda had starred in *The Lady in Ermine*, in which I'd played a short-lived part before colliding with the poor ingenue I was supposed to catch in a dance number.

My mother wrote frequently, often enclosing a draft to help with our expenses. She would write, 'I don't hear of you painting; take some of the money I am sending you and buy canvas and paints.' Instead of buying painting materials, Archie and I would load up with liquor and throw a party.

I decided to give a party for Minnie Chaplin, hoping this might speed Archie's screen test. He invited his friend Leo Beers, who played the piano and did a single. He was a good showman: With his white-gloved hands he always ran his fingers up and down the keyboard; and he was dressed in top hat, Inverness cloak, tails and white tie. He had played London and his repertoire went way back. In fact, he knew every tune from Marie Lloyd's 'She Sits Among the Cabbages and Peas', to 'Lily of Laguna', and this suited George Burns to a tee.

Parties, like chocolates, should be well mixed and well assorted. My party for Mrs Minnie Chaplin was not too well assorted. Sitting up front in my studio were those who felt they were 'of the theatre': Mrs C. Henry Gordon, whose husband had just made a hit starring in *The Shanghai Gesture*; comedienne and wife of Roscoe 'Fatty' Arbuckle, Minta Durfee Arbuckle; Minnie Chaplin; Grace Cornell; and a few others from the legitimate theatre. Jack Benny and his beautiful Ziegfeld Follies Girl Claudia Adell, Gracie Allen and I grouped around the piano while George sang 'Red Rose Rag' and Benny held his sides, roaring with laughter.

It didn't take George long to realise that Minnie had taken an intense dislike to his singing, and when he caught the dried-prune mouth Minnie tossed at him, he played solely to the theatre crowd. Benny became hysterical, and from then on it was Minta and Minnie versus Burns and Benny. Up front, the sofa and chairs were turned around one by one, and when Archie, completely turning his back on us, pulled up a chair next to Minnie, it was a closed set. The class distinction of the Algonquin Round Table had nothing on them – that is, until George Burns hopped daintily into the middle of the circle and sang right in Minnie's face. She got up stiffly, walked to the window and looked out into the courtyard. George then rushed outside and sang up to the window. By now Benny was pounding on the floor. I heard the word *vaudevillians* repeated as if it were a dirty word, as one of the crowd referred to my friends.

There was something about the bathtub gin of the twenties that affected everyone differently. It made me high and happy, so I talked more – if that was possible. But, grouped on their perch like a row of pouter pigeons, all this 'up front' set needed was for agent Louis Shurr to make a wonderful ad for Puffed Rice.

As candles began to drip, I mixed and poured for the Orpheum Circuit around the piano, while Archie tended to the stage and cinema in the front. Somehow I felt the vaudevillians were infinitely better behaved. After a curt goodnight, a certain lady of the drama had only just stepped into the courtyard when Mrs C. Henry Gordon boxed her ears. Later, when I saw my friends to the door, Miss Edna St. Vincent Millay's living room next door was still candlelit in a lovely way. But George, his candle burning at both ends, didn't need the damp morning air to make his voice sound like a distant fog horn as he sang 'Don't Take Me Home'.

As I kissed Gracie Allen goodnight, George went into the Bow Routine, showing how Louie of the Mosconi Brothers dance team milked his audience. Then he did a Grace La Rue, swirling his hat like the vaudeville star, pulling it down over one eye and shrugging his shoulder; with a Mae Murray bee-stung mouth, he sang the last four bars of 'I Love Your Eyes When They Look at Me'. Warming up, he did a take-off of how a legitimate actor ends a sketch: The curtain goes up, catching the back of the actor, who turns and is always surprised to see the audience. As a closing – using Miss Millay's house as his centre-door fancy – he went into a buck and wing, skipping up the short flight of steps to the courtyard, and swung out the bold black iron gates. As I waved goodnight, I heard Gracie say, 'Look, Natie is taking Rena Arnold's three *legitimate* bows.' And he was.

Benny called, 'What happened to Rena?'

And Burns shouted back, 'She's laying off six legitimate months!'

Early that morning Benny's laughter must have been heard all over MacDougal Alley.

After everyone had gone, Archie and I started to clean up the ashtrays and bottles. I certainly didn't think he acted like the horse's head, and told him – who did he think he was? Gracie, George and Jack were my friends, why had he ignored them completely, particularly as he himself was still in red underwear on the Gus Sun Time. Or was he?

That's all I remember – wham! A fist flew, my jaw went up, I went down – and out. Archie's lethal punch put me to sleep for three hours. When I came to, I was sprawled across my bed, fully dressed. A police siren rudely awakened me at 7 am.

Touching my chin, I felt something hard on the outside of my mouth. Jumping up I went into the bathroom and looked in the mirror; I was a hell of a sight. Overnight I had gained a lantern jaw, and hanging over my lower lip was a tooth on a bloody piece of stringy flesh. The bathroom connected both bedrooms. I opened the door and there was Archie, sound asleep in his bed, with a bottle of gin on his night table. Even the police siren hadn't awakened him. Sadie Thompson raising hell in Somerset Maugham's *Rain* was nothing to the noise I made when I took the scissors and snipped off that tooth. I hollered bloody murder while Archie did a back flip and landed out of bed on the floor.

His house guest, Billy Smith, one of his old cronies from The Pender Troupe, was sleeping on the couch in the front room. He was an older man who had looked after Archie when he joined the stilt-walking act. I yelled, 'You and your cockney friend, get the hell out of here!' Mad as blazes, I told Archie to get his little prop bag-o-my-heart tin box and get going!

Before I knew it, Archie appeared with a tray and three glasses of orange juice. My big dramatic scene, of course, had awakened Billy Smith. A few gulps of orange juice and I felt no pain. Later I found out that Archie had mixed one part orange with three parts gin.

Then, what was known in those days as the 'Archie Leach charm' took over. He hadn't been watching those English comedies for nothing, and with his own natural flair for comedy, he went into his act: Drawing back the window curtain, showing the thickly falling snow, he went into a Stan Laurel sad-eyed bit, then a Harry Langdon, then every comedy routine he could think of. He even did a back flip and, taking a leap, ran halfway up the wall and, hanging onto the ledge, looking out the window, likened me to the cruel slave owner in *Uncle Tom's Cabin*: 'You ain't goin' to throw us out into that cold, cold snow, are you, Simon Legree?'

I was beginning to weaken. Besides, I thought to myself, I shouldn't have stuck my chin out the previous night. Everyone knew Archie Leach was very fast with his dukes. In fact, I'd seen him floor the silent star James Hall with one punch. The gin and orange juice thawed me out.

They didn't have to cross the ice.

The following Saturday night, Minnie had arranged a date for Archie with Warner Brothers' test people. Minnie and he were to have dinner together and discuss the test. She asked me coyly if I thought Archie would mind if she bought a shirt and black tie for him. She said that a white silk shirt and black knitted tie photographed best for a test.

'Hon,' I said, 'don't ask, just buy.'

One look at Archie and Minnie said,
'Gawd's truth, but you're 'andsome!'

It was an excited Archie, done up in his new silk shirt, who left for his dinner date, but a very dejected Leach who came back late that evening. Minnie had wanted a shore dinner and, of all places, insisted on going to Coney Island! After dinner she had wanted to see all the freaks. He got by the Fat Woman without being seen. Then Minnie decided she wanted to see the Bearded Lady, who saw him and hollered, 'Hi, Archie!' He hid from the Sword Swallower and persuaded Minnie that she really didn't want to see the Fire Eater. He had spent the entire evening pushing Minnie around corners and dodging spielers – coughing, laughing, talking loudly, doing everything he could think of to avoid his colleagues and their 'Hi ya, Archie!' and 'Get the kid from Bristol.'

'Why run away?' I asked him. 'It would have been so much simpler to tell the truth. Let people like you for what you are, just be truthful, it's so much easier.'

That was another thing Archie and I never agreed upon. I'd never run from anything or anyone, certainly not from my friends.

We sweated out the test. At last the news from Warner Brothers arrived. They said Archie was too good looking, too much the Arrow-collar type, the impossibly handsome models in the advertisements for shirts and collars. So, back he went to the NVA and his pretty blonde, Doreen Glover, who would later play one of the Four Nightingales in the Broadway musical *Boom Boom*. He went with her for about four years until he left for the Coast.

ARROW
DRESS SHIRTS
AND COLLARS

Poor Archie failed his first screen test because he was deemed too much the Arrow-collar type – too good-looking.

CHAPTER SIX

After a few more rounds the right people were doing the wrong things.

WHEN ENGLISH ACTRESS Miss Marie Tempest and her husband, actor Graham Brown, came to America from her Australian tour, she opened in *A Serpent's Tooth* for producer Mr John Golden. A new young leading man – Leslie Howard – played the part of her ungrateful son. Unfortunately the play closed after three weeks, but Miss Tempest was a social success. I was privileged to learn a great deal from this grand lady. All doors were open to her. A representative group of New York's Four Hundred entertained her royally. Once, at a luncheon at the Old Voisin, Miss Tempest let it be known that Art and Aristocracy should be associated.

Through Miss Tempest I met Killian van Rensselaer, president of the exclusive Union Club. Killian would eventually marry my dear friend, the beautiful Lorraine Wood, née Graves. Among the handful of people from the theatre who would be admitted into their home were Miss Ethel Barrymore, Fred Astaire and his sister Adele Astaire, composer Vincent Youmans and Cole Porter. The first time I would meet Lady Peel – the actress Beatrice Lillie – was when socialite Schuyler Parsons brought her to Lorraine's for tea.

But before that, Lorraine Graves was to marry Ben Wood. She told me, 'Marrying Ben will put me out of the Blue Book', referring to New York's social register. She planned to live in France. When Ben was courting her, she took me to his charming East 52nd Street home, which he called One Man

House – a beautifully furnished little town house with a garden in the rear. Since Lorraine was going to Europe, and he planned to follow, Ben wanted to rent his home.

Late in the afternoon, as the three of us were having a cocktail, the butler announced Miss Belle Livingstone. She entered and was introduced.

Belle Livingstone, a showgirl turned speakeasy owner, was a tall, erect, hard-featured woman, extremely well groomed, well mannered and soft spoken. In fact, she appeared almost shy. Later I was to learn that apart from her colourful background, her wit and great humour, she could be bold, brash, defiant, fearless, venal and ruthless. In the years to come I often heard her brag, 'I'm the most wicked woman alive!' Her favourite word was *gracious* and she herself, when the occasion arose, could be most gracious. On this particular afternoon her voice was quiet and well modulated. She talked of her home at Fontainebleau, using more French phrases than even actor Clifton Webb.

Shortly after, Ben rented One Man House to her. She promptly turned it into a speakeasy. This venture lasted only a few months, for as soon as Ben got wind of what was going on, she was just as promptly evicted.

With the help of her Old Guard friends, Lorraine was to sponsor my painting career. To launch me as a painter, Lorraine decided to give a dinner party at her apartment. Beforehand she advised me, 'Now, remember, you've never been on the stage. My friends and I only like actors when they entertain us. You are an artist.' She then mumbled that I was to be sure and tell everyone my family had huge sheep ranches in Australia.

Among her guests were the fabulously rich Louis G. Kaufman, President of the Chatham and Phenix National Bank, and his wife, Daisy; Mrs Oelrichs; Violet Deering of Chicago and Palm Beach; Mrs Crawford Hill, Snr.; and Mrs William Timken of the ball-bearing millions. Mrs Timken in a black velvet gown wearing a long double strand of huge graduated diamonds hanging below her waist fascinated me as much as Mrs Kaufman's Russian crown jewels – her enormous emeralds and fabulous pearls of the Grand Duchess. Two other extra men were poet and magazine editor Charles Hanson Towne and the wealthy socialite Drexel Biddle.

At dinner I was seated next to the Duchess de Talleyrand, the one-time Anna Gould, daughter of financier Jay Gould. During one of the courses, she said, 'Lorraine tells me your people are in sheep.'

'The only sheep I've seen in Australia,' I said, 'was the roast lamb we always had on Sunday, then cold lamb on Monday, and lamb hash on Tuesday.'

The incomparable Fred Astaire and his sister Adele, dancing the
light fantastic on the rooftop of the Savoy Hotel.

My rebel truthful streak must have made some kind of impression, because next thing I knew I was invited to go to Marquette, Michigan, in the Kaufman's private railroad car. Along with Lorraine, Drexel Biddle and others, I was to spend the Indian summer 'roughing it' at the Kaufman's $4 million camp. Late that evening, when I told Archie how it paid off to tell the truth, not only was he unimpressed, but he doubted I'd tried to get him an invitation to the dinner.

The afternoon of my departure, during the long ride from the Village to 42nd Street, my taxi was held up by traffic. Arriving at Grand Central, I heard a Kelly being paged and, hurrying down the stairway, it turned out the Kaufmans had held the train up five minutes for me.

I felt I was going up in the world – I felt even more so when we were all driven to the Congress Plaza Hotel in Chicago, which was owned by the Kaufmans. We were each given a suite and barbers were sent up to our rooms.

On reaching Marquette, we were shunted off to the Kaufmans' private railway station, where we got into motor cars. I've never forgotten the beauty of that drive. Anyone who has experienced an Indian summer in that part of the country knows of the wonderfully brisk chill in the air, while, at the same time, the warm sun beats down. We drove close to the shore of Lake Michigan. The copper-coloured leaves of the huge trees intertwining over the roadway formed a canopy of golden fire. The rays of sun filtered down over us in a network of lacy patterns. Every now and then we caught a glimpse of a deer in the virgin forests – the Kauffman wealth had prevented autumnal slaughtering.

After driving about half an hour through the property, we reached the camp, which stood far out on a rocky point, with huge thirty-foot glass windows cemented into solid rock.

As we entered we found the entire camp was Indian in motif. Two enormous stairways, one either side of the main entrance, were fashioned of huge logs sawed in half, and great open fireplaces ran to the ceiling. The chandeliers were bleached tree trunks; monkeys and birds were carved out of the roots, and lights peeked out from knotted branches. There were no objets d'art – the millions had been spent on comfort. Mr Kaufman wanted peace. The camp had everything but a telephone. Daisy was the first woman to be seated on the New York Stock Exchange, but here in Michigan Mr Kaufman wanted no part of the market news.

Drexel said, 'I've seen all the castles in Europe and the Hearst Ranch, but none compare to this!'

Already in the camp was a nephew of the Kaufmans, Samuel Martin, who at the age of twenty-one had just come into his first million. Young L.G. Kaufman had a twenty-first birthday coming up, and he was to get a million also. He died at twenty-six and Sammy followed soon after. Mr Kaufman had given Daisy a million for every one of her seven babies. She really didn't need the money as she was one of the Chicago Youngs and extremely wealthy in her own right.

Going into the dining room for lunch, we all looked up to see a beautiful blue-eyed, black-haired girl in jodhpurs and a red jacket standing on the stairway. 'That's Joan Kaufman,' Lorraine said.

Drexel looked up and said, 'I think I'll marry her.' Just like that! Three months later, he did.

Numerous house guests came and went. I remember Judge O'Brien's daughter, Mrs Littleton Fox, and red-headed Edith Rockefeller McCormick, a horse-faced horse woman with an enormous square emerald ring and a very disagreeable disposition. And there

"The Great White Way," Broadway, New York City.

was Chesley Richardson, one of Mrs Neily Vanderbilt's extra men; Crawford Hill of the Denver railroad clan, at that time married to Ann Kaufman; and a Vanderbilt or two.

There were two different sets: Mr Kaufman's favourites were invited to have cocktails in his bathroom. By now Mrs Kaufman had asked me to call her Daisy, so I, among others, had my cocktails in *her* bathroom. It was the most un-bathroomy bathroom I'd ever seen; there were huge bear rugs on the marble floor and we lounged or squatted anywhere that was convenient. It seemed so strange to be in dinner clothes, sipping cocktails in the bathroom – but I got used to it and soon found myself perched on the side of the bathtub.

At dinner I always sat on Daisy's right – that is, until Alex Pratt arrived, then I went over to her left.

One evening, towards the end of our stay, Daisy, Drexel and I discussed his forthcoming marriage to Joan. Daisy asked me to get a pad and pencil; she wanted me to drive in the morning to the railway station and phone Marshall Field's department store. The order: 'Ship immediately two Fords, four or five canoes – one untippable – half a dozen fur-lined coats and twenty pounds of bacon.'

Then, not having her glasses with her, she asked me to go over some cheque stubs for her. I came across a stub for one hundred thousand dollars made out to cash. 'Good Lord, Daisy,' I said, 'don't tell me you make out amounts like that to cash!'

She said, 'Look and see if there's a notation.' Then I saw 'FLO' scribbled in tiny letters. 'Oh yes,' Daisy said nonchalantly, 'Poor Flo Ziegfeld is always getting into bad straits.'

I'd painted a few panels and some miniature Indians on the unfinished wooden doorknobs, and I improved a rather frightening Indian someone had painted in one of the alcoves. Daisy wanted to show her appreciation for this work and handed me a bunch of General Motors stocks. Lorraine nudged me to take it, but I refused. Had I kept this stock and sold before the stock market crash, I would have made a quarter of a million dollars!

Daisy, one of the nicest and most generous of the rich I'd known, insisted on giving me a cheque for five thousand dollars for my daubings.

On the way back, in our private car, Lorraine suggested I concentrate on painting but get away from the Village-ites.

Susan's mania was speed!
ADOLPH ZUKOR AND JESSE L. LASKY
PRESENT
BEBE DANIELS
IN
WILD WILD SUSAN
WITH
ROD LAROCQUE
FROM THE STORY
'THE WILD WILD CHILD'
by STEUART M. EMERY
SCREEN PLAY BY TOM J. GERAGHTY
DIRECTED BY EDWARD SUTHERLAND
a
Paramount Picture
PRODUCED BY FAMOUS PLAYERS-LASKY CORP.

Two of my favourite leading ladies, Dolores del Rio and Kay Francis, raising a glass in Wonder Bar, with Ricardo Cortez, Al Jolsen and Dick Powell.

Arriving home I found Archie, with three young fellows, had moved into a basement apartment below my studio. One of his room-mates was Lester Cole, the writer. Archie was off on the road. I decided to move also. I rented the brownstone apartment of some of Lorraine's friends at 40 Central Park South, a few doors up from the Plaza, facing the park. Lorraine loaned me some additional furniture and suggested I give a tea party for Drexel and Joan, who were to be married soon.

I was to learn that one never introduces anyone in the Best Set. The only two outsiders who had been invited were Mrs Chadwick and her sister Helen; Mrs Chadwick and her husband had made the grand tour with Marie, Queen of Romania. After introducing these two friends to Drexel and Joan, I turned to present them to another group when Drexel touched my arm and murmured, 'Don't you know that one's roof is one's introduction?' I didn't.

But I do know the morning after the announcement of his engagement to the lovely Joan, Drexel said to me, 'Thank God I can phone my telegrams and cable my father in Europe at the private railway station, for I haven't *their* price.'

After a few more rounds of extra-dry Martinis instead of the usual tea, the right people were doing the wrong things.

Daisy insisted on giving me a cheque for five thousand dollars for my daubings.

I used a nook in the rear of my apartment for painting. Behind a lovely Coromandel screen which Lorraine had loaned me, I had innumerable odds and ends, prints and cut-outs thumb-tacked to walls. Among my collection was a small Edwardian fan, a white ivory elephant, a piece of turquoise I used as a paper weight, a series of Gaiety Girls pictures from Australia, cigarette boxes and other bits and pieces I thought might be used for a still life some day.

Lorraine had sent me a couple of wonderful art books from Paris; one was Andre's *Study of Renoir*, and the other featured many of the Impressionists. This volume was lying open at a reproduction of Van Gogh's *Sunflowers*. This was the period of Art Deco designer Joseph Urban in the theatre. Many people still professed admiration for the English school of art; others preferred pink cupids and prettiness. The French Impressionists were rarely discussed.

Early one morning, as I was about to start sketching, the doorbell rang. In the hallway stood Belle Livingstone. I had seen her earlier that week and she had asked for my address. I thought it rather cheeky on her part to drop in at such an uncivilised hour.

When I had met her at One Man House, she had worn cinnamon and sables, but the Belle who burst in on me unannounced, before nine in the morning, was something else again. Crumpled and creased, she looked sat upon. In fact, she could have been, for the first thing she said was, 'I've been locked out. They are holding my trunk. I rode the subway all night.'

I'd been out until 4 am myself, and by the time I'd washed my face, Belle had completely taken over. With a tea towel tied around her waist and the coffee pot on the stove, she was in the middle of shaking up a daiquiri. She told me that if I'd wait until a few drinks opened her tired subway eyes, she would make a stack of pancakes.

'Gracious me!' said Belle. 'It is fate that I should pick you, from among all the people I know, to tell you my troubles.' Frankly, I wondered why. It wasn't until a few years later that I realised she had an older woman's crush on an unsuspecting Colonial.

Before I could brace myself for the oncoming touch, Belle said, 'Now, don't worry, all I'd like to do is make a few phone calls after breakfast. If you're ever in a tight fix, Jack, never go to any of your old friends. A perfect stranger will often help you out. The older souls are very understanding, but never when it comes to hard cash.'

She had another drink and went to the bathroom to wash up. When she came out, her little agate eyes glowed as she looked at Van Gogh's *Sunflowers*. Both books being in French, she excitedly read details aloud to me, translating essential information.

'Good gracious,' she said, 'didn't you know I was born under a sunflower, or at least, I was found under one?!' This called for another shot of brandy. It still wasn't high noon.

She claimed one of her true parents had left her in the shade of a tall Kansas sunflower near the fence of John Ramsey Graham's house when she was a tiny infant.

Graham was the owner and editor of the *Emporia News*, and later founded the famous *Emporia Gazette*. He made some unfortunate investments which forced him to sell the *Gazette*. The purchaser was the renowned editor and writer, the 'Sage of Emporia', William Allen White.

'Only my adoptive father,' she continued, 'knew the true story of my parentage, and it went to his grave with him. No matter how I tried to pump him, he always clung to

SAVE THE DATE

THE FLIP SIDE + short film programme
SUNDAY 27 JANUARY 2019
Regent Street Cinema 2pm
Eddie Izzard will introduce the European premiere of his new feature film, set in Adelaide.

LADIES IN BLACK + Q&A
FRIDAY 1 MARCH 2019
Regent Street Cinema 7:30pm
Director Bruce Beresford will join us for the European premiere of his new film LADIES IN BLACK.

LONDON AUSTRALIAN FILM FESTIVAL OPENING NIGHT GALA
THURSDAY 27 JUNE 2019
Regent Street Cinema 7:30pm
Rebranding for 2019, the festival will once again showcase new Australian feature films & anniversary classics.

Belle Livingstone, showgirl turned speakeasy owner, was bold, brash, fearless, venal and ruthless. As she often bragged, 'I'm the most wicked woman alive!'

the sunflower story . . .' Belle's voice drifted as she sauntered over to an empty canvas. I wanted to get my mind off her. Frankly, I was wishing she'd get the hell out. But she didn't have the slightest intention to depart.

'You know,' Belle said, 'I've turned fifty, and I now have the face of a bulldog, and I can be just as tough as one! Texas Guinan told me I couldn't run a "saloon" like a "salon" – well, I'll show her! I've learned a lot in the last couple of months about a whole new world – the *underworld*.' She spoke of her plans to rent a house on the East Side. It would be a totally different type of speakeasy, one where ladies and gentlemen could relax.

She switched to a straight shot of brandy and in no time was talking to someone at the Chase Bank about a lease. I went to my bedroom to allow her more privacy, and my mind went back to my early Australian days when I used to see films such as *While London Sleeps* and *East Lynne*. These melodramas always had an adventuress of some sort. Now, for the first time in my life, I found myself face to face with a real-life adventuress. Here was a woman who had lived all over Europe – in fact, all over the world. She'd been wined and dined by sultans and rajahs, and met King Edward VII and Leopold, King of the Belgians. She had married two wealthy men and one poor Austrian count. Now, with only charm, wisdom and wits left, she'd slept in the subway all night. Yet this very minute she was on the phone talking to the Chase Bank about a lease on an East Side town house!

As I came back, she hung up and reached for a cigarette, making herself very much at home, then she recalled the farewell party wealthy businessman Diamond Jim Brady gave her on sailing to London:

'It was a wonderful supper party. Although I was the only girl present,' Belle said and smiled, 'he gave me an exquisite diamond-studded vanity case. It's in hock right now, but it's been with me all around the world.'

She told me Brady had a habit of setting up his current favourite lady in a little millinery business. His passion and the business usually waned about the same time, and someone would buy back the business for him. His next favourite lady would be set up at the same old stand.

But I'd heard just about enough of vanity and its cases. I told Belle I had a luncheon engagement. She made one more call, to the Vanderbilt Hotel, and this time she, too, had a luncheon date. I called a cab for her and slipped a ten-dollar bill in her hand. This was my first mistake! Little did I realise that a couple of years later I would pay her expenses, and those of her entire entourage, all the way to Reno, Nevada . . .

A couple of weeks later, on a November Sunday afternoon, Belle phoned; she said she wanted to repay my hospitality and asked me to be her guest for supper.

She arrived at 6.30, wearing a well-cut informal black dress with half a dozen sables over her arm, her hair bound with a black tulle headache band – à la Mrs Cornelius Vanderbilt. Four long ropes of very good imitation pearls and a lorgnette on a fine platinum chain were around her neck. She took off her spotless white gloves and told me her plan: She wanted to contact Arnold Rothstein, the big-time racketeer and gambler. 'Let's go across the tracks and see how the other half lives.' I smiled to myself – it was only a fortnight since she had slept in the subway.

'Let's go across the tracks and see how the other half lives.'

She had dug up an Arabian chauffeur somewhere; Belle had lived in France for twenty-five years. Her French was fluent, her German pretty good, and she had a slight knowledge of many other languages. She looked quite at home as she stepped into her rented Rolls-Royce and gave the driver full instructions. We were to stop first at a speak in the Harding Hotel; from there we were to go to Lindy's. It was here she hoped to contact Arnold Rothstein. She told the chauffeur not to hurry when he saw us leave the restaurant. 'I may abuse you, but pay no attention – I have a reason.' From Lindy's we were to go to Dinty Moore's for supper.

We sank back in the luxurious cushions. Belle was talkative; she wanted to open another night spot but was determined to run her 'saloon like a *salon*'. She said Arnold Rothstein had been to One Man House on several occasions. He'd seen some big spenders there who rarely got over to Broadway to gamble. On one of these occasions she'd carefully dropped the name Hester Club – his chin had shot out in startled attention. Belle said Rothstein had gone from poolroom hustling to running his first club – the Hester – and now had become known as 'the Fixer', 'the Pay-Off', 'the Brain of Broadway'.

'He doesn't remember me in my Jim Brady days, but I know plenty about him. He's heard about my plans to open a place on Park Avenue; he overhead me discussing a card room where gentlemen could relax. I'll need money, lots of money; he needs my wealthy friends, he knows it. What he doesn't know is that Belle Livingstone is not going to pay his

outrageous twenty-four per cent interest. I've made it my business to find out all I can about Arnold Rothstein: He doesn't smoke, and he's never taken a drink in his life – that was only ginger ale he toyed with in my club – so I'll never loosen his tongue in that department. However, I found out that with all his asserted five million dollars, he's unhappy and one of the loneliest men on Broadway.' She sighed. 'Gracious, life is so strange – here is that man with all that money, and yet he is morose, calculating, power mad and money mad.'

Through her bootlegger she had learned a certain Big Guy was taking a beating from the gambling fraternity along the Main Stem. Arnold Rothstein and a couple of others had upped his marker, as the saying goes – a marker is a form of an IOU. The Big Guy's markers were being doubled, and consequently at the end of a game he was out twice as much as he should have been. The Broadway boys had been needling him, saying, 'Are you going to let Arnold Rothstein make a rube out of you?'

We arrived at the Harding Hotel and had no sooner been seated when the waiter whispered, 'From the Dutchman.' He placed a bucket of champagne on our table. Belle raised her glass and smiled across the room as she said, 'Cheers, Mr Schultz.' That was the first time I saw Dutch Schultz in person.

This speak was not without notorious characters: Directly across from us sat Joyce Hawley, who had taken a bath in a tub full of champagne for Broadway producer Earl Carroll and his friends. Scattered among the customers paying the high cover charge were undercover boys Big Frenchie and Little Angie. As we were leaving, Ziegfeld Girls Kiki Roberts and Hope Dare came in, followed by lawyer Dixie Davis. Belle whispered, 'That's the Dutchman's mouthpiece.'

When the Rolls pulled up at Lindy's, many curious heads turned. The original Lindy's was a delicatessen on Seventh Avenue; in 1928 it was on Broadway, on the right-hand side going uptown. Later it moved to the opposite side. In those days the show outside Lindy's was as good as the food inside.

It was here one heard Damon Runyon speak of those who had passed on, and the four who had 'burned' – Lefty Louis, Gyp the Blood, Dago Frank and Whitey Lewis, members of the Lenox Avenue Gang who got the electric chair for murder. There were tales of Dandy Phil Kostel, Louis One-Eye, Big Nick Cohn, One Time Charles Freeman.

Standing in front of Lindy's, respectability rubbed shoulders with the underworld. Blackmailers, badger gamers, bootleggers, confidence men, dope peddlers and nightclub operators. Broadway characters stood back to back, touching but not talking to, kidding about but not knowing, the greatest stars and sporting figures of the day.

Belle drew my attention to Iron Sam eyeing Sam Bernard, the vaudeville and motion-picture star. And passing we saw theatre producer David Belasco dilly-dallying with another producer, Charles Dillingham, and artist Dana Gibson, writer Westbrook Pegler, aviator Wiley Post, writer and critic Channing Pollack, the Watson Sisters and comedian Sliding Billy Watson.

Belle herself had become news. Walter Winchell had her in his 'Broadway Through a Keyhole' story, which would later be made into a movie. She had been photographed with Texas Guinan. She had become part of the Broadway scene.

'Let's wait outside for a bit,' I suggested.

Belle's eyes lighted up as she said, 'There's Cantor, not Eddie, but Maurice Cantor, Arnold Rothstein's attorney. We are in luck – A.R. must be around somewhere.'

Towering over vaudevillian Georgie Price and actor George Jessel, Belle spotted Big George C. McManus with his pay-off man, Gillis Biller. 'Good gracious, there's liable to be firecrackers tonight if Big George C. runs into A.R.'

Attending the Sunday night concern at the nearby Winter Garden were: actress and producer Peggy Fears and her husband 'Bloomy'; actress and dancer Peggy Hopkins Joyce; the contract killer 'Pittsburgh Phil'; silent star Hope Hampton; the Marx Bros and flame-haired singer and actress Muriel Hudson; writers Ben Hecht and Charles MacArthur; singer and actress Edith Day; English actor Pat Somerset; impresario Billy Rose; musical comedy star Jackie Osterman nudging vaudevillian Jack Pearl as acrobat Ruth Budd and The Creole Fashion Plate, Karyl Norman, were going uptown; male impersonator Ella 'Burlington Bertie' Shields and female impersonator Stuart, the 'Male Patti', going downtown.

'Here comes the king of them all,' said Belle. Con artist Robert Arthur Tourbillon, alias Dapper Don Collins, alias Rat Tourbeville, and half a dozen other aliases. He was the most handsome, dashing and fascinating man on the Main Stem.

Blasé Broadway grinned as Belle, with her headache band and her ropes of pearls swinging over her ample bosoms, entered Lindy's. The place was jumping; waiters were laden down with Hungarian goulash, cheesecake and borscht. Heads and eyes turned, marinated herring dribbling over lower lips and chins. The Lindy's set stopped eating

At Lindy's, respectability rubbed shoulders with the underworld.
Blackmailers, bootleggers, dope peddlers and nightclub owners
stood back to back with the greatest stars of the day.

to get a look at the lady with the lorgnette from Park Avenue. She knew how to make an entrance; Barnum hadn't offered her one thousand dollars a week to show off her poetic legs for nothing.

Viewing the menu through her lorgnette, she finally settled for a huge order of the best caviar, grated onions and chopped eggs, and thin buttered rye toast.

Belle kept her eyes on the door. Arnold Rothstein was on her mind; she didn't want to miss him. Finally I saw her nod to a man, who later stopped by our table and told her she could have tickets for any Broadway show. When he left she said, 'Back in my Diamond Jim days they called him Boston Sam, but today he's one of the biggest ticket speculators on the Stem. In those days he used to sit in with Last Card Louie – there's another one who made good.' She laughed. 'Louie ended up producing pictures for his own company. One of his sons has become a top Hollywood agent, the other one a big-time producer.'

Belle lingered over her caviar. It was 9.45, past the hour when Arnold Rothstein usually showed up. Finally she said, 'Let's go! Maybe at Moore's I can find out where he is.'

She knew how to make an entrance; Barnum hadn't offered her a thousand dollars a week to show off her poetic legs for nothing.

Belle's chauffeur had seen us waiting outside Lindy's but, according to instructions, he was taking his time. Nudging me, Belle said, 'Did you see that shifty-eyed little shrimp chewing a toothpick and playing with the lapel of his double-breasted coat?' I glanced back and saw him mouth the numbers three forty something, to a man who passed close by him. Belle said, 'That means the big game will be held in room three forty whatever the last number is, at the Park Central Hotel, and Arnold Rothstein will be sitting in.' For the benefit of the onlooker she rattled off a few French phrases.

Stepping into the Rolls, she went into her Arabic routine, and someone close by said, 'She's talking in still another language, yet!'

Dinty Moore's was packed with late Sunday night diners. 'There must be a Detroit Convention in town,' Belle whispered. 'There is Charlie "Chink" Sherman.' Coming face to face with Dutch Schultz's aide, she gave him a hearty, 'Good evening, Mr Sherman.'

Sometime later they buried him in quick lime, and the only way he was identified was by the ring on his finger.

'Well, if I don't see anyone else, the evening has been worth it.' Belle raised her lorgnette and gave a gracious bow to 'Dutch Sadie' and her party. She said, 'My dear, that one has gone a long way since her early Haymarket days. She married a cousin of a great American – for whom I once made a stack of wheat cakes one snowbound night.'

We were seated, ordered our food, then looked around at the famous personalities. There was everyone from Jenny Jacobs to vaudeville writer Herman Timberg. Irving Berlin and producer Sam Harris were in serious conversation; they were trying to hear themselves over the guttural, raspy voice of one of the sisters of a famous act. She had by now no whites, just yolks, for eyes and was weighted down with jewels. She looked like a stuffed seagull.

We finished supper. Belle had kept her eyes glued to the door, but no A.R. appeared.

She greeted owner Willie Moore and wished to be remembered to his mother. Leaving the restaurant, she said, 'We seem to have run into everyone except His Honor James J. Walker, Grover Whalen and Arnold Rothstein.' Getting into the car she gave instructions to drive slowly down Broadway. We both took a swig of brandy from a flask. Belle's mind went back to Rothstein:

'I knew him twenty years ago, when he operated his first gambling place on 46th Street, it was just two blocks from "Honest John" Kelly's West 44th Street place, which was right next door to Rector's restaurant. For those in the know, a door in the back of Rector's led directly into Honest John's gambling room.' She told me that was when Rothstein got to know people like the playwright Wilson Mizner, billiards champion Willie Hoppe, prize fighters, baseball and racetrack players, industrialist John 'Bet-a-Million' Gates, Allen and Canfield. It was off Gates's son that he made his first big killing – forty thousand dollars in one evening. She likened him to the Milky Way: 'He was milky faced with coal-black eyes floating out from under awning-like lids. He was the originator of the floating crap game. His office – a doorway under an awning, any awning.'

Belle eyed every doorway. 'Do you realise, Jack,' she asked me, 'from under one of those awnings stands Arnold Rothstein, surveying the wild undercurrent washing across brazen, brash Broadway?'

As we drove on, Belle said, 'The most beautiful woman in the world is a man,' pointing to a sign on the theatre named for the most famous of the female impersonators – Julian Eltinge.

As a Maxwell car went by, she said, 'Gracious! Every time I see a Maxwell I think of two beautiful girls, and I don't mean Elsa! One waited over twenty years for her friend to divorce.

He died, so she never became the wife of one of America's greatest banking families . . . The other, a friend of one of the famous social families, for whom a hotel is named, waited and waited for many years – but his wife said, "When you find a real lady I'll give you your divorce." '

'Over there,' Belle pointed, 'was where Madame Polly ran a hairdressing parlour. She had a large parrot cut-out in front of her shop. It was the period when long hair was a great attraction and "rats", puffs and pompadours were in vogue. Along with the nice patrons – some were not so nice – often a sweet young thing from the country, with the crinkles hardly out of her plaits, would be sent to Madame Polly's to have her hair fixed before trying out for a show. Polly would call one of the madams and introduce her to the maiden. Pretty soon the madam would be telling the maiden that she knew the nicest elderly man whose wife didn't understand him, but, as she was an invalid, he felt honour bound to stay with her. Why, he'd think nothing of giving a pretty sweet young girl fifty dollars just to take her to the finest restaurants and spend a pleasant evening. He was a perfect gentleman, of course.'

'Of course, Belle, I'm sure it wasn't long before the maiden was no longer a maiden.'

'Exactly,' said Belle. 'Now I must show you where the heart of the Red Light District used to run full force, with big payoffs to Tammany Hall.' She pointed to a section where the notorious Haymarket once stood on Eighth Avenue, with a row of boxes all around. She sighed, 'Many fashionable gentlemen went there for a rendezvous, as they used to call it, and some of New York's best-kept girls got their start right there.'

I thought she was going to throw me out of the car when I asked her if she'd ever been in the place.

'Good gracious, no respectable girl would be caught within a mile of the Haymarket! I got my information from the young sporting bloods who treated me more like one of the boys. They used to call me "a good fella". That's what England's Lord Kitchener always called me, "a good fella".'

I told Belle I had heard she was once very intimate with the famous field marshal.

'Ridiculous,' she said. 'He found me very relaxing and often came to my London apartment, but there was never the slightest indiscretion on my part.' Then, with a knowing look, she smiled. 'If I'd made an advance in that direction I'm afraid he would have run a mile.'

Turning back to Broadway, Clara Bow, the 'It' Girl, dazzled in lights. Noël Coward was blinking off and on in *The Vortex* – his first Broadway hit. Ina Claire shone out in *The Last of*

CLARA BOW

IN
An ELINOR GLYN-
CLARENCE BADGER
Production

"IT"

WITH
ANTONIO
MORENO

Mrs Cheyney. Ethel Barrymore and Walter Hampden were in *The Merchant of Venice*. The Winter Garden had Al Jolson.

Between 46th and 47th Streets, Belle said, 'I. Miller had a tiny shoe shop here. He had six sons, and he made shoes for most of the shows, including the Ziegfeld Follies. Nearby Polly Hyman sold stockings, gloves and lingerie. Up above, Madame Francis had her first small dress shop.'

It was the era of Jack London; gamblers 'Titanic' Thompson, 'Nigger Nate' Raymond and Nicky Arnstein; dill pickles, olives, pigs' trotters; and the Big Woman. Boxers Benny Leonard, Jack Dempsey and Georges Carpentier; Eugene O'Neill's play *Strange Interlude*; actor Clifton Webb and his mother, Mabelle. Fanny Brice in the *Midnight Frolics*; champagne, Welsh rarebits, broiled fat lobsters, Spanish omelettes and newspaperman 'Spanish' O'Brien. All were part of Broadway.

Other big noises on Broadway, besides the whoopee of the butter-and-egg men, were machine guns clattering like monstrous typewriters, the flash of shots in the night, flying windshield glass, skirmishes with the law, stray bullets, 'Mad Dog' Coll, 'Legs' Diamond, Bugs Moran and gang murders. A life could be snuffed out for one hundred dollars. Young Broadway bloodhounds. Morphine- and cocaine-racked minds thirsting for blood blazed up and down and across the blood-red White Way. There was spiked beer, liquor and home-cooked alcohol. Millionaire gorillas; lavish ICE handouts to political fixers to quench America's thirst.

Belle took another swig of brandy from the flask and I followed suit. 'I must find Rothstein!' she said.

After a few drinks at the Abbey, we left for Big Bill Duffy's Silver Slipper, which was housed in a basement on the corner of 48th Street and Broadway; kitty-corner across the street the vaudeville trio Clayton, Jackson and Durante packed them in at the Parody. Here I met Big Bill Duffy and the fighter Primo Carnera, who was much bigger. The brandy was hitting Belle. I nudged her, thanked our host and we left.

Back in the car, we started the drive across town. It was obvious she was tight, for she kept mumbling, 'The fixer . . . the brain . . . the pay-off . . . ' In the middle of her jabbering, a newsboy on the corner called out, 'Extra! Extra! Read all about it! Arnold Rothstein shot!'

Belle jumped as if struck by a bolt of lightning. This news sobered her up and she shouted, 'Stop the car! Get a paper!' I jumped out and bought an Extra. It was Sunday,

November 4, 1928. Arnold Rothstein had been shot in the stomach and was in a critical condition. We checked the time; he had entered Lindy's five minutes after we left, picked up three or four messages from the same person, left and gone straight to the Park Central Hotel.

'What did I tell you!' Belle exclaimed.

The following day this story – one of many versions – travelled the bootlegger route. Belle and I were informed that two of the Big Guy's friends had tried to steer Rothstein away; they were in Room 349 when Rothstein returned his call. By this time the gambler was a wild man, and when they heard that Rothstein was on the way up, they rushed out to head him off. One covered the 55th Street entrance, while the other ran to the 56th Street entrance, but Arnold Rothstein entered by the third entrance, on Seventh Avenue, went directly to Room 349 on the third floor, and to his death.

Damon Runyon wrote:

> *In the haunts of that strange pallid man, during his life you could have had ten to one – and plenty of it – that he would holler 'Copper' did the occasion arise, with his dying gasp. He was often heard to remark: 'If anyone gets me, they'll burn for it.' They felt he would squeal like a pig. When Arnold Rothstein lay crumpled up with a bullet through his intestines, knowing he was mortally hurt, and officers of the law bent over him and whispered, 'Who did it?', the pale lips tightened and Rothstein said, 'I won't tell. Please don't ask me any more questions.' He was game as a pebble.*
>
> *Another sure thing went wrong on Broadway.*

Barbara Stanwyck
Baby Face

CHAPTER SEVEN

'So, you're Kelly the dress designer?'

MY DEAR FRIEND LORRAINE was now Mrs Ben Woods of Paris, France. Mrs Louis G. Kaufman and many others of the social set had been kind to me, but there were too many dinners, too many luncheons and too much bridge in the afternoons, and I had too few dollars left.

I felt it was time I got back to Broadway, and left my swanky address. My bank account just wasn't. I moved back to the Village, near Washington Square, and in no time at all I was working for the Shuberts.

Archie came back from a short vaudeville tour, moved in, and we again shared expenses. Don Barclay, the great comic, gave Archie his first real knowledge of the theatre.

The Shuberts were re-dressing *Diamond Lil* and sending it out on the road. I had an appointment to see Miss Mae West. Sitting through the matinee, I marvelled at how in all seriousness she could portray the character she had written!

After the show I met Miss West in a portable canvas dressing room on stage. There was a lot of confusion; Big Jim Timony sent out for a steak sandwich. Someone was trying to hand her a court summons – just as I would like to have given one to Big Jim for my Texas Guinan *Padlocks* work. On the dressing table, which was covered with cheap lolly-pink sateen, were a brass Victorian comb, brush and a mirror, all mounted with Victorian cupids and baroque bows. Later, in Hollywood, she had everything set in solid gold.

A short woman, she kept on the special shoes which had lifts, inside and out, to give her the famous Westonese walk. She sauntered up and down the tiny enclosure, lowering her lids and heaving her more-than-ample bosom. Curling her lips and looking down over her shoulder, she said, 'So, you're Kelly the dress designer?'

I wanted to say, 'Come, come, honey chile, spring is going to be a bit late this year.' But I thought better of it.

As we discussed business, I began to feel that the reason for Mae West's phenomenal success, apart from her unexcelled timing, was the fact that she took herself so seriously. In my book anyone who is unable to laugh at himself, just as he laughs at others, has no true humour.

Many years later, producer Mike Todd told me that when Mae was appearing in his comedy *Catherine Was Great* she claimed she was the reincarnation of the empress. It seems she'd had a premonition that Catherine herself wanted her to play the part straight and serious. But New York refused to see it that way. In fact, they refused to see the show *any* way.

Mae West was an institution. When she was cast right, and took direction, there was no one like her and no one could put over a number like the girl who said, 'Goodness had nothing to do with it, dearie.'

My social life behind me, I settled down once more to work in earnest.

Now on Shuberts' payroll, I began designing for Mr J.J. Shubert's musicals and Mr Lee Shubert's dramatic shows. I dressed Katharine Hepburn in *Death Takes a Holiday*, and the Shuberts gave her notice after only one week's performance. How foolish they were!

Archie never played the vaudeville circuit. Like my first Sydney appearance, he too was given exactly one line in Oscar Hammerstein's *Golden Dawn*. When this show ended, I suggested he stick around until he got another Broadway show, which turned out to be *Boom Boom*, starring Jeanette MacDonald. In this musical Archie had lots of lines, but the show soon went 'boom'.

Mae West was an institution. When she was cast right there was no one like her. Looking the part here in She Done Him Wrong, *with my old room-mate.*

On trial for producing an obscene play, Mae West receives a little sisterly support and plenty of extra publicity from notorious nightclub queen Texas Guinan.

His first juvenile lead was opposite Queenie Smith in *The Street Singer*. Another young actor, with many gleaming white teeth, also had one line at the finale: 'Shall we dance?' Then he waltzed around the stage and made an exit. It was Cesar Romero. Archie was getting places, with his feet down on the stage at last, and I made a hit with three sets of scenery and costumes for *A Night in Venice*. The star was Ted Healy; with him were The Three Stooges.

In my scene, girls in beautiful white feathered costumes, with a swan's head on one glove, were grouped around a glass lake. Gradually they came to life. The fronts of the costumes were just enough to get by the Boston censors. The critics acclaimed my work. One wrote: 'What happened? The Shuberts have done something with charm and without spangle.'

From then on, 'without a spangle' became a watchword.

Up to this point I'd known little about fashion, and certainly had never bought magazines devoted to it. While many of my ideas and scenery turned into costumes before the eyes of the audience, the clothes actually had little to do with modern attire.

Slaves of Broadway contained one of my ideas: Benny Fields drove right on stage in a hack, or rather, an open Victoria – I'm not sure it wasn't the one I'd made my Broadway debut in!

After one of my transformation scenes got good write-ups, producer George White engaged me to do a New York skyline finale. My first toy theatre was paying off. When the critics praised my finale, the Shuberts re-engaged me; I was called to the office of E. Romane Simmons.

Mr Simmons was Hungarian. He had taste, was well informed and had great musical knowledge. When he engaged me he was quite old. Small and round, he looked exactly like a piece of *blanc de Chine*. At one time he had been pianist for opera singer Madame Nordica. Returning after a concert tour of the Orient, Nordica died at sea and Simmons acquired her magnificent Russian sable coat. Her pearls were never found. The sable coat became the lining for one of Mr Simmons's winter coats. He even sported a pearl or two. Some called him 'Pa', but many called him 'Ma' . . .

The first thing Mr Simmons said to me was, 'Kelly, you a'e much bette' d'ess design' than you a'e scenic. Mist' J.J. suggests you take ove' the wa'd'obe depa'tment at the Mode.' He couldn't pronounce his R's. The Mode was a block-square six-floor building downtown where the Shuberts stored and made everything for their many shows and road companies. For years *Blossom Time* had more road companies than they could find singing soubrettes with sausage curls.

Many people were under Mr Simmons's jurisdiction: a woman secretary; an old-time chorus boy door opener, Ernest Schraffs, whom I replaced; and a bright-faced young mick, Edward Druyer Dowling, who went on to stage *Hellzapoppin'* and *An Evening with Bea Lillie*. We had to check many shows. Eddie attended to the stage managing and I, of course, saw that the costumes looked fresh.

We often made the Broadway tour of all the Shuberts' shows with Mr Simmons in his landaulet. Over our knees was placed a luxurious fur rug and, sitting up front next to the negro chauffeur, was a blond mountain lion. So it wasn't always the winter chill that flushed young Eddie's cheeks, but rather the staring, gaping eye of all Broadway.

The Winter Garden used nudes, and Mr Simmons always ordered me up to the first landing to make sure the ladies had shaven – a chore Eddie often volunteered to do – but he was always sent backstage to check on things more mechanical.

I never really got along very well with E. Romane Simmons, but I found Mr J.J. very fair. Archie and I were both friends of young John Shubert. My early Shubert days stood me in good stead later on.

I was just about to lean back on my laurels, or something, when along came Black Tuesday. As the guard at the Stock Exchange on Wall Street put it, 'Sixteen million shares on the Exchange and seven million on the kerb, set off a panic which eventually wiped out thirty billion dollars in the open market.'

The crash didn't end on Black Tuesday; it wasn't until a Blacker Thursday that *Variety* said, 'Wall Street lays an egg!'

Along with all the other people buying on the margin, wouldn't you know, Belle Livingstone had bought a lease! She'd taken over Robert Goelet's small house at 384 Park Avenue. Almost a year had passed since I'd run into La Belle – now she was with Vernon MacFarlane.

I suggested Archie stick around until he got another Broadway show, which turned out to be Boom Boom. The show soon went 'boom'.

Vernon was born in New Zealand and was what we call a 'fellow Australian'. At one time he was good looking, but in 1929 he was blown up like a Zeppelin. He was full of charm and an acquired soft English accent. His card read 'Interior Decorator', but I found out later his main means of support came from supplying cocaine all the way from Park Avenue through Broadway and some of its top stars, to Tenth Avenue.

The three of us went to the Salvation Army, where Belle bought up a lot of old bug-stained mattresses – she had slip covers made to hide the blood of the bug bites. Soon society found it chic to say, 'I'll meet you on the fourth mattress at Belle's.' She had a point – 'A fellow could get hurt falling off a bar stool.' She didn't count on some of the customers rolling down the stairs, clear out onto Park Avenue!

She had one other unique feature. You were met at the door by a butler who sold you dated booklets, good for that night only. As he sold only twenty-five- and fifty-dollar books, people were often caught with quite a bit of waste paper – I'm afraid Belle's bell was always out of order.

Like Ben Wood, when Mr Goelet got wind of what Madame had transformed his little town house into, her little venture didn't last long. But, undaunted, Belle's bell starting ringing again.

With the five thousand dollars handed to her by 'one of the mob' for her hat and cloak concession – plus all sorts of shenanigans on Babbling Belle's part – she re-did the building, which had once housed John Murray Anderson's School of Dance. Carpenters and job men, none of them Union, were stalled only until the second week's pay was due, then, in disgust, they walked off the job. Her story was that since she didn't trust the American banks; she had placed her money in a bank in Italy. She always had a big bruiser around. It was cheaper to pay him.

Belle, Vernon and I started to plan the decor for the new club. She wanted us to remember that she never swam with the current, always against it. Everyone was screaming for business; she wanted her place to appear so expensive – so difficult to enter – that everyone would break his neck trying to get in.

Vernon suggested completely black floors, walls, ceiling and, of course, mirrored bar. Belle decided to show nothing but champagne. On the black shelves on either side of the mirrored bar she pyramided splits, pints, quarts, magnums, jeroboams and methuselahs.

The entrance had charming, ornate wrought iron gates. We decided to install another pair of gates, which had to be drilled into the stone floor of the vestibule. Behind the first gates a secretary sat holding the Blue Book. As the customers entered she pretended to check their names in the Social Register. After the nod of approval from a front man – a big bruiser in white tie and tails, behind the second set of gates – he would open the door. Many a butter-and-egger or a Seventh Avenue manufacturer thought it flattering to have the blonde on his arm think he was one of the Four Hundred of New York society.

Belle placed *la grande salle* on the rear of the ground floor, which was forty feet high. We planned to surround the entire room with gold-cushioned seats and huge satin pillows in Indian fabrics of red, orange, lime and purple – a revolutionary colour scheme for those days. Directly opposite the stage for the band would be a Royal Box with gold cloth falling from a gold crown, tufted with vermilion velvet.

> Belle wanted us to remember that she never swam
> with the current, always against it.

A couple of days later you could hear Belle's screams a block away. When I got up to the third floor, I found the expensive indoor miniature golf course had caved in and water from the fake lakes had started to drip down all over bitching Belle. This was too much for even Belle's iron buttress.

By the time the leaks were plugged and the golf course repaired, she realised the room off the bar hadn't been touched yet. With no more cash and everyone getting wise to her fibbing, Belle decided to close the room, but I convinced her that this space could be used to our advantage. We painted the whole thing gold, and on the walls I painted the naughtiest vermilion monkeys imaginable – with their backs turned, they appeared to be playing with everything, including themselves. I also suggested that Belle get a tiny gold piano for little Jerry Smith, so she could sing songs to match the mood of the monkeys.

Before the grand opening, I combined a magnificent all-over lace dress with ivory velvet and tulle for Belle's first appearance at her own place. I wisely covered her bulbous arms with the lace and she wore many strands of rather good fake pearls.

The morning of her opening she suddenly realised there was no royalty to sit in the Royal Box, so Vernon and I scurried all over Park Avenue trying to find a title, and we came up with Laura, Princess Rospigliosi. Her sister, Elena, and she came from Cincinnati;

in fact, they were the first two Americans ever to become princesses! I don't think actress Cobina Wright, once courted by Prince Philip, could have done better on such short notice. A young foreigner made up a remarkable fake diamond tiara and assisted in placing it correctly on her head on opening night. Later he, too, was placed on Belle's unpaid list.

At the time I thought Belle could do no wrong. Maybe I was going through my gullible period, or was it my youth? Usually she kept me away from creditors, including the poor workmen. There were times, though, that I overheard things – for instance, Vernon, during one of their fights, called her 'Old Gyp the Blood', the kingpin of the Lenox Avenue Gang. On these occasions she was the injured one and her small grey eyes would fill up quicker than silent star Mary Miles Minter's.

Belle had the great knack of making you feel that you were very special. One of her pet sayings was, 'I don't care whose friendship I lose, but gracious, if you ever walk out on me I'll just have to give up.'

The opening of the 58th Street Country Club was a great success. Among those present from the literary world were Dorothy Parker, Bob Benchley, John Colton, Ray Long, Sam and Edith Hoffenstein, Louis Bromfield, Ring Lardner, Heywood Broun, Floyd Gibbons and one of the Scripps Howard News Service boys.

From Broadway I remember Alice Brady, Miriam Hopkins, John Ringling and Lillian Leitzel, the lusty-throated Libby Holman and McKay Morris.

There were Biddles, Astors and Vanderbilts; Mrs Stanwood Menken and Mrs George Washington Kavanaugh, Teddy de Bernhardt and, of course, actress Fannie Ward and her husband, bearded actor Jack Dean.

Later in the evening, with Belle on one arm and Fannie on my other – Jack had gone home – we went from one end of the bar to the other. Belle accepted each offer of champagne, only she ordered a different brand from the one they were drinking, and after taking a few sips she'd pass on to another party. At thirty dollars a bottle it was no time before she had hustled five hundred dollars. I must say, Fannie would chide her, but she too got a great kick out of Belle's unorthodox antics.

When people left the dimly lit black bar and came into my 'monkey room', they were invariably dazzled by the sight of the mad, leaping monkeys. The newspapers always described this room when they wrote about the club.

Within two days after the club opened to such tremendous business, Belle had Vernon barred, giving strict orders that he was not to enter the club again. Vernon was rightfully vindictive, but Belle was a positive virago. Testy, touchy, she swept down on him like a volcano. One look at the big bruiser behind the iron gates and even defiant, vituperous Vernon turned on his heels and kept walking, or running, for an 'uppie'.

The day after the opening, her barmen, who had worked for weeks setting up the bar and doing other odd jobs, went on strike. What a shame! Here was a woman with a fertile mind who could pollinate an idea into something new and different, but had one great unforgivable fault: she simply would not pay off.

I painted the naughtiest vermilion monkeys imaginable – with their backs turned, they appeared to be playing with everything, including themselves.

Now she was dealing with the underworld. All that nonsense of her liquor being shipped from France was so much pollycoddle. She gallivanted from one bootlegger to another, daring to play one against the other. This foolishness, among other things, finally forced abdication. She was served an injunction, which she ignored. The boys of the Syndicate decided she had taken in more than her share.

The 58th Street Country Club was doing the most business of any place in town. A few days before the 1929 Christmas holidays Belle decided to find out what other top places would cover-charge for New Year's Eve. After our usual number of dry Martinis, Belle and I started out for the Central Park Casino; they were charging twenty-five dollars. Visiting a number of other places, Belle decided she would charge thirty-five dollars. Because of my nips – or perhaps because of my youth – I said, 'Thirty-five is an uneven number, why not make it fifty! Fifty has an air about it.' Belle needed no further encouragement – fifty it was and fifty they paid. Some stood up, but they liked it!

At the last minute she remembered there were no menus. I dashed out, bought some heavy gold paper and stayed up until four in the morning painting naughty little cupids peeing out 'Happy New Year' in little drops all over the front of the menu. While I painted the cupids, Archie helped with the pee! Mark Hellinger wrote up my artwork and Walter Winchell said the menus were the gayest thing.

Belle's Country Club was doing more business than Club Richmond, Texas Guinan's and a couple more put together. Belle was blooming. The Yellow Rose of Texas was falling apart.

One Sunday Belle phoned, asking me over for breakfast. When I arrived, the caretaker let me in through the double set of iron gates and I walked directly up to the fifth floor. Belle, perched in her small bed, was counting the Saturday night take; scattered all over the eiderdown cover were literally hundreds of single-, five-, ten- and twenty-dollar bills.

After a brandy flip I started to help her sort the bills. She seemed to enjoy just toying with them. We had reached the sum of eight thousand dollars when we heard footsteps. Quickly throwing the bundles of greenbacks under the disordered sheets, we looked up to see two sinister-looking men standing in the doorway. They were obviously hoods. Belle sprang from her bed like an adder.

One of them said, 'The Big Boss says he wants to buy in – ' They got no further.

Never in my life have I heard anyone scream louder than Belle did: 'You must have pulled your guns on my watchman!' Stepping closer to them she whirled around and, turning her back, yelled, 'Go ahead and shoot! I am an old woman and I don't want to die of kidney trouble! Shoot me, you yellow so-and-sos!' To our amazement the hoods went hustling down the stairs.

By the time I regained my wind, Belle said, 'Did you see their glassy eyes? They were all snowed up with cocaine or heroin. I'll bet that was the first time they ever came up against an old woman. I guess I scared the hell out of them.'

'Don't forget,' I replied, 'you yelled so loud you could have been heard way over by the East River!'

This was my first direct encounter with the boys from the Syndicate. Through Vernon I had decorated quite a few places for the Syndicate, but I'd never come in personal contact before. I'd received a certain amount of money for each place – or rather, as much as I could get out of Vernon, who was as tricky as they come. I remember only one occasion when a couple of thickset, swarthy characters were talking to Vernon, one of them saying, 'Now don't delinquent on us, Voinen.'

On many of these painting jobs Archie had assisted me because between bookings he could always use the extra bucks.

The Syndicate bought the beautiful home of composer and conductor Walter Damrosch and then transformed his music salon into a gambling room. With Archie's help I painted jade-green frogs on these walls, with sort of a Paul Klee feeling, although at that time I'd not seen his work. Like my monkeys, the frogs looked like licentious old men.

'Go ahead and shoot! I am an old woman and I don't want to die of kidney trouble! Shoot me you yellow so-and-sos!'

I was beginning to wear out the elbows of all my suits leaning on the bars of the speakeasies. I thought it would be cheaper to open my own.

In 1929, John D. Rockefeller planned to build a new opera house, surrounded by a huge civic centre. Of the 229 brownstones demolished to make way for it, the excavators left only one solitary wall of one house, standing for all to see. The house had been at 49 West 49th Street – I hope my next New York one-man show draws as much attention as those naughty monkeys I painted. Exposed to the sunlight and to the public for the first time, they drew huge crowds. Later, of course, the idea of a new opera house was abandoned, and after the Crash, Radio City was built. It was in the middle of what is now Radio City that the Federals used to ring my doorbell and say, 'Joe sent me.'

John Perona had left '49' – this same location – two years earlier for his present address of El Morocco. However, little did I know then that only recently the same address had been known as the Aquarium Bar – that is, before the Feds knocked the hell out of the place and the goldfish tank under the glass bar!

It all seemed so simple; I didn't feel I was doing anything wrong. I was really only going to entertain my friends.

The creed of the time was: Apply prohibition to others – for yourself, a private cellar. No one seemed to take the Prohibition Law very seriously.

'Why, it's a perfect setup,' I told Vernon the day I took over number 49. The whole floor had been opened up except for a room and bath in the back. Vernon suggested I screen off the section where the sinks were located and use this part for mixing the drinks. Wanting the place to look like an artist's studio, I stained the old parquet floor a rich dark brown, added a few beige scatter rugs and some red lacquer lamps. I placed a modest sign by the window: Jack Kelly, Artist. This was the closest yet I'd come to using my given name. I never completely drew the curtains over the large front windows, so that any Federal Agent walking along the opposite side of the street would only be able to see an easel with a half-finished portrait. Behind the front door I hung a palette, a smock and a beret.

Iron grillwork was a dead giveaway, as were sliding panel peepholes, so I decided to take a chance with an unlatched door. I knew the Feds had to have a search warrant to enter, and I would be careful to do nothing to make them suspicious.

Belle's monkey room had met with such success that I decided to paint one wall of my place with these naughty red monkeys – backs turned, they winked, peeked, scratched, jumped and grabbed at each other. I painted two monkeys back to back over the swinging doors leading to the bathroom – one with a monocle resembled actor George Arliss. His companion was a dead ringer for actress Marie Dressler.

I hired a coloured man to serve the drinks. One of Archie's many girlfriends, Helen St. Myer, introduced me to a bootlegger who promised to supply me with anything I needed.

By the time I'd finished the decorating I was low in cash but high in spirits. In order not to have any trouble with the Feds, I decided to entertain only people I knew.

The bootlegger came to see me when my new studio was ready. Feeling no pain after a few Martinis, I gave him a very large order for really good liquor – imported Scotch, bourbon, brandies, Cointreau, rum, gin and wine. The mild-spoken bootlegger wished me all kinds of luck. He seemed so friendly and neighbourly. He admired my photos of the Shubert Winter Garden girls – particularly one of Archie's favourites, Dottie Drum, who posed in a niche nude from the hips up. He also said he would like the pleasure of meeting some of my showgirl friends in 'the cool of the evening'.

I was in business – or at least I thought I was. But my friends never took me very seriously and had no intention of letting me go 'into trade'. I found I couldn't ask them to pay the bill; neither, I learned, could my coloured man.

Then the war of nerves began. I made plans for throwing the Feds off my scent: When the doorbell would ring I'd run to the back of the door and don the smock and beret. With the palette in one hand, I'd open the door with the other.

'Joe sent me,' they'd say.

'What do you think this is, a joint or something?' I'd reply.

No one seemed to take Prohibition very seriously. With more than 32,000 speakeasies in Manhattan alone, including my own modest establishment, the creed was apply it to others – for yourself, a private cellar.

At that time the Palace was playing an act in which Owen McGiveney did an old-fashioned sketch with many amazing quick changes, but his changes weren't any quicker than mine on a busy weekend! No sooner would I get back to mixing drinks when the bell would ring; off I'd dash to get into my smock and go through the whole routine again. When summer came I found it more effective to put my hand on my hip and say, in a minty voice, 'You boys ought to be ashamed of yourselves. I wish you roughnecks would stop bothering me!'

This often sent the Feds scurrying down the steps, saying, 'For Gawd's sake, let's get out of here, quick!'

The ring of my doorbell always made me jump, the way bordello owner Polly Adler did for ages after she gave up house and homing. I began to feel the wear and tear of the ringing doorbell, the rapping, the pounding, the strange faces and odd voices, as late as four in the morning – and I couldn't understand why so many were knocking at my door. I'd heard Commissioner Grover Whalen had made a count; his men came up with a total of 32,000 speakeasies selling liquor in basements, penthouses, Manhattan mansions and every third brownstone off Broadway.

My bootlegger warned me to be on the lookout for Izzy Einstein and Moe Smith, the toughest and most honest of the 1500 Prohibition Agents. Izzy weighed over two hundred pounds and was almost as wide as he was high; Moe was still bigger and fatter. They might pose as baseball coaches, or wear anything from a frock coat to a false nose. They made over two thousand arrests, and the words *Moe and Izzy* were dirty words to those who were trying to quench the thirst of six million New Yorkers.

Late one evening, Daisy Kaufman phoned, asking me to come over. She'd been out doing the bright spots and had hired Harry Richman to bring his band over to her Park Avenue apartment. She had also invited the mayor, His Honor James J. Walker. I told her she had a good combination: one opens them and the other closes them. Of course, Daisy had no idea of the type of business I was involved in.

I accepted her invitation and, for the first time, met New York's Jimmy Walker. Dapper, handsome, born to be called 'Jimmy', he had a puckish grin, true Irish wit and humour. He never forgot a name or a friend.

Before the Crash, the lush years featured whopping welcomes, and Jimmy headed them all. Trips up the river in the *Macom*, New York's official reception ship. Lower Broadway had ticker-tape showers which were usually climaxed by a brilliant and amusing speech by His Honor on the steps of City Hall. He met Channel swimmer Gertrude Ederle, golfer Bobby Jones, world heavyweight champion Gene Tunney, naval officer and polar explorer Commander Richard E. Byrd. He received all the Cardinals, and he married Fanny Brice and Billy Rose at City Hall, with Jay Brennan – of the vaudeville comedy duo Savoy and Brennan – as best man. He was called the 'High Noon Mayor' because he seldom reached City Hall before noon, 'Night Mayor' because he loved night-life, and 'Late Mayor' because he was never on time.

Wall Street had its Black Thursday before the Crash. Jimmy had his black day before the Seabury investigations into corruption in the city. Broadway's bright lights began to dim – His Honor faced a blind alley. The committee began to dig deeper and deeper, and the skeletons began to rattle – and finally came the cutting, razor-edged questions. Before the audience at a banquet, the ever-truthful Jimmy made one of his greatest speeches: 'I have lived and I have loved. The only difference is that I was a little more public about it than most people. After all, maybe it isn't a mistake to be oneself and take chances. With all my misgivings, my countless mistakes, with all my multiplicity of shortcomings, I have a single regret . . . I have reached the peak of the hill and must start the journey downward. I have carried youth right up to the fifty yard mark. I had mine, and made the most of it.'

Of all that was said about Jimmy, I liked the way Gene Fowler put it: 'Jimmy wore New York in his lapel like a boutonniere'.

There were few exciting evenings at my place. Usually I was listening to boring drunks who thought the whole thing a great joke, and when my man presented the checks they wouldn't pay the bill. Some said, 'Tell him we buy everything on margin.' Or, like Will Rogers quipped, 'You stand in line to get a window to jump out of.'

Belle promised to send me her overflow. But, of course, she never did.

After such evenings, in the early morning I would find myself in the Remorse Chamber, trying to find a way out. There were no shows being produced. I'd spent most of my money on my place. I decided to get tough: I would start to ask for money myself.

Then I'd mix a couple of sidecars – it was amazing how they helped!

One wintery evening Belle gave me a hurried call. With snow a foot deep in front of the iron gates, I entered her club. Over a dozen men in tails, white ties and red carnations were at the bar. Belle was disturbed because they kept their top hats on. She whispered for me to follow her up to her apartment, and as she went bouncing up the stairs, the Federals started after her. When we got to the fifth floor, she asked me to reach up and open a small trapdoor which led to the roof. I hiked her up. She had a hell of a time squeezing her ample proportions through the opening. Two or three Feds went flying after her. I stood on a chair and looked out. It was quite a sight! Belle's figure was almost blotted out by the heavy falling snow as she leaped over the rooftops. She wasn't wearing red, as stated in the newspapers, but black satin pyjamas with more of my leaping red monkeys hand-blocked on the jacket. Finally Belle's bounce backfired.

She leaped over the rooftops wearing black satin pyjamas with my leaping red monkeys hand-blocked on the jacket.

It was a very different Belle who changed into a modest street suit before being escorted to the wagon. While changing clothes, she whispered something to one of her men – I guess it was instructions, for sure enough, much to my dislike, the following day a half-dozen cases were delivered to my place.

Belle spent thirty days in Harlem Jail. While there, she still used her lorgnette with the fine platinum chain around her neck. She was given an extra piece of prison striped cotton out of which she made a bandeau for her hair.

Before her release from prison she wrote a letter asking me to rent a Rolls-Royce. Texas Guinan, who had got in touch with her, offered to come up with her Larry Fay armoured car, but Belle wrote, 'I want no part of Texas cashing in on my publicity.' But I could bring Archie, if I wished.

The day of Belle's release, Archie and I drove to Harlem Jail to meet her. I waited in the Rolls while he stood outside the prison entrance. Newspapermen came to the car and wanted my name. I told them I was no one of importance. Was this my car? they asked. I simply shrugged my shoulders. When Belle appeared, Archie took her arm.

Archie threw a fit when he saw the newspapers.
It was the first time he had ever been photographed with
a celebrity, and his name wasn't even mentioned.

The bulbs flashed. The following day Archie threw a fit when he saw the newspapers. He said it was the first time he had ever been photographed with a celebrity, and his name wasn't even mentioned. 'If they'd used my name I might have made Winchell's column!' However, he cut out the picture to show the boys around the NVA – how different from the Cary Grant of later years, demanding his privacy from the press.

I'd often thought of closing my place. I had become immensely popular – why not? I was serving imported liquor 'for free'. It was getting to be too much.

Then, one morning, after a late evening, I made up my mind I'd definitely have to do something – this time the sidecars didn't seem to help the situation. Suddenly a banging on the door made me jump. A loud voice called, 'Open up!' I thought to myself, This is it. And it was!

Opening the door, I was confronted by two of the toughest characters I'd ever seen. They almost pushed me over as they lumbered in, saying, 'We're the accountants, and ya owes seven hundred and fifty bucks. We want da money!'

I told them I was short of cash at the moment and didn't want to upset my mother by cabling twice in the same month. Besides, I only owned two hundred and fifty dollars. One of them said, 'Who gives a so-and-so for your mudder! We want da money!'

They gave me until nine o'clock the next day to get the money, or else I was going on a nice long ride. I knew they meant it. As they jostled me back and forth between them, I got a good look at one of them; he had the neck and shoulders of a wrestler. They both seemed to be wearing suits a size too small – or maybe it was only their thick chests and muscular arms that seemed to shrink up their sleeves. Then, as they talked, one on each side of me, they emphasised their words by running their guns up and down my ribs. They didn't stop until I started yelling with pain. When they left, I looked down; my shirt was bloody. I went to the bathroom, washed off and taped up my still-bleeding sides. Back in the main room I downed a slug of brandy and phoned Belle.

The moment she heard the word *money*, I thought I heard her purse close with a snap. She went into the routine I knew so well – the bank in Italy, and all the rest. Now, she really owed *me* money – she hadn't paid a penny for any of my work, including the painting of the monkey room and everything else.

'Belle, I'm frightened, I'm really scared,' I told her.

'Oh gracious, Jack, there's someone at the door,' she said. 'I'll call you right back.'

Of course she never did. This should have been my cue to cut loose from the Belle of Bohemia, but I didn't.

Late that evening there was more banging on the door. Oh, God! I thought, they've decided not to wait until morning! Then I heard that familiar north of England accent. I opened the door and in bounced Archie.

We were both hungry, and he always had hollow legs for tea. I made sandwiches. He was full of excitement about his own plans; he had saved up enough money to visit his dad in England. I didn't have the heart to dampen his enthusiasm with my woes. It had been so long since he'd been home, and he was so happy. He was full of talk about a new blonde he'd met and fallen for – Mabel Ellis. She was leaving the Deep South soon and would be coming to New York with her friend, Lillian.

It was almost daybreak when Archie turned in on the daybed near the door. I cleaned up the dishes and went to my room. I still hadn't got up the nerve to tell him my troubles.

A few hours later we heard a loud banging on the door. Archie opened up to face the 'accountants'. I think he was almost as scared as I was, for after some discussion about his girlfriend, the one who had steered me to the bootlegger in the first place, he gave them two hundred and fifty bucks. Without getting their 200 per cent they started to leave when one put his head back in the door and said they'd be back. Starting to plan what to do, we knew we'd have to get out before they returned.

Now the thing to do, and quickly, was to get rid of all my draperies and furniture. Vincent Sherman, the same young man who would direct *The Young Philadelphians* for Warners in 1959, had just been married and they bought my things.

Archie and I moved a couple of blocks to an hotel, and got lost . . .

Bette Davis
Ex-Lady

CHAPTER EIGHT

'I'm the most wicked
woman alive.'

THE YEAR BEFORE, I'd gone with Milton Shubert for the St Louis Opera Company season. He had installed a revolving stage, which was quite new at that time; I'd done much more than just costume designing. He wanted me to go with him this year too. We were to leave in about a week.

I asked Milton if they could use Archie. He said, 'He's such a lousy actor.' And he was, at that time. But I convinced Milton that surely Archie would fit in somewhere in the six shows he was to do during the three months' run, and I got him the job.

I went ahead to St Louis and took a suite at an hotel out by the park. St Louis wore a cool, comfortable department store dress.

Archie bought an old convertible and followed two weeks later. That season was Archie's first stock theatre experience. He learned a great deal.

When the summer was almost over, Belle Livingstone kept phoning me from New York. She wanted me to go with her to Reno and help decorate a casino. She said she had seen newsreels of Reno and the gambling; it seemed just like the old days of the West. She was willing to give me one-third interest. Only a little over a year had passed since the Crash, and show business was at a standstill on Broadway. I decided I might as well go whole hog and see if I could get back some of the money Belle owed me. Reno might pay off, after all.

Miss Livingstone arrived in St Louis a few days later than she had planned. Being out and oversized, she'd had a huge wardrobe made in New York before she left, and the morning the dressmaker was to meet her at the bank with the bill Belle was on her way to St Louis! This time, however, she'd met her match: the dressmaker obtained a warrant. Belle was arrested halfway to St Louis and, after spending a night in the local cooler, she paid up.

During Belle's Edwardian days, Beer, the famous modiste of Paris, had to use force with her. He put bailiffs in her flat who seized everything, including exquisite handmade baby clothes, then had her evicted. This story had sounded so cruel when Belle first told it, but now I was sure that Beer had good reason and had probably given her every chance to pay.

After her overnight stay in the jail, and the ensuing headlines, Belle arrived in state in St Louis. She'd made the down payment on a huge custom-made Cadillac limousine which even had a built-in bar in the back. Besides the chauffeur, she brought along her French maid and 'Little Jean', the eighteen-year-old son of a French seagoing captain who had worked at the club. After a late farewell party in our suite, I left the following morning. Archie, Dimples Reid and Guy Robertson waved goodbye. I started my journey with Livingstone through Darkest America.

At our first stop for lunch, we gassed up the car. Belle produced a thousand-dollar bill. The station attendant looked at her in awe, and so did I. That was the first of many tabs I found myself paying. By the time we reached Reno I had spent exactly $1348 for expenses. La Belle never paid me back.

We lost a couple of tyres to blowouts. Stopping at a station, Belle demanded the tyre company be contacted immediately by long-distance telephone. On the wire, she told the company she was 'writing up' the trip for a newspaper syndicate and planned to mention them as the one black blot on the entire journey west. Believe it or not, they gave her two free tyres! Now that she had bamboozled someone, she was in a happier state of mind.

It seemed that every time we stopped to gas up the car, or to eat, it was always too late to reach a bank to break that thousand-dollar bill! When I asked her about settling up, she said, 'I would settle up with you, but I think it would be nice to make an impression on the Reno folks when we arrive by casually pulling out this thousand-dollar bill.'

And so it went – I mean my money!

After long, hot, dusty days of driving, we came to the outskirts of Reno.

'We must be on Divorce Drive,' said Belle, as she pointed to a sign: RENO – THE BIGGEST LITTLE CITY IN THE WORLD.

We found Reno wearing a relaxed calico dress with rickrack buttons and bows. Dear little broken-hearted wives seemed anything but sad as they ambled along in cowboy boots, on the arms of bow-legged, suntanned cowboys – and there were some straight-legged cowboys in fancy outfits, hoping, and often succeeding, in snaring a rich divorcée on the rebound.

Belle instructed the chauffeur to stop at the Riverside Hotel. We were greeted by Cornelius Vanderbilt Jr. We had known him in New York and were glad to see him in this strange territory. We got our bags and went to our rooms. Belle rang for a couple ponies of brandy and handed the boy her famous thousand-dollar bill. This was the impression she wanted to create – which would have been fine, had she not loaded up on corn whiskey two nights later and chemin-de-fer'd herself out of most of her worldly wealth.

It was July the fifth. The night before there had been a big prize fight. There had also been another fight between two of the Big Four who ran Reno. They'd fought it out on the street with guns – and now there were only three.

Every Monday, divorce cases were put on the docket. Reno's Mayor, E.E. Roberts, was the biggest divorce lawyer in town. He masterminded legalised gambling and had put through the six weeks' residence law, which brought people flocking from other states with longer waiting periods for divorce. During the busy season there were as many as a hundred divorces a day. To take care of these cases were two hundred attorneys whose fees varied from one hundred dollars into the thousands. Wealthy businessman Clifford V. Brokaw settled over $3 million dollars on his wife, and the attorneys were reported to have received two hundred thousand dollars!

Mary Pickford was the first motion picture star to go to Reno. She made the whole world Reno-conscious when she divorced actor Owen Moore. Then followed the big stampede, and George Wingfield built the Riverside Hotel. American millionaires who went Reno way included Mrs S.H. du Pont; Mrs Cornelius Vanderbilt; Mrs Curtis Woodruff, daughter of the Standard Oil president; Clare Brokaw, daughter of playwright and politician Clare Boothe Luce; and boxer Jack Dempsey.

Of all the prospectors who eventually became bonanza millionaires, only Wingfield remained in the state that made him millions. Applying intelligence to earth's natural resources, he was the biggest individual taxpayer in the state of Nevada. He owned the Wingfield Bank and most of the real estate in and around Reno. Money made him a power.

Wingfield started out as a bartender and gambler in Golconda, Nevada, and moved to Tonopah, where he opened a gambling–drinking spot and made his first big money. During the goldfield boom he teamed up with George S. Nixon, who later became a senator from Nevada. This team soon owned several of the richest mines in Nevada; in turn, they bought up all the top gambling houses and hotels and became multimillionaires. When the rush was over, Wingfield controlled the whole state. He was responsible for Nixon becoming a senator.

From the first, Wingfield had the reputation of being a square shooter. His games were always on the level and, like his liquor, his word was his bond. He grubstaked many a man in the early days.

Belle had dug up all this information. 'Good gracious,' Belle said, speaking of Wingfield, 'at last I've run across a man who has no ugly skeletons to rattle!'

While Belle had been looking up the power behind the Big Three, they had been quietly watching her every move. Unlike New York, in Reno everyone knew everything about everyone else. She was fenced in. She was out of bounds. Her expensive wardrobe was out of place in these wide-open spaces where the social elite wore slacks and cotton shirts.

By the end of the first week, Belle began to get fidgety. The following Monday we took a drive beyond the outskirts of town. We wanted to look at The Willows, one of the best gambling clubs, located a few miles from town off Truckee Road.

On our way back I spotted a charming little farmhouse with a large barn and a silo at one end. Pointing to it, I casually remarked, 'Now, there's a spot that would make an unusual club. An entrance could be made through the silo. In the barn, huge colourful cushions could be used in the cow stalls and waterlilies planted in the urine drains.' This was all Belle needed.

'Turn in the drive,' she told the chauffeur. We pulled up at the farmhouse. She got out and knocked on the door. An elderly couple came out. Belle put her black magic to work; she said she wanted to rent, or buy, the farm and she talked of her bank in Italy. The conversation, and she, were too much, so I wandered around to the back.

Belle called me; she was all smiles – yes, these nice people wanted to go visit their daughter. They would like to sell or lease. Belle leased the farm, nonchalantly handing over two one-hundred-dollar bills, for good grace. Within two days they moved out. We moved in.

No sooner were our bags unpacked when a man came along in a tow car. He mentioned the word *Cadillac*. Belle took him out in the yard, away from my eager ears. But I saw her gesticulating. She gave him a mother's appeal. But it was to no avail. I clearly heard him say, 'Give me the keys, lady.'

A blushing Belle swept into the modest farmhouse and returned with the car keys. She was full of gripes and excuses – it was that awful corn whiskey that must have fogged her mind; she was unable to function. I told her she functioned pretty well, considering she had talked two nice people out of their home for only two hundred dollars.

'If it is any news to you,' she blurted, 'those were the last two bills I had left!' She had no sooner said this than she was sorry, because she liked to keep everything and everybody in the dark.

That evening we went to one of the clubs. Seeing a youngish man sporting a beard, Belle's eyes lighted up. She introduced me, but I left them alone. He was one of the Scripps Howard newspaper clan and I knew she wanted to do a little gold-digging.

The following morning, after breakfast, Belle and I sat on the porch while she tried to rock away her hangover. We talked of many things.

'Belle, you and I are coming to the end of the line.'

'What do you mean? I'm only a little over fifty.'

'By the end of the line I mean, the end of kidding ourselves. We're not using our brains. As soon as the club is finished, I am going my own way. I don't know what that way will be at the moment – maybe home to Australia. But I'm tired of booze, rackets, racketeers, syndicates, mobs and mobsters. I want to paint, and I want ordered peace.' Then, in my usual flippant manner, I said, 'I wonder what callers we can expect *this* morning?'

She was in no mood for jokes. Just then a car came up the driveway. Out jumped a young man who said, 'I want to speak to Miss Belle Livingstone.'

Belle rose up from under her hangover and suggested they take a stroll. 'I can tell you right here!' the young man went on. 'The telephone company has been looking for you long enough. You charged six hundred and fifty dollars in long-distance telephone calls at the Algonquin Hotel in New York. You used Miss Dorothy Parker as a reference. We have had great trouble locating you.'

Belle started on the same old Italian bank routine. Since the phone at the farmhouse was still in the owners' name, the young man wanted to know where they'd gone. Belle didn't know. Not being able to disconnect the telephone without permission, he left.

That evening we ate at a small boarding house that served family-style meals. Once more I was paying, so I picked the place. Belle had been fighting with the chauffeur; she had no further use for him now, but he wouldn't leave because of back salary. For that matter, no one had been paid – the maid; Little Jean; Johnnie the head waiter, who later worked at Mocambo in Hollywood; or the maître d', who became maître d' at the Beverly Hills Hotel. As the corn whiskey got the better of her, she fired them one by one. The last one to go was Little Jean.

In the meantime Belle dug up money from the slot concession syndicate. Carpenters began to work on the barn, and a doorway was cut in the silo. Enormous pillows in sap green, blue and purple were made for the cow stalls, and waterlilies started to grow in the drains. I painted leaping jade-green frogs around the gaming tables.

Several times Belle mentioned that apparently the Big Three were putting up no opposition. Later I learned they were just letting her play around a little. In fact, they welcomed my new ideas. They'd evidently heard of my work with the New York Syndicate.

We put the finishing touches to the barn. We wanted to retain the rural look. The gaming tables were installed. My jade-green, leaping, lecherous frogs seemed right at home – some were tossing silver dollars into the air, others gazing tensely around, while an odd one or two had a tear in its eye.

With one hundred divorces a day, Reno inspired Hollywood movies, like this one starring Hedda Hopper.

Belle was amazed at the way everyone seemed to be cooperating. Now, for the first time, she really confided in me: 'One thing bothers me,' she said. 'Everything's going too smoothly.' The Big Three had stayed completely away, but you could never be sure they wouldn't step in at the last minute and ask for a big cut.

'You can't leave now. You will have to watch out for my interest, as well as your own,' Belle urged. 'Besides, maybe the people running the tables will cheat on our percentage.'

While shopping in town we ran across Little Jean. She upbraided him: 'I thought I told you to leave town. I'll write to your father in France!' She bought a ticket for him to San Francisco and waited until she saw him safely on the bus. When it pulled out she said, 'Gracious knows what he's been telling people around town.'

That evening, after several Old Fashioneds made from corn whiskey, she told me of her plan. She must have money to make at least a few part payments on her debts, just to show good faith. 'I'll wire ten people in New York,' she said. 'It's a mistake to ask rich people for a couple of hundred, they are liable to ignore that amount. If you ask for a couple of thousand, they think it's urgent. That's it, I'll wire ten people and ask each for two thousand dollars. If three or four fail me, I'll still end up with twelve or fourteen thousand.' She sat down at the desk to word her wire.

I went to my room and soon heard her dictating to the operator: LITTLE JEAN YOU LIKED SO MUCH AT THE COUNTRY CLUB PASSED AWAY TODAY STOP I NEED TWO THOUSAND DOLLARS TO SEND HIS REMAINS BACK TO FRANCE STOP BELLE

This was too much for me! I just stood there and looked at this woman who had bragged, 'I'm the most wicked woman alive.' To me, at that moment, she was. I started to clean up. Maybe I should clear out from the whole filthy mess, I thought to myself as I started putting my things in order. On the table was Belle's book *Belle of Bohemia*, which she had loaned me to read. Flipping the pages, I wondered how she could do such a thing to a young boy of eighteen, left in her care. Then I thought of her own two children, and turning to that part of the book, I started to read: 'This much wisdom I have garnered from my life, that some women are fitted to be mothers and others are not, and that I am emphatically of the latter type . . . but I lacked the tenderness which my parents gave me and which, in fact, I have never given to any human being.'

As I was reading, I heard her sending the other wires over the phone, the same wires to all ten people. I listened, fascinated at the list. One was sent to the son of one of New York's biggest department store owners – would Macy's tell Gimbels? Anyway, they were all prominent people whom I'd seen often in the New York club. She told the operator to sign all the telegrams 'BELLE', except three. To these she added my name – I couldn't believe my ears. One was to a wonderful Back Bay Boston couple who had been overly generous with me when, with Archie's help, I'd painted a monkey bar for them.

I didn't wait. I rushed into the room and the battle was on. All hell broke loose – she told the operator she'd call back. I slammed the front door and went out into the fresh air.

A large aluminium house-car had been parked nearby for several weeks. A salesman named Hal had brought the trailer up from Los Angeles, hoping for a sale. We had become friendly. I think he was almost as broke as I was. I knocked on the door. He was home and suggested we drive into town and have a few beers. On the way he told me a good deal of the gossip that was circulating about Belle. I told him how disgusted I was with her, about the wires, and how I wanted to leave Reno. He said he was going back to Los Angeles in a couple of days.

Later, when we drove back, the farmhouse was in darkness – Belle had locked me out.

Hal let me sleep in the house-car. For two days, having no money, as Belle was still hiding out, I ate nothing but raw carrots from the vegetable garden. On the third morning Hal said he knew a man at the Wingfield Bank and drove me into town. We told this man what had happened and he made out a demand note for the $1348 I'd spent on the trip. The bank also phoned the Vanderbilt ranch, where Belle was staying, and left word for her to come in and sign it. It was a bitter Belle who put her signature on that note.

Hal drove us back to the farmhouse. Silently, Belle unlocked the house and gave me my personal belongings, which I packed and took over to the house-car.

As I stood there, wondering what my next move should be, someone tapped me on the shoulder; I swung around. The man was tall – very tall – and wore a ten-gallon hat and a chequered cotton shirt. He spoke quietly, with a Bronx accent. He said they knew all about me; I was okay. He mentioned the name of a power behind the New York nightclubs.

'You done a couple of his places,' he said. 'The decorations was real great. I loved da frogs you put in da gambling room. You done a real fine job. As for dat old gyp you're tied in with, we want no part of her in dis territory. Dis territory is run on da level – *she* pays nobody. We're railroading her outta Reno.'

As he talked, my mind went back to the 'accountants' who had called on me. It all came back. For a moment I even caught my breath as I felt my ribs paining me sympathetically. Now, this guy wasn't swarthy and pasty-faced like the New York bootleggers; here we were in the open spaces – but there was nothing open-faced about him! Beneath his suntan I sensed a bronze barbarian. He suggested I leave quietly, just get out of town.

'When?' I asked.

'Sundown will be just fine,' he said.

With no hope of selling the house-car, Hal decided to leave for Los Angeles that same evening. He planned to drive all night to avoid the desert heat. I knew the order to leave town had come from the Big Three. All I had to my name was forty cents and Belle's IOU. Having no particular destination, I accepted Hal's offer of a lift to California.

I hadn't gambled in Reno, so as we stopped in town for coffee, I decided to try just one of those one-armed bandits. I put a dime in a machine and hit a jackpot of six dollars! To me that jackpot seemed like six hundred.

The huge house-car had four heavy mahogany bunks which came down, like sleepers on a train. There was a kitchen and shower back of the driver's seat; the back end had a rounded, glassed observation section. I sat up front with Hal.

At sunrise I made coffee for us both. We talked as we rode along. We were approaching the town of Merced, California, and coming towards us at high speed was a huge fruit truck. Without warning the vehicle veered across the white line. Hal swerved quickly, but not quickly enough – there was a violent explosion. A huge hook on the fruit truck ripped open the entire side of our aluminium car. The heavy bunks shot thirty feet into the air; the hot water tank in the kitchen was punctured and poured water all over me. I landed on my back. The driver of the truck admitted he had fallen asleep at the wheel.

The doctor at Merced Emergency Hospital claimed there were no serious injuries to either of us, although my ribs ached so much I could hardly breathe, let alone walk. There were no broken bones.

As the engine of our car wasn't damaged, we started off for Los Angeles. I was still having a great deal of difficulty breathing, so I bound my ribs up with a torn shirt, hoping to ease the pain.

Arriving in Los Angeles, Hal drove to the Hollywood Police Station, where he reported the accident. I thanked him for the trip and went over to the emergency hospital next door for treatment. They X-rayed me and found all the ribs on one side cracked. They taped me up and I left.

At the Warner Kelton Hotel nearby I took a cheap room and deposited my belongings. Then, like all good tourists, I went straight to Hollywood and Vine. To my disappointment I found it like the corner of any two streets in any small town. What's more, it was

The Kid from Kiama, son of a once bankrupt importer of Tweeds and Weeds, had finally arrived in Hollywood.

almost as deserted as a scene from iconic old Hollywood, when its rich black dirt sidewalks were lined with pepper trees. The houses were anything from French chateaus, Italian villas, Turkish delights to the Spanish. All were anything but traditional.

In the early days of the silent movies, within a couple of weeks people from the sawdust, from tank towns, broncos, Brooklyn and Broadway, sprang to stardom. In 1921 Virginia Rappe died at a party; even though he was cleared of her manslaughter, the roly-poly Fatty Arbuckle's career died with her. So, too, did Mabel Normand's and Mary Miles Minter's stardom fade after the shooting murder of actor William Desmond Taylor; though they were never charged, rumours circulated because they had been romantically linked to Taylor. Following the Arbuckle trial, Hollywood became known as a city of sin. When scriptwriter Elinor Glyn was asked about the vice, she remarked, 'If they are flagrantly immoral, hang them' – the same Elinor Glyn who made the work *It* famous, and Clara Bow the 'It' Girl, and Aileen Pringle in *Three Weeks*, and many other pictures that were sizzlers on sex and sin. To clean up Hollywood, Presbyterian elder Will Hays, with his corn-on-the-cob teeth, was paid $100,000 a year as president of the Motion Picture Producers and Distributors of America.

There were bums, brothels, bootleggers. The three Cornero brothers were the Capones of the liquor barges. They sold from the twelve-mile limit, where the deserted coastline made it easy for a fast speedboat to land the booze.

So much for the whiskey and gin . . . now for the women.

Hollywood was one of the first cities to abolish its red-light district. The follow-up was the house on the hill of prostitution. There was a Big Madam in Hollywoodland; you could phone for a redhead, a blonde or a brunette, a fallen star, a high-school girl, or just an extra. Whatever she was, she was a professional. This love market existed despite many exposés. They arrested one madam who had a list of a hundred girls all under eighteen; some were schoolgirls living at home with their parents.

Prohibition was in effect. Many people, left without liquor stocks, resorted to other stimulants – the opium pipe, cocaine, morphine and, of course, marijuana from Tijuana.

Drugs drove beautiful actress Barbara La Marr to suicide; Hollywood couldn't hide the sad morphine-cracked body of screen idol Wallace Reid from his public. Once hailed as the screen's most perfect lover, he became instead 'the man in the padded cell'.

Movie ads heralded beautiful jazz babies, champagne baths, midnight revels, petting parties in the purple dawn. Everywhere were neckers, petters, 'let-ers', white kisses and red

Hollywood was raiding Broadway as talking pictures took over, offering me the opportunity to design costumes for movies like Bordertown.

The Brown Derby was the meeting place for all the gossip writers and stars in Hollywood. More dirt was dished up in the restaurant than food in the kitchen.

kissers, pleasure-mad daughters and sensation-craving mothers.

Movies were made on any street. Men, women and children, their faces smothered in Max Factor's orange greasepaint, blended into the orange-polka-dotted trees; when hungry, they reached up and grabbed an orange. Keystone Kops with walrus moustaches, their cars swaying and screeching. Max Sennett Bathing Beauties in bold black-and-white-striped stockings and stocking-like bathing suits.

The first Biograph Girl was America's sweetheart, Mary Pickford, with her long curls. Hollywood had delicate-faced Lillian Gish; the royal family of Ethel, Lionel and John Barrymore; Charlie Chaplin, The Tramp, with Jackie Coogan, The Kid.

Hollywood Boulevard, the self-named style centre of the world, was a mixture of cropped hair, long hair, satin shoes in the daytime, Russian boots, wolfhounds, women in knickers, pyjamas; dozens of imitation Garbos, Crawfords and Connie Bennetts; Bebe Daniels, with a live white cat around her neck, strolled the Boulevard.

Mae Murray in Panama hat, sweater and white knickers, stepping into her chauffeur-driven Lancia sports car. Loretta Young was photographed with a spotted dog matching her spotted outfit. Gloria Swanson drove her own long Lancia sports car. Pola Negri and Olga Petrova in their respective Packards. Tom Mix was the flashiest of all – everything on his car, like his bathroom, was gold-plated.

Of the clubs, there was the Embassy, and the Montmarte, near Highland Avenue, frequented by the three Talmadge sisters (Norma, Constance and Natalie); Myrna Loy; Norma Shearer; Jean Harlow; Joan Crawford; Dick Barthelmess; Corrine Griffith; Katherine MacDonald, the 'American Beauty'; Colleen Moore; Molly O'Day and Sally O'Neil; Nita Naldi; Theda Bara; Laura La Plante, Polly Moran, rubbing shoulders with Wallace Beery; Rod La Roque; Monte Blue; Richard Dix; J. Warren Kerrigan; Conrad Nagel; William S. Hart; Will Rogers; Buster Keaton; William 'Buster' Collier; Moran and Mack, the 'Two Black Crows' – and everyone wanted to dance with Valentino.

Around the corner on Vine Street was Al Levy's. Opposite was the Brown Derby, where playwright Wilson Mizner made his home. This was also a meeting place for the gossip writers; more dirt was dished up in the restaurant than food in the kitchen.

There were terrific feuds – if there weren't any, the stars or their agents made them up. One reminds me of the fable of the Kilkenny cats, who were supposed to have fought until only their tails remained. Everyone who had been around at that time knew of the famous feud between Gloria Swanson and Pola Negri on the old Paramount lot. I'm not sure which, but one of the two was a great lover of black cats. The other was terrified of them; she was superstitious and claimed they were bad luck. Both stars were of equal importance then. One said she wouldn't work if the feral cats remained on the lot; the other said they certainly would remain. It really wasn't up to either of the stars – cats being cats, they had their way and soon multiplied in such numbers that the studio was infested with leaping, darting, hissing black pussies.

In 1930, one year before I arrived in Hollywood, the *talking* pictures really took over.

Hollywood raided Broadway. As to salaries, the sky was the limit. Helen Hayes starred with Gary Cooper in *A Farewell to Arms*. Soon Ina Claire, Ruth Chatterton, Tallulah Bankhead, Jane Cowl and Alice Brady were basking in the California sunshine.

Garbo's Swedish accent broke through the barrier in *Anna Christie*; she became the screen's greatest attraction. Ronald Colman, with his wonderful voice, had no trouble bridging the gap. Nor did Bert Lytell, Lewis Stone and others. Miss Barrymore joined her brothers, John and Lionel, in *Rasputin* at MGM.

The movie moguls realised the two most vital cogs in the whole mechanised set-up were writers and directors. Young stage directors, like George Cukor, were added to Lubitsch, Vidor, Ford, Milestone, Stevens, Borzage, Wyler, Wilder, Goulding and Clarence Brown. John Colton, who adapted Somerset Maugham's *Rain*, was engaged by producer Irving Thalberg. Zoë Akins, author of *Déclassé*, which starred Miss Barrymore, joined Paramount to write for Ruth Chatterton. Ben Hecht and Charles MacArthur joined other screenwriters – Frances Marion, Adela Rogers St John and Sonia Levine.

George Cukor sent for more and more Broadway personalities – Constance Collier, Gladys Cooper, Billie Burke, Mary Boland, Florence and Mary Nash, Lucille Watson and Lenore Ulric. I will never forget Grace Moore in *One Night of Love*.

The English made an invasion. Laurence Olivier, Leslie Howard and Herbert Marshall joined Ronald Colman, already in residence. Four magnificent voices and actors. The brilliant Noël Coward, his crisp clipped accent giving you every R and every G. Diana Wynyard's performance in his *Cavalcade*, as the little child on its toes, looking down at Queen Victoria's funeral cortege, saying, 'She must have been a very little woman' was unforgettable.

This distinguished English contingent was followed by other Englishmen who seemed to have packed their odd socks and vests in great haste, because the further away from home they were, the more British they became. I can think of nothing worse than a second-rate Englishman.

Character actors have long been married to their medium. These knowledgeable performers, with years of study of their craft, are really the backbone of our greatest movies, and it was these sturdy worthies who lifted and kept the pace and tempo for the sexy sweater girls – and the handsome leading men who stumbled and yapped their way across the screen.

There were terrific feuds – if there weren't any, the stars or their agents made them up.

The hotel Chateau Elysee housed many wonderful character actors and actresses: C. Aubrey Smith, with eyebrows like my Sealyham dog; whimsical Roland Young; baffled, bewitched and bewildered Charlie Butterworth. And there was one-of-a-kind Bob Benchley of the Garden of Allah hotel set. Spoon-faced Una O'Connor, the kitchen maid; Edna May Oliver, a Grant Wood study in a high-backed chair.

Broadway's top stars may have become Hollywood conscious in 1931, but none of my old friends had yet made the trek west – with one exception, Frank Joyce, who had managed the Coolidge Hotel on 47th Street. His sister, Alice Joyce, was a silent star. Frank had joined forces with Myron Selznick and was now a top agent.

Sid Grauman, creator of the Chinese Theatre, had started the idea of a stage show or prologue along with the picture. Brother and sister theatrical producers Fanchon and Marco, who had the downtown Paramount Theatre, followed suit and played their units all over the state. This was right up my alley, as I had been supplying many of the ideas for the Shuberts' shows.

George White once paid me $1500 for just one idea for the finale of one of his Scandals revues. The scene opened with a lone Indian girl, almost naked, sporting an enormous white headdress. She stood on the top of a series of irregular platforms which were painted to look like barren country. One by one, showgirls wearing headdresses representing all the countries in the 'melting pot of America' appeared and stood in formation. When they turned, the backs of the headdresses formed the whole skyline of

New York City, the lights dimmed and tiny ships on wires moved across the stage, giving the effect of boats on the Hudson. As the stars in the backdrop lighted up, a beautiful girl draped in white jersey, representing the Statue of Liberty, ascended on a hydraulic elevator up to the flys. This finale was given write-ups *above* the Folies Bergère idea which George White had imported from Paris.

Since I'd become known for my ideas in New York, I was sure Fanchon and Marco would be interested here in Hollywood. Armed with drawings of three complete sets of scenery and costumes – carted from New York via Reno – I called at their business office. After a long wait the office girl asked me to leave my sketches for Miss Fanchon to see. I didn't think it was a good idea, but with less than a dollar in my pocket, I took a chance.

I'd read in the newspapers that George and Gracie were billed to open at the Orpheum, so I took a street car downtown and watched the act from backstage – I didn't have the price of a ticket, anyway. I hoped they would take me to dinner after the supper show. They did, and it was the best meal I'd had in weeks. I might have been too proud to ask Gracie for a loan, but I was not too proud to do any kind of work. That's another thing I've never understood – people who borrow money. We have two hands and can wash dishes or drive a truck. At least one can keep one's pride.

I had three or four hundred dollars owing to me by various people to whom I'd loaned money in New York, apart from Belle's note. I wrote Larry Reilly, my friend from the Hotel Coolidge days, asking him to try and see if these people would send at least five of what they owed me. He, too, was far in debt to me. He called everyone, but no one had seen a five spot in ages – neither had he.

Of all the people I'd loaned money to, Jack Benny was the only one who ever paid me back. He wasn't broke at the time but had just run short as he was going on tour. As I remember, a few months later, when he got back from the road, he called saying he'd moved to the old Claridge. If I'd drop around he'd pay me back that ten bucks. I dropped around.

Now, the following day after seeing George and Gracie, I read a small piece on the front page of the newspaper: Bankrupt Australia had sent her last shipment of gold to America. She could no longer repay her war debt. The Government Savings Bank of Sydney was to pay so much on the pound to its creditors. I realised why I hadn't heard from Mother regarding my request for funds.

I went back to Fanchon and Marco's business office, and after sitting around half the

Gracie Allen and George Burns in cracking form. Gracie was my
first friend in New York, and we all became lifelong friends.
They were a rare man-and-wife combination, on and off the boards.

morning, the secretary said she wasn't sure Miss Fanchon could use my designs. I guess I made a great mistake saying I was broke and asking what they would give me for the lot. She went into the office and then returned to say they'd take the sketches if I'd care to sell the lot for *fifteen dollars*. I was flabbergasted! I told her George White had paid me $1500 for only one finale. But, with rent to pay that day and nothing in my pocket, and only coffee in my stomach since the Burns and Allen dinner, I took the money. I gave them all my sketches and ideas of scenery and costumes, representing many months of work. Some time later I went to the downtown Paramount. Fanchon and Marco's whole presentation was built around just one of my ideas. They surely got a bargain for fifteen bucks!

Many years later I met Miss Fanchon – or Mrs Lyman, as she was then. She said, 'Oh, I'm so glad to meet you, Orry-Kelly.' I told her my name, at one time, was 'Jack Kelly', and how she'd picked my brains for fifteen dollars, and I wasn't so sure I was glad to meet her.

One morning a big old tired convertible stopped in front of the Warner Kelton Hotel; Archie Leach and Phil Sharack, a songwriter, had driven across country. Archie had played with Fay Wray in a short-lived Broadway show, *Nicki*. Fay told him he would do well in pictures. Archie took a room at the Warner Kelton for the night, and the next day found an apartment on North Kingsley Drive, in the older section of town, between Hollywood Boulevard and Franklin Avenue.

He had a letter of introduction to an agent, Walter Herzbrun. Marian Geering, a foreign director who had made a big hit with his last picture, was going to test his wife for a contract. Herzbrun got Archie the chance to test opposite her. The lighting was focused on Geering's wife, leaving Leach in shadows; the shadows brought out the cleft in his chin, sharpening his jawbone, making him appear older. When the heads of Paramount saw the test they said, 'We've got another Gable.' He was signed to a seven-year contract, with six months' option.

Unlike another young hopeful, Randolph Scott, who had just signed at the usual seventy dollars a week, Archie's salary started at $350. After all, he had been in Broadway shows – and the fact that Walter Herzbrun's brother was Paramount's attorney didn't hurt either.

Archie Leach became Cary Grant.

When the heads of Paramount saw Archie's screen test they said,
'We've got another Gable'. Archie Leach became Cary Grant.

Hedda Hopper's famous sense of style shows in her early days as a silent movie actress before she became one of Hollywood's most powerful columnists and a bestselling author.

Cary had no sooner signed when he began worrying about whether they would take up his options.

Neither of us were known in Hollywood, so every evening we'd meet at the corner drug store for a sixty-five-cent dinner. Once a week we'd go up to Vine Street for an eighty-five-cent seven-course fish dinner.

One day we bumped into Frank Joyce. I introduced Cary. Frank needed an extra guy for a dance at the Hotel Mayfair and invited Cary to join him. The same Saturday night the hotel manager where I was living decided he must hold my key – I was several weeks in arrears. I'd already shown him the letter from my mother, saying she'd send me money the moment she was able to collect from her tenants, but the hotel had grown tired of waiting. Somehow I was never able to tell Cary of my predicament. Every time I'd start to say something during dinner, he would be full of his own plans. Other times, taking a drive after dinner, I'd pluck up the courage, but before I'd get started, he would say, 'Kelly, you talk too much – I'm thinking.'

Cary went to the Mayfair dance. That was the only night during the entire first six months that we hadn't dined together. I thought to myself, Why did the manager have to take my key so late at night, and on such a cold night? What was I going to do? I thought of Belle and her night on the subway. I decided to walk around to keep warm – there were no all-night picture houses in those days. I was almost exhausted when I arrived at Cary's apartment on Sunday morning. He wasn't overjoyed at my early call, but I guess he had other things on his mind, plus a hangover. I made some coffee and cooked breakfast. Then he said, 'Okay, Kelly, get your so-and-so out of here! I've got to write to Doreen.'

Completely done-in from my all-night walk, and having nowhere to go, I broke down and told him I'd been locked out. I also told him of my mother's letter. Lord knows, she'd been pretty decent to both of us through the years in New York. He said he was sorry, and for me to go and sleep on the couch in the living room, which I did. The following day we found a nice sunny room in a private house a couple of doors away for seven dollars a week, including breakfast. Cary advanced the seven bucks and I moved in.

Shortly after that, Al Rosen, who shared an office with Walter Herzbrun, got me a job decorating B.B.B.'s Cellar on Cosmo Alley, near Hollywood Boulevard. Ye Gods!

Wouldn't you know – they'd seen and heard of my monkeys! I pleaded, 'Let me do anything else.' But, no deal, they wanted the naughty red monkeys. They got them.

During the first six months in Hollywood, Cary made one picture, a smallish part in a Lili Damita film. One evening, after we'd had our usual sixty-five-cent dinner, we drove towards Western Avenue. Cary looked in a doorway and saw a pool table. He exclaimed, 'Ah, beeleeards!' His voice was north-of-England mixed and Americanised at the NVA with a dash of the cockney of the Pender stilt-walking troupe he used to perform with.

I said, 'What do you mean, "beeleeards"? It's billiards!'

He flushed. 'I'll bet you a milleeeon dollars that "beeleeards" is correct.'

I told him they had a school at Paramount where he could learn diction. That's all, brother! The car came to an abrupt stop. I was arsed out – but I was used to it by now. We'd been having these silly brawls since 1926 and by now, 1931, they were more like brotherly arguments. We really were trying to help each other. So I went to a movie and forgot about it – I had to as Grant was, for the first time, buying the dinner, or so I thought.

During these first six months Cary had more days off the sound stages than on. We would often drive to the beach; he wanted to listen to the spielers on the Pike at Venice. At this point he hadn't yet washed the carnival out of his hair. On one of these drives, shortly after Paramount had picked up his option, I began to notice Grant was taking over Leach. Out of the blue, Cary said, 'The woman I marry is going to already own a mink coat, and a diamond bracelet.' Then, sort of thinking out loud, he asked me if he should marry Doreen.

I told him he shouldn't have to ask me, or anyone else for that matter. 'After all, you've gone steady with her for four years, she's a lovely, natural blonde, and a really nice girl. Why not?'

'Well, you know,' Cary mused, 'Doreen is of German extraction. Germans get fat. In ten years I may be a big star and she may be a big fat blonde.'

'Oh, for Gawd's sake, Cary, don't marry her. You can't love her!'

Once more I had opened my big mouth without thinking first, and Grant just as quickly opened the door and out I went! By now I was getting used to walking home.

Some time later Walter Herzbrun took me, armed with my sketches, to see Rufus Le Maire at Warner Brothers Studios in Burbank. My designs were shown to the powers that be. They were to call me . . . After forty-two long days and longer nights of waiting, I got word: Yes, the studio would engage me as their designer.

The first time I drove through those big gates of Warner Brothers, my thoughts went back to Kiama, where I was considered bush. Once a week was 'picture night' at the Odd Fellows Hall – a serial, usually starring Pearl White, and a two-reeler with Flora Finch and John Bunny. Now here I was in Hollywood, engaged to dress film stars brighter than any I had seen on the flickering screen at home. The Kid from Kiama, son of a once bankrupt importer of Tweeds and Weeds, was entering one of the biggest picture studios in the world!

This was to be my home for the next eleven years.

843.   WARNER BROTHERS WEST COAST STUDIOS, SUNSET BOULEVARD, HOLLYWOOD, CALIFORNIA.   KFWB.

Kay Francis
Another Dawn

CHAPTER NINE

She became known as the best-dressed woman on the screen.

LORETTA YOUNG WAS very young when I designed my first motion picture dress in 1932. It was a B picture, but it broke the ice for me – and almost my heart.

The one evening dress I was proud of and liked, she didn't. It was thrown out of the picture. Later I was told she bought it at half price. Not wanting to have it ruined under the hot arc lights, she pretended not to like it. It was really a compliment to me, but at the time I didn't think so.

While marking time for my first Kay Francis picture, the studio assigned me to a George Arliss epic about a mythical kingdom. I was excited at the opportunity of knowing this great actor. I was one of his avid fans. I admired his beautifully modulated voice, and while he possessed great authority, there was something timid about him – and I was soon to learn he was henpecked. His wife, Florence, had all the say. She saw to it they had an iron-bound contract, and that no one played opposite Mr Arliss excepting herself. She demanded and saw to it that her part and dialogue were always a sweet family portrait. No one on screen appeared as kind and gentle as she.

The first day of shooting, Mr Koenig, Warner's production head, excitedly ordered me to dash down to the set. 'There's something wrong with Mrs Arliss's hat. She's holding up a set that has hundreds of extras. We can't afford a minute's delay.'

Mrs Arliss had everything and everyone jumping, and she, too, was jumping while pounding her umbrella on the stage. She threw her handbag on the floor. She tossed her hat in the air . . . I arrived just in time to catch it, and Florence's tongue: 'I thought I told you in the fitting room, Mr Kelly, not to cup me under the saddle!' She was referring to her rump, of which she had more than a sufficiency. While all of this was going on, Mr Arliss stood in a corner, quivering, trembling and shaking. Mrs Arliss snapped at the wardrobe woman, who was having trouble making her stand still while the snaps were moved over – way over. Continuing her rampage, she said, 'And my hat, Mr Kelly, I distinctly told you I wanted it trimmed with the male bird of the wren!'

The property man must have seen the baffled look on my face; he beckoned me over to his corner. 'The male bird's tail should have gold on it.' Casually dipping the tail of the wren into some gold paint, he handed it to me. When I returned with it to Mrs Arliss, her eyes lit up. A sudden calm came over her face as she adjusted her toque, with its shimmering gold wings. Looking at herself in the mirror, she exclaimed, 'Ah, the male bird of the wren.' Mr Arliss, in his corner, stopped quivering. Hundreds of hussars straightened their high-peaked hats and brush feathers. The tights of two crotch-bound lackeys were adjusted. They opened the double doors. Mr Arliss, looking exactly like a very old English walking stick in a hall stand, stepped out, adjusting his monocle.

The director called out, 'Lights! Camera! Action!' The superb actor went into his act.

Now that I was working, Cary thought we should take a house and share expenses. I rented a duplex on the way to Warners. By now I wasn't so sure I wanted to live, and eat, the way Grant wanted. At number 10 Commerce, in New York, my studio apartment was very modern for the twenties. I had an electric kitchen – I never did care for sitting at drug store counters, particularly at dinnertime. So, just as Grant was about to move in, I suggested he take an apartment nearer Paramount and share it with Randy Scott.

After the Loretta Young picture I dressed Bebe Daniels in *The Silver Dollar* – a period piece with Edward G. Robinson based on the Denver legend Baby Doe, once dubbed the 'best dressed woman in the west'. Bebe became my first Hollywood friend, and the first star to invite me to her home. One day I introduced Cary to her while he lunched at

Cary thought we should share a house and expenses. But I suggested he take an apartment nearer Paramount and share it with Randy Scott.

Warners. Shortly after this, Bebe invited Cary and me to a sit-down Sunday dinner at her beach house for, of all people, Elsa Maxwell, the gossip columnist known for her high-society parties. At five-thirty I telephoned Cary about picking me up. He sounded as if he'd been nipping; he said he wasn't going and I could make the apologies. I hit the ceiling: 'When in hell are you going to learn manners? At least call Bebe.'

Then I was taken aback. Cary said, 'Who the hell do you think you're talking to? You owe me three hundred and sixty dollars and forty-eight cents!'

I couldn't believe my ears. '*For what?*' I asked. Then I remembered that little red book he kept; often I'd seen him make an entry after we'd had dinner. And there were the fights twice a week, at $3.30, which I'd thought were a treat, making up for the many fivers I'd handed him, insisting he keep up his treatment with the doctor. I know nothing of his later LSD 'kick', but I do know he knew plenty about PSP – the pounds, shillings and pennies he hoarded. Just as he saved and collected string, which he tied in neat little balls, pieces of brown paper were neatly folded and saved. Book matches were put in another carton until one day, wanting to use the top drawer of my highboy, I chucked them all out. And boy, was there a brawl!

Some weeks later Cary called me. He was sorry – after all, we were old friends. Some actors from the St Louis Opera were coming up for a party; I should come too. No sooner had I arrived at the party when in walked Randolph Scott's girl, Vivian, who later became Mrs Ernst Lubitsch. With her was a beautiful blonde with milky white skin; she wore a mink coat and a diamond bracelet. Her name was Virginia Cherrill. Catching Grant's eye, my mouth on the bias, I mumbled, 'The mink coat and the diamond bracelet.' He gave me a hard look and I knew he would have liked to kick me in the shins. Gone was the Archie Leach full of fun. He was adjusting the mask of Cary Grant – a mask that became his career, a career that became Grant. He would indeed go on to marry her.

A little later I called him aside. Neatly wrapped and held together with a rubber band was the $360.48 he had claimed I owed him. As I handed him the wad, for a moment he seemed like the Archie I knew. 'I was tight,' he told me. 'You really don't owe me this.' But he took it.

One evening, much later, Howard Hughes, Randy Scott, Cary and I went to a party at the Coconut Grove. I can't remember the girls – they were starlets – that is, with the exception of Wendy Barrie. Randy had just finished a picture with Kate Smith. Cary and Randy had moved to the beach, where they rented Constance Talmadge's beach house.

But the two of us drifted apart, as so many people do in Hollywood. Our friends were different and we seldom ran into each other, except sometimes at the fights, which I often attended with George Burns.

Through Bebe Daniels I became friendly with movie columnist Louella O. Parsons and her husband, Dr Martin, the commissioner of the fights. For several years I went along with Doc, as Louella wasn't fight crazy. His seats were in the second row, and directly in front of us sat actress Lupe Vélez, known by her fans as the Mexican Spitfire.

Fight nights were as colourful as any opening night in Hollywood today. Everyone was there, from Damon Runyon, boxing manager Willie Bernstein, to boxers Jackie Fields, Slapsie Maxie and Max Baer. The referees were former boxing champions Mushy Callahan and Frankie Van.

Directly opposite Dr Martin's seats, Mae West would make an entrance, one arm weighted down with rings and bracelets of huge star sapphires and diamonds, the other arm weighted down with Big Jim Timony – the same Jim, as you'll remember, who still owed me for the Texas Guinan *Padlock* sets and costumes.

There was no one like Mae and, I must say, the crowd watched her as much as they watched the fighters. When the big brutes entered the ring, Mae's eyes would flash like her enormous star sapphires as she looked over their focal points.

After the fights everyone went back to the Brown Derby, where most of them had dined. Over beer or highballs, the picture stars – all the Marx Brothers and too many Ritz Brothers – would go over the evening bouts.

My first assignment with Kay Francis was *One Way Passage*. William Powell was her co-star. I think it was the best picture she ever made for Warners. It took me several years to know this very down-to-earth, genuinely nice person. During the eight years I dressed her, we had no misunderstandings; she was well mannered, cooperative, easy to please and knew exactly what she wanted. She became known as the best-dressed woman on the screen.

One of the few frugal stars, Kay Francis lived behind the Sunset Towers in a tiny house on De Longpre, where the rent was seventy-five dollars a month. Later she moved to a small charming cottage across the street, next to the Towers.

Some years later, I couldn't help overhearing Kay returning the telephone call of a big star who had squandered all of her money after leaving Warners. The fallen star was still living in the grand manner at the Pierre Hotel in New York. I heard Kay say, 'Now, don't worry dear, I'll send you five thousand dollars in the morning.'

Not only was she generous and understanding in this way, but she liked and helped little people. She bought a Ford for Ida, her little old wardrobe woman.

When I first arrived in the movie colony, I studied the work of the two top designers – Adrian, and Travis Banton. Later, Omar Kiam came out for Samuel Goldwyn.

Goldwyn was supposed to have said of Kiam, 'I thought he was a writer, but he's a dress designer too.'

Starting with Kay Francis, I designed simple, unadorned evening gowns . . . At first only those with taste were impressed. Luckily Kay was the essence of good taste.

Adrian used elaborate embroidery on Garbo, Shearer and Crawford, while Banton dressed Colbert and Lombard in all-over beaded gowns. I decided the only way to be different was to avoid glitter. Remembering my motto, 'without a spangle', I made up my mind not to use a single bead or spangle.

Starting with Kay Francis, I designed simple, unadorned evening gowns – black velvet, white, beige and black chiffon or crepe. I introduced what was the forerunner of the shirtmaker dress, for evening: taking the daytime sportlines with kick pleats, I dropped these to the ground, using tailored arrowheads where the inverted pleats met. At first only those with sensitive taste were impressed. Luckily Kay was the essence of good taste.

I had won over Kay Francis. Now my big problem was to please Ruth Chatterton, who was getting three times Kay's salary. Miss Chatterton, who had made the successful transition from silent films, was being paid $125,000 per picture, with three pictures per year. Each picture took eight weeks to make. In 1931, with no taxes, her salary was astronomical.

Making my point to star Ruby Keeler (centre) about her wardrobe choices in Go Into Your Dance.

She was about to divorce her actor husband, Ralph Forbes, to marry another actor. Ralph was 'Rafe' to Miss Chatterton, whose accent was more English than the English. As she said, 'I'm being civilised about the whole thing. I am presenting Rafe in a play which I shall direct and produce.' And, with a smile, she added, 'Then I am presenting myself with a new husband, George Brent.' It all ended up veddy 'Noel-ly Poly', with Rafe meeting Mr and Mrs George Brent at the station upon their return from their honeymoon.

Warners wanted to get the clothes underway for her forthcoming picture, *The Rich Are Always with Us*, which would also feature an up-and-coming actress called Bette Davis. Production head Mr Koenig arranged for me to take my sketches and a letter of introduction to Miss Chatterton, who was rehearsing in Santa Barbara, where the play was to break in before moving on to San Francisco and Los Angeles.

I arrived early at the Samarkand Hotel in Montecito. I was jumpy – and my stomach jumped more. It was important for me to make a good impression. The letter was sent to her bungalow. Half an hour later I saw her pass through the lobby with her entourage and get into her car. The desk clerk said he had sent my letter. I followed her to the Lobero Theatre, where they were rehearsing, and sent in my name again, by the stage manager. The company broke for lunch, and finally so did I.

Late in the afternoon I phoned the studio and was told to leave the sketches with another message. I was just about to leave when a friend from my New York 'Old Guard' days, Chester Arthur, grandson of the American president of the same name, came into the theatre. I told him, unhappily, my plight.

He suggested I stop in and see his mother, who lived in Carpinteria, on my way back to Los Angeles. I did, and while having a cocktail, the phone rang. Ruth was coming over to see Mrs Arthur; they suggested I stay and meet her. I came back to Hollywood. I had never in my life used a letter of introduction, and didn't want to start by using the daughter-in-law of an American president as a premise. I realised Miss Chatterton had also had a hectic day, basting and tying together the strings of her turkey.

The studio got a letter from Miss Chatterton from San Francisco, saying she was delighted with my sketches. I, too, received a charming note to go ahead with the wardrobe. Then, as now, I've always found that it doesn't pay to act smarty-pants and have that 'I'll show her' attitude. In the long run, people appreciate the sensitiveness of others.

Now I had taken both Francis and Chatterton away from costume designer Howard Greer.

Later, when I met this really big person, I found Greer charming and most amusing. I sent him Gracie Allen, among others. Gracie in turn brought him Mary Livingstone, fellow comedienne and wife of Jack Benny. Mary was as good as a dozen customers, for in those days she ordered everything she liked in her three favourite colours.

I was a little scared of Miss Chatterton. I needn't have been; she was wonderful. Of course, she was always very formal, just as she was with everyone. I was 'Mr Kelly'. Her secretary, Miss Grey, always called if there was a delay for a fitting. Miss Chatterton became my biggest booster. In fact, she stopped ordering Patou clothes from France and had me make many of her personal things.

We had a mutual friend, screenwriter John Colton. Once she told him, 'Mr Kelly makes ladies' clothes.'

'Ruthie, dear,' Colton replied, 'Kelly makes *well-bred* clothes.'

Towards the end of her contract she made *Frisco Jenny* – the picture she didn't want to make made the most money. Jack L. Warner had engaged Wilson Mizner to work on the script. The period was 1914. I arrived at the Chatterton bungalow with my sketches and some yearbook copies of *The Theatre* magazine, which had only just come from Research. In fact, I only had time to glance at the magazines.

Her bungalow was huge, with bedrooms, baths, sitting room, special make-up room and kitchen. While going over my sketches and showing swatches of fabric, I opened up a *Theatre* magazine to show how authentic I'd been. In her very English accent, Miss Chatterton said, 'Now, don't tell me, Mr Kelly, they wore those peg-top dresses!' As I turned the pages, she kept saying, 'Oh . . . it's too much . . . Now, really . . . look at those upper shoes . . . I really can't imagine . . .'

I turned one more page; there was Miss Ruth Chatterton in *Daddy Long Legs* staring up at me! Thank God the phone rang.

Miss Chatterton was wanted on the set. Saved by the bell, I left the sketches but took along my *Theatre* magazine!

As I had not become an American citizen, I planned a trip home to Australia to get a quota number. The day I bought my ticket the headlines in the papers announced, 'BANK MORATORIUM'. Banks across America closed.

The shipping company, however, accepted my draft, payable on sight. Fortunately I'd not yet cashed the previous week's salary, knowing I would need some money for the trip.

My boat was due to sail from Wilmington, Los Angeles, at 10 pm, and at 7 pm an earthquake struck. The roads were blocked, but finally I made it to the Wilmington docks and started the voyage.

In Sydney I took Mother to the Randwick races, where she dearly loved to go. Once more my past caught up with me. We made a bet with our favourite bookie and were about to join our friends when I heard a familiar whistle. Turning around, I recognised the figure standing a little apart from the crowd. I took Mother back to our friends and excused myself.

I might have known I'd run into Gee Gee. On my last trip home I'd cleared shy, but now, on my second visit, he caught up with me. At thirty-eight Gee Gee was mature; gone was that element of dandyism which accompanied the period after the First World War, when he had been the handsomest figure on the turf. Now he appeared reserved, thoughtful and rather restrained. Even his clothes were more conservative. Only his eyes were restless. All the racetrack detectives knew him as the notorious pickpocket they hadn't been able to catch red-handed. He'd been arrested only once, and when they'd asked him his occupation, he replied, 'I'm a gentleman'. The police, no doubt, had heard rumours that he had the blood of a king running through his veins.

After a warm handshake we went into the bar and, as of old, Gee Gee insisted he shout. I looked at his skilful, sensitive hands. As if reading my mind, he said quietly, 'That's all over, I'm no longer on the cross. I'm a prosperous businessman running a late-night club. I quit before they got a single rap on me.'

Talking so civilly with Gee Gee, my thoughts went back to the turbulent days of my youth in Sydney. I asked him about some of our old cronies. He said that big, wholesome Alice O'Grady and one of the girls had been killed in a motor crash, but Ralph, my old actor friend, was only injured. Lena the Fox, still very much alive, was troubled with arthritis in her hands. I smiled – Lena's hands had often given her trouble; they were always in hot water.

It was getting late and, anxious to go back to my friends, I promised Gee Gee that I would stop by his place one evening. Joining my mother I decided I had no desire to be involved with the underworld. America had knocked all that nonsense out of my head.

Warners wanted me to get the clothes underway for a forthcoming picture that would feature an up-and-coming actress called Bette Davis.

Preparing Kay Francis for her close up. Kay might have been a major star but she was easy to please and knew exactly what she wanted. She became known as the best dressed woman on the screen.

I remained in Parramatta until my visa and quota number came through. A few days before sailing, after hitting the bottle pretty hard with my favourite barmaid, Miss Mac, at the Australian bar, I weakened and decided to see Gee Gee.

Word had travelled fast – in no time at all, Lena the Fox, Spanish Nell and a few more cronies of bygone days came in to see the local boy who had made good in Hollywood. The dazzling, gaudy Rosie Boot – still using the name of her favourite London Gaiety Girl – arrived, and Gee Gee led us discreetly to a dimly lit corner. If anything, Rosie's expensive clothing was more ravishingly garish than ten years before, when she was the leading Two-Guinea Girl. Maybe it was only the smokey cabaret cellar, or my own hazy condition, but my past seemed completely unreal to me.

Rosie gave me the lowdown on everybody: Gee Gee, far from giving up the underworld, had simply gone underground. He'd built a respectable front, then, starting with a couple of privately owned cars, he transported the harlots back and forth. This arrangement was faster and more profitable in the long run, as the girls would never use trams.

'God's truth,' said Rosie, 'they get bumped as 'tis, without 'aving to get bounced and shook up all the way to Kings Bloody Cross, or Bourke Street!'

Lena's respectable niece, Leonora, had married into a respectable Melbourne family, and was no longer respectable. It was inevitable that one day Gee Gee and Leonora would meet. And they did. She would often come to Sydney on the pretence of visiting Auntie Lena, who was now in her seventies, but, of course, she was really carrying on a hectic affair with Gee Gee. Sometimes the poor girl would dash back to Melbourne with a nervous headache, but more often Gee Gee would walk out on her.

To Gentleman George, a sheila was still a tabby – a cat – and all cats were alley cats to him. The end of this affair came one night at the Australian hotel, where they'd been dining. As they came out into the cool night, the doorman chased a flower girl away from the entrance – the girl was Cammie, dressed by Port Wine Pansy in a ragged dress with one toe out of her shoe. The pale-faced Raggedy Cammie caught Gee Gee's eye; he left Leonora standing alone as he pretended to buy some violets from the flower girl. He was fascinated by this beautiful eighteen-year-old. Behind him, Leonora, who was no fool, knew what was happening. Furious, she jumped into a cab, leaving Gee Gee with her ermine wrap still over his arm. He calmly watched her go, shrugged his shoulders and turned back to the girl.

'I've seen you somewhere before,' he said. 'What's your name?'

'Cammie.'

'Cammie what?'

The girl smiled. 'That's what I used to ask me aunt, but she'd always say, that's all there is. And then I'd say, but what will I tell people when they ask me last name? And she'd say, just tell them your name is Cammie and to think of a Cameo, that's you.'

Then Gee Gee remembered her. 'You're the kid who used to call cops for Alice O'Grady, aren't you?' Cammie smiled and nodded her head. 'Look what a beauty you've turned into!'

Just then Port Wine Pansy came around the corner with a new supply of spring flowers and violets. Gee Gee turned to her.

'You've got this kid decked out like 'Liza Doolittle, Pansy, but you're a quarter of a century too late.' Then, throwing Leonora's ermine around Cammie's shoulders, Gee Gee took her to see *Sweet Nell of Old Drury*, which was playing a few doors down the street, leaving Port Wine Pansy alone on the corner.

Sitting in the stage box, Cammie toed herself out of her old shoes and sat entranced at the play before her – no doubt identifying herself with the ragged, barefoot lass on the stage. Later, I heard that Cammie, wrapped in ermine and sable, was the most beautiful creature in the theatre, before or behind the footlights. And, as time went by, Gee Gee for the first time in his life found himself talking gently to a woman.

The following week I sailed for America. That first night out I was introduced to the Earl of Beauchamp, one-time Governor of New South Wales and King's Counsellor, who invited me for cocktails. He'd never been to the United States, and when he found out that I lived in California, he was anxious to learn all about Hollywood.

After he had ordered champagne, I confessed that I couldn't reciprocate, as my money was tied up. Being an international figure, he knew all about the Depression difficulties and was very understanding of my plight. His Lordship couldn't have been kinder, and he seemed to get a kick out of news of Hollywood and my Kellyisms.

While getting dressed for dinner, I thought what a hop, skip and jump I'd made this time – from Gee Gee, the notorious Sydney underworld character, to the former Governor of New South Wales.

The banks had reopened since my departure; I was glad I didn't ask Mother for additional money. She had been so good to me all during those early days with Archie in New York. I'd planned to give some suits to the stewards in lieu of tips.

During the voyage, as I became more friendly with the Earl and his attaché, I learned that he had rented Zane Grey's house in Tahiti for six weeks, then he was going on to Los Angeles to visit his son, the Honourable Hugh Lygon.

After a couple of weeks at sea, one morning we saw a tiny dot in the vast ocean – Tahiti. Passing through the atolls and reefs, seeing the white houses with window boxes of red geraniums, the Earl remarked, 'This could be a bit of Montmartre transplanted to the middle of the lush Pacific.'

Immediately after breakfast, the male passengers assembled in the smoking room and the women gathered in the lounge. The ship's doctor told us of the beauty of the island girls, but also warned us of the astronomical percentage of syphilis.

I went ashore alone.

Tahiti is not the South Seas paradise of Dorothy Lamour's films. The GIs found that out during the Second World War, and on my previous trip in 1923 I found Tahiti more the way Gauguin wrote about it.

Like Cézanne, Paul Gauguin worked frantically 'to realise'. In his search he drew from his contemporaries, but they were all dominated by his own personal style and transferable secret. Much of his early stuff had the silhouette of Ingres, the line of Degas, the unbroken contour of Van Gogh; and Cézanne's planes were evident in the modelling of his fantastic flat patterns with their stained-glass designs. Surfeited with civilisation, Gauguin journeyed to the South Seas, extending his free way of life and free love.

Born of rebel blood – a mixture of Spanish, Inca, African, Arab and Celt – he wrote in his suppressed *Intimate Journal*, 'Your civilisation is your disease, my barbarism, my restoration to health.' He told of French traders and found a handsome race of people, with the graceful elasticity of wild animals. 'The women's bodies were sculptural and large. Their feet large. The men effeminate – but not all.'

Taking a wife in Tahiti was as simple as reaching up and plucking some luscious fruit. Gauguin plucked Tehoura, 'a large child of thirteen, slender and strong and wonderfully proportioned'. When her mother finished extolling the virtues of her golden-skinned daughter, the candid, coarse, cruel Gauguin asked the child, 'Are you in good health? Are you clean? Do you love me?' He wrote, 'The answer to the last question must wait, for no Maori girl could love a man unless his nuptial addresses had proved satisfactory.'

He detailed it all in his *Noa Noa*, a Tahitian word meaning any form of scent. The egotistical, witty artist who, at times, wrote as brilliantly as he painted, would have you believe he astonished Tehoura with his physical talents. In his writings, describing his paintings, some passages are composed with poetic fervour. But likening himself to Superman in parts of *Noa Noa*, instead of scent it smells of Sunday journalism written by Elsa Maxwell, that outsized old gal with the oversized ego.

Tehoura was the beautiful bronze-skinned girl he painted stretched out naked on a crude couch. She was the inspiration for a whole series of voluptuous studies in happy moods. His masterful canvas, *The Spirit of the Dead Watching*, captures the real terror and fear of Tehoura for her gods.

On a whim he deserted her and their unborn child, to return to Paris.

In 1923, on my first trip to Tahiti, I heard a legend of the island: Tehoura had named her son Emil, the same as Gauguin's legitimate son who was living in Copenhagen. Her *tāne* – her big white lover – never came back.

Wanting to retrace my steps of ten years before, I inquired of Emil's whereabouts, but no one seemed to know. I rented a car anyway and followed the same route. On my first trip I had learned that Emil had grown up to be a stalwart fisherman. When not fishing, he acted as a guide, for a fee. I had engaged him and we had toured the island. He showed me many out-of-the-way spots. Casually, I told him I painted, spoke of Gauguin, careful not to have him think I knew of his relationship.

Without mentioning Gauguin's name, but referring to him as *he*, Emil pointed out various relics – Gauguin's crude jungle studio, the tinkling home-made doorbell. On the inside of the door he had painted, in the Tahitian language, one of their mottos: 'HERE ONE MAKES LOVE'. Scattered about were a boomerang, shells and some coral. The artist-barbarian had painted the entire studio chrome yellow, the same yellow he took from his friend, Van Gogh, and painted his yellow Christ. In bright daylight the blazing yellow room seemed to conform with Gauguin's palette.

Driving home, I had asked Emil to pull over by the beach; I wanted to watch the sunset. As Emil and I sat on the hot sands of Tahiti, I experienced a sunset I shall never forget: Like a flash, the luminous gold sky blotted and bled into a crimson lake. The gunmetal sand of the beach became puce pink, the colour Gauguin painted it.

I looked at the virile twenty-nine-year-old Emil, born with all the elements of his father's blood and the tropical beauty of his Polynesian child-mother; his liquid eyes gleamed like black leopard dots as he gazed out across the purple Pacific. The sky turned to ox-blood, everything went pitch black . . .

Much later, as Emil's jalopy rattled towards Papeete, he spoke of Gauguin; now he wanted me to know Gauguin was his father. There seemed to be so much cooped-up human emotion when he said, 'He never came back to my mother, but went twenty miles down the west coast.' For a long time he never knew about his father, but his mother had made him do all the things she was so proud of Gauguin doing when he was here. 'She had me climb the most rugged mountains, and swim a black volcanic lake.'

After Gauguin had left Tahiti, Emil learned he had wandered through other neighbouring islands, finally settling in the Marquesas. Slowly the hatred drained from Emil's face as the peaceful Tahitian pointed to the far horizon, saying, 'He died at Hiva Oa, Dominique Island of the Marquesas.' The Marquesans were described by Melville as 'the fairest of men, surpassing all in beauty and form'. Gauguin found them ill-formed, many hideous with elephantiasis, a dwindling, decaying stock wasting away with consumption, leprosy and syphilis.

Paul Gauguin never lived to be acclaimed, but when he died, his exotic pictures startled and excited the art world. He became famous and infamous. Calling himself a savage – a wolf in the woods – and a sun-lover, the last picture he painted on his tropical island was a snow scene reminiscent of Brittany.

He died as volcanically as he painted, from a tropical disease that often accompanies tropical love.

Getting back to Papeete, I went aboard ship and changed into a tropical tux. I was to dine with the Earl of Beauchamp and his attaché at the Blue Lagoon Hotel, which was built on sticks, partly over the water. The ship was not leaving until the following morning; the locals had been slow in loading the copra. After dinner we went to the Officers' Club. The Tahitian men and their women were a handsome mixed race. The men wore white mess jackets and a frangipani over their right or left ear, signifying either they had a friend, a lover, or were free, or maybe looking for one. Many rums later, and before the evening ended, I had one over each ear.

Not wanting to sleep in my stuffy stateroom, and being too late to disturb His Lordship, I slept atop Zane Grey's house with only the stars for cover.

The following morning, after a wonderful breakfast, I went back to the boat and we set sail for San Francisco.

The Earl had asked me to get in touch with his son as soon as I got back to Los Angeles, which I did. Hugh Lygon introduced me to Lady Bridget Carlisle of Carlisle Castle, Carlisle – I may as well do the whole bit. She was passing through California after a sojourn in China, where she had acted as hostess for her brother.

The day His Lordship arrived, Lady Carlisle and I drove down to Wilmington to meet him. I had taken over the old Clover Club for the evening for the Earl's welcoming party. Apart from the picture stars I knew, dressed and undressed, I had invited such wits from the silent movie days as actresses Aileen Pringle, Dorothy Mackaill and the beautiful Kathryn Carver – then married to actor Adolphe Menjou. And, of course, Norma Talmadge, who had been one of the biggest box office stars of the silent movies. The party was quite a success.

Later that week I invited the Earl out to see Warner Brothers Studio. He must have enjoyed his Hollywood stay, because for years I received a note from him each Christmas, thanking me again and again for his visit, which was, evidently, one of the greatest thrills of his eventful life.

Bette Davis
The Rich Are
Always with Us

CHAPTER TEN

'That kangaroo hide of yours is tougher than any two agents' put together.'

'**KELLY, YOU ARE** an extraordinary dress designer.' It was Jack Warner toasting me on my return from Australia. 'And why the hell I insisted on talking business to you instead of to an agent, I don't know. That kangaroo hide of yours is tougher than any two agents' put together.'

I said, 'You mean as tough as –' My boss didn't let me finish the name of a female agent who had a hyphenated fanny.

Warner said, 'And now that you have doubled your salary after only two years of apprenticeship, I expect some extraordinary work.'

Previously I only had a visitor's visa. Now I had a quota number. It wasn't easy; an American earning a salary comparable to mine must enter Australia before I could re-enter America. As there were none like me, or earning my salary, Senator McAdoo, through Washington, arranged for my passport. It was termed *Extraordinary*.

At option time when Jack Warner wouldn't talk to my agent, I had told him I wanted double or nothing, $750 a week. After six weeks of wearing me down – making appointments but mainly breaking them – he finally settled for $737.50. As I was leaving his office, I turned at the door and said, 'That's such an uneven amount, make it seven hundred and fifty. I need the twelve dollars fifty for dog meat.' Pressing a button, Warner hollered, 'I'll make dog meat out of you, you dressmaker, if you don't get going.' I got.

From 1933 to 1940 there was an intense period of mass-produced pictures, and Jack Warner saw to it that I earned my weekly $750. No sooner would I get through one movie than I would start on another. I often designed two and three pictures at a time. When I saw some of them years later on the late show, they looked it! Apart from the dressy films, there were the bread-and-butter pictures. In the casts were usually Pat O'Brien, Frank McHugh, Allen Jenkins, Guy Kibbee, Hugh 'Woo-Woo' Herbert, Ruth Donnelly and Glenda Farrell. I christened them 'The Warner Irish Stock Company'. This talented group often backed pictures that starred Jimmy Cagney and Joan Blondell.

When I first set eyes on Joan, in 1932, she looked like a big beautiful Kewpie doll out of a penny arcade. In fact, it was the Broadway play *Penny Arcade* that got Joan and Jimmy Cagney a Warner contract. Everything about Joan was rounded, from her top to her bottom. Big glass-blue eyes shone from under her tousled golden brown hair. When she smiled, her round dimpled cheeks set off her capless pearly teeth. The nape of her neck was salt cellar–less. Two rose-pink buds swelled from her bosom like full-blown cabbage roses. No wonder she was nicknamed Rose Bud when, in her teens, she won a Texas beauty contest. Like all rounded figures and naughty French postcards, she looked better in the altogether. Clothes cluttered her up – or down.

I had my troubles dressing her. Still, I could never get angry; she was always so fey – full of mad dishy fun. No wonder we became such great chums. Neither of us spoke in the conventional way. At parties she was 'front' for my back talk.

Joan was the original 'give until it hurts' girl. If she wasn't paying some faded star's debts, she was taking care of an extra's hospital bill. Then there was her mother, father, brother and sister – they all came first. Anyone could have her last nickel, and some took it.

While lunching with Joan in the studio green room, the stately Kay Francis entered, wearing a white jersey evening gown I had designed for the picture *Another Dawn*. The neckline was a first for the screen, or anywhere else for that matter, its narrow V-neck slit to her waist. Like bubbles in a stein of beer, Miss Blondell's eyes almost bubbled out of their sockets at the daring neckline on the elegant Kay. Joan could turn night into day, and did the moment my back was turned. After lunch, on the sound stage, she called for Cora, her wardrobe woman, to fetch her the scissors. She slashed the modest neckline of her street dress down to her navel. Not satisfied, she made a spread eagle out of a couple

Joan Blondell was full of mad dishy fun. No wonder we became such great chums. At parties she was 'front' for my back talk.

of rhinestone clips and opened up her below-the-waist line. Then, for an added touch of colour, she tucked in a rosebud to cover her button, and off she went to the corner store for a loaf of bread and the sack of potatoes the script called for.

At the preview I wanted to hide under my seat when I saw how Joan had turned a day dress into a night dress. The following day I lectured Josephine, the head of the Finished Wardrobe, about Cora and other set women.

'They should always tell me when changes are made on the set,' I told her.

Cora was superior looking, forever adjusting her pince-nez. Her lips were pressed so tightly together one felt she used alum in her drinking water. Ever since she was Miss Blondell's maid of honour, when Joan became Mrs Dick Powell, there was no standing or sitting Cora.

I said to Josephine, 'You must speak to Cora. She should know better.' Josephine looked at me in amazement. 'Mr Kelly, I wouldn't dare speak to Cora – Cora's from Boston.'

Another set woman came in, wanting a character shirtwaist. 'They are *acrosst* the way with the frayed and *toren* shirts,' Josephine said. I looked to where she had pointed – a shelf Josephine had marked 'TOREN SHIRTWAISTS'.

I made up my mind never to criticise other designers' incongruous get-ups, no matter how they may appear on the screen. And I wondered just how some people became heads of departments. But, I was in Hollywood, and in pictures, and I mustn't bite the hand that scratched me.

I went back to my office. My door opened and a voice said, 'What's new for spring, Toots?' It was Alice White.

'Not you,' I replied, looking her over in her bit of black lace.

At one time Alice was Warner Brothers' biggest star, earning four thousand dollars a week. At this point she was trying for a comeback with Rudy Vallee and other guest stars. I liked Alice. I re-dressed her, exposing her two best points.

The job of discussing a star's defects is both difficult and delicate. Few are perfectly proportioned. The camera points out their many defects. One shoulder may slope more than the other – one bust may sag a bit, or be less rounded. Often one hip may be inches higher or lower than the other. Some are knock-kneed while others wear their legs in parenthesis. And so it goes – all the way up, down and across.

If a star possessed real humour, I would often ham it up a bit, using English stage terms such as *prompt* or *O.P.* (meaning opposite prompt, or the opposite side of the stage where the actors used to be prompted when they forgot their lines). When I said, 'Helen, dear, your O.P. needs an infinitesimal touch of padding,' Helen Morgan, who was guest-starring with Rudy Vallee, said, 'Darling, they are in your hands to do as you wish with them.'

Along with Belle and Texas Guinan, I had known Helen back in my speakeasy days. No one had Helen's alabaster skin, slightly tinged with green, nor her mop of black coq-feathered hair. Her sensuous nostrils quivered; her gaping moist mouth trembled when she sang, as no one else could sing, 'Why Was I Born?' It was late in Helen's career when I dressed her. She always carried a large-sized bottle of 4711 Eau de Cologne in her purse; it had a distinct Courvoisier aroma.

I'll make dog meat out of you, you dressmaker, if you don't get going.' I got.

Another well-rounded figure was the ultra-sophisticated, yet still a little girl, Dolores del Rio. She came from good stock. Her mother, constantly at her side, took Dolores on her sixteenth birthday to Spain and had her *presented* at Court. She had the curried look of a pedigree filly.

She was the first in the movie colony to own a modern house with all-white decor. I shall never forget the day I draped her naked figure in white jersey. She wanted no underpinnings to spoil the line. When I finished draping her, she became a Greek goddess as she walked close to the mirror and said, 'It is beautiful.' Taking a few steps closer and gazing into the mirror, she said in a half-whisper, 'Jesus, *I* am beautiful.' The *Jesus* was said with reverence. Narcissus? Maybe, but she spoke the truth – she was unbelievably beautiful.

In contrast, when the talented, down-to-earth Barbara Stanwyck came to that same fitting room, she usually wore a short leather jacket, a sweater and a shirt. She had wonderful skin – no make-up, no to-do of any kind, and at this period no enthusiasm about her clothes. There was something sad and melancholic about this really nice girl. So many in this business go from love to stardom, but seldom can they find the road back from stardom to love – if ever a girl deserved love, Barbara did. She had the love of the crew with whom she worked, but that isn't enough.

Bad Girl made actress Sally Eilers a rich girl. When I first dressed her she was starring opposite Richard Barthelmess and was the wife of cowboy film actor, director and producer Hoot Gibson.

In Hollywood, some husbands and wives swap annually. As the six-year-old child of a movie star said to another, 'How do you like your new daddy? He was my daddy last year.'

A year later, Sally, no longer hootin', was now the wife of Harry Joe Brown, a Warner Brothers producer. I liked Harry Joe. It was different the day he put his okay on my sketches for *First Lady*. It starred Kay Francis, Verree Teasdale and Anita Louise. He raved about the first four sketches, and as he looked at each one he said, 'Oh, that's great. That would look great on Sally,' or 'Gee, Sally would look wonderful in that.' When he came to the fifth sketch his voice changed as he shouted, 'I don't like that!'

'What's the matter?' I yelled back. 'It wouldn't look good on Sally, eh?'

He tossed the sketch into the air, and when it landed on the floor he stamped on it. Then we both went up in the air. I don't remember who grabbed who first, but Harry Joe's face got caught in a pair of old-fashioned women's split drawers that were hanging on a rack. From the look in his eye I knew he was about to haul off at me. I hollered, 'For hitting a hemstitcher you'll get much more than seven years' bad luck!'

As Harry Joe Brown stepped from his corner under the ropes, he was laughing out loud.

> *For hitting a hemstitcher you'll get much more than seven years' bad luck!'*

By now I was dressing sixty pictures a year, with very little help. Some, of course, were minor designing jobs. Eddie Robinson playing a Portuguese fisherman, with an earring in his ear. A girl in rags. A few period costumes out of stock. Still, they all took up my time.

I was buying a home and went on the wagon for two years. It wasn't until later the bottle almost got me, as it does so many connected with pictures. I made a rule – and never broke it: 'Never take a drink during working hours.' The studios were paying me for a job, and I did the job. There were days of awful hangovers later on, but I always stuck it out until five o'clock. Too many times I'd watched the stars kid themselves with those morning 'pick-me-ups'.

The job got tougher when the early musicals made such a hit – *42nd Street, Gold Diggers of Broadway* and all the other Buz Berkeley pictures. These films made little Ruby Keeler,

Barbara Stanwyck owning the role in Baby Face. Yet when she came
to the dressing room her look was as down to earth as she was.
No make-up, no to-do of any kind.

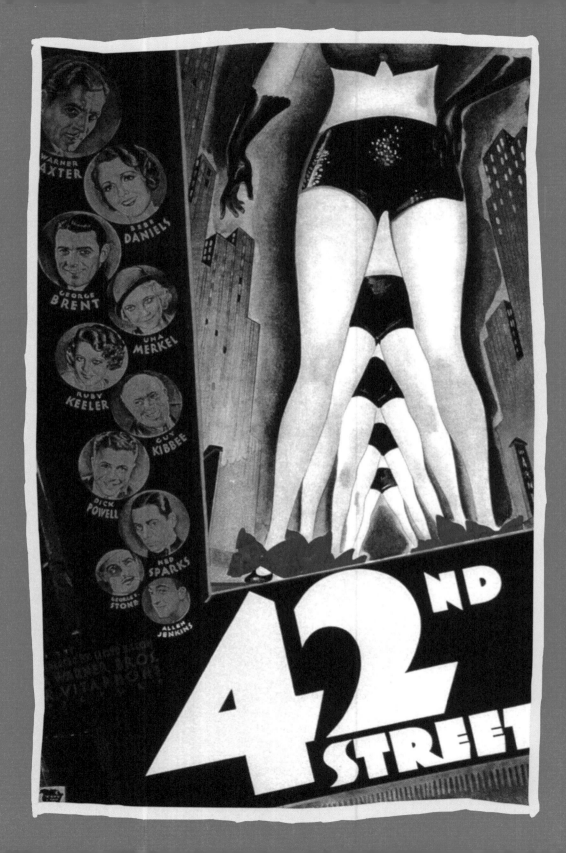

then Mrs Al Jolson, a big star. In real life Ruby was just what she looked like on the screen, unassuming and down-to-earth. A genuinely nice person. But she was much more at home in her golf shoes on the golf course than on the set with her tap shoes.

One Saturday evening, to soothe our nerves, we did the town. (Buz Berkeley was between marriages.) In the early hours of the morning, after too many Canadian Clubs, a very surprised dressmaker was introduced to madam Miss Lee Francis and her girls. Lee's high-tone establishment catered to the cream of Hollywood, and she always kept champagne on ice and caviar on hand should officers of the law make an appearance. After going into, over and under the cold facts of life, I invited Lee and a blonde to the Brown Derby for Sunday morning breakfast. Then I drove them home – Lee didn't live in the same house where she carried on her business. A few days later, Brown Derby owner Bob Cobb kidded me, saying he regretted not being present to welcome such 'distinguished' company.

Later, when Lee knew me better, she said she was sorry she didn't include me in her book, *Ladies on Call*. It seems I was the sole representative of the designers who became a patron!

There was no doubt about it, the days of the Warner musicals were happy days. Key men of the studio arrived earlier than usual; they found it necessary to be on the set early of a morning as the Berkeley girls dashed around as scantily dressed as the censors allowed. William Koenig found time, between his busy job of running production, to fall in a big way for a platinum blonde named Barbara. She had a beautiful firm body and a firm belief she would one day marry my boss. And did. She began buying her clothes from Bess Schlank. Bess was a very fat, very round little woman who always wore dark glasses and a black dress that completely hid the big round padded pouf she sat on. Her favourite line to her customers when they tried on one of her dresses or fur coats was, 'Honey, you look so beautiful I want to cry.'

One morning, while going over some costume details in Koenig's office, Bess Schlank was on the phone. 'All right, Bess, but how much?' My boss hollered. 'Is that really your rock bottom price?' A wonderful calm came over his face. His eyes moistened as he repeated, 'She has the coat on – she looks so beautiful you want to cry.' Then, this old man who had really gone over the hill but wouldn't admit it, put his hand over the phone and asked me, 'Is two thousand dollars a steal for a full-length white ermine coat?'

I replied, 'It would be if there weren't a few Australian rabbits hanging around.' I left him to haggle.

A short time later he married Barbara, and in a shorter time still they were divorced.

It wasn't long before Jack Warner himself appeared on the Berkeley set one morning and chased all the executives back to their offices. And to work!

I was in Hollywood and I mustn't bite the hand that scratched me.

Few teenagers had the figure of Miss Ginger Rogers. I dressed Ginger in some of those early Warner musicals. She loved to do imitations of other stars in the fitting room. Tiger-eyed, squaring her mouth and shoulders, she would go into her favourite routine: flattening herself against the wall and slinking up to the mirror, she would give a devastating impression of the big Hollywood star, singing 'My Melancholy Baby'.

But, in those days, her personal clothes had the touch of loving hands. With a cartwheel hat outlined by black-eyed Susans perched on the back of her head, her momma, Lela, on one arm and director–producer Mervyn LeRoy on the other, the corn was green. Then one day a sad Ginger came in for a fitting. Miss L.O. Parsons that morning carried a scoop in her column – Mervyn LeRoy was to marry Harry Warner's daughter. True to his promise and Hollywood tradition, Mervyn told Louella first – not Ginger.

It was Irene, the designer, who first took her in hand and gave her good taste in clothes. Later, her head severely coiffed, simply and elegantly dressed by Jean Louis, she was a far cry from the early days when she played opposite Joe E. Brown and Allen 'Farina' Hoskins.

Hollywood discovers few in its own backyard. When Santa slid down Lana Turner's bougainvillea bungalow and left her a sweater, she changed the whole picture. Until then the star was usually dressed in huge transparent organdie puffed sleeves; backed by overhead lights, they pouted and pecked at each other. When the long, long kiss donned a sweater, the lighting took on a low key, but when the camera turned on luscious Lana's profile, the audience looked more at her sweater.

Lana wasn't much more than sixteen or seventeen when she walked around the Warner lot for a year. Mervyn LeRoy gave her a few lines and made a milkmaid out of her in a period piece. When he left Warners he took Lana and her sweater to MGM, where she milked her way to stardom. Too much of any good thing is more than enough – a couple of inflated dames tucked in their sweaters and brought on a rash of Bourbon Street bad taste.

In the early days, technicolor was used mainly for outdoor films. Blue is the one colour that intensifies three times in value. That's the reason so many skies looked the colour of

A young and cheeky Ginger Rogers in Gold Diggers of 1933.
She loved to do imitations of other stars in the fitting room.

Ruby Keeler in Gold Diggers of 1933 with Dick Powell. In real life she was much more at home in her golf shoes on the course than on the set with her tap shoes.

a castor oil bottle instead of a heavenly blue. Olivia de Havilland spent a great part of her early Warner years in a horse hat, waving goodbye to Errol Flynn as he rode off in a cloud of technicolored manure. She rebelled after playing Melanie in *Gone with the Wind*; and then it was lovely Anita Louise, done up in mediaeval headgear, who was waving goodbye to Errol Flynn from drawbridges and garret windows.

When Olivia was cast opposite Leslie Howard in modern clothes, I then began dressing her. What a difference between her and her sister, Joan Fontaine; they were direct opposites. Olivia was kind, considerate, sincere, loyal and full of charm. I dressed Miss Fontaine as the young girl in *The Constant Nymph*. On screen she was charming.

MGM loaned beautiful Virginia Bruce to Warners for several pictures. She had the intelligence to know that she only had to underplay her clothes to look ravishing. A trick Grace Kelly later learned.

Glenda Farrell, her own worst critic, did more with less. Always a good performer, she always looked smart.

Marie Wilson – kind, generous – but always too much out in the open.

The 1942 picture *The Hard Way* starred Ida Lupino and Joan Leslie. Clothes-wise, Joan Leslie: no. Ida Lupino: yes. When Miss Lupino was kept in tow, she looked extremely chic. Explosive, but fun. Not a mean bone, as they say.

Take away Eve Arden's great big checks, plaids and stripes and she would have been an unhappy gal. Punching out her lines as Our Miss Brooks was one thing, but everything *big*, including the bags she carried, was too much.

Along with the stars, I often dressed the character women: May Robson, a fellow Australian, once chased me with her black ebony walking stick when I accused her of sleeping in her three dog-collar chokers.

The wonderful, funny Helen Westley, a past pillar of the Theatre Guild, loved to tease the dignified Constance Collier. Before a crowd, like a screeching old parrot, Helen would call out, 'Connie, there's a couple of old tarts in Cukor's next picture that would be great for you and me.'

Darling old Skippy – Alison Skipworth – with her henna-pack hair and lavender lace dress. In the fitting room she always said, 'Don't bother turning your back. I've got me petticoat on.' Through the years it seemed to be the same mouse-coloured flannel petticoat. I could always tell when Skippy was coming up the wardrobe passageway – the scent of lilac perfume and musty, dusty flannelette.

William Randolph Hearst brought his Cosmopolitan company over to Warner Brothers from MGM. I often took wardrobe sketches to San Simeon – the Hearst Ranch – when a script had been submitted for approval.

Travelling back and forth in the chief's private plane was quite an experience. I met many famous and interesting people. Edward Hatrick, the president of Hearst's newsreel company, introduced me to Joe Connelly, head of King Features, who became a good friend. In fact, Hatrick encouraged me to write this book.

On one of my trips I met the great newspapermen Arthur Brisbane and Paul Block. Once I flew up with Franklin and Eleanor Roosevelt's daughter, Mrs Anna Boettiger; Lady Plunkett and dear old caustic Nanny Tiffany of my 'Old Guard' days; also Senator McAdoo, who helped get my American quota.

I'll never forget the day I draped Dolores del Rio's naked figure in white jersey. 'It is beautiful,' she said. Taking a few steps closer to the mirror, she added in a half-whisper: 'Jesus, I am beautiful.'

I slept in the Richelieu bed and all the bungalows and suites, including the Celestial – high in the tower. But the greatest experience was meeting and getting to know William Randolph Hearst himself.

I found him a great gentleman, although much has been written about him to the contrary. He had a most wonderful manner, inherited from his mother, no doubt. He was a stickler for good taste and good behaviour. When a guest got overly loud or tipsy at dinner, and you inquired about him or her the next day, someone would remark, 'Oh, haven't you heard? So-and-so's off the hill.' The procedure was always the same. The offending guest was told quietly by the valet, 'Your bags are packed. The car will take you down the hill.' You were given train reservations.

Once, during lunch, the subject of actors and actresses came up. Mr Hearst addressed me: 'Mr Kelly, perhaps you can tell us – when is a star on her best behaviour?'

'And her worst?' Mr Brisbane added.

'During their first and last three months in pictures,' I explained. 'Coming in and going out, they'll do anything you ask – fit and re-fit, be photographed, give interviews. In the interim they can be pretty difficult.'

Barbara Stanwyck giving glamour an edge in Gambling Lady.
Whatever fate her characters on screen suffered, behind the camera she
had the love of any crew she worked with.

Tiger-eyed Ginger Rogers in Gold Diggers of 1933. Slinking up to the mirror in the dressing room, she could give a devastating impression of a big Hollywood star singing 'My Melancholy Baby'.

A very English voice said, 'May I come in, Old Boy?' My fitting room door opened just a fraction. Edmund Goulding's blue eyes, with a thousand tragedies beneath them, gazed at me from under their drop-curtain lids.

He was a fine women's director. Back in my Sydney days, the cockney help always carried an extra hanky every other Thursday when they saw a Norma Shearer picture directed by Eddie Goulding.

Goulding was brilliant, kind, overly generous and wickedly witty. He liked nothing better than stirring up a wicked brew. Taking two femmes fatale – egging them on – he delighted in more ways than one in seeing them end up having a go at each other.

He composed and wrote the words to the song 'Love, Your Magic Spell Is Everywhere' for Gloria Swanson. She sang it in an early talkie – *The Trespasser* – which he wrote and directed. Later he came to Warner Brothers, rewrote it for Bette Davis and directed it along with some of her best pictures, including *Dark Victory*. At the time I speak of he was preparing to direct *The Great Lie*, which Henry Blanke was producing.

Goulding was a great raconteur. He would take a current dirty story, change or add to it, often adding my name. No wonder my reputation began to smell not so mighty like a rose. Even though I knew Eddie was in the habit of selling me down the river if it meant getting a laugh, I still liked him. He had so much charm.

The previous night we had both heard Gladys George wildly applauded after her small scene in a small part of a very small picture. Eddie had a plan. A good friend of ours, Lawrence Riley, wrote *Personal Appearance*. It had starred Gladys George, who hit the jackpot with the stage play, which was later turned into a movie. Recently she had hit the bottle. 'You must do for Gladys what you did for Wini Shaw,' said Eddie. Then he went into a devastating imitation of how I acted the first time I saw Wini in a slip. In my cups I must have told him of the Parker House rolls around her waist, and the side of bacon on her back. With more than slight overtones, he mimicked me telling Wini not to come back until she'd lost ten pounds. 'You made her cry, Old Boy!'

'Okay, Eddie,' I replied, 'I brought the tears, but she was also tearful the day Jack Warner took up her option after he saw her all slimmed down in a shimmering sheath, singing "Lullaby of Broadway". And after that she went into *Sweet Adeline*, starring Irene Dunne.'

'Exactly, Old Cock,' said Goulding. 'Then do the same thing for me with Gladys George. The part of the concert pianist in *The Great Lie* is equal in size to Bette's, and it's a bitchy

The impeccable Irene Dunne in *Sweet Adeline*. Her clothes had to be simple in line and authoritative. No wonder she fit into the United Nations so well.

part. She will be great. Bette will be all for it. You know how she's always giving someone a lift, particularly when they are talented. Make her a special black dinner dress. I shall pay for it personally.'

Opening the door, he turned, and with the look of an old tomcat that had just swallowed a mouse, he called out, 'Whip her with your tongue, Kelly – it's something I hear you're quite good at.'

The following noon Goulding phoned; he was sending Miss George around to my office. Minutes later she appeared, wearing a sat-on, off-the-face hat. Her cheap black rayon taffeta dress had a powdered-over sweetheart neckline – there was something terribly pathetic about her whole get-up. But worst of all was the frightened, hopeless look of a lost traveller – a look I'd seen before in my early Sydney days. We spoke of Riley and fun parties, but for the life of me I couldn't bring myself to hurt her. Then I got an inspiration; I would take her down a couple of doors to Mark Hellinger's office. For years he had written about just such situations. He hadn't arrived yet, and his secretary was out.

On entering Hellinger's office you were faced with two solitary framed photos of Imogene Wilson – one when she was a ravishing Earl Carroll Beauty; the other, after starring in pictures when they arrested her for dope. Gladys George's eyes seemed glued to the wall. She shook and shivered from head to toe. For a long time neither of us spoke. I managed to say, 'Tragic, isn't it? But no one could help her – she wouldn't help herself.' Trying to cover up, I told her Mark Hellinger was the only person Jack Warner allowed to have a bar in his office; he had to, Mark drank a quart of brandy a day. Making conversation, I said, 'I thought maybe Mark would give us a nip before lunch, but I guess he's in a production meeting.' We lunched. Then my fitter measured her for the dress. I suggested she soften her canary yellow hair with an ash rinse. At the second fitting she was in bright and early. I felt I had made her see the light.

The day arrived to show Goulding the new Gladys George. From another part of the wardrobe I was phoned to come quickly to my office; they were having trouble getting Miss George into the dress. I found poor Gladys hanging on to her fitter's shoulder, swaying back and forth. She gave me a blind look and asked thickly, 'Where am I, and who are you?'

I replied, 'You're at Warner Brothers Studio in Kelly's fitting room.'

'Kelly who?' she burped.

'What the hell, I'm not Patsy,' I told her and sent out for lots of hot coffee.

I phoned Goulding and he said, 'Alter the dress to fit Mary Astor. I'll take your suggestion and give Astor the short cropped hairstyle Kay Francis originally made famous.' He made another test of her.

After Blanke saw the clean, slick look it gave Mary Astor on the screen, he realised I was right. It wasn't her figure, which was neither good nor bad – it was her hair. Until then it hadn't set off her lovely angelic face.

When the public saw her performance as the concert pianist, opposite Bette Davis, in *The Great Lie*, it won her an Academy Award nomination. Mary Astor's shingle shuttled her to an MGM contract and a brand-new career.

No, I never received a thank-you note, nor a Christmas card, from Miss Astor. I've learned to take it in stride. I'm paid for my work and realise many of the poor dears feel they are doing you a favour letting you dress them. Every now and then a Kay Francis, a Kay Kendall, a Marion Davies, a Bette Davis, a Roz Russell or a Miss Ethel Barrymore comes into our life and heart – and that's all that matters.

Serene, impeccable Irene Dunne always knew the correct way. She never made the mistake of letting fashion become a gross indulgence. I only had the privilege of dressing Irene in *Sweet Adeline*, but I realised immediately there was never overemphasis. Her clothes had to be expertly fitted, simple in line and authoritative. No wonder she fit into the United Nations so unobtrusively when Eisenhower appointed her as an alternate American delegate. She served the flag, but never wore it.

I had met screenwriter John Colton during my New York social hop. He lived in a rambling house, up a flight of moss-covered stone steps, up a canyon. The first day I called on him in Hollywood I was introduced to poet and novelist Mercedes de Acosta. She was standing astride, her legs spread like an upside-down Y, while being fitted to fly-front trousers by a tailor from MacIntosh. MacIntosh was on Hollywood Boulevard and was known for dressing some actors, prize fighters and Filipinos. Her fitting over, she donned a long black cape over her two-piece strictly mannish suit with its padded shoulders. Pulling what resembled a jockey's cap with a large beak over her own large beak, she seemed to swoop down on the canyon as her black cape flapped in the breeze.

HUMPHREY
BOGART

MARY
ASTOR

THE
Maltese
Falcon

by
DASHIELL
HAMMETT
Author of
"THE THIN MAN"

GLADYS GEORGE · PETER LORRE
BARTON MACLANE · LEE PATRICK · SYDNEY GREENSTREET
SCREEN PLAY BY JOHN HUSTON · A WARNER BROS. – FIRST NATIONAL PICTURE
Directed by
JOHN HUSTON
Presented by
WARNER BROS.

For The Great Lie, I gave Mary Astor the cropped
hairstyle Kay Francis made famous. By the time we reunited for
The Maltese Falcon the shingle had became her signature look.

Colton told me, when he first arrived he shared a house with her. 'She was too much,' said John, 'and when she called the bootleggers "gangsters", and complained because they sat around after they delivered the booze, someone had to go. It was Mercedes.'

I had taken an instant dislike to her – the white lead skin, the slit for a mouth, her manner, and particularly her manner of dress. I said to John, 'Watching her take off down the trees in the gulley, she reminded me of some weird wild Australian fowl.'

'Bravo, worthy Kelly,' Colton exclaimed in his Olde English terms. 'How right you are. Garbo once called her a plucked chicken.'

John Colton, producer Irving Thalberg and writer, director and producer Paul Bern shared a house at one time; that was before Thalberg married Norma Shearer. Now John had a house directly below me in Hollywoodland. He had begun to mix the little pill bottle with the booze.

John Colton had asked me to design a party dress for his dear friend, actress Mrs Leslie Carter. At the reception, the snobbish Mrs Carter gave Sid Grauman a short 'How do you do.' Grauman, who didn't think she heard his name, said, 'But Mrs Carter, I'm Sid Grauman.' Mrs Carter paused, looked at him and, in one breath, rattled off, 'And I'm Mrs Leslie Carter and your fly's undone.'

One evening John, the beautiful socialite Geraldine Graham Dabney from Santa Barbara, and a few others, had just finished dinner at my house. I noticed Colton's glassy eyes when he started pounding the table. He shouted, 'They can't do this to me! I won't allow them to change my story!' He got up from the table and left. About an hour later he returned with a still wilder gleam in his eye. He told us that he had gone to MGM and burned down the set. His voice echoed all over Hollywoodland: 'There will be no augmented dialogues used on that set tomorrow!'

Later I was shown a letter from his friend Irving Thalberg saying that as much as he regretted it, he could do nothing more for John at MGM.

Colton seemed to pull himself together for a time; we continued being friends.

One day he phoned. He was taking a group of us to see evangelist and faith healer Aimee Semple McPherson's performance at the Angelus Temple. There were very few days Aimee 'Give, give, give 'til it hurts' McPherson and her famous 'Ma' didn't make the headlines. Yet, somehow her faithful followers ignored her shenanigans and continued to pin paper money on the clothesline, rigged up for collection at the temple.

Someone must have warned Sister Aimee, or else she recognised John when he waited in the vestibule to meet her after the service. Possibly she had seen his Mother Goddam, the brothel madam in his play *The Shanghai Gesture*. Surely she had seen his stage adaptation of Somerset Maugham's *Rain*, starring Jeanne Eagels as a lady of the night, or maybe she'd memorised some of the Reverend Davidson's memorable seduction scenes. In any case, she wanted no part of Mr John Colton. She flew the coop.

Later on I met this good-looking Canadian woman who had been lost on a beach, presumed drowned, and turned up in a desert saying that she had fled kidnappers who'd held her captive in Mexico for five weeks. I had the pleasure of being introduced formally to the Temple Goddess in Mrs Alexander Pantages' box at a marathon dance. The evening was anything but formal. It was still prohibition. Aimee shared the bottle of Scotch we hid on the floor. We sipped the bootleg hooch from Dixie cups as we watched the tireless couples dance through the early morning hours.

Whip her with your tongue, Kelly, it's something I hear you're quite good at.'

Every other weekend I went to Santa Barbara, and on occasion Colton and I went as guests of the art collector and philanthropist Wright Ludington, whose magnificent house in Montecito was one of the finest in the West. Formal gardens, thirty-foot hedges, a lake with a lonely black swan whose mate had died – unlike humans, it would never love again. In those days former *Harper's Bazaar* Paris editor Louise Macy and Wright had a crush on each other. Later she married politician Harry Hopkins and eventually became Mrs William Gage.

I spent other weekends at Montecito with eastern friends who had moved west. While other cities reminded me of dresses, Montecito seemed more like a tea-gown of old rose crepe de Chine. Over its haughty, aristocratic shoulder hung a scarf of Brussels lace, a reminder of the many crossings in calmer days. When a good book was set aside, she donned gardening gloves and pruned the Belle of Portugal rosebush that climbed clear to the top of the high walls, a protection from those who didn't belong.

In these solid surroundings of Old Guard atmosphere, of libraries, Jacobean furniture and tuberoses, John Colton and I met many of the grand old ladies and the menfolk in tweeds and weeds. Here, also, one name must never be uttered to disrupt the calm, orderly lives of these American dilettantes, completely oblivious to the breadlines seen in downtown Los Angeles. The name: *Roosevelt*.

I committed that deadly sin. A darling old beetroot-faced hostess, whose husband had been an ambassador to many countries, reached for the long corded tassel. With its jerk, a butler appeared, dressed in a bottle-green uniform – once ivory-black – and handed me my hat. However, there were many other places I could go to.

One could always stop at Katherine MacDonald's, the 'American Beauty' of the silent screen, then Mrs Chris Holmes. I went there one Sunday morning, wearing an oversized hangover. Sipping a sidecar, I felt a hand on my shoulder. Looking up I discovered a huge chimpanzee – one of Chris's playmates from his enormous menagerie. As I leaped through the estate towards the gate, I yelled loud enough to have been heard down in Echo Park.

Here, too, resided opera singer Ganna Walska and her enormous emeralds. The Fleischmann's Yeast millionaire and his two polo fields. Robert Cameron Rogers wrote the poem 'The Rosary' here. And, when there's a ring around the moon, 'tis said you can hear Mrs Danvers as she wanders through Judith Anderson's Palladian house, high up on a hilltop in Carpinteria. Often I had tea with Mrs Chester Arthur in Carpinteria.

If Cary Grant wasn't invited out the first six months of picture work, he wasn't an isolated case. George Burns and Gracie Allen, and Jack Benny and his wife Mary Livingstone had been out here several years before they made some of the parties.

Before one of Marion Davies' famous birthday parties she asked me who I wanted to bring. I said, 'Would you hate me if I told you I want to bring *two* people with me, Gracie Allen and George Burns?'

'Oh, I want you to,' said Marion. 'She's a cute Mick. I'd like to meet her and her husband.'

When Louella Parsons heard they were invited she suggested we all go together, as they were practically neighbours. This invitation made Gracie and George one up on Mary and Jack, for in those days in Hollywood, if you weren't invited to Marion's, you hadn't fully arrived.

Gracie Allen parading for me, Edith Head, Howard Greer and George Burns. Gracie was still wearing same size dress as when we first met decades before. And Gracie's head size had never changed either.

The previous night it so happened that Fanny Brice's brother got involved in a $100,000 gambling escapade which, naturally, put his sister in the headlines. As we were about to line up at Marion's buffet, I saw Constance Collier standing with Fanny. I caught a pained expression in her eyes. 'Gee, kid,' she said to me, 'I just wish I were home. I'm sorry now that I came.'

I said, 'Let me take you home, Fanny, I'd much sooner be with you anyway.'

Her face lit up like her character, the toddler Baby Snooks. 'Gee, kid, you really mean that?'

We waved goodnight to Lolly, Doc, George, Gracie and Constance, and went home and raided Fanny's icebox. Looking back, I think that evening in 1935 cemented our friendship. I knew deep down that this wonderful woman, who had been hurt so often, had been snubbed by someone.

Shortly afterwards George and Gracie set up a tent in the garden and gave Mary Livingstone an elaborate birthday party. As Fanny and I entered, she looked the tent over as if she were 'counting the house' in vaudeville. She said, 'Five Gs.' Peering into the supper tent, Fanny looked up at the posts, massed with American Beauties and camellias, and said, 'Ah – ah – six.'

I said, 'Six what?'

'Six grand, kid, that's what this party will set 'em back.'

This was the first Hollywood party where top eastern talent entertained. George had seen to that. I had dropped in the day before and heard George talking it over with Jack Benny – what they would do and how they would do it, just as if they were playing the Palace.

The night of the party it all seemed impromptu, Blossom Seeley singing 'Breezin' Along With the Breeze', Benny, Cantor, Jessel, and 'you ain't heard nothin' yet' – Al Jolson! It was quite a shindig! And, from then on, the Bennys were in.

Nowhere in the world, at any one time, was so much beauty assembled in one place as at Marion's birthday parties which, incidentally, were rarely held on her natal day. Her parties had a different theme each year: One was a circus party where an enormous tent was erected on the tennis courts adjoining the house. There was a full-sized carousel, complete with sideshows.

Another year the motif was Spanish. I remember so well the original platinum blonde, Jean Harlow, wearing a white fringed evening gown. Her escort was William Powell, who had left her with me while he joined the Richard Barthelmesses. Like all femmes fatale, Jean was never completely happy. While we were sipping champagne, she said, 'Now watch this.' She pointed to a female star who had sidled up to a couple of top box office male stars. 'Now, if I were to join that little group' – Jean smiled – 'their wives would be on my neck!' Just then the other star left.

I said, 'Well, there's your chance to prove it.'

With an impish twinkle, Jean sashayed her fringe over to the reigning king of the box office and his chum. Sure enough, a few yards away I saw his plump wife nudge her companion, and simultaneously they turned and called, 'Don't you think it's time we joined the others?'

Jean threw her hands in the air. 'What did I tell you?' She laughed.

We joined William Powell and a group of people in Spanish costumes and mantillas. And what a group! Dolores del Rio, Connie Bennett, Eleanor Boardman, Marlene Dietrich, Ann Warner, Jean Harlow, Carole Lombard and Hedy Lamarr. I challenge the youth of today to name a more exquisite eight. They may say, 'Why does that old fogey keep harking back to the good old days?' Well, this old fogey was dressing glamour girls then.

This female group at Marion's Spanish party was just as unique as people as they were beauties. Life is female, and these beauties were all fatally feminine. With one it might be her meticulous good taste; another, her elegant company; others, their wit might dazzle like the jewels they wore.

Carole Lombard sparkled like the huge star sapphires she wore, and with her affectionate, impulsive nature she had the courage to live and speak as she chose, setting up her own standard of values and abiding by them.

The intensely engrossing grey, blue and at times green eyes of Eleanor Boardman were never meant to be lulled by security into a dull life. Classic features and modern vision, she lacked neither fantasy nor biting satire.

Looking at the haughty haute couture of Connie Bennett, whose eyes were as blue as lapis lazuli, one would never believe she had sued – and been sued – more than anyone else in filmdom.

Dolores del Rio – a wild anemone watching her own reflection by a lake.

Hedy Lamarr had never been able to quell the storm since the world saw her 'September Morn' in *Ecstasy*.

Ann Warner, wife of studio head Jack Warner, had the gentle features and aristocratic look of Queen Alexandra. Scholarly and refined, she delighted in collecting Egyptian and Chinese objets d'art. And, if there was a human being who needed help or understanding,

Ann Warner, wife of studio head Jack Warner, and the finest friend anyone could wish for, had the gentle features and aristocratic look of Queen Alexandra.

The one and only Marion Davies. Nowhere in the world, at any one time, was so much beauty assembled in one place as at Marion's legendary birthday parties.

she collected them, too. She wrote strangely sensitive poetry. No wonder her house – the finest in Southern California – was a poem.

Jean Harlow's platinum pulchritude gave her the look of a shimmering white aigrette. Poet and novelist Gabriele D'Annunzio claimed few women could stand up to a greyhound; Jean Harlow had what he described, of the perfect breed, 'a small head, a swan's neck, a stomach like a lyre, and long, long, nervous legs'. Mama Gabor's pretty ducklings may have pretty faces; too bad her Zsa Zsa had such short stocky limbs. And Marilyn Monroe suffered from the same trouble. Marilyn and Zsa Zsa may have been able to stand up to a 'hound dog', but never to a greyhound.

Marlene Dietrich, the bird of paradise, had all that the great Don Juan described, and legs that not even a greyhound could stand up against. Yet Marlene, the world's most glamorous and exciting woman, refused to let any man clip her wings, regardless of his wealth. She possessed few jewels. Freedom was her pearl of great price.

When any of these exquisite eight emerged in their solitary grandeur, they were exquisitely beautiful.

An invitation to Marion Davies' for Sunday evening supper was a command performance. If you told the secretary you had guests of your own, you were asked to bring them also. Forty or fifty guests often had supper in the dining room, redolent of Grinling Gibbons' ornate 18th-century wood carvings.

Adjoining the dining room was the smaller Green and Gold Salon. Beyond that was the large Cream and Gold Salon which was the drawing room. In it were hung priceless Sir Thomas Lawrence paintings – one was a portrait of Emma Hart, who later became Lady Hamilton, whom Marion strongly resembled. Here you might meet still other guests who had dropped by to watch a movie in the Pickled Deal Library. It was always a relaxed evening. Often we watched movies while sitting on cushions on the floor.

Lords and dukes sat down at table with politicians, professors and members of the Fourth Estate. Lord and Lady Mountbatten, Lady Plunkett, Winston Churchill and his son Randolph were guests at various times.

At her beach house, one day Marion was wearing an enormous square-cut emerald ring. I said, 'The only emerald I've seen that compared with that was on Edith Rockefeller McCormick's finger at the L.G. Kauffman camp in Marquette, Michigan.'

She smiled and said, 'It's the same one. After she died it was given to me as a present.'

The first time I'd seen Marion's angelic face I was at once reminded of Sweet Nell of Old Drury. The faces must have been very similar. King Charles II, of course, fell madly in love with the sight of the beautiful young Nell, so overflowing with life's youthful sap. And Marion, too, was so vivacious and full of fun. She had a natural pink blush to her cheeks, and when this little miss from little old New York smiled, her big turquoise-blue eyes lit up and sparkled as much as her Irish wit – the same wit George Bernard Shaw found so enchanting. During a visit to England, Marion went to lunch with GBS, who was a strict vegetarian. When her rare steak was served, GBS looked up and said, 'Here comes the corpse!' Needless to say, Marion's appetite was ruined for the rest of the day.

When Shaw was a guest at MGM Studios, John Barrymore requested an autograph for his son. 'How old is he?' asked Shaw.

John replied, 'A year and a half.'

Shaw laughed. 'He's much too young to appreciate it!'

Later, to avoid autograph hounds, Marion ducked the Old Man down an alley, where they ran into make-up man Cecil Holland, who also asked for an autograph. Shaw turned to Marion: 'What does he do?'

Marion replied, 'He's an artist.' Shaw gave him the autograph and Marion said, with a twinkle, 'I wasn't lying, he does paint – faces!'

Shaw then visited Miss Ann Harding's set. Upon introduction, she said, 'Mr Shaw, I did your play *Androcles and the Lion*.'

Shaw looked at her and said quietly, 'It must have been a pirated version, my dear.' Whereupon Miss Harding rushed to her dressing room in hysterics and was unable to work for the rest of the afternoon.

Word spread to Louis B. Mayer, who phoned Marion. 'Get that character off the lot, he's holding up production!'

President Coolidge came to lunch one day. As he was a complete teetotaller, Marion served him some Tokay wine. 'It's very rare and very old,' she said, 'and it's made from non-alcoholic grapes.'

At first he sipped it cautiously and then drank the entire glass. Smacking his lips he said, 'Why, it's wonderful. There should be more of that stuff around.'

And there should be more people around with the stuff that the incomparable Marion Davies was made of.

In 1938, Miriam Hopkins made a great hit when she played opposite Bette Davis in *The Old Maid*. The strange human chemistry between these two came across on the screen. But, as great as she was, Warners felt her demands in all departments were too much; they decided to use up her contract making love to Randy Scott in a Western. At the final fitting it was an angry little woman who stood stock still before my mirror as I dressed and undressed her in calicos.

'Do you know what I'm going to do?' she foolishly confessed. 'I'm going to make such a fuss, Curtiz will have to stop shooting the picture this afternoon when he comes here to okay my clothes. I'm going to make them look so ridiculous I won't be able to go on location in the morning.' She thought a moment. 'That will give me time to have my part rewritten. I'll stand like this,' she said, and slumped her shoulders, caved in her chest and bent her knees. 'Look at me! He would never okay this outfit. I'll do the same with all the others.' A big delay would cost the studio at least $100,000 in lost production time, and it would be the first time I'd fallen down on my job. I said nothing until we started showing director Michael Curtiz the wardrobe.

True to her word, Miriam did everything she said she would do. She gave a convincing performance; her diaphragm caved in, the material crinkled, her shoulders slumped, the dress wouldn't fit.

Mike said, 'Stand up straight, Miriam!'

Her face became defiant. 'This is how I always stand.'

I took my cue and spoke up: 'Oh now, it isn't! The little lady just wants the script rewritten.' I grabbed her shoulders and straightened her up. Her little eyes became littler.

She hollered, 'Let me go – you're hurting me!'

'Not half as bad as you would have hurt my reputation,' I told her.

She still persisted in trying to make the clothes look ridiculous with her slouch. And each time, as I approached her, she'd scream, 'Don't you dare lay a hand on me!'

With Curtiz away from the set we had held up shooting one hour, for which the producer, Hal Wallis, blamed me.

When Hal Wallis was head of production under J.L. Warner at Warner Brothers, he rediscovered Lola Lane. Lola had been a silent actress. For a while we got a Lane a day as, one by one, she sent for her sisters. First Rosemary, and then Priscilla, who were both on the road with Fred Waring's band. The Lane Sisters became very popular. They made a picture with a brilliant young actor, John Garfield, called *Four Daughters*; it was a great success. A sequel was made: *Four Wives*; but not *Four Mothers*. Soon, a street in Burbank – with the aid of the publicity department – was renamed Priscilla Lane. Another was called after Rosemary. But Lola, who started it all, must have made a wrong turning.

A different studio came along with a picture *Four Sons*. Unfortunately the sons became more popular than the daughters. Pretty soon there were no more Lanes and no more Lola.

Life is female, and these beauties were all fatally feminine.

When silent-movie great Norma Talmadge told 'China' Harris, the lovely wife of theatre producer Sam Harris, to 'always put your foot against the closet door', she was kidding me. In fact, for years after she married the doctor, her last husband, she would say, 'It was all your fault, Orry. You should never have shut the closet door that evening.'

That evening was a dinner party she gave in 1939 for her one-time sister-in-law, Pansy Schenk. I remember Norma taking a guest's coat. The butler had gone to fetch a new light bulb for the clothes closet. Helping her to hang the fur coat in the tiny dark closet, the door shut – or maybe I kicked it. We had both been nipping champagne, and between one thing and another in the dark room, Norma mistook a negative for a positive. Before I was exposed to the light, Norma had proposed to me. After all, she had been a reigning movie queen. Royalty always does the choosing – and with five million bucks in her beaded bag, it figured!

The following evening, during dinner at the home of actor William 'Buster' Collier, with her sister Constance present, Norma announced we were to marry. Constance's jaw jutted and her big beautiful brown eyes popped more than mine. Norma was married to actor and singer George Jessel at the time. Jessel's trunks went out the window. He phoned Mamma – and I went to Australia to get my palm read.

Columnist Louella O. Parsons wrote hundreds of wonderful stories about me, but I also felt the sting of her quill. Returning from my hurried trip to Australia, I dined with Norma Talmadge on my first night back home. She showed me a clipping, written during my absence, from LOP's column in which she'd said, 'Norma Talmadge and Orry-Kelly are just good friends, but she would no more go to the altar with him than she would with Charlie McCarthy.'

I had just finished reading the write-up likening me to Charlie McCarthy – ventriloquist Edgar Bergen's famous wooden dummy – when the phone rang. It was Lolly, making sure that Norma would attend the wedding of her daughter, Harriet, which was to take place in a few days. Norma said, 'Just a minute, Lolly, my fellow has just returned from Australia, and I've shown him your story. If he'll take me, I'll go.'

When I got on the phone, Louella said, 'Oh dear, I hope you didn't mind what I said.'

I replied, 'Oh, that's all right, Lolly, seeing your daughter is about to marry Mortimer Snerd, we're even.' Snerd was another of Bergen's dummies, often appearing alongside Charlie McCarthy.

Miss LOP called out, 'Don't you *dare* say such a thing.'

When the Australian press picked up the story, my mother was just as incensed at Lolly's remark as Lolly was at mine. Anyway, this was one time Louella was dead wrong. I've always been truthful, too much so for this town where everyone and everything is 'lovely'.

With Norma dead, this is no time for me to start to lie. But I assure you, Miss LOP, you were dead wrong regarding Norma and me. Everything seems to have been different in my life. Norma had proposed to me. She even had her will changed and asked me, much against my wishes, to look at the new document she made out in my favour.

However, Lolly wasn't the only one who took a crack about Norma and me. A New York columnist asked George Jessel if it were true that his wife was going to marry Orry-Kelly. Georgie replied, 'Oh that's too bad, I would have liked to have married him myself.'

And no one laughed more than I did.

Bette Davis
Now, Voyager

CHAPTER ELEVEN

'Kelly, I've been a devil this last week, haven't I?'

IN 1942 I DESIGNED *Now, Voyager,* and although she looked well in *Dark Victory,* clothes wise I think it was Bette Davis's best picture. The tiny waist, broad shoulders and small bodice of the pre-Civil War period of *The Old Maid* showed off Bette's neck, shoulders and bosom.

Her feminine figure always looked so well in the Victorian period. In fact, there was something almost Victorian about her behaviour at times.

Bette and I didn't agree on some of the more dressy evening things. In fact, during three different fittings they hung on the hanger without being tried on. Each time we fitted, I told my cutter-fitter, Miss Keady, to bring in the gowns and hang them on the rack, and each time Bette looked at them as if to say, What! Are those things still here? She was in one of her moods all that week. I flew to the bottle, and my hangovers didn't help either.

The following Monday was the final fitting. Bette arrived looking like the old Bette I knew; the tormented look was gone. Without saying a word, she examined the evening dresses she'd ignored all the previous week. 'Let's try that one.' She indicated a cream wool dinner dress with bugle beads of streak lightning. It was for a strong dramatic scene. She tried it on; it looked great. 'And that one,' she cried, pointing to a white chiffon evening dress with a red wool cape with a butterfly motif embroidered over the shoulder.

When the fitting was over, she turned to me and said, 'Kelly, I've been a devil this last week, haven't I? I've been almost out of my mind; my sister Barbara has been terribly ill.'

That's the way Bette was with everyone. It made up for everything. It didn't matter if I'd jumped in my sleep all week, or that I was hitting the bottle – I didn't need an excuse for that. In the end she was always so fair and considerate.

Ilka Chase was also cast in the picture as the kind sister-in-law to Bette's downtrodden Charlotte Vale. Her mother, Edna Woolman Chase, for years, was the Grand Old Lady of *Vogue*, who ruled with an iron will and who, I'm sure, read her daughter Condé Nast's *Vanity Fair* every night instead of children's stories. I saw Miss Chase at times looking well turned out, and I saw her wearing what was in vogue, turned inside out. When I heard that she was going to play in Bette's picture, I wrote her to go to my good friend, and hers, Arthur Falkenstein, who in 1942 had the smartest clothes in New York – in fact, he was the only one who made money on custom clothes.

Miss Chase arrived for *Now, Voyager* with many things, all good. But she knew nothing about what would photograph. One simple black dress was lost and looked drab; others looked too spotty on the screen. What did the most damage were the hats. When Hal Wallis saw her profile under some of those silly little hats, he threw up his hands. She looked somewhat like a penguin about to take off. One has only to read Miss Chase's writings, which are so delightfully caustic, to know that the lanky daughter of Mrs Edna Woolman Chase looked down her not-so-paper-thin nose at Kelly, the Hollywood designer. Let's say she tolerated me.

The true artist is perpetually searching for the new. Few can understand it at first sight. Even Émile Zola, the literary champion for the Impressionists, looked at Cézanne's works askance, often hiding in his closet the paintings Cézanne gave him when other artists visited him.

Carmel Snow had a 'feel' for the new. After serving her apprenticeship with Mrs Woolman Chase of *Vogue,* she chased over to *Harper's Bazaar* and became editor-in-chief. Mrs Snow had a nose for fashion. She could sniff a new trend in the air before it became vogue, which at times must not have sat too well with her teacher. Carmel Snow had something of the artist combined with the shrewd foresight of the connoisseur. She was quick to grasp something Balenciaga grabbed out of the future, which Seventh Avenue just as quickly often made an end of. That was when bad taste set in.

As my friend, actor and writer Jay Brennan, used to say, 'Some people like mutton, others like lamb.' If Ilka Chase didn't like my 'cut', I didn't like the cut of her shoulder-of-mutton sleeves.

Bette Davis transforms from downtrodden spinster to elegant woman of the world in Now, Voyager. Of all the many pictures I designed for Bette, clothes wise I think it was her best.

But Irene Castle and I cut quite a figure the night we did the town. To me a trip to New York has always been a refresher course. Seventh Avenue may make the American woman the best dressed in the world, but so much of the French is often lost in the crossing. The Seventh Avenue label is the result of a compromise often in the modification. To my observing eye, much of the freshness is lost.

It was right on Seventh Avenue that I ran smack into Irene Castle. Irene was as tall as the gods and divinely fair, lithe but not lanky, with the neck and the grace of a swan. Anyone who had spent a lifetime caring for dogs had to be kind and considerate. She could be brittle, but never had a bite.

Irene and husband Vernon had started a dancing craze in America, popularising dances like the tango and their trademark Castle Walk. Dubbed 'The Aristocrats of Dance', they made several films together before Vernon was killed in a plane crash in 1917 during the First World War.

Years back, producer and screenwriter Gene Markey had arranged for Irene to come out from New York to test. She naturally bought her own clothes but was delighted to listen to my advice regarding the camera, and used what I'd dug out of stock for her test.

On this trip she was doing a corset demonstration at Gimbels, or maybe it was Macy's across the way. Not having brought any dinner dresses with her, a mutual friend, Roy Bradley, had arranged she buy some informal things for $49.50 wholesale. 'The only trouble' – Irene laughed – 'they're four inches too big around the waist.' I suggested we do the town that evening. She arranged to stop by my hotel to see some sketches. Getting into the cab she called out, 'I'll wear the lime and white chiffon. You can get me a posy to cover the safety pin I'll have to use at the waist.'

Irene arrived. I covered the safety pin with a corsage of green and brown orchids. She had hiked her dress up at the left side, giving it ten times more chic. Looking in the mirror she said, 'I'll be moving around – it will float.' No one I know could float into a room as she did, unless perhaps Ina Claire or Miss Ethel Barrymore.

That evening, as she floated across the dance floor, the dress looked like $490. Here was a woman with enough assurance to be able to put on a $49 dress that didn't fit, and forget about it.

Those who knew or remembered her stopped dancing. Even the young lovers stood fascinated as they watched her glide across the floor as no one else could. In an early

Ingrid Bergman, the most un-actressy of all the actresses I have dressed, looking radiant in Casablanca. She wore no make-up; her lovely face didn't need it.

movie, *Castles by the Sea*, she had become my idol. As much as I would have loved to have one dance with her, somehow I couldn't ask for that privilege.

Strolling back to her hotel that morning, I couldn't help but realise what a full and rewarding life Irene Castle had. Here was a beautiful, socially prominent, well-bred woman. She had worked all day in a department store on 34th Street, stripped of her privacy, allowing thousands of curious morbid women to watch her model corsets, just so she could have a little more money for her pet charity – dogs!

If Seventh Avenue didn't inspire me, Fifth always did. I could learn more about women's hats in five minutes listening to the good-looking Miss Jessica at Bergdorf's than I could listening or looking at any other five mad hatters. It was Miss Jessica who hatted Kay Kendall for *Les Girls*. But it was Kay looking at Miss Jessica for the first time who said, 'My, what a raving, tearing beauty she must have been!'

I had never taken a trip east when I hadn't learned a great deal or been inspired. The Menken girls, Helen and Grace, were always first on my list. Both had long been two of New York's best dressed. Helen, who was then Mrs George Richard, used to show me all her original Balenciagas. But in recent years all her interest, time, and often her own money, had gone to the American Theatre Wing, of which she was president.

One evening, in my twenty-fifth floor apartment, I was getting high in the sky when my phone rang – the studio had signed Ingrid Bergman. Fly back at once.

Casablanca starred Ingrid Bergman and Humphrey Bogart. Miss Bergman was the most un-actressy of all the actresses I have dressed. Off the screen she wore simple peasant-style skirts and blouses, and always low heels, even with evening dresses. She wore no make-up; her lovely face didn't need it. The one request she made was to have her hair dressed on the set. She disliked listening to the gossip in the make-up department.

A year after the release of *Casablanca*, Mrs Magnin of high-fashion department store I. Magnin told me I should have collected a percentage on all the jumper dresses the New York fashion houses put out when they saw my white sleeveless jumper and white French sailor sweater which Miss Bergman wore in the film's casbah scene.

When she wasn't attending to details concerning the picture, it was Miss Bergman's home, and mainly her daughter, that seemed to be her chief interest. I was putting her into a white dinner dress on the sound stage one day, and checking for last-minute changes – the playback machine was playing 'As Time Goes By', Bogart's voice came on, saying, 'Play it, Sam'. Then the song came on again: 'The world will always welcome lovers . . .' I can see the lovely alive face of Miss Bergman now, smiling and saying, 'What a lovely theme'.

Schiaparelli had squared women's shoulders. Hollywood, who does nothing in halves, four-squared them. I never approved, using them only when the star insisted.

Everyone was going to the movies. Everyone saw Hitler's marching army in the newsreels, but no one did anything about it. Huge, braided and beaded epaulets adorned women's evening gowns. Was this a hysterical display? Both men and women wore the widest and squarest of shoulders – a forerunner, a prediction of the squaring of America's shoulders for the Second World War.

I remember so well the arrival of Lady Mendl, also known as Elsie de Wolfe, in California in 1940, just after she had fled France and Hitler's marching armies. I had met the famed interior decorator many years before at Miss Bessie Marbury's house, on Sutton Place in New York. Now, after a short period of house-guesting with Ann and Jack Warner, Elsie was living in Fred Astaire's guest house. I went to see her often, and we'd drink what she called her 'house cocktail' – gin, Cointreau and grapefruit juice. She never drank in the manner that Bemelmans's vulgar portrait of her in his book *To the One I Love the Best* would have you believe.

Over the years I've collected many rare china cats; an extremely impudent one was given to me by a famous French madam in Sydney; others I've picked up in Suva, Tahiti, Pago Pago and New Orleans. One evening, when Elsie and Sir Charles were also my guests, Miss Barrymore and Cole Porter chuckled merrily when Elsie exclaimed, 'Ah, dear Kelly, you collect these naughty cats that coined that nasty word *cathouse*.' She especially loved a very early Victorian pussy with a wrapover Sadie Thompson taxi dress and high button shoes which were painted by E. Gallet in 1840, in Nancy, France. In fact, as I am writing these words, the cat is sitting here on my table and it's still the nanciest cat you ever did see!

On another occasion, Elsie wanted to dine at The Players, then a newly opened restaurant. I invited Admiral Ike Johnson, his wife Nell, Judith Anderson, Fanny, and a couple of other people. Elsie amused Ike when she told about receiving a letter from France telling her about Goering taking over her beautiful estate at Versailles. 'Admiral,' she said, 'that gouging Goering brought a lot of his boy-girls with him and they got into my lovely Mainbocher gowns and splashed under the fountains!'

'Now, Elsie,' I chided, 'surely Goering couldn't squeeze into your little size eights.'

'Not he! His naughty boy-girls! Although I have the feeling that he would have if he could have!'

After dinner, the subject of art came up and Nell said, 'Orry, your paintings hang on the walls of some of the best homes in America.'

'True,' I said, 'but never in the name-buyers' houses.'

Elsie rapped on the table emphatically. 'Who knows, your little daubs – as you call them – will probably remain when some of the more exaggerated schools of art are past and forgotten.'

'You may be right, kid,' Fanny said, 'but you see, Orry is paintin' this world and my son Bill and I are paintin' another world.'

I asked Elsie, 'In that other world Fanny's talking about, do you suppose you'll get all of your things exclusively from Mainbocher?'

'My dear, everything that's good is right down here on earth, and what's more, it's getting more expensive every day!' To prove her point, Elsie gave me an excited dig in the ribs with one of her fingers which was beginning to look like a tie-back for a window curtain.

Darling Elsie, in her late eighties, did everything to hide her age, but she could do nothing to alter her hands, except to keep them covered with spotless white gloves. In fact, she was a white-on-white study even as she sat propped up in her hospital bed the day that Margaret Case of *Vogue*, George Cukor and I visited her before she was to return to her beloved Versailles. She wore a delicate white hand-tucked batiste nightie, a white chiffon bandeau around her head and, of course, her spotless white washable cotton gloves. She might have been the model for all of Marie Laurencin's paintings. Elsie was ageless, and had a juvenescence which clung to her straight through maturity into ripe old age. Even then she retained the fresh bloom of youth.

She loved people. Many Hollywood hangers-on sneaked under her tent at cocktail time. According to Sir Charles, one agent's wife, along with her Blum's candy, even let Elsie, who loved to win at cards, win and gin her. But this lady's high losses still did not win her a place card at one of Elsie's small dinners.

She was so feminine and so personal that you could never compare anyone to her. To use a quotation from a fragment of Sappho, Elsie may have sprung without any masculine help from 'an egg hidden under a hyacinth blossom'.

In 1941 the publicity department of Warners, headed by Robert Taplinger, selected a group of twenty men to meet, wine and dine at the Los Angeles Town House. There was one of everything there: The late Dudley Field Malone, the great attorney; an ace football player; a banker; and all the way down the line to dance director Buz Berkeley. And for a dash of extra flavour, a dress designer – Kelly.

Annie-pie, as we used to call actress Ann Sheridan, the only female, sat at the head of the table. We were to vote her as having the greatest amount of 'oomph'. Dudley

Field Malone, after too many nips, decided that the whole arrangement was suddenly too phony. He became brutally unfair to Ann, who didn't want to be there any more than the rest of us. I finally got my Aussie up and quieted the one-time great Malone.

'Gentlemen,' I said, 'all those in favour of Ann Sheridan having the most "oomph", please stop guzzling and say "aye".'

So, Ann Sheridan became the Oomph Girl. It wasn't long before a gas station in Burbank was advertising a gasoline that had 'oomph'. Mr Warner decided it was time Ann was put in a major movie, *The Man Who Came to Dinner*. William Keighley, the director, complained her clothes had no oomph. He visualised leopard-skin coats and bizarre dresses. I prefer to dress colourful characters in black and sable and let their own oomph oomph its way through. There was a fuss on the set: Monty Woolley jerked his beard, Jimmy Durante twitched his nose, Bette Davis sent for tea, and Jack Warner sent for me!

'Why are you holding up a picture? Meet me in the projection room.'

When the tests were run off, Mr Warner did a rare thing in my presence; he got on the phone and told Keighley to go ahead and direct his picture, but 'leave the dressing of Sheridan to Kelly. He has taste, that's what I'm paying him for.' Then he ended with, 'Whatever the hell this oomph is, she's got it now!' Then, with a wink, 'If I weren't so in love with my wife Anne . . .' Then he became my boss again: 'Seriously, Kelly, it's the first time she's looked bigtime.'

Rita Hayworth appeared in *The Strawberry Blonde*, with Olivia de Havilland and James Cagney. She was always professional, prompt, very quiet and almost shy in those days. Later on, when she was married to Orson Welles, I dined with her at Cole Porter's. She reclined on the couch, content to listen. For someone who had been so well publicised, Rita couldn't have been more unassuming. Jean Louis later made her many beautiful creations, mostly strapless evening gowns. There was no padding used in Miss Hayworth's clothes; she needed none. As a party broke up early one morning, Louella Parsons came into her playroom, saying, 'Would somebody be good enough to take Rita Hayworth home? She came alone.'

George Burns said, 'That's one for the books! Who would believe Lolly would have to beg someone to take the glamorous Rita Hayworth home?'

Then Lolly said, 'I know – find Cesar Romero.'

Annie-pie, as we used to call Ann Sheridan, was the original Oomph girl. She stole all her scenes in The Man Who Came to Dinner, here with Monty Woolley.

Talking wardrobe with Ann Sheridan. Jack Warner decreed, 'Leave the dressing of Sheridan to Kelly. He has taste, that's what I'm paying him for'.

A star spends most of her time getting dressed. First, she dresses to go to work. During the average working day she may dress and undress four or five times. Then, she dresses to go home. For relaxation she gets all dressed up in a fancy dress to attend a party.

One thing is certain, if it was a fancy-dress party, Elsa Maxwell would be in men's trousers. Little Elsa dressed as Little Lord Fauntleroy or as Little Eloise of the Plaza was one thing, but Big Elsa at a party, in men's pants and sporting a beard, was something else. For one who has devoted his life to making feminine clothes, I know of no more nauseating sight than a rear view of Elsa in trousers. But then, I understand Elsa was never little – she never grew up, she simply spread out.

Elsa's young childhood is foggy and clouded as the Rock in San Francisco Bay. Her father had an insurance office in the small town of Sausalito, across the Bay. Rumour has it, at one time he was a jockey. That fits. Elsa went to James Denman public school. She was exceedingly bright in all her lessons. She made her first New York social connection when she swooped down on Mrs Belmont's cause – women's suffrage. Elsa wrote the music for Belmont's suffrage opera *Melinda and Her Sisters*. And sisters, I want to tell that when Elsa became an accompanist, while she didn't have a light touch, she could sing an octave lower than anyone in skirts – natch.

It was under the guise of patriotism that she first got in with the Park Avenue patrons, by organising or appearing at gala parties.

When you think of Elsa, you immediately think of stuffed shirts, gilded ballrooms, opera boxes, music, masks, souvenirs, French francs, dollars, dinners and dough in any form, including nuts.

The day of the American expatriate is over. The rich sons of department store families who followed the sun, the nouveaux riches, the watchers, those that had everything, went everywhere, saw everything but produced nothing. These idle rich that poor Elsa so desperately hung on to.

I've often thought if Elsa had taken some of the thousands she spent giving a name dinner, and for once gave it to the poor old bent women working through the night scrubbing offices, or to old grandmas bundled up on windy streets selling their papers, how much more worthwhile it would have been. And but for the grace of God, Elsa could so easily have been one of them.

Elsa made the front page, threatening to use her quill to influence Americans to boycott France. On numerous occasions she laid bare the private lives of the Windsors, the Aly Khans and all the rich who didn't favour her.

Apparently Elsa wasn't an admirer of columnist O.O. McIntyre, whose creed was 'Never abuse the power of the pen', because Elsa house-guested at the drop of a tea cosy and hardly unpacked before her chops began chopping her hosts to pieces, as she threw open their windows for a peephole view of their doings. She really should have opened her own casements – or would it be too draughty?

Elsa was a curious mixture of naïveté and malice, a lover of the arts, music, ballet, poetry and painting. When she painted her portraits, there was never a brush stroke, only the trowel and the knife. They were really not paintings at all, they were woodcuts.

During the Second World War, on a train trip to New York, Supreme Court Justice Murphy – then a colonel on a special Roosevelt mission – and I had hardly seated ourselves in Mrs Jack Warner's drawing room when down the passageway, like a southerly buster bursting at the seams, came Elsa, cards in hand, announcing, 'Let's play gin, I must recoup my Hollywood losses, five cents a point.'

'My God, Elsa,' I said, 'I've never played more than a quarter of a cent. I can't even shuffle cards well.' But Elsa was adamant. The three of us – Ann Warner, Elsa and I – settled down to our game with Frank Murphy looking on. I won one blitz after another, as Elsa would say, 'I can't stop now, I'll score later.'

Later, for Elsa, was always when Frank was busy telling the lovely Ann something about the war. And later also was when she accidentally (so she said) tore up all my blitz scores. This was too much for Frank's justice; he suggested he keep score, but Elsa refused to burden him. With my unprecedented run of luck, I stood treat for dinner while Elsa screamed for every imported delicacy. I stayed lucky until 2 am.

By now Elsa's hair resembled a built-in Charley's Aunt wig, and as she toddled off to bed she looked more like an untidy package sent slow freight. The next day was warm and she appeared in a housecoat with voluminous sleeves. I've always wondered what the score would have been if so many of my recorded blitzes hadn't disappeared into their capacious depths. As I remember, it was the wind this time that was to blame.

By the end of the second evening Elsa's face resembled a cold suet boiled pudding that had been hanging too long. She waddled off to bed, but not before I heard her whisper to Ann, 'He's a terrible man, and something horrible is going to happen to him.'

Rita Hayworth in Strawberry Blonde. There was no padding used in Miss Hayworth's clothes; she needed none.

Bette Davis in the 'red' dress I created for the scandalous ball scene in Jezebel. The film was black and white but the tone of the dress had to suggest shocking scarlet.

I had three days and nights of winning everything but money, blitzes torn up; others got lost up the sleeve and still others got huffed and puffed away. I ended up with $1.49.

There's a postscript to this titbit. (I can hear Elsa screaming, 'Titbit my eye, I'll bury him in my column tomorrow.') Let me tell you about the little milliner, Leah Barnes, who executed and brought to life the hats for *Les Girls* and *Auntie Mame*. Elsa ordered some personal hats from Leah, and after waiting a full year with no response to her registered letters, Leah finally realised all she got for the money she laid out, and her time, was Elsa's autograph on the return receipts.

I didn't care when Elsa went after the rich, but when she ignored and refused to pay people who couldn't afford it, I'm afraid it was a bit more than too much.

There used to be a simple side of Elsa that I once liked. I remember having lunch with her and her lifelong friend, Miss Fellowes-Gordon – called Dickie by her intimates. It was at Elsa's hideaway, as she called it, just around the corner from the Waldorf Astoria. It was a brownstone and they each had a floor. One had the basement with the yard. I can't remember whether Elsa was on top of Dickie or Dickie was on top of Elsa, but the roast beef was good. After lunch Elsa wandered out into the backyard, and as I caught her peeping over the back fence, I couldn't help but feel that this was her real milieu.

I can hear Elsa screaming, 'Titbit my eye, I'll bury him in my column tomorrow'.

Later we talked of many things. We told many stories. This is one story that's been told from Biarritz to Burlingame, but never in front of Elsa.

It happened on a liner. Two prominent socialites were crossing together, and one said, 'Oh, dear, I've just had to send poor so-and-so five thousand dollars to bury her mother,' to which the beautiful wife of a famed composer opened her purse and, taking out a wire, replied, with a sad sweet smile, 'Oh, did you get one of those too?' as she showed her an exact duplicate. It has been said that three others got a similar call to arms.

After twenty-odd years of watching Elsa operate, I came to the conclusion that if you had Elsa for a friend you didn't need an enemy.

Elsa got her wish when I returned home: A letter from Uncle Sam was attached to my door. It was my draft notice.

The first thing I did was to phone Bette Davis. I told her we had better get a move on and dress her new picture, as Uncle Sam was about to dress me. Bette took me to lunch in the green room. She'd asked me to read the script of *Old Acquaintance*. When we sat down to eat, Bette asked me, 'Well, who do you think should play the other part?'

'Miriam Hopkins, of course,' I said. It was obvious Eddie Goulding, the director, who was sitting on the other side of the green room, had written it with her in mind.

Bette called over to him. 'You win, you devil, you double-crossed me. I know she'll be a big headache, but get her anyway, she will be great in the part.'

A little later, it was a gay and charming Miss Hopkins who came dashing into my fitting room directly from the plane. 'Darling!' she exclaimed, throwing her arms around me and kissing me on the cheek. 'Please, Miriam, we don't like each other,' I said bluntly. 'I'll do my best to dress and please you, but no kissy-kissy, please.'

She became Becky Sharp. 'Aren't I awful, Orry-Kelly? But I just can't help myself.'

Now, what are you going to do with a belle like that? Difficult or not, I think she was an exceptionally fine actress when cast correctly.

I was about halfway through *Old Acquaintance* with Bette Davis and Miriam Hopkins when I decided that the Army would be a cinch after putting up with the shenanigans of Miss Hopkins.

My last chore on the lot before donning olive drab was completing the wardrobe sketches for Lauren Bacall's first movie, *To Have and Have Not*. Director Howard Hawks took her 'New Yorkese' high voice and lowered it until he hit her rock bottom. Then I lowered her neckline.

Anything but chesty – but lots of guts – when she leered at Humphrey Bogart's character and said, 'You know how to whistle, don't you, Steve? You just put your lips together and . . . blow'.

Everyone around the world wanted to see and hear more of 'Baby'.

Bette Davis in The Letter, breaking all the rules of a leading lady, as always.

Irving Berlin's

This is the

Army

CHAPTER TWELVE

I gathered my few loose ends, untangled a few threads, and joined the Army.

I'VE BEEN AROUND FOR two world wars. Old men make them; young men fight and die. I was a bit young for the first, but the second, after my first long day of induction, I felt like, and in fact was, the oldest private in the Army Air Forces, which would later become the United States Air Force.

After Pearl Harbor, Hal Roach Studios was taken over by Special Services. Many connected with the film industry joined the Special Service units; they were of great value to the war effort. Colonel Jack Warner, Colonel Darryl Zanuck and others made great contributions to the war effort.

But there were so many others, particularly relatives, pulling strings to join this unit that some wag christened it Fort Roach. Disgusted at all the angling, I gathered my few loose ends, untangled a few threads, and joined the Army. I decided that this, too, would be a challenge and an adventure.

After giving away four or five expensive watches, rings and other jewellery, I took the rest of my loot, including a platinum and diamond dress watch and diamond stud set given to me by Marion Davies, to the vault, closed my house, and off to the war I went. Anyone who knows anything about the Aussies knows we have spunk and spine. Too bloody right we have!

I left for St. Petersburg, Florida. The slow train got lost, and so did I, with the help of sloe gin, which I got from the porter when we went down a siding and ran out of track. After endless days and nights we arrived at St. Petersburg.

At the aptitude test I was a complete washout; both my eardrums had been broken and my hearing wasn't the best. I couldn't even drive a car! I was also told that my IQ was the lowest out of 1700 men stationed at St. Petersburg, and that included a handful of Mexicans who couldn't speak English. Now, with a bucket, brush and broom, I seemed to have the rating of a downstairs maid. Nevertheless, I cheerfully scrubbed the basement of my hotel quarters which, like all the others, had been taken over by the Army and stripped of everything.

Four bunks, upper and lower, were installed in all the single rooms. My chum below me was a harmless moron. He was a Polack from Intercourse, Pennsylvania. His mind had been on a lay-off during its entire run. He took a fancy to me when he wasn't griping about how he missed his wife, Sadie. On introduction he said, 'Just call me Moe. What'll I call you?'

And I said, 'Kelly.' From then on, morning till night he asked me what I was doing, as he watched me do what I was doing. The morning started off with:

'What're yur doin' Kelly, lighting a cigarette?'

And I'd say, 'Yes Moe, lighting a cigarette.'

Then, 'What're yur doin' Kelly, makin' your bed?'

'Yes Moe, making my bed.'

'What're yur doing Kelly, washing up?'

'Yes Moe, washing up.'

When I had occasion to rush into the boys' room. Moe hollered, 'What're yur doin' Kelly, takin' a –'

I interrupted, 'No Moe, I'm just sitting here picking my nose!'

Then a voice imitating Jack Benny hollered, 'Now, cut that out!'

For quite a while I hid the Orry and the dash in my name by just using the initial O. One day along came a guy from the base newspaper. He'd worked on *Boys Town* at Warners and recognised me underneath my fatigues. Before I knew what was happening, I had been photographed sweeping up the alley. A few days later I was featured on the front page along with a brief résumé, which included my salary at Warners. Everyone on the base was quick to notice that I had been getting more than all the head brass put together. That was all, brother! A little swallow of a Southern second lieutenant called on me. He was very full of himself, and also a little movie mad. He arranged that I should do pit duty the following day, which meant up an hour earlier and hustled into a truck with forty others. Being slow on the jump, I had to lean halfway out, and during the half-hour ride to the pits my toes were squeezed like anchovies as I hung on for dear life. On arrival at the pits I was assigned the special duty of filling in a huge open-air Chic Sale, or outhouse. The little swallow had flown over to keep me company and get firsthand information about glamorous Hollywood.

His greeting was, 'Ain't your name Kelly, and don't you come from Hollywood and have something to do with women's dresses?'

'Yes sir,' I said.

'Well, now you're going to have something to do with . . .' pointing to the Black Hole of Calcutta.

I was determined not to let him get my goat. Then his curious little mind turned to the female stars. He plied me with questions such as, 'What kind of dame is Ann Sheridan?' and 'Can so-and-so be made?'

The wind was starting to change, and after about half an hour of this obnoxious shavetail and his questions, I really didn't care about the outcome. I started to tell him a really juicy bit about a star and, like a cat with a mouse, I led him on until he came closer and closer, and finally was standing right next to me, in spite of the unbearable odour. Then I veered just slightly on my next shovelful so that his tailor-made olive drab looked like a Jackson Pollock splash job. Manure on manure.

The following day I shall always remember. I was given KP – kitchen duty – and during both rest periods I had to carry sixty-pound bags of flour from one end of the mess to the other. About seven that evening, having been up since 4 am, with no rest in between, old Kelly surprised everyone as they saw me dancing home – they didn't know I had downed a pint of bourbon on the way. As I entered, someone told me to go to the bulletin board. I was on fire duty for the rest of the night, and I had to start for the pits in the morning, without any rest at all. This was against Army regulations.

After three months of this I had an informed taste of Army life. When I first entered, I had been dead serious. But no one took me seriously. I had stepped forward when volunteers were called for. Being a non-citizen I couldn't be sent overseas, but by stepping forward I showed my willingness to serve. Somewhere along the line I had heard the word *goldbrick*, a soldier who shirks his duties. At the time I had scoffed; now the Aussie was ready to enter into the gentle art of goldbricking.

It was near the end of the month and I was told we weren't welcome at the Jockey Club – a hangout for the top sergeants – but I knew they would be broke. What the hell, I thought,

'Don't you come from Hollywood, and have something to do with women's dresses?' The second lieutenant then plied me with questions like: 'What kind of dame is Ann Sheridan?'

I've got to learn the score. I was right. Most of the thirsty sergeants were broke, and by midnight I had succeeded in pouring enough bourbon into a Polack top kick by the name of Zeek to be told that I was his lifelong friend.

In the morning he had me transferred to his hotel, and I became one of the thirty-seven most hopeless cases in the Army Air Forces, where everybody was nobody and nobody was anybody. Officially we were termed Group O. More commonly we were called The Crippled Commanders. All the other thirty-six had something chronically wrong: an injury of some kind – an arm, a back, a leg, a trick football knee. In my case, I was just too darned old. None of us should have been in the Army. After morning rollcall, my newly found friend instructed me to dash back to the quarters and hide flat on my back under my bunk until the others had marched off. Then Zeek and I would go out of bounds for a decent breakfast. I was living again! After breakfast we played rummy. Zeek was an honest man and didn't believe in borrowing money. Instead, he would win a minimum of five dollars from me each morning. Once, while playing, he said quietly, 'Private Kelly, unless I get an ace you go back to the pits.' Needless to say, he got an ace.

In the back of the hotel there was a mound of dirt, and into this I had built a tunnel of tin, similar to the one Alice O'Grady had on Bourke Street in Sydney. Every night I placed a bottle into my Alice O'Grady, and every morning, when they hollered, 'All down, you lazy mother so-and-sos,' I would dash to the Coke machine, grab a bottle, half empty it and fill it up with bourbon. Then I would grab a broom and work like mad, to the puzzlement of the rest of the company.

The day before Christmas we were scheduled for a short-arm inspection. I imagine the Army wanted to make sure we were nice clean boys before having our turkey. Of the thirty-seven men in the company, only seven were well enough to march across town to the place of inspection.

Most of the old tourists who came to St. Petersburg to rest and sit on the many benches along the streets had gone, but there were a few left. On reaching our destination we joined the end of the long line, which looked like a huge caterpillar winding out into the street. Suddenly a corporal came dashing out, hollering, 'Get 'em out and have 'em ready!' We all unbuttoned and stood there in the Florida sunlight, with our short arms out, when around the corner toddled two darling old Helen Hodgkinson Garden Club ladies; one let out a noise like a train dashing through a tunnel. The stronger-willed of the two said,

'Now, control yourself, Miss Minnie.' Then she turned on me and screamed, 'Why, you dirty old man, you, you ought to be ashamed of yourself – and at your age!'

'There's a war on, ma'am, and orders are orders,' I said.

Bending the corner, to their horror, they caught sight of fifty other people's persons. With stifled screams they about faced and started down the street at a slow canter.

After the inspection, a corporal with a double-breasted Eddie Robinson mouth, came along and told us he had been ordered to see that The Crippled Commanders got back safely to quarters. At the first intersection we crossed, he saw a Salvation Army lass ringing her bell. The Christmas spirit must have swept through his semi-abstract mind. With an awful jab in my ribs he ordered us to start singing.

'What?' sez I.

'Christmas carols,' sez he. And, in the off-key voice of boxer Slapsie Maxie, he proceeded to lead 'Jingle Bells' between his 'Hup, two, three, four!'

I started to laugh and the more I laughed the harder he dug my ribs. By the time we reached quarters I had to lie on the road as he'd punched me way below par.

The following day was D for Danger. Forty of us were loaded together into a truck and off we went to the pits. About four in the afternoon, back at quarters, a dead soldier was taken out. Before long four more followed. It was highly contagious spinal meningitis. They had all been in my truck. Nothing happened to me. The doctor said I was saved because of my age, and possibly because of the fact that I was pickled in alcohol.

About that time I started wondering why I didn't receive my discharge. The President had signed the Bill releasing all men over forty-five from active duty. Where was my discharge? I had spent more than nine thousand dollars for whiskey and fried chicken by this time, besides the fifty a month Uncle Sam paid me. It was no wonder my application never left the base.

However, a few days later my papers arrived and I went back to Warners for Irving Berlin's *This Is the Army*. Heavyweight boxing champion Joe Louis had been added to the film, and he and I would pass the time by playing gin rummy.

One day, while playing, we watched the chorus-boy soldiers rehearsing the finale, 'The Army's Made a Man Out of Me'. Looking at them, Joe drawled, 'That ain't the way I see it.' When Colonel Warner saw the rushes he must have agreed, for the next day a group of real soldiers marched into the studio and onto the stage, in front of Berlin's not-so-manly chorus boys.

Dear Ray

Sorry to take so long with papers but the army keep on busy.

Looks like they will be sending us old guys back pretty soon

Regards,

Pvt Orry Kelly

Shortly afterwards I lunched with Ann Warner and Justice Frank Murphy. Alexander de Seversky – who wrote the book *Victory Through Air Power*, which anticipated the method of winning the war – was also a guest. I told Frank some of the doings of those permanent duty officers in St Petersburg. A week or so later a letter arrived from one of the staff down there, saying all hell had broken loose. It seems some redheaded Colonel Murphy with bushy eyebrows like labour leader John L. Lewis had pulled a surprise visit; not even the pot-bellied used-car salesman, the company commander, had been alerted. My Army friend said the colonel must have had a big pull in Washington, because he had ordered almost all of the entire permanent corps transferred overseas.

I hadn't yet been mustered out of the Army. My work with *This Is the Army* was finished, but I was still in uniform. Riding my bike around the Warner lot, I ran into Cary Grant. He was making *Arsenic and Old Lace*. I told him of the party Lady Mendl had given me when I passed through New York, at which I had been informed by a high official that Britishers must either join up or go home. Cary didn't let me get any further. In a rather supercilious manner he told me of chatting with Lord Lothian, the British ambassador to America, in Washington. Then *I* didn't let him get any further. I could see now that Grant had gone to the point of no return. He no longer wanted my opinion or advice. Making an excuse, I circled off. That evening I told Miss Barrymore about it, and she replied, 'That's all right Kelly, he Lord Lothian'd me too.'

When I finished my chore with *This Is the Army*, my commanding officer, Colonel MacCabe, sent Peter Gunn, who was then plain Corporal Craig Stevens, down to City Hall, where I swore my allegiance. It was simple in wartime. I had tried once before and got George Washington mixed up with Dick Whittington or Guy Fawkes in my nervousness, when answering the questions. Now that I've been a naturalised American citizen for seventeen years, I feel I can criticise as an American: When Sid Grauman died, they called him Little Sunshine, and Will Rogers always said he never met a man he didn't like. Well, I have . . . and a couple of women that were horrors, too. Even though I didn't go overseas, I volunteered. My short say in the regular Army made me regain values.

Being born British, I realise the British have long been used to being disliked by other nationals. Now, realising how much we give to help other nations around the world, I wonder if it wouldn't be better for Americans not to try so desperately hard to be liked. Pollyanna was never my cup of tea.

CARY GRANT

Frank Capra's "ARSENIC and OLD LACE"

Bette Davis
Dark Victory

CHAPTER THIRTEEN

'No matter what anyone may say, Orry is a very moral boy.'

TO CELEBRATE THE ALLIED victory, Lady Mendl gave a gala at After All, the name she gave her home. It was my first party back in civvies.

First I took Norma Talmadge and Constance Collier to dinner at Mike Romanoff's old restaurant and then went on to Elsie's. Everyone was there. Perched up on stools at the tiny bar were Olympic figure skater turned actress Sonja Henie and Cary Grant. When I asked the bartender for the drinks, Grant half turned his shoulder and, looking over my shoulder, gave me a half-hearted 'Hi'. I knew Grant had heard and read my mother had visited me. She had just gone home. He had forgotten the many drafts she had sent me, which went for food and liquor. I hadn't! My dander was up. I felt the least he could have done was to send her flowers. Mother had always mentioned him in her letters to me way back in the Archie Leach red underwear period.

Looking into the mirrored bar at him, I said, 'Look here, Cary, if and when you are in the mood to say hello, do so. If you are glad to see me, look straight at me – preferably in the eye. But never, never again half-turn and give me that half-English half-cockney half-arsed "Hi"!'

It wasn't the first thing I'd taught the kid from Bristol, but it was the first time I did it publicly. I felt Sonja Henie's eternal Bird of Paradise wanted to take off as I took off, but not before I reminded Cary of my mother's visit.

Then Grant made a magnanimous gesture – one I've seen other stars feel takes care of everything. He would send me an autographed photo, inscribed to my mother, which he did the next day.

Somewhere among a lot of old press cuttings is a photo of Cary inscribed to me. Actors did that in the Roaring Twenties. It says, 'To my finest and closest friend'. But except for an occasional low 'hello' – but no 'hi's – his finest and closest friend rarely heard a peep.

Out of uniform on a Friday, back in the Wardrobe Department on a Monday, my eye was not yet focused for frills.

Few stars have the selective eye. Fashion often goes off in three different directions. Jane Wyman went with it, but always in three different shades. Rarely did she wear a dress designed with one piece of fabric and one shade. Talk about the lady sawed in half, she was cut up three different ways. I was lucky I never had to design her pictures, until I got back into mufti and was assigned *Dough Girls*. It was being produced by Mark Hellinger, with Ann Sheridan, Alexis Smith, Eve Arden, Faye Emerson and Jane Wyman.

The 'early' Jane had been married to a downtown wholesaler connected with clothes; she knew all the terms and spoke in their lingo. Remarks such as, 'I was on the Boulevard and I got me a stop-red formal and an aqua spectator sport.' Once she described a 'suspencer' dress that had three rows of 'bric-a-brac' around the skirt.

'Oh, I mean rickrack,' she added when she saw me jolt.

'What goes with the suspencer dress?' I asked her. 'Or would you be referring to suspenders?'

Both Leah Rhodes, my one-time assistant, and two other designers, had important pictures to do. I was being used as a doctor, going to the rushes with Mr Warner and correcting their mistakes. *Dough Girls* was my only picture.

Although we had never worked together before, I was good friends with Mark Hellinger, who made his name as a New York theater critic and then as one of the first nationally known Broadway columnists. After one of his stories adapted for the screen became a success, Jack Warner hired him as an associate producer. He came into my

Things had changed since the war. The 'hotcha' girls like Jane Wyman were in demand, and could make demands.

office one day and told me they were taking me off the picture, but he wouldn't tell me the reason. I told him I was halfway through my work and if he, or anyone else, thought I was running a school to teach others what I'd taken years to learn, he had another thing coming. This was a hell of a way to treat someone just out of the Army.

Things had changed since the war, and so had taste. The 'hotcha' girls were in demand. Jane Wyman had a cute puss, and she began to change her diction. She was in demand. She could make demands.

With reluctance he finally said, 'Jane Wyman won't do the part unless her Little Favourite dresses her.'

'Okay,' I said, 'let him cut her up in three shades of blue and I'll do the rest of the picture.'

Mark said, 'No dice.' I would have to go.

I told him where to go.

Mr Warner was a very busy man and must have been guided by the men under him. I was misquoted to him by the production office. Word got to him that I was trying to run the studio. I had better quit. 'Okay,' I stormed, 'tomorrow is payday, have my cheque ready!'

In all fairness to Mr Warner, I must say that he sent for me. He had his two key men right there with him. Mr Warner couldn't have been fairer. I told him my side of the story; I thought I had been double-crossed. Looking one of his men right in the eye, I said, 'I guess all big companies have one SOB, are you the one?' He started to rise from his chair and his face went the colour of a purple plum. I alerted myself.

I think the story had gotten around Hollywood that I was a fighting dressmaker. While I have little muscle, an Aussie can kick like a mule, and I was aiming where Warner fired.

In the eleven years I had worked for Warners, this was my first flare-up. Mr Warner asked me to stay; by this time it was too late. As I was leaving, JL called out, 'If it's any consolation, Kelly, and if I know you, you'll double your money.' Within a year I more than doubled it.

The day after I left Warners I signed with Darryl F. Zanuck at 20th Century Fox. I had worked for him when he was at Warners in the thirties. Betty Grable, the number one pin-up queen and box-office star, had the good sense to know that the studio designer at Fox was not for her. I was to do two pictures a year with Miss Grable, and outside films as well.

Jack Warner, head of Warner Brothers, told me when I left,
'If it's any consolation, Kelly, and if I know you, you'll double your money'.
Within a year I more than doubled it.

Let's face it, no one had more beautiful gams or a cuter chassis than Betty Grable, offering a glimpse of those famous legs in Mother Wore Tights.

I did *Mother Wore Tights* and *The Dolly Sisters*, and others. The latter film was so unlike the real lives of the identical twin Broadway stars, it might as well have been the lives of the Cherry Sisters, the five sisters famous for the scathing reviews of their vaudeville touring act. I found Betty Grable more interested in her husband, her children and her racehorses than in motion pictures. Of all the people I've dressed, she had less enthusiasm about the making of a movie itself. Not that she didn't have her mind on her work – the moment she was on the set she turned in a good job. She was professional and considerate with everyone concerned. And, let's face it, no one had more beautiful gams or a cuter chassis than Grable.

Towards the end of filming *Mother Wore Tights*, Betty's pregnancy became obvious. Musicals take a long time to make. The dance numbers were all shot at once, as soon as she became aware of her condition. Louella O. Parsons, of course, was the first to know. While I've always made it a point never to tell personal or production secrets to Louella, or anyone else, now and then, being a good friend, Lolly would pump me when she thought she had a hot story. In fact, word got around that Betty might have the baby at any minute. One morning Miss LOP called: 'I hear they're standing by to take Betty to the hospital.' Not wanting to be scooped by an afternoon paper, Lolly, in her vague manner, continued, 'I hope she can hold off until the morning edition.'

Like myself, Louella Parsons walked, talked and went around in circles. Cole Porter once said, 'Kelly often starts a story with the soup, forgets about it, and then finishes it up with the salad.' Louella attended every Hollywood party and missed nothing, from the fruit cocktail to the nuts.

Miss Louella Parsons was the first woman motion picture reporter. She was the most maligned, misquoted and misunderstood woman in Hollywood. She was tough, sure she was – she couldn't have reached the heights of top newspaper reporting without garnering a few enemies along the way. Like all personalities, she had many sides. In fact, she was as contradictory as Scarlett O'Hara – and her sash was just as colourful! Louella's floral sash was varied and had many moods. One side could be pretty, petulant, peeved, never petty; the other side could be gay, hospitable, always lovable. But the centre was tied with a naïve, yet shrewd, knot. She missed nothing. She saw all the sides of the bows and beaux.

Lolly's greeting was, 'Hello dear, any news?' Invariably while saying this, she was looking over your left shoulder, and nine times out of ten had already spotted someone on your wing who was news – they were the ones who made the bulldog edition. One should never have been fooled by Lolly's vague expression, for she was quicker on the draw than Billy the Kid.

One evening, long ago, I called at Lolly's house to take her to a party. Collins, her faithful butler, asked me to go straight upstairs. Sadie, her coloured maid, a woman of good taste and judgment, said, 'Miss Parsons is almost through dressing. She'll be with you in a minute.'

Louella came out wearing a lovely powder-blue Bergdorf Goodman evening gown. I looked at her in the full-length mirror and said, 'Lolly dear, you look charming.' Sadie adjusted her, shook her head and pinched her mouth like a dry prune. Catching Sadie's look in the mirror, Lolly's smile disappeared. 'What is it, Sadie?'

Sadie, who always included herself in all conversations, said, 'We would look much prettier in pink, and we would have a much better time in pink, Miss Parsons.' Lolly's eyes went up and her mouth went down as she called out, 'Get me out the pink satin, Sadie.'

'No, Miss Parsons, we would look better in the pink peau de soie.'

By this time Lolly was getting tired as she looked at Sadie over her shoulder. 'All right, Sadie,' she sighed, 'get the ruby and diamond set Docky gave me and my gloves and bag and everything else. I'll never get there.'

Eventually Lolly was lolly pink from head to toe. As we came downstairs, she called out, 'Goodnight, Sadie, dear!' She hardly got the 'dear' out when she whispered to me, 'At times I could kill that Sadie.'

After her Hollywood Hotel program – which combined music, an interview with a star and a sketch from a current movie performed by the stars – she began another radio series, featuring each week an interview with a different personality. Claudette Colbert opened the season, and I followed her. Believe it or not, my appearance sent Miss Parsons' ratings up and mine down. The Associated Press carried my quotes. I'd opened my big mouth and taken a slam at Hollywood.

I was working at Fox then for Darryl Zanuck, whom I greatly admired, but Bette

Louella Parsons, the most maligned, misquoted and misunderstood woman in Hollywood. Lolly's greeting was always, 'Hello dear, any news?' This time Marilyn Monroe is in her sights.

Davis would not return to Warners for her next picture unless I dressed her. My non-exclusive contract with Fox allowed me to do outside work; I was paid a flat sum for the Davis picture. This put me in the two-thousand-odd-dollar-a-week bracket – then the highest any motion picture designer had ever been paid.

The pre-scripted Parsons interview was written by Hollywood reporter Miss Ruth Waterbury, who informed me before the show that Louella would ask me to name the ten best-dressed women. Miss Waterbury said, 'You are not going to tell me you think Bette Davis is well dressed.'

I told her I thought I had done a pretty good job on *Dark Victory*. Later, I would see Miss Davis in *Now, Voyager* on television, almost twenty years after the film was made, and the clothes still stood up. I told the little Miss Waterbury that since Bette was my bread and butter, she could at least write that Miss Davis was much more interested in her acting than fussing about clothes.

I told her I thought I had done a pretty good job on Dark Victory . . . Miss Bette Davis was much more interested in her acting than fussing about clothes.

I arrived at the broadcasting station and was introduced to the announcer, Marvin Miller. Now, in the parlour or a drawing room, you can't shut me up, but give me an audience and I freeze. The mike has always scared the devil out of me. We ran through the show. I likened most Hollywood stars to amateur chefs: 'They all have wonderful ingredients – some too many – and what they don't wear they carry.' Then I asked Lolly, 'Where's the paragraph mentioning Miss Davis?' Very nervously Lolly said, 'Now dear, you're not going to change the script ten minutes before airtime and get me all mixed up – and another thing, when you talk to me, look up now and then, like Claudette did when she was on. It sounds more natural.'

'Claudette is tops in her profession and her smile's her own,' I said. 'I have five American teeth in the front and, besides, if I look up and smile at you, I'll lose my place – like you just did, Lolly.'

We went on the air. I don't know who was more nervous, Louella or I. Anyway, the minute the program was over we both made a dash for the john.

Ten days later, I was due at Warners for a Bette Davis film which had only about three changes. I got a message from producer Henry Blanke. 'S'feethart,' he said in his broken German accent, 'we will not need you on this picture, we are going to buy the clothes.'

I remained good friends with Mr J.L. Warner, but I'm not kidding myself when I say that he was delighted with their turn of events. Bette remained at the studio a year and a half longer, and I lost sixty thousand dollars. I never explained to Bette, or complained to Louella since this certainly wasn't Lolly's fault.

But it is unfortunate that Miss Waterbury was unable to rise above her likes and dislikes. I have known many players who have not been fair with me, but when it comes to working, I've given them my best time and effort. Now, not only did Miss Waterbury not see fit to write up my clothes for *Les Girls*, but she wouldn't even mention Roz Russell's wardrobe in *Auntie Mame*. But then again, I'm not an isolated case. She reviewed *Suddenly, Last Summer*, and other than mentioning Kate Hepburn's name she said nothing at all about that magnificent performance. Still, when it comes to clothes, maybe it was just as well that Little Miss Waterbury didn't mention me. I saw her in some quaint little tulle numbers that made her look like a toby jug on a mantelpiece.

It's impossible to write about Louella Parsons and not mention her one-time assistant Dorothy Manners, a Hollywood columnist. I knew her for decades. She had peaches-and-cream skin – she herself was just as peachy. A wholesome, earthy laugh and a good writer, she often subbed for Lolly. Shortly after the war, when singer and actress Frances Langford, who entertained the troops with Bob Hope, was still doing her 'Purple Heart' column, a few of us were driving by the Sawtelle Veterans Hospital one night, feeling no pain. Dorothy kiddingly called out to the driver to slow down in this territory because 'Frances will bury us all in her column if we come within ten feet of one of her beloved veterans!'

One of the earliest and best of the talent tooters – press agents – was handsome Margaret Ettinger. She may not have been as spectacular as Russell Birdwell in some instances, but in the long run no one was more consistent. She kept more Hollywood names up in lights, in newspapers and in magazines, on radio and on television, and featured on billboards alongside more fences than Burma-Shave, whose signs advertising their shaving cream were everywhere on the highways. Margaret engineered clever publicity that remained for many years in the minds of the public about producer Irving

Thalberg. Mr Thalberg was a modest, sensitive and charming man, but he also had occasional disagreements with his studio. This time he had taken his star wife, Norma Shearer, to Europe.

He never allowed his name to appear on the screen or be used in publicising the pictures he nursed under Louis B. Mayer's empire at Metro-Goldwyn-Mayer. When the Thalbergs returned to New York, Margaret met them, and started the publicity wheels turning. The public read for the first time about the modesty of this brilliant young man. Mr Thalberg was publicised as the man who shunned publicity, and the public ate it up.

It had taken a lot of persuading for my mother to make the long sea voyage to America. Finally I had coaxed her by offering to shout for her little old Scotswoman friend to accompany her. (Here she is above, left, with her friend Eleanor.)

They had arrived just as the studio saddled me with another important picture. After seeing the studios, radio shows, dining at the Riverside Inn and trips to Santa Barbara, their six weeks' holiday ended.

The evening before their departure I arrived home. Mother was sitting in one corner of my living room, in a high-back chair, looking as rigid as Edna May Oliver, the character actress renowned for her acerbic spinsters. Her little Scotch friend, Eleanor, with her Victorian body and Adam's legs, squatted far across the room. Entering the room I felt a tenseness. 'Now Mother, don't tell me you and Eleanor have had a tiff on your last night?'

Mother drew herself up, as only Edna May Oliver could, as she said, 'It's only one of the biggest universities in the country.'

'What is?' I asked.

'Purdue,' Mother replied. Over the years I'd forgotten to answer questions she asked about Purdue University. Her little Scottish friend had taken Mother to the Los Angeles Library.

'What would you like to do, Ma, go to Purdue and be photographed standing at the entrance?' I asked.

'I certainly would,' Ma replied, as she started giving me her Purdue family history.

Kidding her, I said, 'What's wrong with the Kellys?' There were only three original families in the Isle of Man – the Christians, of which the mutineer Fletcher was one; the Callows; and the Kellys. Then my ma hit below the belt. I was carrying a load, so I joined in with her as she started: 'If you'd drink like a Purdue . . .' We didn't finish. She didn't let me. Taking the floor she said, 'You're exactly like your father – hot of head, quick of temper.'

'Hot or cold,' I said, 'the boat sails in the morning.' And it did.

With ten outfits my Miss Keady made for Mother, hats by Leah Barnes, and six sables I put around her neck the following morning, my loving mother, Florence Purdue Kelly, went merrily on her merry way.

My mother was the original Morse code. She loathed wasted words. She had great penmanship and was a brilliant speller. Her bold style was very readable, until she got to the juicy bit, when it became so small it was almost illegible. Of course, this was always maddening. Her gossip was always followed by a large, powerful, 'However, it's nobody's business.'

Over the years every letter ended in precisely the same way, except for the flowers she described in my father's rambling garden. They told the change of seasons:

The primroses bordering beds dotted with daisies buttercups
snowdrops phlox forget-me-nots look like upstairs hall carpet.
Everywhere masses of maiden-hair fern jonquils daffodils and iris
be sure to keep your bowels well open you'll never get appendicitis

> *I remain*
> *Your loving mother*
> *Florence Purdue Kelly*

No, mother wasn't calling me Iris – like myself, a comma, a colon, and particularly a semi-colon meant little in her life. In this letter she forgot the full stop after iris.

One sad thing about an amateur writing a book is that just as you begin picking up the loose ends, putting things where they belong and start bundling them all together, you suddenly realise you're only starting to learn to write. It's been eighteen months since I've started my story. I wouldn't want to live through this again. There has been pain in reliving my life, and yet, I wouldn't have wanted it any other way. But, I've learned the value of the little dot, dash and particularly the full stop. It finalises everything.

'If you'd drink like a Purdue you'd be a gent, but you drink like a Kelly.' This time it wasn't Mother's words ringing in my ear. It was I yelling it out in my drunken sleep, until my Man Friday, almost shaking the daylights out of me, woke me up.

I now lived in a duplex. While he went downstairs to fetch my breakfast, I said, 'Bijou, this is it! The end! Finis, full stop! Mother was right. When I drink, I'm not a gent.'

I used to be a chain smoker, but I'd thrown away the cigarettes two years previously. No tapering off. I just got tired of spitting up that filthy grey blancmange of a morning. Now I would throw away the bottle. And did. Many asked how I did it. Well, I never cared to drink for at least an hour or so after dinner. The first night I dined at 5.30 – the hour I usually flew at the bottle. I never drank on a full stomach. Within a week I was dining at my usual 7.30. I've had no desire to take a drink since. I never *will*!

Nobody dished and dug up more Hollywood dirt than Miss Edith Gwynn. She was the den mother of Mike Connolly's 'Rambling Reporter' column in the *Hollywood Reporter*. It was during Marlene Dietrich's trouser period, and the night of the earthquake in 1933, that Miss Gwynn wrote, 'Marlene Dietrich rushed into the Beverly Hills Hotel dressed on the wrong side.'

Marlene could wear anything, including the tuxedo she wore that evening, and still look utterly feminine. In fact, anything and everything sat well on her lovely shoulders. Over a quarter of a century later, Marlene was still sitting pretty, while Miss Gwynn – who once had Clark Gable, Cary Grant and all the top stars at her little dinner table in her little house on the fringe of Beverly Hills – now just sat on her fringe.

Marlene's case was not an isolated one. Miss Gwynn went to work on me. My mother had always been so proud of the good press Sydney had given me. Isolation and extremes, heat and thirst, toughened the sports-loving Australians. I am anything but typical of the lean sun-drenched horse-borne Aussie.

For centuries Australia lay hidden while ancient civilisations were born, built and buried. For a rugged country with such a short history, they spoke well of their male designer of women's clothes.

When I first returned to my homeland as Warner Brothers' designer, the press looked me over. They gave me the works, and although it seemed a bit odd, decided I was fair dinkum.

I had made eight trips, thirty-six days by water, leaving me only about ten days to visit each time. But I was trying to repay my mother for all she had done for me. After the war a plane service opened. I flew home several times. Then a relative cabled saying Mother had contracted cancer of the jaw from a faulty plate – it would strike the brain within nine months. Miss Gwynn was short a line at deadline. A fellow Australian, Gordon Currie, cartoonist and columnist for the *Los Angeles Mirror*, later told me how a few lines almost broke my mother's heart. Miss Gwynn's twisted tale travelled across the Pacific to Australia. What started out as a gag I had said about myself now lacked that razor's edge – the difference between good and bad taste.

Some wretched creature was unkind enough to show it to my mother – at the same time comforting her by saying she was sure it wasn't true. Shortly before Mother died, she said, 'No matter what anyone may say, Orry is a very moral boy.'

I was fifty when Mother passed on, but I guess to her I was still her little boy.

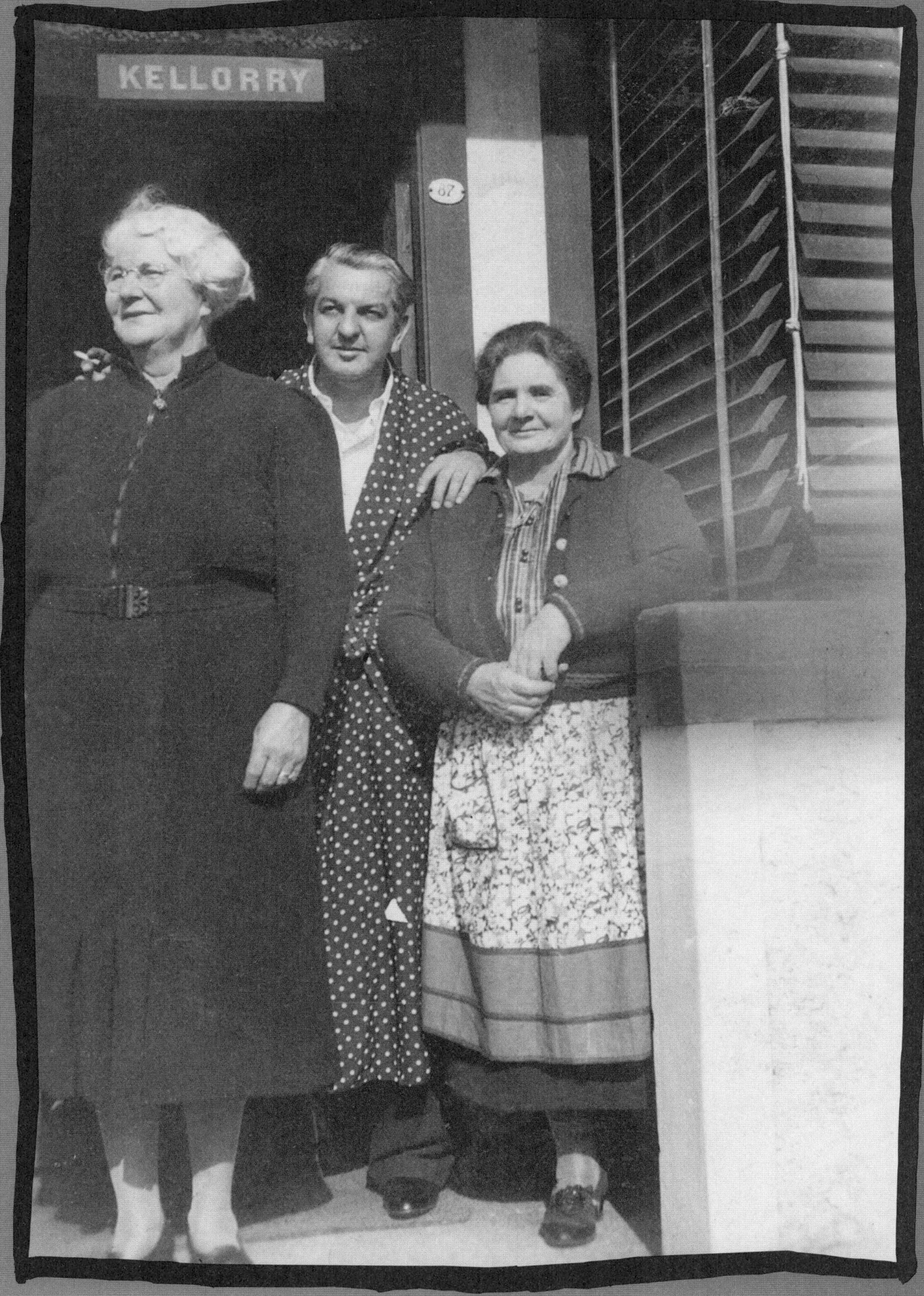
KELLORRY
67

Jack Lemmon and Tony Curtis
Some Like It Hot

CHAPTER FOURTEEN

'It's the finish that counts, kid.'

ALTHOUGH I DON'T HAVE loads of friends, I have been fortunate to keep those I have over a period of twenty years. I've shared the same affection with some of the little sewing women I worked with as I did with Miss Barrymore and Lady Mendl. I was just as fond of comic character actor Rags Ragland, known mostly for playing likeable oafish characters, and Joe Frisco, the vaudeville comedian and jazz dancer who made his natural stutter part of his act, as I am of George Cukor and Cole Porter.

Holidays, particularly Thanksgiving, I always got together with Joe Frisco. For years Joe wouldn't work for anyone under $1500 a week, and he wouldn't take less than fifteen bucks when he put the 'B' on Rags Ragland and me – and others he liked, for he wouldn't ask for or take money from anyone he didn't like.

Shortly before he died, the Masquers community theatre gave him a benefit. Actor and comedian Ben Blue sent a cheque for twenty-five dollars. When Frisco heard about it he said, 'Send it back – I don't like Blue.' Although he'd get mad at actor Charley Foy, he was fond of him, and Charley was his best friend right up to the finish.

The previous year I had taken Frisco out for Thanksgiving dinner – just the two of us. His last Thanksgiving, friends had invited him out. We had arranged to meet at the Firefly, a Vine Street bar. After we had downed our before-dinner quota, the gang began to leave. Actors Cully Richards, Joe Kirk, and 'Coat' Ralph (he had more coats than old-time vaudevillian Ned 'Clothes' Brown), called out, 'Come on, Frisco.'

But Frisco said, 'Wait for me at the corner, I want to talk to Orry.' That was the first time he ever used my Christian name. Frisco called me, like most other people, anything from Herman to Hermes Pan. Just as he once called out to Louella Parsons, 'Well, if it ain't little Ruby Stevens', which was Barbara Stanwyck's given name.

With the brawdy brandy boys gone, and alone with me, Frisco said, 'No, this time it ain't a touch, I want to buy you a drink.' He told Danny, the bartender, 'Give the Hawaiian beauty, Luka, one and pour one for yourself.'

There was something pathetic about the natty little Joe – by now Joe was little; cancer had shrunk him to one hundred pounds. His snappy bow tie shirred his shirt collar that was now three sizes too big.

Joe stuttered a bit more than usual when he said, 'I can't stop losing weight. If you see Marion Davies over the holidays, tell her Frisco thinks he could put on weight in Palm Springs. The last time up there I stayed at her hotel, everything was on the house. She gave me a couple of eggs when I arrived, and when I left I got another egg.' With Joe, an egg was a thousand dollars.

'The doctors told me I had ulcers. How come then, Orry, after my last X-ray they told me I can drink again?' He hadn't been looking at me. Looking up, he said, 'Do ya think it's the Big Casino and they won't tell me?'

He gulped his Manhattan and slowly drained the bottom of his glass. Busty Luka put a dime in the music box. Roberta Sherwood hurled out 'Lazy River' – the number Frisco and I so often used when we kidded doing our stuff. He tipped his hat over his eye. His cigar twirled up in the air, landing on his chin; he somersaulted the lighted end into his mouth. As Joe Frisco started to tap, I went into my Louise Groody 'Tea for Two' bit. We danced out on Vine Street and halfway up to the corner of Hollywood and Vine.

After the holiday dinner, Charley Foy took Frisco to the Motion Picture Country Home. Two months later he was laid to rest in the Hollywood Cemetery.

Standing between producer Harry Joe Brown and actor Walter Catlett, we heard comedian Julius Tannen's simple touching eulogy. There was no drama – that is, until

I realised the faint faraway quivering organ music. It was not a hymn, it was Joe's theme song 'Darktown Strutters' Ball'. There were moist Irish eyes – actors Pat O'Brien, Wally Ford, Lee Tracy, Tom Dugan and Pat Buttram.

Across the aisle stood Polly Adler, the Broadway madam. Joe was a bachelor, you know.

We danced out onto the street and halfway up
to the corner of Hollywood and Vine.

My day's work finished at Fox, I'd make a beeline for Vine Street.

I must say, my Vine Street days were among the happiest I've ever spent. Even if the spangles were a little frayed and dimmed, the view from Hollywood and Vine shone brighter and was dusted with more stardust than the hills of Beverly.

'Outside the Plaza Hotel' became 'Outside of Lindy's' – Hollywood and Vine was now the street of broken dreams. I christened it 'The Street of Disappointments'.

We were a closely knitted group: Rags Ragland, boxer Barney Ross, movie producer Mort Brisken and 'Wild' Bill Morrow, the creator of the Jack Benny perennial formula.

When Barney Ross arrived in town, all the ex-pugs started ambling around on Vine from the hotel where they lived, a place I called 'The House of Forgotten Men'. About fifteen feet apart, one by one they'd touch Barney for at least a ten: he always had a fat roll. Every time he bought a drink, he would give the bartender a buck. I had to call him on it because he made it tough for the rest of us. In fact, some of the bartenders started to act like B-girls.

Often it would cost Rags Ragland and me a fiver in one-dollar bills just to cross the street from the Plaza to the Derby.

One time Rags took a handful of the labels I used for women's gowns and had them sewn into his suits, sport coats and hats. He entered the Brown Derby carrying his coat inside out, showing the Orry-Kelly label. Everything including his jacket and hat carried my label. This was all done with that deadpan look of his.

Rags remained my friend until the end, which was much too soon. The day after he got back from visiting restaurateur Toots Shor in New York, I got a hurried call. On the way to his house in the Valley I stopped and picked up another of Rags' old friends, the irrepressible Martha Raye. One look at Rags and somehow I knew it was the end. I wanted

Fanny to get him into Cedars of Lebanon Hospital. I called her, but she was in one of her vague moods: 'What about his own doctor?' Disappointed, I hung up. I asked someone to call Frank Sinatra. Within ten minutes Frank had made arrangements at Cedars and the ambulance arrived.

There were many other good things Sinatra did which he never discussed – like going on the radio special 'Tribute to Ethel Barrymore' and insisting they pay him five thousand dollars, which he then turned over to that great lady, as did others, like Claudette Colbert. Frankie was quite a guy in my books; like Toots and many more, he shared my affection for Rags Ragland.

It was not so much what Sinatra sang, said or did, but more the manner he did it. Deeply lyrical by temperament, like the early Impressionists, he was a solitary rebel.

Frank Sinatra sat on top of the heap at the head of his clan. He was the *sun* with his pack – like so many planets revolving around his generous warmth. There was brittle, brilliant Shirley MacLaine. The Dean – mellow, mild, Martin. Sammy – you name it, he did it – and for those who wanted it, there was always a little of Peter Lawford.

With Frank, the rebel, it was never a question of good or bad taste. Whether it be cruel, crafty or kind, he did what his heart told him. At times his art was spotty, but his show was always well done, be it medium, rare, or sunny-side up. His idiom was an art of its own.

Frank Sinatra belongs with giants.

Often we wonder where a story starts or how a word is coined. During the early part of the war, the columnist Ed Durling gave me credit for being the first to use the expression *boo boo*, but actually it was vaudevillian Jay Brennan. His partner, Bert Savoy, and he created many phrases, sayings and gags. 'Let your hair down' was first used by Bert one Monday at the Palace; and columnist O.O. McIntyre, who only publicised Caruso and Savoy and Brennan, dashed backstage and quickly coined the phrase. When Jay visited California one spring, Fanny Brice, Norma Talmadge and myself flipped a coin to see who would be lucky enough to have him first for a house guest. Much to Fanny's disgust, I won.

The first night he arrived I gave a dinner party and invited, among others, Louella Parsons, who wore a floral print and a couple of silver foxes. Norma Talmadge lingered for

Even if the spangles were a little frayed and dimmed, the view from
Hollywood and Vine was dusted with more stardust than the hills of Beverly.

some more talk with Jay and me after the others had left. I had a Sealyham dog, Stymie. Suddenly Norma exclaimed, 'Why is Stymie sniffing at the closet?' as she opened the door. In plain view was a large silver fox tail, obviously belonging to Louella's double foxes. Jay grabbed the tail and, waving it around, called out, 'Get the boo boo, get the boo boo, Stymie.' The excited dog started tearing around after Louella's silver fox tail, which Jay then hid under the sofa. 'Where's the boo boo?' he asked Stymie. The word struck both our fancy, and Norma and I, with our brandy glow, got hysterical.

The next morning, when Jay came down for breakfast, he went through the same routine while Stymie went mad. The dog didn't need the fox tail anymore – the word *boo boo* was enough to make him frantic. Louella never knew that Stymie with the fox tail in his mouth put his head into a gopher's hole, and that ended the tale of *The Little Foxes*.

At five o'clock that same afternoon I went to the Brown Derby on Vine Street, where I met my pal, Rags Ragland. At our 'round table' was the usual gang: Joe Frisco, Bud Abbott, Barney Ross, Mort Brisken and Rags. I had no sooner seated myself than a very weird blonde dame, with a surprised look, came in and looked up and down the bar, mumbling to herself as if she was looking for someone. A seat at the bar opened up next to an Air Force officer. She darted for it. As she went by, still talking to herself, I said, 'Get the boo boo.' Rags caught the inane look on the blonde's face and practically fell on the floor. When Rags came to, I was pointing to a man with his hand on his hip. 'There's another boo boo.'

Rags said, 'Are there both men and women boo boos?' No sooner had I spoken than the man turned towards us. His face was as tough as Wallace Beery's. 'Uh oh,' I exclaimed. 'I made a boo boo!'

Two nights later, on their radio program, Bud Abbott's partner, Lou Costello, boomed out, 'I made a boo boo.' Jerry Lewis's writers took it from there. Soon every Jerry and Joe in the nation was using it – but it was really Jay Brennan who invented the expression. In my cups, I'd simply twisted it around.

Every January, for years, I attended the joint birthday party for Bebe Daniels, producer-director-actor Hal Roach Sr, and Dr Martin, Louella Parsons' husband.

All these years ago dreaming of Bebe Daniels in Sydney with GG and here I was attending her birthday party. This is one of the gowns I designed for 42nd Street.

Actress Verree Teasdale wearing an evening gown I designed for her that reflected my preference for simple, unadorned elegance 'without a spangle'.

One year I was to take the actress and comedienne Bea Lillie, who was house-guesting with Fanny Brice. Fanny was supposed to have come with us, but backed out at the last moment. I'd given my chauffeur this Saturday night off and had rented a Tanner closed car.

The moment we arrived, actress Cobina Wright got on to Bea's train. On Cobina's train was Judith Anderson's ex, whom I didn't care for – Judith had told me many tales. After they'd tagged along for about half an hour, the nips got the better of my disposition. I looked at Cobina and said, 'Honey chile' – I used one of Bea's favourite expressions – 'you must have cut that dress out with a knife and fork.' Bea let out a yell, but Cobina's face went beetroot.

Frankly I don't remember much more until later. With Cobina's friend at the wheel of an old rattle trap, we went jogging up the hill to Fanny's. After dropping Bea, I vaguely remembered my rented Tanner and asked to be let out in front of the Beverly Wilshire Hotel.

It was a blind night, not a star, and I was blind drunk. I stood in the street, hailing what I thought was a black-and-white taxi, when out jumped the driver and said, 'What do you mean by standing here in the middle of the street? Don't you know it's four forty-five in the morning?'

In a very cheery mood I replied, 'Well, I'm not standing here picking my so-and-so nose!'

Bang! I got hit with the officer's night stick and pushed into the back seat. Now I realised they were officers of the law; I suggested they drive me home and we could talk it over. Bang! I got hit again. We pulled up at the Beverly Hills Police Station.

I had no money on me, no identification except my Marion Davies platinum and diamond dress watch and diamond stud set.

It was all much clearer when the coffee awakened me early Sunday morning. I was in jail. Someone came by and said, 'You are allowed one telephone call.'

I called Dr Martin, who asked me what the charge was. I turned and asked the desk sergeant, 'What's the charge?'

'Drunk on the street,' he replied.

I called out into the phone, 'Drunk on the street.'

'Okay,' said Doc, 'I'll send Collins over with the twenty.' And he did.

I was sitting on Doc's bed, giving him a full account, when Louella arrived home from early Mass. When she'd been brought up to date she said, 'Oh oh, no one must know about you being in jail. I'll stop the press.' And she certainly did.

Doctor Harry Martin was Norma Talmadge's doctor. I was very fond of Doc, and through the years I found him to be a real friend and quite a character. He was – as the saying goes – as Irish as Paddy's pig, and there was rarely a party that Norma and I didn't end up in a corner listening to Doc. On one particular occasion he was telling us of Ireland and its asses. 'And you can't always trust the ass you sit on,' Norma interrupted as she pointed towards a famous star, recently widowed, who was leaving early with a well-known wolf.

'You must have cut that dress out with a knife and fork.'

After the Grable picture at Fox, *Mother Wore Tights*, I went to Universal International to do *Ivy* with Joan Fontaine for director Sam Woods, with whom I'd worked on *Kings Row* at Warners. The clothes in *Ivy* were Edwardian, a period which I'd always felt only Cecil Beaton should do. I think it was more the close cooperation of art director William Cameron Menzies plus Miss Fontaine's frail beauty which made the gowns I designed a success.

Louis B. Mayer, impressed with my work and designs on this picture, offered me a two-year contract at Metro at $102,000 plus vacations. Wanting to just freelance, I thanked Mr Mayer, but told him I had reached the point where I knew that to do a real job one must do only one picture at a time.

Shortly after being invited to take over at MGM, I was signed for *Pat and Mike*, starring Katharine Hepburn and Spencer Tracy, with Cukor directing.

In the studio commissary during lunch, I found myself back to back with costume designer Helen Rose, still not quite thawed out from her job with an ice show. She had skated over to MGM and taken the place of the talented and outstanding designer Irene. Or had she? On introduction, Miss Rose said, 'You know, I don't mind outside designers coming onto the lot.'

I thanked Miss Rose for benignity, and while tossing my salad I thought, how little she knew.

Mr Mayer's wife at the time, Lorena, an actress, was previously married to Danny

Danker, the former West Coast head of J.Walter Thompson Company. We were great pals. I'd known and had a great fondness for Lorena since her Warner Brothers contract days. There was something of the early Norma Talmadge look about Lorena, which is rare. Maybe that was why movie executive Joseph Schenck was so fond of her. Like her beauty, Lorena's friendship was rare.

When Danny Danker died he left her over a quarter of a million dollars' worth of comfort. Having a fine executive mind as well as her figure, J.Walter Thompson gave her an executive desk and a large expense account. She continued to live in her $750-a-month bungalow at the Beverly Hills Hotel with her little daughter Suzanna.

When Mr L.B. Mayer courted Lorena, he also paid court to Suzanna. First he won the child's affection and eventually Lorena's. It was some years after their marriage that Mr Mayer had a sad falling out with his daughter Edith, from his first marriage. Lorena did everything – but to no avail – to bridge the gap.

L.B. Mayer, like so many rich fathers with power, position and possession, raised his daughters like little Hollywood princesses. He gave them everything except real understanding. Irene, also from his first marriage and the stronger willed of the two, was always able to stand up to her father when he tried to bamboozle her. Edith was more feminine, and I knew of the fond affection she had for her dad, as she always called him. Before and after he died, it was hard for me to fathom how a father could hurt his daughter, who was the apple of his eye, the way Mr L.B. Mayer did.

I had great respect for Mr Mayer – what he did and stood for. His speeches at parties were something else again. I always felt that, like any sentimentalist, he 'lowered the coffin'.

During the Christmas holidays, the last eight years of Mr Mayer's life, Lorena always gave a pre-Christmas party, inviting her old friends – not all top drawer. At each party, when Mr Mayer made his speech, he would look at Lorena and say, 'The only real happiness I have ever found has been with Lorena.'

No one is easy to live with twenty-four hours of the day. I have always felt there is no compensation for boredom. If Lorena was ever bored during her marriage, no one will ever know. Lorena was like that.

Yet when L.B. Mayer died, in his will he left her only $750,000 but $7,000,000 to undesignated charities.

After every Paris opening, many Hollywood designers come out panning the blazes out of the 'greats' of this business. It's a cheap way to get their names in print. Then, within six months, after their eyes have been accustomed to the newness of the same designs they panned earlier, they themselves come out with an inferior copy. Thank God by the time the pictures are released, Paris is off on another style and the Hollywood copyist is caught with his or her pants down.

Let's face it, people seldom like their contemporaries. Al Jolson really was never as friendly with George Jessel as Jessel would have you believe. He respected Eddie Cantor because Eddie was a great Ziegfeld star. But frankly, Jolson in his heyday was a bit of a snob. I know, I designed some of his Winter Garden shows.

New York designer Hattie Carnegie always referred to Sophie Gimbel, designer at Saks of Fifth Avenue, as 'that woman up the street'.

I was all for Irene Sharaff, Oliver Messel, Cecil Beaton and Jean Louis.

Since 1935 designers tried to get together to form a union. Way back they called us 'The Big Four' – Adrian, Banton, Omar Kiam and myself.

For my money Kiam was by far the greatest. Time is the best test – Omar's clothes hardly dated.

The attorneys for the International Alliance of Theatrical Stage Employees called the four of us in to their office. After feeling the chill, they decided they weren't ready for designers. I guess they realised we were out of a different mould.

Then, later, all the studio designers met at costume designer Howard Greer's old Sunset Boulevard shop. As they entered one by one, I got to giggling. I guess the giggle water I imbibed didn't help. Greer, sitting on a small gold chair in the middle of the room said, 'What's so funny, Kelly?'

'Us,' I replied. 'I have never seen us as a group before.'

Then Greer said, 'It's no laughing matter. We must all get together.'

'Uh uh, spread out,' I told him.

And they spread out ever since. At least I did.

Good taste went out the window when a major studio engaged a tired New York hemstitcher. He had a little New York dress shop. Dressing little, and not so little, near-sighted old women was his specialty. He also specialised in dressing the circus. This tasteless creature, when not dressing pictures, dressed the boss's little wife – he cut her

*A rare gathering of movie studio designers at the West Coast Style Show
in Los Angeles in 1941: me, Bernard Newman, Travis Banton,
Edith Head and Irene.*

up in two. She ended up with one white and one blue bust. And one half of her bottom was white – the other blue. When I, like so many other designers, had to leave the studio, I told him, 'You dressed the circus and the horses looked pretty.'

Talk about the politicians getting out and hustling votes, they have nothing on Hollywood dress designers. Scheming, plotting and publicity campaigns are planned in the dark.

During my Army stretch, one female designer phoned my assistant, Leah Rhodes, and said, 'If you vote for my black-and-white picture I'll vote for your coloured one.' Leah justly deserved her Oscar for *Don Juan*. The other little woman added still another Oscar to the large collection of the Oscars she admired through dark glasses – including the one Givenchy should have been given for all the exquisite clothes he designed for Audrey Hepburn in *Sabrina*.

Just as I was taking bows after the release of *Ivy*, an important man in the industry phoned. At a dinner party the night before, where among others Mr Samuel Goldwyn had been a guest, my name came up in conversation. Miss Fontaine had insinuated that I wasn't around on the set when I was wanted. When my friend said, 'I thought Kelly was always reliable and on the job,' she quickly admitted such was the case, but then mentioned a woman designer at another studio. 'So-and-so's down on the set every morning when I am dressing.'

Miss Fontaine's husband at that period was Mr Bill Dozier, vice-president of Universal. I'd found him affable and always fair. I was doing additional pictures – in fact, two at a time.

The following morning I sent a message to the set by her wardrobe girl, telling Miss Fontaine that I was too old, too tired and too successful to fetch and carry for her on the set. Naturally, I never dressed her again.

One of the last weekends I spent at Fanny Brice's beach house, late in 1951, we talked into the early hours of the morning. The nurse was off and Fanny made up a daybed in the living room adjoining her small bedroom.

That afternoon Fanny and I played gin and the cards had run my way. Anything to break her losing streak, she said, 'Come on, kid, I've been promising this guy, Ludwig Bemelmans, I'd come over and see him all season.'

To you with Love me Tammy

We called on the writer at his beach house built on Maxwell House coffee tins. He opened a bottle of champagne for the occasion. I don't think we'd been there fifteen minutes when Fanny gave me the high sign. Out loud, she said her writers were waiting for her. As we passed through the small hall on the way out the back entrance, the bathroom door was open; we could see that rust had corroded the once white tub. The immaculate Fanny shuddered.

Bemelmans stammered, 'Fanny, what could that be in the tub?'

'I dunno, kid,' said Fanny, 'but it looks like _____ to me!'

Some years later, in his book, *The One I Love the Best*, Bemelmans spoke of having to take a sponge bath at the Hearst Ranch because the bathroom taps didn't work. I chuckled. With all the dozens of bathrooms at San Simeon, I don't think he tried very hard! His description of his overnight stay at the ranch was as full of fabrications as his reference to Elsie Mendl's drinking. Anyone who knew that great lady knew she never got tipsy; the only thing she ever drank was her 'house cocktail' – a little champagne. He also said Elsie called herself 'Mother' during her conversations with him. Most un-Elsie! I think he had great impertinence speaking of Lady Mendl as he did, and even greater impertinence to refer to himself as a painter. His daubs are half-ink, half-water, half-oil, half-arsed. No, I'm sorry, not half, three-quarters! He was eighth-rate Dufy – that is, the early Dufy, when he designed dress prints for Paul Poiret.

Dufy at this time allowed his paintings to become entangled with his textile designs; the results were arabesques. The Impressionists called him 'a milliner in paint'. Later Dufy produced some pictures with guts, and was smart enough to catch the same train as the avant-garde.

Fanny had a wonderful collection of paintings, all of which were painted by children about the age of Snooks. Bemelmans' work fitted in perfectly. Fanny said, after we reached home, 'You know, kid, I'm awfully glad we called on that guy today. You know me, I don't want anyone dropping in on me here at the beach.'

We then spoke of playwright and screenwriter Moss Hart and comic actress Helen Broderick, who had great affection for each other. Two complete opposites, yet they respected each other's talents; Moss was a gentle man, Helen was an arch exponent of caricature. If she cut anyone down, it was never on the bias, and never the little fellow. Yet, this woman with answers as short as a Manx's tail had a great self-persecution complex.

When Moss came to California in 1950, he bought several of my paintings, including a large one which he wanted to place over the mantel of his New York apartment. I was very flattered, and also glad to know he wasn't a 'name' buyer.

'I want to see Broderick,' Moss said, 'and Clifton Webb tells me she only goes to your place and to Fanny's.' Although Helen had starred with Clifton Webb and Marilyn Miller, she always said, 'I cannot go to his house, he's been the butt of my jokes for too many years.' Helen was honest. Following Moss's great success working with playwright George Kaufman, she continually goaded him. She would say, 'You don't need George Kaufman, why rely on him? There's nothing you can't do alone.'

When Moss's first child was born she immediately wired, 'You see, you don't need George Kaufman!'

Then Fanny and I started to talk about Hollywood and various people from the studio and their habits – both good and bad.

'Why do all dress designers drink so much?' Fanny asked. 'Look at so-and-so, such a charming woman, yet she's always going into a sanitarium. And Vera West, whom everybody loved, drowned herself in her own swimming pool. And little Bobby Kalloch, who took an overdose of pills? Why kid, why? Is it because most of you guys who do a woman's work feel that you're misfits?'

I shook my head. 'Maybe we feel if there isn't a place down here for us, maybe there won't be a place up there either . . .'

Fanny had already taken a sleeping pill. She was in the habit of talking or listening until she was ready to doze off. Usually she'd say, 'Okay, kid, scram, my pills are working.'

That night she rather groggily mumbled, 'Goodnight, Orry. Goodnight, Bijou.' Fanny's pill had worked; she was sleeping. It was late, but little did I realise how late.

The last conversation I had with the great Fanny Brice began one morning at ten minutes to ten. She usually complained of a backache or something. On this particular morning she had neither aches nor pains. She was in great spirits. As usual, the curious Fanny told me something about her personal early life, hoping I'd swap her a more juicy bit about mine. Then, for no reason, she said, 'Stick around long enough, kid, and the deal will come around to you. We all do many things which are not always attractive; sometimes in our youth we get away with them, but as we grow older we learn those same things and that same behaviour are most unbecoming. It's the finish that counts, kid.'

Unable to sleep, I went outside where I could smell the eucalyptus trees at the back of my house. Like me, they had been transplanted from Australia.

Poor dear Fanny was going down the stretch when she said, 'It's ten past ten, kid, I gotta scram. My nurse is out – I'm expecting my daughter Frances – I gotta get into the tub.'

Frances had only just arrived when her mother called for Alka-Seltzer. She had a gas pain. Then she keeled over. Four days and nights Fanny was in a coma. Dr Myron Prinzmetal, who diagnosed a cerebral haemorrhage, never left her side at the Cedars of Lebanon Hospital. Nor did her son Bill and her daughter Frances.

The fourth night, unable to sleep, I got out of bed and walked out onto the upstairs verandah. I smelled the eucalyptus trees in the back of my house. Like myself, they too had been transplanted from Australia. The planetarium was silhouetted against Griffith Park. Beyond was Hollywoodland – its thirty-foot electric sign lighting the gully below, where a young disappointed starlet had leaped to her death.

It was a few minutes before dawn and a flight of sparrows swarmed down into the trees. Like an orchestra, the birds began warming up – there seemed to be much confusion and commotion in the pit. A tapping sound rang out; sopranos, tenors, altos, basses – all chirping and whistling as they sounded their A notes. This is the hour, the moment, when life is at its lowest ebb. Life is given and life is taken.

Suddenly there was a chill in the air and a deathlike silence. A lone swallow took off and floated into the dark heavens. I might have imagined it, but I thought I heard a faint voice saying, 'Goodbye, Orry. Goodbye, Bijou.'

Fanny died early that morning.

Ava Gardner
One Touch of Venus

CHAPTER FIFTEEN

'Don't forget, Kelly, use lots of nice little clean four-letter words.'

ONE EVENING, JUST BEFORE Miss Claire Booth Luce left for her assignment in Rome as America's ambassador to Italy, Merle Oberon invited me to an intimate dinner, only six of us – Merle, Beverly Hills physician Dr Rex Ross, Miss Ethel Barrymore, Mr Cole Porter, Miss Luce and myself.

After dinner, when the coffee was being served, we sat round the fireplace. Miss Luce launched into a long dissertation, taking us down memory lane with stories of Mrs Cornelius Vanderbilt. She told us how 'Her Grace' only wore a pair of gloves once, etc. In fact, this went on and on, getting dull after a time. Miss Luce was telling things which Miss Barrymore and Mr Porter could possibly tell her! She even got to a point where she was describing the exclusive private Bailey's Beach at Newport, Rhode Island.

'One's social status,' she said, 'could be recognised according to how close one was to Mrs Vanderbilt's cabana.' She went on, 'There were always three eligible gentlemen surrounding her.'

I couldn't resist any longer. Looking over to Miss Barrymore, I said, 'Ethel, they could only be, first, Charles Hanson Towne; second, Schuyler Parsons; and the third one, I'm sure, would be Chesley Richardson, "Her Grace's" favourite extra man.'

Ethel replied, 'My God, Kelly, wherever did you dig up Chesley Richardson? I haven't heard of him in years.'

Dressing the luscious Ava Gardner in One Touch of Venus. Her multi-millionaire suitor at the time bypassed his usual diamond bracelet and gave her a Cadillac.

Miss Luce, realising she had been telling us a tired tale, shot me a look that only Sylvia from *The Women* could give.

There were stretches when I didn't visit Miss Ethel Barrymore, but I phoned her two or three times a week. She would listen and give suggestions. Like all amateurs, I over-described my characters, using two-guinea words when a two-bob one would have been much better. That was when Miss Barrymore would say, 'Don't forget, Kelly, use lots of nice little clean four-letter words.'

Once I enquired as to the whereabouts of her son Sammy. Miss Barrymore replied, 'Oh, he's up at Santa Barbara where no one uses that four-letter word W-O-R-K.'

At Universal-International Studios I had a very understanding and fair boss in William Goetz, president of the company. During the several years I worked there, I never had a disagreement with the democratic Mr Goetz, who was 'Bill' to many, and everyone spoke well of him.

But I had a slight to-do with Mr Goetz's production man, Jim Pratt. They were starting a new picture during a time when the axe was being used. I've forgotten the excuse this time; there have been so many periods of studio retrenchments.

Although the studio had two other designers under contract, Mr Goetz suggested I dress Ava Gardner in *One Touch of Venus*, but I'd have to take a cut in salary. Long used to those demands over the years, I suggested a better way to cut. There was a short scene in the script where Miss Gardner was supposed to go to the powder room; I suggested they save the money of building that set. 'Cut the can, don't cut me,' I told them. Bill Goetz has a good sense of humour besides a good business head. He cut out the can and I dressed the beautiful, talented Miss Ava Gardner.

Ava has something of a Greek coin beauty; her swan-like neck emerges from her shoulders in much the same manner as the young Ethel Barrymore of the Sargent drawing. Draping Ava's naked body in white jersey for *One Touch of Venus*, I'd never seen nipples tilted like hers – except perhaps on twelve- or thirteen-year-old Samoan beauties.

Don't believe all you might have read about her. She may have been tactless in some of her interviews – she happened to be honest and outspoken and, let's face it, with all that beauty, the hags were bound to hack. Early in her career I met her once for coffee before going shopping. I was giving my usual advice to young players. 'And another thing,' I said, 'if you ever go out with that multi-millionaire, get a diamond bracelet first, for he is notorious for wanting people to like him for himself.'

'You're a bit late with that' – the luscious Ava smiled back at me – 'he's already given me a Cadillac' – she sighed – 'but we had a spat. It was towed off yesterday morning.'

By the time I got to Deanna Durbin, she was at the 'I don't care' stage. She soon left for France and retirement.

Lenore Ulric was very colourful as Merle Oberon's maid in *Temptation*. Lenore was way ahead of her time in her Broadway days with producer David Belasco, wearing winter white; but she was way off the day she dropped into Bendel's and instructed the Custom Department, 'Make me the simplest type of travelling suit – in orchid satin!'

By now I was designing pictures at a flat fee. It only took me three weeks to earn my ten thousand dollars for *Night Song*.

The shape of a star is one of her major factors. There are rare exceptions, but a few great actresses don't care what shape they're in. There are the out-shaped, the over-shaped, the vulgar with little talent. There are no ends to which some stars won't go if it means attracting attention. Bosoms seem to burst out all over the wide screen. Paraffin had been used in this regard since the turn of the century, but it was very dangerous to inject, and vinyl plastic had been substituted. The advantage of using vinyl was that when the doctor inserted it into the breast, the plastic interlaced with the tissue, giving a sponge-like quality.

I dressed a singer – which I shouldn't have – and while explaining to my fitter the bustline effect I wanted, I took hold of the bodice at the cleavage. I thought I had taken hold of two apples as hard as rocks.

I can remember the time when it was easy to spot a strumpet. Today, externally there is very little difference between the nice women and the other kind. The dress and the make-up are the same. The only real difference is the behaviour, which, in the case of the extremely clever tart, is better and more discreet than the good little woman. The beautifully clothed and magnificently bejewelled courtesan of old was despised. Today she is envied and admired and invited everywhere. Not only the tabloids, but most newspapers and fashion journals, print her portraits and feature her gowns and jewels along with the elite of society. The best performances of these women are no longer restricted to a crib, but their own town houses. Every sweet young thing throughout the length and breadth of America – and the world for that matter – tries to look like, and copy, these well-heeled trollops who happen to be little smarter than the laced-mutton ladies of my Macquarie Street days in Sydney. They do exactly the same thing – only with fewer and richer men. They are allowed to appear on informal late TV shows and flaunt their prosperity under the guise of being actresses.

Toulouse-Lautrec painted the circus and the whorehouses. With the folding of the big top, Cafe Society is now a three-ring circus.

Zsa Zsa Gabor heard about a black-and-white outfit I had created for actress and one-time fashion model Joan Caulfield to wear at a Damon Runyon charity fashion show. The dress was a great hit, or rather the lovely peaches-and-cream complexion of Joan helped it to be a great hit.

The following morning my phone rang. It was Zsa Zsa. 'I must have zat drezz, dahleenk.'

I had never met Miss Gabor, but I had admired her lovely face for years. It reminded me of the faces on chocolate boxes I used to see when I was a child. She wanted to know 'zee price'. I told her the dress belonged to Miss Caulfield and I didn't care to discuss the price. But she was adamant. Finally I told her it cost $750, not including my fee.

'My gott you iss expensif!' There was a pause at the other end of the phone. Then she said, 'Oh vell, I go to Helen Rose. She iss only hav expensif as you.' And with only half my talent.

'Like yourself, Miss Gabor,' I assured her, 'Miss Rose is only just graduating from the Ice Follies! And speaking of *ice*,' I said rather loudly, 'which one of your remarkable family possesses the most?'

In the background I heard a dog barking into the phone. Then Zsa Zsa said, 'Oh, I'm so sorry, but the dog she do not seem to like vot you say – and my secretary say I am vanted on zee ozzer phone.'

The receiver clicked in my ear. I have a hunch Zsa Zsa knew she was dealing with an old established firm.

Yes, we had both been in business for quite a while.

I can remember the time when it was easy to spot a strumpet.

Shelley Winters, with George Cukor's training, became an excellent actress. Then the studio cast her in a remake of a Marlene Dietrich South Sea movie. This was too much! The pads began to fly. They were trying to make a young Mae West out of her. Shelley was very excitable, and so are designers. I saw her, in her excitement, before going in front of the camera, stuff two falsies in one bosom and three in the other – no wonder she looked lopsided at times! When Shelley went in for pads, which she actually didn't need, I went back to the bottle – screwdrivers, this time. I was getting cunning; you can't smell a vodka hangover.

After two years of Shelley's pouting and pecking, I couldn't take it any longer. I turned down a year's contract at Universal-International.

Hedda Hopper – whose book *From Under My Hat* was just out – meant well when she called and advised me to sign with the studio, as conditions were getting pretty bad in the picture business in 1952. 'If you don't sign,' Hedda said, 'what will you do?'

In my meanest morning hangover voice I said, 'Oh, I guess I'll just wear a funny hat and write a book.'

There wasn't a more beautifully shaped head in Hollywood than Hedda Hopper's. For someone who had belonged in the beauty class so long, I asked Hedda, 'How come people said you laid an egg in pictures?'

'I came from Quaker stock,' Hedda said, 'and being nimble on my feet I could get around the bosses' office desks much faster than they.'

If Hedda laid an egg in pictures, she certainly laid a golden egg when she Mother Goosed herself by dipping her quill into an inkwell. Writing about the stars instead of trying to remain one gave her a golden nest egg. Decades later, Hedda, by now no Quiz Kid, could still stand in the Hollywood beauty line.

Fearless, she consistently used red ink when writing about Red actors, writers and producers. Never one to sit on the fence – if she were to, I'm sure we'd discover she wore red, white and blue drawers.

If Hedda Hopper laid an egg in pictures, she certainly laid a golden egg when she dipped her quill into an inkwell. Here she shows her peerless style leading the cast of Midnight.

Hollywood columnist Hedda Hopper holding forth, wearing one of her more demure signature hats. Hedda was never one to sit on the fence – if she were to, I'm sure we'd discover she wore red, white and blue drawers.

In a day and age of sloppy joes and sloppier jeans, robot dancers shaking their fists at the Lean Angry Young Women, becoming more like the Angry Young Men, it was a delight to see Miss Hedda Hopper beautifully quaffed, hatted and gowned in her *Hedda Hopper's Hollywood Spectacular*.

Viewing her show, critic R.H. Sherwood remarked, 'Somehow the word as well as the condition of "elegance", seems to have disappeared, except among a few high echelons of society, who have not yet, at least, surrendered to 'T' shirts, sloppy plaid pants, pony tails and ballet slippers. Miss Hopper was elegance itself.'

Hedda was an elegant woman, and when it came to wearing clothes she could hold her own with all comers and ages on the TV screen, in the drawing rooms of Hollywood, New York, the San Francisco Opera or Barnby Blarny. And of course her love of hats became legendary.

When it came to hats, put any kind of frosting atop of Ann Sothern's cute pussycat face and she looked well; and once Lucille Ball threw away her cartwheel hats she was a different dish.

Carol Channing was a big blonde rag doll stuffed with talent instead of sawdust. She was more Tallu than Tallulah, more wicked than Dietrich and had not quite as much Sophie as Tucker.

Carol had inexhaustible energy and talent, and if she weren't so tactful you could have gone mad getting the effect she wanted. Her clothes had to be utterly simple. Not even a button, earring or glove must detract from her act – as if anything could have detracted from those outsized eyes!

CHAPTER SIXTEEN

Like murder and morphine, fashion has become front page news.

FASHION HAS ALWAYS HAD its shape. Women have sometimes shaped history. Few have shaped fashion. Like murder and morphine, fashion has become front page news. It has often been a barometer. The times and conditions, economically and politically, have had their effect on fashion.

The painted butterflies – the actresses of the stage and screen – may be copied by the midget moths, but rarely affect fashion in the main.

Until the twentieth century, fashion was governed by royalty. As the sun never sets on the British Empire, English queens and members of their family have had good and bad effects. There was a time when one would never dare criticise clothes worn by royalty.

I prefer to put the blame for a rash of bad taste on the Court designer Norman Hartnell – thank goodness it ended with the marriage of Princess Margaret. It is quite evident the charming little princess informed Hartnell she would have none of the butterflies, spangles, beads, seed pearls and rhinestones he splashed all over her sister's bouffant court gowns. Hartnell obviously didn't know that rhinestones don't go well with the priceless Mountain of Light or Star of Africa diamonds, any more than salted butter goes with fresh beluga caviar.

Bad fashion, and its shape, all began way back with Princess Margaret's great-grandmother, Queen Victoria. During Queen Victoria's reign, Anglo-

Saxon taste was at its lowest ebb. Her Majesty's clothes were as busy, and had the same 'mess' of detail, as her buildings and arcades. Not shaped for clothes, she was more interested in building an empire than the building of her hoop skirts and bustles. Having no family plaid, Queen Victoria designed her own, which was unfortunate because it made her look even more roly-poly.

Queen Victoria had married off seven of her children, all of whom were first taught to speak German, to petty and impecunious German princes and princesses. Behind the scene a big family feud was brewing, dating back to the Queen's daughter. She was a high-spirited girl of seventeen. There was the question of her marriage to the German Emperor being performed in Prussia. Queen Victoria wrote caustically to Lord Clarendon, ambassador in Berlin: *Whatever may be the usual practice of Prussian Princes, it is not every day that one marries the eldest daughter of the Queen of England!*

Princess Victoria did go on to marry the German Emperor. She took his name, Empress Frederick, upon his death, when their eldest son became Kaiser.

When Edward, Prince of Wales, succeeded Queen Victoria, who died in 1901, the Court took on a new look. Before he took over his royal responsibilities, he often attended his favourite theatre – The Gaiety.

After he became King Edward VII, the strict Victorian customs disappeared. His gay companions had style along with beauty. The lovely Lillie Langtry, Lady Londonderry and Lady de Grey were far outshadowed by his magnificent enamelled Alexandra. Only a chosen few are born with the subtle refinements of true chic. It is born in one, rarely acquired. Queen Alexandra had it, and so did the Duchess of Kent. And, much later, the Duke of Windsor's Wallis.

It was an age of elegance and ecru – almost everything was in the palest eggshell tones of ecru, the softest of Charmeuse satins, taffetas, brocades, chiffons, sheer mulls and moted veilings, laces of Battenburg, Brussels, rose point, Valenciennes, and Val.

When calling in their carriages, their only once-used kid gloves were held daintily in a small gold mesh bag; a tiny gold pencil was always attached to the engagement book; cards with turned-down corners signified they had been left in person.

Life was calm and gentle. The soft folds of their skirts were as graceful as the wearers. It was known as the Mauve Decade, but it was the men who wore mauve gloves – well, not all. But most men wore cornflowers and rosebuds in their buttonholes.

The Kaiser with his modern-made Germany wanted Russia as an allied vassal. Austria was a subject nation and France an impotent weakling. With Germany's growing population, the Kaiser demanded a more powerful fleet to take care of the country's rapidly expanding commerce. He also sought to make his English cousins a second-rate naval power.

On May 6th, 1910, King Edward VII – known to the man in the street as 'Teddy' – died at the age of fifty-nine. 'The King, Edward VII is dead. Long live King George V.'

There was great advancement mechanically leading up to the First World War, and there was great prosperity. With everyone earning more money, there was fun, but behind the fun was fear; yet no one seemed to do anything about it.

There is no fight like a family fight, and no race is more stubborn than the German race – and the way the Duchess of Teck, the Dowager Queen Mary, later treated her favourite son, the Duke of Windsor, proved that she, too, had a stubborn streak. When King Edward VII died, it was difficult for Queen Mary to follow the magnificent Queen Alexandra. The English – particularly the middle class – like the queens rich and royal. The Tecks were far from well off, Queen Mary's father being the son of a prince of Wurttenburg. There was much fuss as to Her Majesty 'not being a considerable royal personage by birth'.

Short in stature, King George V complained of her large plumed hats. When the Queen concocted a crown-like velvet toque, chose powder blue for daytime frocks, carried cumbersome handbags and umbrellas, and wore two-tone low-heeled unbecoming shoes, she truly was a royal dowdy dresser. Furthermore, wanting to be comfortable, she used her royal rights – no one dared argue with her.

Gone were the soft folds and graceful flowing skirts of what may one day be called 'The Beaton Period' – the Edwardian years that Cecil Beaton recaptured so handsomely. In its place were the stiff, staid skirts of Queen Mary.

France must have felt the pressure of the Kaiser as he tried to slow down the other European nations. Paris came out with the hobble skirt. Gone was the freedom of Edwardian flounces. The long skirts were buttoned at the ankle, slowing the pace. Women began decking themselves out in the most frivolous fashions: gold brocades, dripping pearls wound around the body, climaxing in fish or caterpillar trains bordered in everything from skunk to chinchilla.

The creator of these and other 'lampshade' fashions was Paul Poiret. He was the first designer of the twentieth century to completely revolutionise fashion.

Poiret was born in a section of bourgeois Paris but was smart enough to move to another quarter, where he began his career by opening a small umbrella shop. He had a talent for many things, but his greatest talent was collecting *other* talent – like Drian, the great illustrator, and Dufy, who designed and painted his fabrics. But it was Bakst whose wonderful oriental designs and theatrical costumes influenced Poiret most of all.

He never used a toile; he didn't believe in cutting the piece. The stuffs he used – sumptuous brocades from the Far East – were wound around the body, ending in a long tapering train. Trailing up and down staircases the wearers looked like caterpillars. His things weren't dresses – they were costumes.

Then Poiret shortened the corset and loosened women's busts. At the same time he shackled them with the hobble skirt.

Women have sometimes shaped history. Few have shaped fashion.

Paris must have heard the clanking of the Kaiser's sword as he bullied and belittled his in-laws, because, in 1914, the peg-top skirt made its appearance. Never in fashion history had anything been quite so bold. The Kaiser himself got bolder, politically, as the skirts split up to the knee, and even the Queen's sombre toque couldn't quell the rising hemline, or the revealing mode of dress. As international tensions grew worse, the tight hobble skirts unbuttoned and burst wide open. Poiret's slinking fishtail trains disappeared, along with the common sense of the public.

Reasoning became futile. Diplomacy abdicated. After the murder of Franz Ferdinand and his wife, Europe erupted like a steaming volcano into a bloody, terrible and futile war. At midnight on August 4th, 1914, Great Britain declared war on Germany. Women for the first time donned sailor middies and soldier jackets. Designers, cutters and fitters put away their scissors, pins and needles.

By the end of the war, the people of England realised the unexpected brilliance of their practical queen in organising war work. Snobbery and European nepotism disappeared and Queen Mary emerged a very popular and beloved queen. Unlike the monarchs who had come before her, she spoke without a German accent. When she wore regal robes of state, with one of her three diamond crowns, a nine-strand pearl

dog collar and Mary Queen of Scots-style ropes and ropes of huge pearls, she was every inch a queen.

The First World War came to an end in 1918 and hundreds of thousands of girls, ready to take over men's jobs, were ready for change. But Poiret, who had reigned over fashion throughout, refused to alter his ideas.

Madeleine Vionnet, the first designer to make a seam count, introduced the basic bias-cut black dress. She was also the first architectural designer and her clothes were sculptured. Like smoke which surrounds but never touches the body, her clothes had ease.

It was Gabrielle Chanel, better known as Coco, realising the coming economic change, who practically put Poiret out of business overnight. Chanel came from Saumur, France. She was one of three motherless sisters raised in the country by nuns who, luckily, taught them to sew.

In 1913, she opened a little hat shop in northern France. After the First World War, with her uncanny intuition, she sensed feminine emancipation and realised that women who had worn uniforms and middies would now want freedom of dress. She began designing all the basic and functional things she had seen in the country as a young girl. She adapted the little box coat which the porters wore. The simple white blouses with collars and cuffs – a fashion that was still in vogue forty years later. She also sensed the long daytime skirt was impractical for women taking over men's work in civilian life. Having pretty legs, she hiked her skirts up to her knees. One of her sisters had a boyfriend in the French Navy. One day Chanel borrowed his striped T-shirt and brought the look of the French sailor into the George Cinq hotel in Paris. She was a sensation overnight.

As Chanel became rich, she began collecting oriental pearls in all shades, except black. It was Chanel who taught the rich it was smart not to look rich – not to wear their riches on their backs. She put them in a simple little wool jersey, using the greige – the fabric's natural shade. But she put a fortune around her own neck when she wore her oriental pearls with her daytime sweaters. Still later, as she became richer, she added huge chunks of emeralds scattered among the pearls. She started the vogue for costume jewellery, and people around the world also sniffed Chanel's No. 5.

Not only did she put Poiret out of business, but the entire corset industry as well. She built houses and a luxurious apartment. She had many admirers, among them the Duke of Westminster. When Hoyningen-Huene, the great fashion photographer for *Vogue* and *Harper's*, was discussing clothes with her, Mlle Chanel asked, 'Do you know what elegance is, Baron Huene?' Tapping her clavicle with her forefinger, she replied, '*I am elegance itself!*'

When the Duke of Westminster asked her to marry him, she told him, 'There have been several Duchesses of Westminster, but there is only *one* Chanel.'

Fashion is frivolous and flighty. Who would have thought that a little tricornered hat could almost put the great Chanel out of business? But that's exactly what happened. When Greta Garbo wore her Empress Eugenie hat in *Romance*, women the world over wanted to emulate her. This tricornered hat did not go with Chanel's clothes. Mlle Chanel went out through the swinging door of fashion and in came Balenciaga.

Along with the romantic period influence came Balenciaga's black and brown Goya period. He said, 'Woman is a flower.' Romantic clothes were back!

Cristóbal Balenciaga was born of simple parents in a fishing village near the Bay of Biscay. Fashion is always going somewhere, and Balenciaga was the unrivalled leader for twenty years.

Carmel Snow of *Harper's Bazaar* was quick to realise Balenciaga would become the leading designer of the haute couture. She consistently boosted him. He had his first showing in 1937; and in 1946, when Dior opened his salon, Balenciaga hinted at the full long skirt, gathered at the waist, with rounded hips. However, he made only a few models and unfortunately didn't follow through. So it was Dior who came out with his New Look in 1947.

Christian Dior was born in Granville in the province of Normandy. His father was a wealthy chemical manufacturer. One of France's largest fabric houses got behind Dior. He was a new name and this company wanted the New Look because he used enormous amounts of materials. He lined and interlined dresses to warm, to cover up and to thaw out the knees and legs of France.

Poiret, Chanel, Balenciaga and Dior were the four giants – the royalty of twentieth-century fashion.

There have been many minor royalty, in fact too many to list. Often a designer will create a new silhouette. He knows only too well that the press can make or break him. Preferring criticism to oblivion, he does not include something he has started the year before and another designer may come along to give the original creation a slight twist.

He gets the credit. Whether Balenciaga thought of the New Look or not, he was the reigning king of twentieth-century fashion. Should he have abdicated, Givenchy, his Crown Prince, would take his place. Till then, Balenciaga would remain the Font of Fashion.

Best-dressed lists can be as tiresome as Fauvist painter Vlaminck's cold wintery skies. These lists are usually tied in with gimmicks and guilds. There is nothing original – including sin. There are only eight notes for a composer to arrange variations of in order to create a new melody. There are just so many necklines. Only a few select women with true chic could take something Balenciaga plucked from the future and, wearing it her own way, add a personal touch to make it appear different. But the same women could be just as alluring in a Charles James heirloom ball gown, a Falkenstein or a Zuckerman suit; anything the brilliant Norell made, an ageless Mainbocher or something gorgeous from Galanos.

My twentieth-century Best Dressed List includes socialite and author Rita de Acosta Lydig, who went by the nom de plume Mrs Philip Lydig. Others are The Countess Salm – the former Millicent Rogers, the Standard Oil heiress. The Duchess of Windsor. Heiress Mrs Harrison Williams, who became Countess Harold von Bismarck. Actress and dancer Irene Castle. Broadway comedienne and film actress Ina Claire, who became Mrs William Wallace. Socialite and *Vogue* fashion editor Babe Paley. Mrs William Randolph Hearst Jr, and Mrs Ray Stark – the daughter of Fanny Brice.

My worst first, second and third are: actress Fannie Ward, socialite Mrs George Washington Kavanaugh and silent movie actress and producer Hope Hampton.

Mitzi Gaynor,
Kay Kendall and
Taina Elg
in Les Girls

CHAPTER SEVENTEEN

You wouldn't want to have angry bosoms, would you?

EVERY NOW AND THEN I take a breather. It's been a long time since I started this book. Most autobiographies must travel the same ground. I found myself asking advice – should I tell of this or that? If it was about someone my friends didn't particularly care for, they would invariably say, 'Kelly, you must tell that.'

I told them of the evening Jack Benny's wife, Mary Livingstone, looked down the bar of J.L. Warner's playroom and said, 'Tell me, do I look like half those dames along the bar?' I took a look and – seeing Marlene Dietrich, Dolores del Rio, Hedy Lamarr, Ann Warner and her house guest Lady Diana Manners – replied, 'From the shoulders up . . . no!'

Then those same people said, 'Oh, I wouldn't write that, you may lose readers. Jack Benny is so popular.'

But designers don't always remain popular. Everyone has a selfish bone or two in his or her body.

Stars are fickle. The designer goes in and out of fashion with them, just like off-the-face hats and roller skating.

A national magazine was giving me a large spread. They wanted a photo of Dolores del Rio and myself. Warners weren't sure they would make her third picture – her second one had flopped. I phoned Dolores. After a long, long wait a servant told me, 'Miss del Rio she is walking in ze jardin.'

A week later the studio decided to go ahead with the third picture. The phone rang bright and early. It was Dolores. I excused myself to *find myself*. Still talking into the phone I said, 'Come, Bijou, we go find Mr Kelly.' Then, after a long wait, I told her, 'Mr Kelly he is walking in ze jardin.' That afternoon, when Dolores entered my office, we simultaneously threw our arms around each other.

As I write this I find myself talking to myself. Should I tell this titbit on Dolores? Why not! We have always been genuinely fond of each other and, anyway, orange juice in the morning often sours one.

I don't know whether it was orange juice in Merle Oberon's case the morning I called her. Merle was no longer in pictures; she was now Mrs Bruno Pagliai. I knew she was in town. She had called Louella with some news. This particular morning Merle was short. Hell, not short – abrupt. She had no time to speak to me. She had to meet Bruno at the airport in an hour. I quickly explained I was just checking on a story about Elsa Maxwell.

'My God,' said Merle, 'surely you're not going to print that in your book, are you?'

'Why not, Merle, it's the truth.'

'I know it's the truth, Orry dear, but I wouldn't write about it if I were you.'

I told Merle I was telling the truth about myself and about others, including herself.

All of a sudden she was in no hurry. 'Orry dear, why don't you dine with Bruno and me this evening?'

When I hung up I jotted down exactly what I've just written. Bijou stirred at my feet. Looking at him, I asked, 'Should I tell it, Bijou?' Bijou wagged his tail.

That evening, with dinner on a tray and Bijou at my feet, I wrote into the night.

If you hear someone say that Joan Crawford – with all her success, wealth and glory – was a very unhappy girl, don't you believe it.

If the Hollywood stars had a sweepstake, I'd put my money on Joan Crawford and Cary Grant for the daily double.

For decades their names were in lights, blinking on and off, and the world's presses flashed headlines about their doings – what they did, with whom, and even why. When

Dolores del Rio, looking gloriously imperious in one of the costumes I designed for Madame Du Barry.

I read, or rather heard, of some saccharine sister's sick story of how she had been hurt, I had to laugh.

Joan Crawford was never even bruised, much less hurt. She saw to that when she shed her cocoon and spun the golden web. From the very beginning she would stop at nothing if it meant furthering her career; and she herself became her career. To achieve success meant complete dedication, a great deal of study and years of hard work.

Crawford swam and exercised every bone in her body. The beautiful bone structure of her face made her one of the world's most talked about women – at least over the longest period. Joan had mean beginnings. I don't know how many changes Crawford had as Lucille LeSueur when she danced in the Shubert Winter Garden. But I do know Cary had just a little tin box and what was on his back. Even then he was never shy or reticent – always alert and aware. He was just as indestructible as Joan. He might have started out as a bad stage actor but he studied and learned the magic of the magic lantern. Like Joan, there was nothing he didn't know about screen technique. Once she was filthy rich, she went from gauche to grandeur. Yet both she and Grant were afraid to tackle the stage.

After seeing Grant walk down the stairway with Kim Novak at the Academy Awards finale, I realised why; there was just a suggestion of the bent knee and slight pigeon toe about his stage walk. This doesn't happen on screen. At that time I asked him if he would do a stage play. His answer: 'Never!'

But while Cary Grant was worth millions and still had his first twopence, the overgenerous and extravagant Crawford had spent more than her last nickel.

Joan Crawford spent a fortune on clothes. She had a personal dressmaker on her payroll. She bought the finest fabrics, brocades and embroideries, but somehow – maybe by intention – she dressed for the taste of her multitude of fans, the same fans she continued to inform of her whereabouts, the time she would leave her apartment, what theatre she would attend, what street she would walk, what nightclub she would be in, even what was cookin' and what have you! Her fans copied and demanded her *Letty Lynton* sleeves. She squared her mouth and the mouths of many other screen personalities. It became a worldwide vogue from the time her waistline was lower than Ward Bond's in *Wagon Train* – but it took Kay Kendall in just one picture, *Les Girls*, to wipe it off the screen with her Gainsborough Cupid's-bow lips.

Actors never stop acting, even when their careers are ended. They still 'get on'. They all have implicit faith in themselves. In Cary's case, his faith ended with himself. When we were both young, our biggest brawls were over his *not believing*. He had no *faith*. I realised his torture. For many years his mother had been mentally ill. When I told him, 'You must have faith of some kind,' the battle would be on. Later, I don't know how he felt about faith, or about the truth. Nor do I know of Crawford's faith – except the faith she had in herself.

Joan Crawford's oldest friend was William Haines. He had an enormous respect and deep affection for the lady he called Miss Cranberry. When Haines was a star, Crawford was his leading lady. He had two careers. He was a silent star. Then he talked when the talkies came in. But he made a much bigger career as an interior designer, talking the stars into redecorating their homes. He was the last word in elegance and good taste, and he would take your last nickel. As Fanny Brice once said, 'He ain't cheap, kid.'

And I replied, 'But he's worth it.'

Shortly after Easter one year, Bill Haines rang me up, 'Kelly, I attended Joan Crawford's last supper.'

I choked a laugh with, 'Just a moment, Bill, there's someone at my door.' Of course there wasn't. Grabbing a pencil and paper I decided this was my chance to get the final analysis on Miss Crawford. Later, when I tried to read my own illegible scribble, only bits of the witty, caustic Haines remained. He was more than caustic – he could be as cutting as the French artist Sem's wicked caricatures of celebrities of the belle époque. He told me Joan phoned saying, 'Please come, dahling, and have Easter supper with just the children and me – there's something I want to tell you. Also please bring your little sister, Lillion, as she might enjoy just being with the family – very informal, dahling.'

Billy stands six foot one and his little sister is only a few inches shorter. He had accepted Joan Crawford's invitation, as he had been doing for the last thirty-five years. 'Knowing from all those gathering years of Crawford's very informal fiestas, Kelly, I warned my little sister to wear a dinner dress, and I wore a tie, adding a carnation for the bunny.'

There were fourteen guests, two butlers and two maids, for an elaborate dinner. Among the ones at the table were *Dragnet*'s Jack Webb and wife; Jule Styne, the songwriter; and other faces he had never seen before. Then Joan told her secret. But,

Bill said, she directed her tear-stained words to him: 'Willie, dahling, I wanted you to be the first to know that I have sold this house in which I have lived for the last thirty-one years to Donald O'Connor.'

'Something pulled at the corner of my heart, Kelly, and I knew I had to reply as all those faces were looking to me for an answer. I did not get up when I lifted my glass, but said, "I would like to drink a toast to This Old House. I have been coming here for years to these little family dinners, and I feel that This Old House and her mistress are part of my blood and bones. It was the mother and father of my career, and it makes me sad to see them go. It's like the passing of an era – to me it's the passing of a true and capable friend. I remember when I first started work on This Old House, it was about Crawford's four husbands ago. After each husband it was scrubbed, tubbed and recovered, deleted and added to – I won't admit to myself that you are pulling up all your roots here. I know you're not, because I have a little cottage where I live for your return and, as the Spanish say, *esta casa es su casa* – this house is your house. There is a guest room there waiting for you – your room – without notice come any time. But, the day you move in, Cranberry, is the day I move out". '

Producer Sol Siegel of MGM Studios engaged me to design his production *Les Girls*.

Mitzi Gaynor had exactly the right amount up front. When Mitzi's many ringlets and curls were brushed out and up, George Cukor said, 'I never realised Mitzi has such a beautiful neck and shoulders.'

It was Cukor who saw Taina Elg walk into the studio cafe for lunch. He liked her fresh young looks. He tested her. Sol Siegel had already engaged Kay Kendall and Mitzi. He gave Taina the other part in *Les Girls*, which George Cukor was to direct.

Cukor, the discoverer of subtle talent, I'm sure got bored with being called 'the great woman's director'. Nevertheless it was true. He was something of a magician. His alert eye revealed a latent beauty which the average director rarely sees. To emphasise his point to an actor or an actress, his right hand rose in rapid movement as his wide gestures sought to clarify and induce the illusion he sought.

Since the stage gave him his early training, his shelves were crowded with a

November 9th, 1957
Vol. 69   No. 1806   Every Tuesday

Picture Show
THE PAPER FOR PEOPLE WHO GO TO THE PICTURES

& FILM PICTORIAL

4D.

GENE KELLY *with* MITZI GAYNOR
KAY KENDALL *and* TAINA ELG *in*
"LES GIRLS"

For designing Les Girls I had a dream cast with Mitzi Gaynor, Gene Kelly, Kay Kendall and Taina Elg, and a magician in director George Cukor.

wealth of books and pictures dealing with the theatre. He recognised and was devoted to those with superior talent. His house, like his magnificent gardens, had roots. He had five dogs. Scattered throughout five sitting rooms were many paintings, pictures and bibelots.

It was a warm sunny day. George invited Merle Oberon and myself to Sunday lunch. He was having the Sitwells, who were to give a lecture the following evening at Royce Hall, UCLA.

Cukor said, 'Kelly, if you will shut up for a change and listen, you may learn something.' Difficult as it was, I took his advice.

Dame Edith and her brother, Sir Osbert, and a secretary had come directly from the Los Angeles railroad station. The great English poetess sat on her host's right. Her long aesthetic countenance resembled a monk of the Middle Ages, but what fascinated me most was the medieval headpiece which had more veils than even impresario Minnie Maddern Fiske loved to wear. Her tiny eyes were searing and haughty. For long periods her head, neck, shoulders and body seemed immovable. But the most disarming thing about this patrician creature was her magnificent sensitive hands which were mostly in repose; when she raised her hands in gesture you saw the third fingers of both hands were weighted down with six enormous turquoise rings. The shock over, you realised that, unlike her face, which is that of an old soul, she had the hands of a girl. She wore an ankle-length dark dress covered with two voluminous coats with bat-like sleeves; the outer one was fur trimmed. She had placed her fur gloves on her lap. She kept both coats on while she lunched.

I sat between Merle Oberon and Sir Osbert, who had some coddled egg on the lapel of his tweeds. Although I was directly opposite Dame Edith, I had great difficulty hearing her, and watching her mouth was of no help, since she hardly moved a muscle of her magenta lips. Much of her conversation was said while gazing at the lovely Merle. Such a wonderful study in contrasts: two ladies with a past. Both, I felt, had definitely been on earth before – they could have lived centuries ago.

Dame Edith, an extraordinary, almost mystical figure in the world of letters, often wrote in the rhythms of Sappho; but her spoken observations were more down-to-earth. She said, 'I do not have that lady's unfortunate disposition. I am a throwback of my Plantagenet ancestors and I know I look it. My mental life is so violent that I have no physical life to speak of. I am like an unpopular electric eel in a pond full of flat fish. I am simply alive. Nobody has been more alive than I.'

Two babies were born around the same time in Hobart, the capital city of the tiny island of Tasmania, Australia: Merle Oberon and Errol Flynn. They were destined to light up the sky around the world just as the Southern Cross lights up the heavens Down Under.

According to the story Merle told early in her career, she was born Estelle Thompson O'Brien and she was the daughter of a policeman. The family moved to Launceston, where her handsome mother ran a hotel. When Merle was seven, her mother took her to India, leaving copper O'Brien in Tasmania. Later it was revealed that Merle was actually born Estelle Merle Thompson in India. Her mother was Indian, and her father, Arthur Thompson, was a railway engineer who later went into the British Army.

Whatever her origin, it was inevitable that Miss O'Brien would become Miss Oberon, the international beauty and movie star. She belonged in the big world. Her almond-shaped face was one of a kind. Her jewels were fabulous; she owned the Empress Josephine emerald and diamond necklace, which seemed so at home on her throat. I saw her wear other diamond necklaces, two at a time, and on Merle they seemed right, while on someone else they would look vulgar. Everything she did seemed to be to the manor born. Everything about her had been carefully planned – her poise, her dignity, her manner of speech. And, topping it all, she had the most devastating charm.

I felt the Grand Old Lady of English Poetry, who looked like a Spanish conquistador, was searching within the beautiful Merle. Narrowing her piercing eyes, she seemed to be thinking: 'Someone with *so much* must have a secret barricaded deep in her soul.' Maybe the great dame was wishing she could trade actual experience with Merle instead of having to write about her own emotional problems.

The pain of early youth conditions some people to remain perfectly calm and without emotion – like Merle. All of us have memories hovering about in the back of our minds that we would like to forget.

Everything Merle Oberon did seemed to be to the manor born – her poise, her dignity, her manner of speech. Topping it all was her devastating charm.

The searching look in the 'Old Soul's' eyes got me to thinking: Maybe Merle could really have been Napoleon's Josephine, or Lord Nelson's Emma. Then again, she could have been the one out of a thousand and one nights of *Scheherazade*. I was dying to say, 'A penny for your thoughts, Dame Edith.' But of course I couldn't; it would have been impertinent. And, besides, I'd promised my host to keep my mouth shut.

The following evening the Sitwells gave their lecture in the large college hall, and many earnest students paid to hear them. When Sir Osbert asked the audience if they could hear him, many called out, 'No, no, no!'

'Pay more attention, then you will,' Sir Osbert replied in a matter-of-fact tone.

This whispering seemed to be a family trait, for as I write this, a recent clipping from the *London Daily Mail* stated:

When the galleryites of the packed Lyceum shouted, 'We can't hear you!' Dame Edith Sitwell broke off her poetry recital at the Edinburgh Festival, wagged a heavy jewelled finger at her audience and told them: 'Get a hearing aid, I am not going to shout with my own voice. Don't you think after all the reciting I have done I don't know my onions?'

There are many kind people in this town of Hollywood who help a lot of people, but somehow this 'kindness' always seems to get into the movie columns. George Cukor, our host that night with the Sitwells, was not only the kindest man in Hollywood – for he untiringly helped so many with their careers – it was the manner in which he did it. His infinite tact and deference while he generously helped the aged made him a rarity in the eyes of the true elite.

I got to know the great Garbo at some of Cukor's dinner parties and Sunday lunches. She also visited Cole Porter and Miss Ethel Barrymore.

One Sunday, when Miss Barrymore lived way down at Palos Verdes, a good three-quarters of an hour's drive, I picked up Miss Harriet Brown – a name Garbo liked to use when travelling. I found her completely relaxed. She had brought along her Hauser Diet lunch in a crushed little brown paper bag. I told her she mustn't bring her own lunch to Ethel's. 'Oh,' she said, 'maybe Miss Barrymore might be insulted?'

That Sunday Miss Barrymore's son Sammy Colt made extra-strong cocktails, a thing he could do well. Garbo ate and laughed heartily.

During the long drive back the great Garbo became completely relaxed. She laughed a lot and I found her to be sensitive, modest and wise. She asked, 'What is the most important thing a designer must have?'

'Integrity,' I told her. 'I've always felt that everyone should be surrounded with a wall of discretion. Designers are a sort of mentor. We are, or should be, bound by professional secrecy and, uninvited, we have no right to penetrate into people's private lives.'

The longest eyelashes in the world swept up. Looking at me, she took hold of my hand and said, 'Ah, you funny man you, one minute you make me laugh and now . . .' She didn't continue, but there was a sort of communication in the way she looked at me and squeezed my hand. I felt it was a great privilege to become so close to this great woman.

George Cukor gave a large Sunday luncheon for his friend Irene Selznick, the Broadway producer. Garbo and I sat holding hands, as she said, 'with her funny man'. Opposite us sat Edith Goetz, wife of movie producer William Goetz, fascinated by the beauty of Garbo. It was quite obvious Garbo in her slacks and sweater wore no bra – and, like her beautiful face, there was no sag to her firm bosom.

As people began to arrive I kidded, 'Maybe we'd better stop holding hands. People may talk.'

The modest Garbo tossed her head back and said, 'Oh, no, everyone knows we are just a couple of old fogies.'

Visiting my studio one day, she was fascinated with one of my pictures. In fact, she was about to buy, then she shrugged her shoulders: 'What's the use, I only have one room furnished in my house. I would only turn it to the wall. It is so lovely, someone must have it – that others can see and enjoy its beauty.'

Back in 1946, George Cukor was to direct *Razor's Edge*. Darryl Zanuck had engaged me to design the clothes. Somerset Maugham had been house-guesting with Cukor.

The day before Maugham departed for home, I brought my sketches to show him. There were just Lady Mendl, Cukor and Mr Maugham lunching. Fanny Brice reneged at the last minute. Later, when Cukor took Lady Mendl to the gate, Maugham turned to me and said, 'I am sorry Fanny Brice didn't come to see me. She's one of the few women I've been really fond of. I won't ever see her again. I am seventy years of age. Tomorrow I go home to make peace with my Maker.'

Wanting to protect Fanny, I said, 'Mr Maugham, with Fanny it's really not a case of being selfish, it's more thoughtlessness on her part.'

Maugham stuttered a little more than usual when he repeated the preface of his book: 'There is only a razor's edge between selfishness and thoughtlessness.'

When I told Fanny, that weekend at her beach house, what Maugham had said, she had nothing to say. But the following morning when I came in for breakfast, she had plenty to say when she told me, 'Orry, I've had a helluva night's rest. I wish you hadn't told me what Willie Maugham said.'

Maybe this is why Fanny liked me – she always knew I told her the truth.

I put a sign over my door: 'Have leash, will travel.'

When Rex Harrison took a holiday from the 1957 stage production of *My Fair Lady* – wanting to be near actress Kay Kendall, whom he would later marry – he came to the coast. He shared a house with Terence Rattigan, the brilliant English playwright. George Cukor gave him a dinner – about ten or twelve people. Leaving my house I got disturbing news about an eastern friend's health. Still, that was no excuse for me getting so 'potty'. I remember little after I switched to wine during dinner. In fact, the only other time I blacked out was when I called the cop car thinking it was a black-and-white taxi.

Later I was told – but not by Cukor – that I mimicked Clifton Webb. If I shot my head high up in the air, looked down my nose, tilted my chin, squared my shoulders, threw out my chest, sucked in my gut and pointed my toe at an angle of forty-five degrees, and told Clifton, 'I, too, were born in first position.' So what? I did it to his face. I admit to being two-sided but not two-faced.

I've seen Clifton and his mother, Mabelle, as high and kicking as kites. Higher than when it has been said they both danced as brother and sister in the same chorus in New York – that is, when New York was Little Olde New York.

If Merle Oberon saw me under the weather that night, that mattered little. She, too, was born Down Under.

As Isabel Jeans said when I was draping her neckline in *Tovarich*, 'Be kind to my neck.'

It was only the neck of the beautiful Isabel that showed age. At Cukor's dinner she said, 'Mr Kelly, let's sit down and have a nice little chat. I know you are busy with Miss Oberon, but I, too, am important. In the West End I am Miss Isabel Jeans. In America Merle Oberon is Merle Oberon, whereas in London she is simply a Miss Thompson, and I don't mean Sadie.'

Then I said, 'Isabel, when you were so friendly with a duke, did Noël Coward say, "Isabel, you're a lady in your own wrong?" '

Rex and Kay were too much in love to pay attention to my nipping, as Kay said too following Sunday at brunch, 'Sure you were good and potty, but you were good and funny too.'

If my behaviour in front of Lauren Bacall at Cukor's party was wrong, that, too, is of little consequence. When I first dressed her she was Betty Bacall – Betty fresh from Brooklyn was both flippant and fresh.

The thing that distressed me for days and really put me in the Remorse Chamber was behaving as I did in front of people like Kate Hepburn, the eminent fashion photographer Baron Hoyningen-Huene, and Cukor's house guest, the distinguished historian the Honourable Steven Runciman. But mainly it was George Cukor himself. I had taken advantage of an old friendship – a friendship I didn't want to lose.

For once Cukor never chastised me, only his look told me of his disappointment. But I continued to work for him designing his pictures.

What a joy it is to work with people like Kay Kendall.
Somehow it isn't work; it's just great fun and it shows on the screen.

I have been fortunate enough to be able to please a great many of the people for whom I have designed. Most of them have been very well mannered. None had more beautiful manners, nor was more kind and considerate, than Miss Kay Kendall.

Even on first introduction to the lovely Kay a warm glow seemed to reach out to you. As she became excited, the 'pink of the peach' penetrated though her olive skin. Like her hair, her eyes were golden brown. In fact, Kay was a golden girl, and her wonderful humour was a case of the right person saying the wrong thing in a well-bred way.

What a joy it is to work with people like her. Somehow it isn't work; it's just great fun and it shows on the screen. No hours would be too long to work for people like her. It's always been the in-between people, the vulgar, the ill-bred people with whom I seem to be less successful.

Kay Kendall had the wit of Carole Lombard, the glamour of actress Gertie Lawrence and some of the mimicry of Fanny Brice, all bundled up with such great beauty and chic.

Her career and personal life were always slightly hectic, but I don't think she wanted it any other way. She wasn't the type to sit down, be calm and quiet. She thrived on excitement, turmoil. Whether it was Connie, her corgi dog, the butler, the cook, or being separated from Rex Harrison, there was always excitement.

Kay was sort of alone in Hollywood. Although she had friends like the David Nivens, she was terribly lonesome for Rex Harrison whenever he was away. Fellow English actress Gladys Cooper had given Connie to her. For days before the start of the picture, the dog had bowel trouble – after all, Connie had sat through weeks of costume fittings for *Les Girls*. In fact, she seemed to frown at me when I placed a naughty blue bow on Kay's bottom. Kay shrieked with laughter as she said, 'Darling, don't you think you point it up too much? Mitzi Gaynor has such a lovely figure, maybe my bum is too big. It's round, you know.' Kay, who had a beautifully proportioned figure, was forever tearing herself to shreds: 'Like all English girls, I don't have large bosoms.'

I said, 'You wouldn't want to have "angry bosoms", would you?'

'What do you mean by "angry bosoms"?'

'Just that. There's nothing delicate about them, they're simply overinflated and angry. And the people who have them usually possess little talent.'

I felt Connie cringe at my Australianisms. After all, she'd been brought up with the soft cultured voice of her mistress, Gladys Cooper. Connie had gotten to know me rather well, but she still remained rather snooty about Hollywood people in general.

There is always twice as much tension and excitement on the first day of shooting any movie, but the dazzling Kay made the opening day's shooting of *Les Girls* doubly exciting. While she was dressing, I walked Connie for her. But, no luck!

Kay made her entrance onto the set; she looked so elegant in black, with a large velvet hat. Just then she was called to the phone. It was Rex Harrison. Suddenly Connie looked up at her mistress with a strained expression, as if to say, 'I wanna go.' Kay whispered to me, 'Would you mind, dear?'

Again I took the leash and walked Connie to the nearest lawn, tree and hydrant. I'd tried them all before. A few moments later I returned. Dozens of people were cluttered around on the set near Kay, who was talking to Rex. With opening day nerves, her very British voice seemed to have more resonance than ever. The conversation went something like this:

'Yes, I know dear . . . I know . . . but Connie's constipation has been driving me almost out of my mind. The poor darling . . . it's been going on for three days now . . . as a matter of fact, this is the fourth. Yes . . . she's tried everything . . . even Doane's Little Liver Pills . . . but to no avail.'

Just then I came through the crowd of electricians and cameramen. Mr Cukor waited patiently, a broad grin on his face as he took in the conversation. Suddenly I caught Kay's eye and nodded. She screamed excitedly into the phone, 'Oh Rex, darling, she's done it, she's done it!' as Connie, now full of life, broke leash and dashed to her mistress. Saying goodbye to Rex, she gave the dog a hug: 'Connie, you be good now and keep quiet.' For the first time the extras and the rest of the people on the set knew who Connie was! The assistant called for quiet.

Later, when I was adjusting Kay's coat, Mr Cukor walked over to give her some last-minute instructions as to the quality and feeling he wanted in the first scene. He told her, 'You're distinguished, elegant, self-possessed. You're being sued, but you're about to' – then he stopped suddenly and pointed at Connie – 'do what Connie just did.' And Kay, without batting an eyelid, in her crisp matter-of-fact voice, said, 'Why, of course, of course.' Then Cukor hollered loudly, 'Lights, camera, action!' and *Les Girls* went to work.

I put a sign over my door: 'Have leash, will travel.'

As *Time* magazine so aptly put it after Kay died years later from leukaemia, 'A blithe spirit is gone.'

Holding on to the hand of her husband, she whispered, 'Darling, I love you.'

No one knew that better than I.

After her success in *Les Girls*, with offers of huge salaries for the first time in her career, she said, 'Orry dear, I never knew real kindness until I met Rex. I just want to go back to England, get a house in the country and be Mrs Rex Harrison.'

Once more I had to revise my telephone book. More and more of my good friends were dropping off. Actress Lilyan Tashman said, shortly before she herself died, 'One never thinks of death until one's contemporaries begin dying.'

Too many of mine have gone – others have become bitter – I must never break my banjo. I'm in the testy sixties. Now I understand what mother meant when she always answered, 'And a healthy New Year to you too.' As one grows older it is good to have some young people around.

Mrs Jay Paley, wife of tobacco giant William Jay Paley, once invited movie executive Joe Schenck over to spend Sunday: 'Come to our house Sunday, Joe, no big to-do, just young people and cold cuts.' When someone admired the same Mrs Paley's gorgeous emeralds, she replied, 'My dear, they're last year's emeralds.'

No one I know of stayed younger than Miss Barrymore – her mind in particular. Cukor called, 'When did you last see Ethel?'

I told him, 'It's been some time, but I talk and read stuff to her for my book every other day.'

'Go see her, Kelly. Kate Hepburn was shocked at the change in Ethel just before she left for Europe.'

George Cukor had been rushed to Europe to take over *Song to Remember*. Miss Barrymore had begun to fail, she seemed lost without George, and Kate Hepburn was in Italy. Ethel's son Jackie Colt had made unfortunate headlines ten years previously. He had been drinking. His mother never forgave him. When others weren't around I always spoke of Jackie, hoping she would relent. More and more she clung to my words, but only when I broached the subject first.

I phoned 'her Anna', her nurse. Did Miss Barrymore need flowers? Yes, she had just emptied the ones Miss Hepburn arranged to send in her absence. I stopped by the florist and gathered up all the pink carnations, sweet peas and Cecile Brunner roses, for her all-pink bedroom.

Three days later Miss Barrymore went into a coma during the night. Early next morning the priest was sent for. But she was already unconscious.

Jackie and his sister arrived at the coast and joined their brother, Sammy.

Although Miss Barrymore hadn't been to church, or been given absolution in years, she was given High Mass. There was something about Queen Ethel like the unbending Queen Mary and her behaviour towards her favourite son, the Duke of Windsor.

It was only when she was with her dressmaker that she spoke from the heart. When I said that her son Jackie was so understanding, even when he was a very young man, she would say, 'Oh, he was, Kelly, he was. If only he had not married a woman so much older than himself.'

'But Jackie always liked older women,' I told her.

'You're telling me? He was only seventeen years of age when he was running around with Mary Duncan,' said Miss Barrymore. Actress Mary Duncan became the wife of champion polo player Laddie Sanford.

After the funeral I told Jackie how often his mother spoke of him and with such affection.

'I know you haven't heard from your mother in all these years. And while she was unable to tell you herself, somehow I felt she knew I would tell you of her love.'

Then I told him how her faithful Anna had called, saying she knew Miss Barrymore wanted to talk to me. 'But please only say a few words. I have to hold the phone up for her – she is sinking fast.'

I shall never forget Miss Barrymore's wonderful voice. But as long as I live I shall always remember the voice that was now just an echo coming faintly through the phone when she whispered, 'Goodbye, Kelly dear. God bless.'

to natural
waist line

#5
Sc. 189

Marilyn Monroe
Some Like It Hot

CHAPTER EIGHTEEN

'It was such a good party. Everyone wasn't rich.'

ART AND MUSIC ACCOMPANY each other. I have been very fortunate in having the friendship of three aristocrats of the music world – Cole Porter, Oscar Hammerstein and Vincent Youmans. All three had much in common. Like Cole and Oscar, Vincent Youmans was an extremely modest, disciplined artist. They all looked 'within themselves', never relying on preconceived methods.

When Vincent produced *Great Day*, he not only wrote and produced it, but he took over a theatre. Apart from designing the costumes, he used several of my ideas and injected them into the show. Without attending any calls, he had me select all sixteen showgirls. Two of them were Mabel Ellis, Cary Grant's latest crush, and her friend Lillian, who later became Mrs Fred MacMurray – I taught Mabel and Lillian to walk like showgirls. They were so beautiful, that's all that was needed.

Although there was no smog then in Los Angeles, Hollywood didn't notice the modest Oscar Hammerstein II. But then again, Hollywood often loses its bifocals. They had nothing to offer 'that wonderful man', as Miss Barrymore always referred to him.

So much has been told of Oscar, but I like best the story of how playwright and screenwriter Moss Hart kidded Irving Berlin. It was in New York. When looking out of the window of the River House apartment building, he pointed to a barge coming up the East River and said, 'Irving, look at that barge laden with gold bars. It must be Rodgers and Hammerstein's royalties from *Oklahoma!*, *The King and I* and *South Pacific*.' It's been said Irving Berlin didn't look.

And I like to remember Dorothy, Oscar's wife, saying to me, 'We had so much fun last night. It was such a good party. Everyone wasn't rich.'

And I shall always remember that during my 'slack period', it was Dorothy Hammerstein who gave me my first New York one-man show. All thirty-five paintings were sold.

As I completed this book, Oscar Hammerstein II – Broadway's Poet Laureate – left us.

They dimmed the lights on Broadway for two minutes while the heavens were lit up for Oscar's entrance.

One night I may have been on Vine Street with no tie, the next I'd be wearing black tie and a red carnation to Cole Porter's.

Cole Porter was the very essence of theatre, for Cole *was* theatre. He was its entrances and exits. He was where the dream began and reality ended. He transported you into a realm of magic fantasy: not just for a few hours, for his melodies lingered on and on. This refined artist, with his own peculiar instinct and ease, was not of the Tin Pan Alley school with their ready-made tunes. He belonged with the giants. Somehow he saw to it that his melodies wouldn't become 'Fords' overnight. His wonderful words, his swift phrases belonged with the Impressionists, out in the sunlight.

'I Get a Kick Out of You' gave me the same dizzy sensation I got when I had my first ride on a merry-go-round. I've seen the wild rhythm of the Samoan boys in Pago Pago dancing the beguine with their devilry mixed with loose love and lust. For a long time 'Begin the Beguine' didn't catch on. Naturally it was recorded, for it was a Cole Porter song. One interpretation after another was grafted onto the original orchestration, each one as right as the other, but it took Artie Shaw's rendition to make it an overnight sensation and become the classic that it is. Through the years, a Cole Porter tune – just like any truly creative art – is rarely understood at first sight or hearing.

Like the poets, Cole himself had the gift of eternal youth. And like the true artist, there was much of himself in his words and his music. Brimming over with intelligence, he was fun-loving and loving, critical and kind, caustic and courteous, generous, plucky, and had more spunk than anyone I'd ever known. Though he had over thirty operations on his leg after a fall from his horse, no one ever heard him complain. But on at least three occasions Cobina Wright complained bitterly to me: 'Cole never invites me to his house. I knew him before Elsa, and I always write him up in my column.' At the third telling I felt Cobina must have meant me to mention it, so I did. Cole's big expressive eyes smiled as he asked Max, one of his menservants, for his engagement book, saying, 'I must have Nela and Arthur Rubinstein for dinner next week. I'm devoted to them both.' He was referring to the great Polish pianist and his wife.

Born rich, Cole Porter had always known luxury. His theme could quite easily have been, 'Give me the luxuries and I can dispense with the necessities.' Endowed with the most subtle refinements, 'He lives like a king, for he is a little king'. That remark was made by Marie Louise Wanamaker Munn. The fact that she herself was given one thousand dollars a day pin money by her father, John Wanamaker, the department store giant, gives one an idea of how Cole lived, when he could awe someone like Louisa. Miss Ethel Barrymore once told me Louisa's father bought her everything her heart desired, except the Duke of Spoleto, whom he could not buy. Just as no one can buy or bully their way into Mr Porter's realm.

Dinners at Cole's were usually from four to eight or ten people. His drawing room in the Towers in New York, with much of Linda's – his wife's – pieces, augmented with his own, had an atmosphere of Europe and its old-fashioned graces. There was the feeling of the days of the literary salon. His California house was simple, but he lived in the same grand manner.

He had a wide and varied circle of friends. It wasn't necessary to belong to the best set for Cole to like you. He liked you for what you were. One thing is certain, you would never meet a tedious or boring person at his table.

One of the few who was permitted to name the guest list was Fanny Brice. Apart from his great respect for her artistry, both he and his wife had known Fanny for years and had a great fondness for her and her frankness. These were always small dinners, for Fanny's guest list was always small: Constance Collier, Kate Hepburn, George Cukor, Ina Claire and myself.

Cole Porter was fun-loving and loving, critical and kind, caustic and courteous, generous, plucky, and had more spunk than anyone I'd ever known.

I remember one evening in particular: Fanny, as usual reversing things, phoned and left a message for Mr Porter not to dress for dinner as she was wearing slacks. There was just four of us – Constance Collier, Fanny, Cole and I, and we had four serving us. Cracked crab was a first course. Fanny loved crab. In a loud stage whisper she said to me, 'I hope that guy sticks around with the cracked crab, I feel like making a whole meal of it.'

Mr Porter's eyes gave a glint as if to say, 'He's not leaving town,' and went on with his meal. Then she repeated it, this time addressing Cole: 'Gee kid, this is the best cracked crab I ever tasted.'

'I hope,' I joined in, and we did a George and Gracie as we both ended with 'that guy sticks around with the cracked crab.'

During these conversations in front of his servants, the suave Cole, his sense of order maintaining his rigorous rules of etiquette, withdrew behind his impenetrable wall of dignity and reserve. A reserve that even dear Fanny found impossible to break through.

After dinner, as we sat with coffee and liqueur, Fanny got started on performers and their worth. Cole said, 'As much as I hate the word *genius*, I think Danny Kaye comes closer to being one than anyone I know.'

The ever-honest Fanny, referring to Danny's wife, Sylvia Fine, said, 'Yeh, Danny is great and Sylvia writes great stuff, but somehow I feel she never quite got away from the borscht circuit.'

On another occasion, just Fanny and I dined with Cole, and afterwards listened to the Academy Awards. Miss Ruth Chatterton's very English accent came over the air: 'And from Twentieth Century *Faux* – '

Fanny said, 'You know, kid, I knew her before Henry Miller made her a stage star. She did an act in vaudeville with a dog, and she talked just like you and I.'

What a shame the theatre has turned into show business. So many write at the top of their voice, slick and brash; themselves mediocre, they cater to the masses.

Cole always wrote with a voice that didn't particularly desire or demand to make itself heard, but more to please and charm. But after all, Cole Porter was a man of considerable charm.

Some years ago I was dining at Cole Porter's. The ladies had gone back into the drawing room while the men sat with their coffee and cigars. Broadway producer Gilbert Miller, Douglas Fairbanks Jr and David Niven were discussing Cary Grant. I turned to Doug Jr. 'Tell me,' I said, 'I've always wondered if the story Eddie Goulding tells about Cary is true.'

It appeared that many years before, when Cary and Randy first shared Constance Talmadge's beach house, Cary gave his first party for actress and singer Gertrude Lawrence. She was visiting Hollywood. Gertie and Doug Jr had been great friends at one time. Doug suggested that Cary and he give the party together and share expenses. This suited Cary. When he sent Fairbanks the bill, everything was itemised, down to cigarettes and paper napkins, and, as there were two bathrooms in the beach house, the list ended with 'two rolls of toilet paper – 20 cents'.

Doug shook his head and with a rather sheepish grin said, 'I'm afraid, old boy, it's the truth.'

Cole Porter once said that most of Errol Flynn's women somehow never seemed quite housebroken. Between Errol's marriages, he often dined at Cole's, who usually invited him as an extra man.

One evening Miss Barrymore, Mrs Ray Milland, Clark Gable, Errol Flynn, two others and myself had a superb dinner. Then the ladies went to the drawing room while we had after-dinner drinks in the tiny bar off the sitting room. Errol was in rare form as he proceeded to mix the B and Bs. He told us how he'd started smoking the opium pipe, then mentioned his early cocaine addiction. Cole left us and joined the ladies.

Errol's descriptions were so fantastic, yet told in such a gay manner that Cole, fascinated by the tales, kept stopping by the bar, also hoping we'd remember to join the ladies. Half an hour went by when suddenly we heard the rustle of Miss Barrymore's gown as she walked directly to the end of the room. Looking at Clark, her head high, she said, 'Good evening,' in a rather haughty-vexed tone. Errol got the same 'Good evening.' Peering around the corner where I was sitting on the bar stool, she said, 'Ah, Kelly, I might have known.' Ethel was treating me like family, scolding me, but also showing King Gable and Crown Prince Flynn her disapproval of our bad manners. She left.

Clark wheezed, 'I'd hate to have to run up against her.'

One night I'd be on Vine Street with no tie, the next I'd be wearing black
tie to Cole Porter's, or dining alongside the beautiful Bebe Daniels.

The moment the rest of the ladies had gone, Cole got to the bar just in time to hear Errol say, 'I guess I was bored but I've completely cured myself of the habit.' I looked at his glassy eyes and knew it wasn't true.

Boredom to Errol Flynn was the greatest sin in the world. Mentally he had to create fresh excitement every day. In his prime I spoke of him as a beautiful man. Writer H.L. Mencken once remarked, 'The moment a man puts make-up on his face he becomes less of a man.' But not so with Errol. He was as much a man's man as a ladies' man – with or without make-up. He loved being a film star and everything that went along with it: yachts, imported tweeds, black brocade dinner jackets, made-to-order shoes, king-sized beds with mirrored ceilings, fur-lined bedspreads, caviar, wild duck, whole suckling pigs, rare wines, champagne, brandy and a bidet.

> *Errol Flynn was as much a man's man as a ladies' man – with or without make-up. He loved being a film star and everything that went along with it.*

In the early thirties I dined with Lili Damita – his first wife – and him, both at my place and at their place on many occasions. I liked Lili. I'd dressed her in *The Match King* back in 1932. She had French chic, a keen eye for fashion, continental sureness, and her aim was mighty sure when she conked Errol over the head with a bottle of French champagne. Their son, Sean, had the combined good looks of his parents. After they divorced I often told Errol how well Lili was rearing his son and how she was forever singing Errol's praises to him. Errol said, 'Oh Kelly, if she weren't so chic and so mad about clothes, you'd dislike her as much as I do.'

Money was always at the bottom of Errol's trouble, and money was eventually his downfall. Devoted as I was to Errol, I was always aware of this not so uncommon parsimonious trait among Hollywood male stars. In fact, if they had their way, everything would be on the house – food, liquor, clothes, even Polly's house. No wonder female stars regard Hollywood as a man's town.

When I introduced Errol to Rags Ragland at the Derby, the forthright Rags said, 'You're the one that's just got to end up behind the eight ball.' This didn't sit too well with Errol. When Rags and I had both bought a round of drinks, the ragman said, 'Come on,

I had dressed Lili Damita, Errols Flynn's first wife, in The Match King. She had a keen eye for fashion and her aim was mighty sure when she conked Errol over the head with a bottle of French champagne.

crumb bum, your turn to buy.' Rags was sitting in for his good friend Toots Shor with that remark. But Errol, like many stars, carried no cash.

As we proceeded to pin one on, Errol submerged himself in self-pity. He said, 'Look at Kel here, he plays around in more ways than one and never gets into trouble.' Touching wood, I told him about an occasion a few nights before when a young secretary jumped at the chance to visit him at his hilltop home on Mulholland Drive. That same evening, just as the Derby was closing, she came into the bar to borrow cab fare from me to get home in the rain. 'But she wasn't a tramp, Kel, I couldn't offer her money,' Errol said.

'Any female, highbrow or lowbrow, will never be offended, Errol, when the taxi driver tells her that Mr Flynn has already attended to the fare.'

Errol was a great joker, and I'd been on many escapades with him, but I was lucky enough to have escaped one – the 'porthole' excursion. He'd planned to lock me in irons in the hold of his yacht *The Zaca* and not let me out until the boat reached Ensenada, Mexico! I got wind of the scheme and phoned Aileen Pringle, my date, and told her we wouldn't be going down to the dock for cocktails.

It was for allegations about events during this trip that he was later charged with rape. I learned to know the real Flynn in the days leading up to the infamous 'porthole trial', so named because of the courtroom debate about whether the moon would have been visible through the porthole in Flynn's cabin – the reason he gave for taking an underage girl down there.

Although Flynn was born in Hobart, Tasmania, he'd worked in Sydney in his early days. Even though I was ten years older than he, we had mutual women friends in the racetrack set.

The day before the verdict of the trial, we lunched in the green room at the studio and then walked down to the back lot. He seemed to want to avoid everyone. We talked of our early Australian doings. Errol had caused quite a stir Down Under when he was a young chap. I kidded him about his early 'Shanghai Gestures' with the natives of Australia when he silvered Australian pennies so the natives would think they were two-bob pieces.

As the trial proceeded, people in the know offered little encouragement. He'd had bad press. The court proceedings had gone on for five months. I tried to cheer him up and told him we would be celebrating his victory at the Vine Street Derby in a couple of days. I remember he said, 'I'm afraid we won't, Kel.'

Errol was never happier than when partying and everyone was having a good time at this opening party: Ann Warner, Lili Damita, Marlene Dietrich, Jack Warner and Errol.

We had been walking around a deserted Western set at the studio. Suddenly Errol grabbed my hand; my knuckles cracked like dry biscuits. 'Jesus,' he said, 'I'm scared.' I looked at him. Gone was all the bravado. He wasn't confessing these true feelings to one of his old cronies like actors Guinn 'Big Boy' Williams, Raoul Walsh or Bruce Cabot, or writer Gene Fowler, or the painter John Decker, or agent and producer Pat DiCicco – no, it was me, Old Kel, just another bleeding Aussie from his native land.

He was furious with Jack Warner for avoiding him all during the trial.

'Wait a minute,' I told him, 'you can't ask Jack to condone your behaviour any more than I would. We get into these scrapes by ourselves, we've got to get out the same way.'

The following afternoon Errol called me at the Derby from the courtroom and told me he was acquitted. He arranged to meet me in the rear of the large dining room; for once he didn't want to be seen in the crowded bar.

We had hardly finished our first round of drinks when Jack Warner telephoned to congratulate him.

I must say, we put one on for a couple of hours, drinking them neat. Resolutions were made – the phony kind that one makes on New Year's Day. 'If I ever get over this one, I'll never . . .'

Warners had three Flynn pictures in the can with about five million wrapped up. Errol agreed it had been a close call. The cashier at the desk brought in an Extra. There he was, splashed all over the front page. Flynn started to smile again. He told me about meeting a policeman's daughter during the trial. He brought out his little black book and picked up the phone. He called all of his friends – big men, little men, yes men and, of course, a whole crate of pullets . . .

Some time later Kay Francis gave a wonderful party. In the early hours of the morning, finding it impossible to get a cab, Errol suggested I spend the night at his house. It was almost sun-up as we drove up to his Mulholland house. He was leaving for Washington the next day to see about a war correspondent's job. Before turning in for the night, he suggested we have a nightcap, Black Velvets.

We sat out by the pool drinking, looking down on Warner Brothers Studio. Again we went back to our early Sydney days. I told him how Gentleman George had introduced Black Velvets to me. He had heard of him. Of course, he knew of Lena the Fox and Terrible Tilly. He was amazed that, like himself, I had played around the Loo.

I mentioned the name of a wealthy married woman who used to take me to Tango Teas and slip me a fiver – the same sophisticated red-haired beauty Errol later described in his book. I said, 'You know, Flynn, after I made good I took a trip home and our mutual wealthy lady friend told me all about you. That was in 1933, you had just left for England.'

Errol looked straight at me as he said, 'You know, Kel, I never stole that emerald necklace. She gave it to me.'

The years went by. He married several times, settled, unsettled. He got into trouble and out of trouble.

In 1956 I went back to Warners to design the clothes for the film, *Too Much, Too Soon*, based on Diana Barrymore's autobiography. Henry Blanke, the producer of the picture, was more concerned with *The Nun's Story*, which he was to do next in the Belgian Congo. I felt Errol Flynn was the only actor to play Diana's father, Jack Barrymore, in his twilight days in *Too Much, Too Soon*. (Lord knows he was acting enough like him off the screen to give an excellent portrayal.) To get a good picture, I kept sticking my nose in where it didn't belong: I bothered the director, who was new on the lot; I went to Blanke, who was getting ready for his trip. He said he had bigger worries and, besides, Flynn had misbehaved before he left Warners. I said, 'I misbehaved, but Jack Warner took me back. Besides, he is fair, and I'm sure none of you suggested Errol for the part.'

Mr Warner was in Europe. I knew they all wished I would get back to my hem stitching. Luckily Ann Warner called me from New York that evening. I told her Errol should play Barrymore in the picture – a few days later Mr Warner engaged Flynn for three weeks at thirty thousand a week.

Meanwhile, with a cut in budget, the picture slipped from an A production to a B, finally ending up a Z.

When Flynn arrived on the set, I exacted a 'no drinking' promise from him. Outside of looking haggard he seemed in pretty good shape. He didn't have an agent; his attorney had handled the deal. He was staying in the Huntington Hartford guesthouse, just four blocks from my studio on La Brea.

The first few days of shooting he behaved wonderfully well. Several nights he drove me home, stopped in and had a drink. One night he called Mrs J.L. Warner in New

York. J.L. had returned and he thanked both of them. Everything was fine – except the phone bill I got at the end of the month!

After that week, with the help of vodka, Flynn wasn't much use after three or four o'clock in the afternoon. I gave him hell. I felt I had a right. He was cheating, laying down on the job. Why kid myself? Errol was still immature – the years he had been away from Warners had been no help. I did my best to make him go easy on the vodka, and I made it my business to drop by the set after lunch.

One afternoon I was taking the sun on the steps of his portable dressing room, which was parked on a street outside of the sound stage. Errol was inside, changing. A couple of cuties had been parading up and down in front of Flynn's bungalow. One of them was wearing skintight white Capri pants; she was blonde, pretty and terribly young. I called out to her and told her I thought I could get her four or five days' work on the yacht sequence in Mr Flynn's picture. She came over to where I was sitting. Just then the door opened and Errol appeared. I asked the blonde what her name was, and she said, 'I'm Beverly Aadland.' I introduced her to Errol.

Then, for some unknown reason, I asked her what her father did. She replied, he was a policeman. I shook my head and looked at Errol. Nora Eddington's father was a policeman; she ended up as Errol's second wife. I thought I recognised the look in Flynn's eye when I said, 'That's all, brother. This was where I came in.'

Before the holidays they put *Too Much, Too Soon* in the can. I didn't hear from Errol that Christmas. I guess he was bored with my Mrs Danvers bit. In fact, I didn't hear from him again until two years later.

In November of 1958, I was in New York, and Errol had just returned from Europe for the opening of his picture *The Roots of Heaven*. He called me at the hotel several times. When I returned his call a young girl answered – as usual. I left a message, then I heard her say, 'Don't you remember me? I'm Beverly.'

I don't want to take any responsibility for that association. The way she had been pacing up and down outside his dressing room, she would have met him one way or another, anyway.

In *The Summing Up*, Maugham says, 'The spirit is often most free when the body is satiated with pleasure; indeed sometimes the stars shine more brightly from the gutter than from the hilltops.' No one's spirit was freer than Errol's. Like the Australian giant

Hollywood star Verree Teasdale wearing a gown I designed for her.

eucalyptus tree, the sap was tapped early and flowed freely down its trunk. He cared little for the disdain of his many critics, but seemed to cry out, 'Love me for my faults, not my virtues.'

Poor Errol, he made hard work out of a hobby.

Hollywood junkets set well for quite a while. When Errol Flynn headed the Dodge City Junket, it was Humphrey Bogart who curdled the headlines. At this point Bogart was married to Mayo Methot. It was during the unattractive period of dress-alikes. Mayo had me doll her up in an identical black-and-white cowboy outfit her husband was wearing. 'Bogey and I should get a big newspaper spread,' she explained to me.

Like Bogart, she left for Dodge City a study in black and white. She returned black and blue. Just to make sure they returned a matched pair, she black and blued both of Bogey's eyes.

Then, everyone, including the hotels, began making junkets. As each new Hilton hotel opened, Hollywood stars found it great fun and jumped at the chance of the free ride. I remembered not so long ago the same stars would run a mile before taking off on a non-paid trip. Those on top still wouldn't.

Cobina Wright was called in to mix up a few royal junkets. Her Mexican junket had hardly set when Merle Oberon, who had gone along for the ride, announced she would marry Bruno Pagliai – a nice little man with a big bank account. Then Merle was serving junket to her two adopted Mexican children. Most actresses will drop everything and run at the chance of making a movie. All I hoped was that the phone didn't ring and producer Jerry Wald offered Merle a picture while she had both children in her arms.

Natalie Wood
Gypsy

CHAPTER NINETEEN

'The great trick is not to let your public get wise to your tricks.'

RECENTLY I CAME ACROSS a portfolio marked: 'Brush Strokes from My Hollywood Canvas'. The spoken word is one thing, but for an amateur to write is something else again. However, using my pen as a brush I will attempt to paint a few portraits . . .

Miss Ethel Barrymore was born of elegance; her profile, a Greek coin. For over thirty years I knew and had a deep affection for this great woman. It was around 1929 when they named and opened a theatre in her honour, and I felt I'd arrived when she asked me to design the production.

Full of subtle and intriguing simplicity, her canvas needed little colour or elaborate frame. Even when it was for *Variety*, 'The 12 Pound Look' – a simple charcoal sketch – she deliberately left unfinished areas and threw away the line that her audiences may fill in at their whim. Her full-length portraits, with no craft-fuss, reminded me of El Greco's sweeping brush strokes and powerful feeling of grandeur.

Her discerning palette was never the conventional colours. Hers were the vibrant ultramarine blues and violets; at other times, pure white blending into dove greys and liquid blacks. If her composition called for pastels of flesh and sand, they were delicate, but never sentimental.

Her personal and private world rarely broke through the picture for she was both modest and shy. Her behaviour was always impeccable, and crowning all this, the poetic voice, unlike any other, a signature all her own.

Whether she was behind footlights or in front of a camera, her beautiful bone structure needed none of the artificial Hollywood shadows that belong with so many beautiful flat faces, and voices that match.

Her canvas here on earth will never be finished as long as one person remembers the exciting timbre of her voice, or a single stage program remains in a collection somewhere in the world, or one film throws her shadowy image on a screen in the archives of the Museum of Modern Art.

There was no one similar, and her successor shall be difficult to name.

Judith Anderson was born in the colourful garden city of Adelaide, Australia, a town where every other block consists of a pub, a church and a garden.

Although the continent of Australia is known mainly for wheat, butter, beef and bad voices, it has produced some of the most God-given vocal organs: sopranos Dame Nellie Melba, Gladys Moncrieff and Marjorie Lawrence; actress Coral Browne; and, of course, Judith Anderson.

Without her golden voice I wonder if Miss Anderson would have scaled the heights of stardom – even with her blood-splashed Jackson Pollock canvas. Her first appearance in America was in a play called *The Dove* and on opening night she had no billing. The second night her name was on the marquee. True she gave a great performance, but it was her voice that turned on the lights. Judith's voice could have the fury of the pits of hell one moment, and be tender the next.

She had more personal triumphs in mediocre plays than any other actress. It would indeed be difficult to forget her portrayal of a variety of women in *Cobra, As You Desire Me, Behold, the Bridegroom* and *Family Portrait*.

Her milieu, the literary bearded giants: Shakespeare, Ibsen and Chekhov. Somehow she seemed more influenced by the painter Edvard Munch then by Pollock, because her work often appeared darkened by death; ghostly shadows rose and fell only to turn into a flame-dusted hurricane. This was so apparent in her greatest success, *Medea*, which was adapted for her by her great friend the American poet Robinson Jeffers.

Miss Ethel Barrymore's profile was a Greek coin. Whether she was behind footlights or in front of a camera, her beautiful bone structure needed none of the artificial Hollywood shadows.

Judith was a small woman, just as her mother was small before her, yet in rags or regal robes, when she strode across the stage, from the ball of her foot her magnificent body rose and stretched like gutta-percha into an elongated tall and stately figure.

After the thrilling opening of *Medea*, some of us were discussing her technique. A white woolly bearded man who came to dinner and late to the theatre turned up his celebrated nose.

'Granted she was great,' he snarled acidly, 'but it took two thousand years to find a witch big enough to play the part!'

Be that as it may, one evening after watching her play Lady Macbeth, I walked her to her hotel. I said, 'Judy, how rewarding it must be for you to have the critics all down on their knees acclaiming you as one of the world's greatest actresses!'

Her head shot up in the air and she proclaimed, '*The* greatest.'

She slipped a bit, or maybe I pushed her off her perch, when I said, 'There's always Miss Lynn Fontanne.' There was a pause; her little eyes got littler. I think Miss Anderson realised she was up against Mr K, another bleeding Aussie like herself and with just as much spunk and cheek.

Then, in the simplest and most earthy manner, she confided, 'Frankly, Orry, it all sounds so great, all that applause, all those curtain calls. It's all very touching, but look at me! I now go back to a lonely room. Who wants a woman with a hawk nose and a wart?'

Once Judith became a dame, she had something else in common with Scottish singer Sir Harry Lauder. Judith was of Scottish ancestry and held the world's record for house-guesting.

Tallulah Bankhead engaged me to design her clothes for her play *I'm Different* – and she certainly was!

Recently married to actor John Emery, she instructed me to be at the Lost Angeles Town House at 8 am. My cutter-fitter Miss Keady and I arrived punctually. Miss Bankhead was one lady I did not have to undress. She opened the door of her suite wearing only her mules. Unashamed and with a Rouault-like candour, she led us to the sitting room. Through the open door of the bedroom we caught a glimpse of the tousled head of her husband, emerging from a very unkempt bed. He looked exactly like something out of Toulouse-Lautrec!

Gulping a quick second breath, my little grandma fitter zipped the actress into the first quick-change costume. Miss Bankhead approved the dress and then explained that she hated to wear hats.

'Brandy has enlarged my head from size twenty-two to twenty-three and a half,' she drawled, 'and Lord knows, darling, people think my head is big enough already.'

'Well, Miss Bankhead,' I tactfully replied, 'why don't you just carry the hat? After all, you have pretty hair.'

'Pretty hair?' She let out a scream which I'm sure awakened everyone on Wilshire Boulevard. 'Why, you stupid dressmaker so-and-so, I'm one of the few natural blondes in this country! You don't think that Hollywood star we saw last night at the preview was born with hair that colour, do you?' She was referring to a top star who had just finished a role in an elaborate costume picture. Tallulah gestured explosively with her right hand and tossed her head about until her natural blonde hair was in ringlets. 'I mean, even when she gets out from under that Louis XIV wig!'

She became calm, realising that she had just frightened the hell out of one otherwise fright-proof dress designer. Then, pensively she began to record that famous star's performance of the night before.

'You know, darling,' Tallulah said rather tenderly, 'I thought she looked awfully pretty in her lovely Adrian costumes and she was awfully pretty when she cried, but then the stupid so-and-so cried so often.'

The new gown was fitted and as Madame was unzipped I turned my back and strolled to the window – more out of respect for dear old Miss Keady than Miss Bankhead – when suddenly the explosive actress shouted, 'What the hell's the matter, Kelly, are you afraid to look at me in the altogether?'

'I love to look at nature, Miss Bankhead,' I said, for by now I had chewed some acid pills of my own. 'Green trees and unspoiled youth.' And I pointed to the little park below. She gave a grunt – no, it was a snort.

Two hours and five changes later we said goodbye to Miss Bankhead and prepared to go back to Hollywood. As I helped the staunch little grandma-fitter into the car she suddenly broke into tears. I joshed Miss Keady – after all, I've always felt anyone

Tallulah Bankhead was one lady I did not have to undress. She opened the
door wearing only her mules. No matter how dull or dreary the subject matter,
you could count on Tallu to explode it like a firecracker.

connected with the wardrobe department has a little of the gypsy in them. 'You've heard most of those little four-letter words before. Besides, she is giving you two tickets for the opening, and actually she couldn't have been nicer to you, Miss Keady.' Miss Bankhead was giving me The Treatment, and in my case, I realised it was more in devilment.

That was a rare not so 'still life' of Tallulah. Her professional portrait was framed in kindness and consideration for everyone in her company and, what's more, she was prompt and, of course, well mannered.

She had not the canvas or the technique of one artist, and while she encompassed all of the violent exciting colours and even the self-destruction of Modigliani, she reminded me more of Rouault, that poet-painter who had a horror of hypocrisy.

When this dynamic star exhibited her portrait of Regina in *The Little Foxes*, she was approaching perfection and the reputation for which she had striven for so long. Then, just as swiftly, her perfectly organised canvas sidetracked with the abandoned zigzag brush strokes of Fauvism. She moved into another period, a period of undisciplined sketches, but even these she made exciting.

No matter how dull or dreary the subject matter, Tallu could suddenly loom up like a black menacing cloud and explode like a Fourth of July firecracker, never failing to send her audience into gales of appreciative laughter.

Her blinds were never drawn, to the delight of some, annoyance of others, and even at the expense of her secretary. She had much to say, much of which was about herself – for Tallulah never lost sight of herself.

This turbulent artist etched a bold self-portrait, exposing her passions for all the world to see.

Tallulah, daughter of Senator Bankhead, Speaker of the House, from Jasper, Alabama ...

Bette Davis used the staccato brush strokes of Van Gogh. The boisterous colours she chose from her varied palette were used with great sensitivity. Watching her creations surge to floodtide on the set was an illuminating experience and then later, in the movie theatre, they seemed to burst all over the screen in one mass of pure delineated form.

Her piercing aquamarine eyes had a luminous quality which brooded like the dark areas at the entrance of a cave. She never had any regard for critic or criterion, only her own satisfaction and that of her few peers.

In the old days Fanny Brice always had me take her to the Davis previews. She was fascinated by Bette's capacity to create such dramatic intensity at the drop of a handkerchief. 'It's that unexpected, that different,' Fanny would say, 'that little-known touch that gets me, kid. She's got tricks and I'm going to find them! We all have tricks – you, a dress designer, and me, a comic. Yeah, kid, but the great trick is not to let your public get wise to your tricks.'

Bette was the breadwinner right from the start. Her first concern was always for her mother, Ruthie, and her sister, Barbara, and I'm sure a great deal of her money went to provide for their comfort. She had four marriages. She never lived in the Hollywood-accepted grand manner, nor did she care for jewels or a large wardrobe.

Somehow, in the 1930s she seemed happiest at Butternut, her cottage in the White Mountains of Vermont; she later lived at Witchway, her home at Cape Elizabeth, Maine.

In 1939 I created the costumes for her first technicolor picture, *The Private Lives of Elizabeth and Essex*, with Errol Flynn. One afternoon she dropped by wardrobe and asked if I'd like to view the finished product. Later, when the lights came on in the projection room, she confided to me, 'You know, Kelly, I played Liz just ten years too soon.'

'No,' I replied, 'that's not the problem, Laurence Olivier should have been cast opposite you to catch the ball.'

It was hectic working for Bette, even though she was a loyal friend and a really nice person. Often I jumped in my sleep. And I saw little men jump on the set, and others drop their hammers from catwalks during a battle between Bette and her director. But she had a right. If it weren't for her, this man who was once a dialogue director might have remained a dialogue director!

Twenty-five years after I first worked with Miss Davis I found her, as always, the same good friend. I saw Bette do a real earthy character on the television show *Wagon Train*. She played a dance-hall queen, and it could have been one of Van Gogh's women in the field. Her brush strokes were relaxed and finely etched; she had pared the character down to basic essentials. I felt that she had reached maturity. With the years, she learned to express more with less. Her keen eye taught her that she couldn't have everything in life, but it's been that way since time began.

Bette Davis and I worked together on countless movies and became good friends.
But there's no denying it was hectic working for her. Often I jumped in my sleep.
Twenty-five years later I found her, as always, the same loyal friend.

Whether she was playing comedy in The Philadelphia Story or
Shakespeare, Katharine Hepburn was always bold and brilliant,
yet you were aware of a curious tenderness under the surface.

Bette Davis remembered that while Good Queen Bess had one thousand dresses, she had no bathroom.

Few great artists live 'to realise'; most of the Impressionists didn't. They had great heartbreaks, and so did Bette Davis. It took the simple and meaningful poems of Carl Sandburg to give her the material to create a whole new medium of theatre. I created four gowns for her *World of Carl Sandburg* tour. With a bare stage and a few props she was able to convey *all*. Bette Davis had 'realised'!

Katharine Hepburn had the same natural elegance as Miss Ethel Barrymore. Miss Hepburn's palette and its use differed from others. Nothing was borrowed. Always capable of doing things differently, she never had a Kodak look. Here again were the beautiful bones which needed no overhead lighting to enhance the panes of her aristocratic face. Her voice, unlike any other.

I dressed her in her first Broadway play, *Death Takes a Holiday*. The grace and movements of a fawn seemed to call for the fawn tweed dress and cape she wore to rehearsals. I thought at the time how indeed like a frightened fawn she looked. Even in this first sketch, her lines, thin and unsure, the superior quality of her mind, came through. It wasn't long before her art, with its intense colour, exploded around the world when Hollywood discovered her and gave her an Academy Award for *Morning Glory*.

The perceptive director George Cukor was responsible for much of her best work. With his sure guidance her forms were no longer laboured, and her vision mellowed and ripened with each film. As she progressed she discarded the fine-pointed brushes, the meticulous stippling, replacing them with the palette knife. Where once there were muted tones we now found shining vermilions, acid mustards and humid African jungle-sap greens. Feminine without fuss, she belonged with the early rebellious Impressionists – in face, she had a great deal of Cézanne's early impetuous defiance and candour.

After years in Hollywood she went back to the stage in 1939, choosing Constance Collier as her coach. The play, *The Philadelphia Story*, was such a success that it placed Kate back in the box-office top ten when George Cukor directed the film version.

Along with studying her art, she studied being a human being. Her respect and thoughtfulness in the last days of Ethel Barrymore would not be soon forgotten: No matter where Kate was – in New York, Rome, Paris or London – she arranged for flowers to be sent every week to that great lady.

Her frequent rejections of this or that were not an act of denouncing this or that, but rather a declaration of the high standards of her art. She had great integrity.

Whether it was the high comedy of Philip Barry, such as *The Philadelphia Story*, the classic beauty of Shakespeare, or the dramatic intensity of Tennessee Williams, her canvas was boldly painted, yet you were aware of a curious tenderness.

Miss Katharine Hepburn was a confident, organised and seasoned artist.

Every painter has an unfinished canvas or two turned to the wall, and throughout history there have been unsigned portraits. Here is one of mine . . .

To my small out-of-the-way maison came one of the shrewdest and wealthiest stars in the movie world, a woman who placed money above everything. Let's call her Madame X. On her arm was Mumma, and on Mumma's arm were a couple of Seventh Avenue beaded dresses.

As I showed them 'my things', it suddenly occurred to me what Madame X really wanted was my fitter who had made her clothes at the studio. However, I said nothing. She gave me the old personality treatment, saying she would place an order upon her return from Palm Springs. Meanwhile could my fitter re-do these beaded dresses?

Now, while it was perfectly true that I was 'in trade', I had not yet reached the stage of taking in alterations! As Mumma unfolded the shoddy machine-embroidered dresses, I could see where the 'essence of armpit' had stained the bodice, and they hadn't been to the cleaners. The star smiled her lovely smile which had thrilled millions, tossed her girlishly long pageboy bob, took Mumma by the arm – Mumma also had a long, girlish pageboy bob, only Mumma's was honey coloured. As they departed she announced she would like her things altered by the end of the week. That's what *she* thought!

That evening, over coffee at Fanny Brice's, I related the story. As coincidence would have it, the phone rang. It was a radio writer who was romancing this selfsame star! In fact, he was calling from her home. With a Baby Snooks wink, Fanny said, 'Oh, she's right there with you, eh, kid? Well, I'm sittin' here with Orry. Ask her if she ever knew a guy called Whitie.'

There was a long pause. Then Fanny rode him a bit. He often kidded her about her fondness for a young man on the Snooks show. 'You're going with a broad who's over fifty, kid,' she said. He hung up.

Fanny laughed. 'You see, Orry, in the very early twenties, this gal was married to Whitie, a conman. Mumma and she used to work the boats, luring the pigeons to be fleeced by her husband.'

That was only part of the seamy side of Madame X. From 1931 to 1950, she starred in pictures, but she got her early breaks in the twenties as a Ziegfeld beauty and later, in the thirties, as a Goldwyn Girl. Married four times, one marriage helped her become a star. Her husband was one of the most creative men ever to come to Hollywood. He was an astute guy; from the very first he collected mementoes of her shady past, which he carefully kept in a vault with his many millions. When they divorced, the money settlement was as mysterious as the whereabouts of the marriage license.

During her apprenticeship at Samuel Goldwyn Studios she went to a Beverly Hills jeweller and picked out a tray of perfectly matched diamonds; each gem cost $1500. She told the jeweller, 'I'll bring my various friends here and just ask them to buy me one.' And she did! One by one, she brought them in. She worked fast, for it was no time at all before she had acquired her first diamond necklace of perfectly matched stones.

But, collecting ran in the family. For money alone she started to assemble the paintings of Miró, Braque, Modigliani, Rouault and Picasso – the same time other people were building collections of the not-so-good periods of Utrillo, Dufy and Marie Laurencin. Our star travelled to other countries and spread her charm throughout the colonies so that she could learn something of art herself – not for the love of Van Gogh's golden sunflowers. Her interest was, and always will be, the gold standard.

Her portraits were pretty and pert. Amazing when you think early in her career she was past forty. I can think of no artist she resembled. Her work always borrowed, her canvas always repeating itself; pretty but never beautiful. With her violent background colours, it was inevitable they would seep and bleed through the layers of tired flesh.

When daughter and Mumma arrived to collect, we placed the still unaltered dresses, wrong side out, on Mumma's arm, showing the wide half-moons of perspiration stains.

The beautiful cat eyes of Madame X flashed. 'What do I owe you?' she hissed.

I replied, 'An apology for coming here'.

Fanny Brice was the theatre's Picasso. No wonder her name was up in lights for over thirty years; it never dimmed.

Like the extraordinary precocious Picasso, she had the same naïve, almost childlike quality, combined with relaxed matchless technical sureness. And, like the great painter, she seemed inspired by the earliest forms of art, with her odd and surprising face and body distortions.

The last fifteen years of her life Fanny played Baby Snooks, a precocious kid, and Fanny herself called everybody 'kid'.

Everything was a 'girl' with Fanny. Only the initiated knew what she meant. With Fanny, cushions, couches, chairs, tables, cars and people were all a 'girl'. At the preview of a horror picture, when the camera got too close to the six-foot-three moustachioed heavy, Fanny detected a slight minty quality. She broke up everyone with her loud whisper, 'Gee, kid, he's a big girl, ain't he?' And he was.

She had many offbeat phrases: If some woman didn't make any particular sense she'd say, 'Gee, kid, she sounds oogly boogly to me!' In fact, Fanny's conversation was offbeat long before the Beats became offbeat.

From the time Fanny Brice was about eighteen years old she never changed the tone of her C note. She knew instinctively that if she ever ceased being honest, something would happen to her great sense of comedy. Once, when I found myself laughing at Titus Moody on the Fred Allen radio show, she said, 'You know why you like that little guy, kid? He's honest. He's a real person and that's why everything he says and does is right'. And through the years I would hear her argue with her clever writers. 'No, no, that ain't real, a kid Snooks' age wouldn't think like that'. Or, 'Snooks would say it like this . . .' And she always had an illustration handy.

Fanny was brilliant. She was always the centre of things. She had tremendous energy, courage and quick wit – and, while she could swear like a man, this strange, complex

The brilliant Fanny Brice. No wonder her name was up in lights for over
thirty years. On and off stage, her quick wit, boundless energy, courage
and fierce loyalty to her friends made her a true star.

woman possessed innate good taste. Somehow her cussing never seemed objectionable; she was more like a naughty child repeating a naughty word.

Several times a week I'd go up to the 'Big House', as I called her seventeen-room mansion in Holmby Hills. Once Fanny said, 'Gee, kid, find another name for the place – that hits home!' We'd talk and play gin rummy. I think Fanny liked best to play with me because I was the only one of her four favourite opponents she could always beat. The others were Eddie Cantor; her doctor and great friend Dr Myron Prinzmetal; and her close friend and agent, Abe Lastfogel. While Abe was unassuming and spoke gently, he was one of the most influential men in show business.

It is difficult to write about Fanny and not include a very dear friend of hers and mine. He was a Ziegfeld chorus boy in 1915. A couple of seasons later Fanny joined the Ziegfeld Follies. The chorus boy and the star soon were firm friends, and he became the greatest drawing room comedian in America, rating with Chaplin as a pantomimist.

Everyone has friends who become too possessive or agree to disagree. When I began to write this book, he decided to tell me nothing and he wanted no part of it, nor did he want to be in it. One year later he and I were still enjoying one of our strange interludes. During the war, *Time* magazine quoted, but didn't credit me, when I said, 'He went to Fanny's for a cup of tea, and stayed twenty-six years.' After reading it he didn't speak to me for six months.

When Fanny was in the Ziegfeld Follies she was forever doing something for other people. She would take home some other principal's stockings after the matinee, dip them a shade darker and have them back in time for the evening performance. They brought their jewellery and fur coats to sell when they were in a pinch. Marie Stevens, a Follies beauty who later married actor William 'Buster' Collier, bought a squirrel coat Fanny sold her as a good buy: The squirrel must have been double-crossed by a rabbit. It was the period of wrapover coats with no buttons. Marie got just one evening's wear. When she complained the fur had come off, leaving an imprint of her right hand, Fanny said, 'What do you expect, kid, for one hundred and forty-five bucks?'

When Fanny played the midnight Follies on the Ziegfeld roof, a chorus girl brought in another fur coat to be sold. Bert Savoy, the female impersonator of vaudeville duo Savoy and Brennan, said, 'Oh Fanny, let me wear it at the end of the show.' During the finale they all went down the ramp singing – Bert modelling the coat. Fanny, trailing behind him, called out, 'It's a bargain at three hundred and fifty bucks – there's a kid backstage who needs the money for an operation.'

Years later, during the Shuberts' Ziegfeld Follies, a newspaperman came to interview Fanny in her dressing room. He reminded her of the evening Bert Savoy modelled the coat and said, 'I wonder whatever became of that fur coat?'

Jay Brennan, who was also in the dressing room at the time, took out his pince-nez, and, adjusting them on his nose, replied, 'It's in vaudeville and is now known as Sam the Skating Bear.'

Fanny always remembered her old friends. Loyalty was an integral part of her make-up. She often sent for actress Ann Pennington, who lived in New York, to come and stay with her. One evening, while she and little Penny were reminiscing about their Follies days, I heard about the dog fight with Lillian Lorraine.

The beautiful Miss Lorraine was once a great favourite with the public and with Mr Flo Ziegfeld. During a performance of an early Follies, Fanny was patting Miss Lorraine's dog. Lillian passed by and said, 'Don't pat him, he doesn't like Jews.' Fanny never answered her, but when the final curtain came down she and Lillian had the darndest fistfight on the stairway.

Years later, after Ziegfeld died and Miss Lorraine was down and out and on the skids, Fanny picked Lillian off the street, took her home to her apartment, cleaned her and dressed her up in brand new clothes. As the one-time famous beauty was leaving Fanny's apartment, she started to thank her. Fanny just looked at her and then said, 'Don't thank me, I didn't do this for you, I did it for Flo.' Flo Ziegfeld took Fanny out of burlesque and made her a great Ziegfeld Follies star. They had a great admiration for each other.

Fanny was happiest in the summertime when *The Baby Snooks Show* went off the air for the season. She loved the informality of her small beach house, instead of that 'big girl' on the hill – her home.

She surrounded herself with a few close friends – all were opposite in type to herself. Actress Alla Nazimova; heiress Marie Louise Wanamaker Munn; Kate Hepburn and the very English, dignified Constance Collier. Through the years Constance would say, 'I do wish Fanny wouldn't use that naughty four-letter word starting with the eighth last letter in the alphabet.' But she really adored Fanny and pretended not to

The very English, dignified Constance Collier adored Fanny but constantly told us, 'I do wish Fanny wouldn't use that naughty four-letter word starting with the eighth last letter in the alphabet.'

hear, or else she would 'talk over' her with, 'Darling, Millicent Sutherland wrote me and said she had been to tea at Sandringham,' or 'Queen Mary sent me a charming message.'

One evening, after dinner, Constance Collier, Fanny Brice and I were discussing life. Constance, the wise soul, said, 'Life is in thirds – we are one third young, one third growing old and, let's face it, darlings, the last third we are old and we may just as well make the best of it.'

Fanny got into her act of the whys and whats, and what makes people do this or that. 'Why, Connie, did your friend Charlie Chaplin get up at that rally in Madison Square Garden and demand a second front, and he an Englishman?' Chaplin was indeed among those calling for the Allies to bring relief and support to Communist Russia during the Second World War.

Constance thought for a moment. At first she didn't want to discuss it, as Chaplin had been very kind to her; she had stayed at his house. Constance said, 'I must explain something, Charlie has two sides to him.'

Fanny said, 'Don't we all?'

Constance continued: 'But Charlie has a strong right hand and his left is smaller and weaker.'

I said, 'At that rally he must have been speaking with his left hand.'

I also remembered some years later dining at Cole Porter's. After dinner Louisa Wanamaker Munn and myself were sitting directly opposite Chaplin. He was gesticulating with his right hand as he spoke of the first time, at the age of eighteen, he had gone to Paris and met the renowned comedienne Mistinguett. He was saying, 'There was I, knowing no one, just eighteen years of age, with nothing except my extraordinary talent.' He paused for effect, then he repeated, 'with nothing except my extraordinary talent'. Louisa had been nudging me during this not-so-modest speech coming from the world's greatest comedian, then she whispered, 'The left hand.' I looked – sure enough it was smaller and rather like a claw.

This interested me, for in my costume research I've found that a deficiency – or a drawback – right throughout history has been the reason for many of the great to dress up, to hide their embarrassment. When Constance appeared before the Kaiser at a command performance, he gave her a piece of jewellery. She told how he loved to have his picture taken at a discreet distance, never showing the left arm and hand.

His favourite pose was to have one foot on a huge buffalo, wearing his elaborate hunting uniform. 'Uniforms, always,' Constance said, 'but never a civilian suit. On occasions he covered his hand with a huge sable muff.'

Then I told what Daisy, Princess of Pless, wrote in her private diary about the Kaiser: *There is an old superstition that body and mind grow to match; if the body is not quite symmetrical, neither will the mind be. In my judgement there were large tracts of the Emperor's mind that matched his defective arm. The arm and hand were perfectly formed and healthy, but they had never grown.*

Constance, with a far-off look, as if she had 'taken stage', said, 'Then since the heavens have shaped my body so let hell make crooked my mind to answer it.'

Fanny said, 'Gee, kid, that could be Shakespeare.'

And Constance, smiling, said, 'Could be – *Richard the Third*.' Constance continued discussing the Kaiser's love of getting all dolled up. 'Green was his favourite colour – that is, next to gold. Even his newspaper was printed in gold.' Then, with a wise look, the knowledgeable old Constance said, 'Let me tell you about Napoleon and what they found out at the autopsy.' She looked at me and said, 'Now, Orry dear, I know you don't mean it but if I tell you, please don't rush out and tell it at the first dinner party you go to that Constance said at the autopsy they found that Napoleon was extremely deficient at certain parts of his person.'

Fanny never forgot the Lower East Side of her childhood. When people got too uppity, particularly those she knew were born in the ghetto, she delighted in taking them back to their early beginnings.

When Fanny took up decorating she could often be found in a little shop called Home Silk. They sold silks and woollens and also had a bargain counter. It was to the bargain counter Fanny started bright and early, as she would say, 'before the best of the junk gets picked over'.

It was a summer morning; Fanny had asked me to meet her there. When I arrived a clerk had just dumped a bundle of calicos and cottons on the remnant counter. Fanny beamed over the colourful cottons. 'Gee! Orry, this bargain counter sends me back to where I was raised.' She went on describing the ragged and patched kids darting in and out under horse carts, their bells jingling and jangling, the pushcarts laden with fruit, sweet potatoes, herrings, potted plants and calico.

She told of the marble games she played on the streets, 'Often garbage wrapped in newspapers tossed out of windows would just miss us. The fat mamas, in knitted shawls and bandanas, talking to each other. Other mamas sitting or standing on stoops laughing and gossiping, whining, wailing, arguing back and forth.

'It was the whining ones I could never stand, kid. But I used to stand and look at the little men with long black beards and skullcaps, softly talking; and the organ grinders, the monkeys. I would gaze at the sunflower seeds, cheese blintzes, pickled tomatoes, Turkish halvah and gefüllte fish.'

At the bargain counter there was a certain little man she liked to wait on her. She would wait for him if he was busy – just as he was this morning. I asked her why.

'Why, kid? I'll tell you why; he reminds me of a whole lot of little guys on the East Side, but one in particular who had an apple cart. I used to mimic people walking along the street, and when he'd turn to take a second look, that's when I'd swipe an apple. He caught me once, but he didn't seem to mind, I'd made him laugh so much.'

'That was where you got your early training,' I told her, 'your classic burlesque of Pavlova's *Dying Swan* – the ballet and fan dancers, cockneys, Indians and duchesses.' In fact, all of her satire that became the highlight of the Ziegfeld Follies. No wonder she could sing songs about Rose and her second-hand clothes, and 'My Man', leaning against a lamp post.

'It was this time of year,' Fanny said, 'hardly a night went by I wasn't awakened by the fire engines screaming in the night. I would look out the window and see half the neighbourhood sleeping on the hot tin roofs. I guess I was always looking up, even when I was a kid. I liked to look up at the tenement windows, the watering cans, potted geraniums, sweet williams, patchwork quilts, bedding, baggy underwear and feather mattresses being aired.'

She stood for a moment, repeating, 'Feather mattresses – that makes me think of Momma when she came from the Old Country with her feather mattress. Gee, she was a good mother! She worked so hard. When she was young she never had time to learn to read or write.' Fanny saw my eyes blear. Neither of us had a hell of a lot of time for our fathers, but our mas, that was something else again.

I remember so well the day her mother died. I called on the phone around 8 pm; would she like me to come to her house? 'Oh, would you, kid?' In no time I was there, and I remember every word that was said. She was in the playroom with her two children, Frances and Billy, whom she adored so, and they her.

I remember her brother-in-law saying, 'Why can't Carrie come over, she's your own sister, and you have Orry here?' Fanny looked at him and said quietly, 'I'll see and hear Carrie tomorrow at the funeral.'

The phone rang; it was Dr Myron Prinzmetal. She seemed hazy. 'You want what, Myron, for research? Oh, please,' she pleaded, 'don't ask me to let them do that to Momma. Oh I couldn't – I just couldn't.'

Fanny left the playroom and walked through the long drawing room. When she neared the entrance hall – thinking she was out of sight – her whole body began to quiver and shake as she hastened her steps and finally ran all the way up the circular stairway. I followed her and waited in the small sitting room off the entrance hall. Half an hour later Fanny came downstairs. I got up and met her. She said very tenderly, 'Come on, kid, let's try and play a little gin.'

The burial was the following day.

Now, as everyone knows, Fanny was not a beauty, but I swear to you, the day I rode with her to her mother's funeral she had a look I had never seen before. Pain and sorrow had swept away all the ribald, hoydenish hilarity, her undisciplined sense of the ridiculous. In its place I saw a striking woman who, as always, was thorough about everything. She sat there in a simple black dress with no theatrics, no outward emotion; her expressive sensitive hands, her soft white skin, the proud tilt to her chin. She wore a large black straw hat with a brim that shaded her eyes. That was it, I thought to myself, it was her eyes that made this magic transformation; they had taken on a wonderful glow, a most peaceful look, the look of a thoroughbred.

Way, way back, when society looked down on actresses, no wonder Helen Dinsmore Huntington, then wife of prominent businessman Vincent Astor, looked up to Fanny.

Another close friend of Fanny's was Helen Broderick, mother of actor Broderick Crawford, and one of New York's greatest comediennes. She starred with Marilyn Miller and Clifton Webb in *As Thousands Cheer*. Helen adored her husband and son. She was kind and understanding to the few she considered good friends. Others she could finish off with less words than Alexander Woollcott holding court at the Algonquin's Round Table.

*Fanny Brice goofing around with two other big kids and our
old friends and fellow conspirators, comedians Gracie Allen
and George Burns, at Fanny's birthday party in 1939.*

Never have I laughed as much as the weekend Broderick – as we called her – stayed at Fanny's beach house. Her world-weary owl eyes and purposely expressionless face made her brittle cartoonlike word pictures all the more amusing. During dinner, when the chicken in a glass casserole was placed on the table, family style, Helen casually remarked, 'Every time I see chicken under glass I think of banquets and then George Jessel,' referring to the actor's fame as a toastmaster on the banquet circuit.

I said, 'That's where he belongs – under glass, would you please pass the salt?'

After many devastating descriptions of people, all done in fun, we started to discuss stars and their qualifications. Someone mentioned the word *stardust*. Helen said, 'Just how do you define the word? I know many people from the New York stage who have it, and yet there are others whose names have been up in lights for years, yet somehow I don't feel they really belong. I think it's more a case of clever handling or publicity, or great press, or maybe a rich guy behind them.'

And I said, 'Or in front.'

I started to talk of the arts. Fanny said, 'Hold on to your hat, Helen, here he goes again. Orry's talkin' in circles.'

'But,' I said, 'the art of painting, sculpture, poetry and music go hand in hand with the theatre, because I feel that if an artist has the true perception of the essentials and the power to express it, the result is stardust. For direct observation, let's start with the theatre: The proud craftsmanship of Lynn Fontanne, an artist all actors and actresses should study, just as academic students go to the Louvre. I go to music to illustrate her. Her ample, profound voice is full of orchestra. Music, like painting, works with the purest elements of form, and there are none purer than Miss Fontanne's; her dynamic swoop of emotion is like Beethoven's Fifth Symphony – the moment the first chords are struck, the conclusion is reached. She and her husband, Mr Lunt, both achieved early fame, but only on their own terms.

'Who could ever forget the golden-voiced actress Helen Menken, who shook up Broadway in *The Captive*, in which her character leaves her husband for another woman? Like Miss Fontanne, Helen glided from tragedy into comedy, making it impossible to detect the bridge which unites them.'

'What painter does Katharine Cornell remind you of, kid?' asked Fanny.

Describing the great stage actress, I told her, 'She had the resonant, rare vigour of Daumier. Sumptuous colour, never afraid to experiment with the new. Beautiful poetic hands, beautiful sensuous face. She belongs with the giants of the theatre.'

The early portrait of *Coquette*, on the stage, was the first time I saw Helen Hayes, who proved you can become a star in America even if your voice has a Midwestern twang.

And, who was more like the fantasy of Chagall than the wonderful stage and silent-movie star Laurette Taylor? Like English stage actress Mrs Pat Campbell, she 'saw a moonbeam and floated beyond the acid satire, far from this whirling vortex to a calmer and more peaceful world'.

Broderick wanted to know who her dear friend Jeanne Eagels reminded me of.

'That's a tough one, kid,' said Fanny.

I ransacked my brain but could think of no adequate words to describe the evening I sat in the gods witnessing her electrifying performance in *Rain*.

Excitedly Fanny said, 'Now, wait a minute, Orry, you've been on long enough, I'll call George, he'll tell us.'

She dialled; was told Mr Cukor, the director, was dining. Putting her hand over the phone she said, 'He's got some dame there.' Then, speaking into the phone again she said, 'Tell him I've just got to have an answer to one question.' There was a slight pause and then she said, 'Hold your horses, George, I gotta repeat this.' And then she quoted, 'Jeanne Eagels had the look of a depraved Botticelli who came out of Kansas City.'

Helen exclaimed, 'But that's where she was born!'

Fanny said, 'Gee, kid, I'm sorry I interrupted you, George, but who's the dame you got there? Who, kid, who?' Then, with a surprised Snooks look, she aha-ed, 'The dame is Dame Edith Sitwell!'

Fanny poured us more coffee. 'Gee, Orry, you've been reading – getting up in the arts.'

'I save my eyes for painting,' I told her. 'The only reading I do is about the arts. Rouault, who was known as the artist pamphleteer. Van Gogh's letters. Gauguin's *Noa Noa*. Rodin. Da Vinci. In fact all those who combine art and letters.'

I thought of the actress and comedienne Bea Lillie and said, 'Your friend Bea could have been the early Dali, with his dreamy, witty, mad world of butterflies – that is, before he became a mixture of Catholicism and Baroque-like Vermeer.'

And Fanny added, 'And his surrealism with the Chic Sales peepholes.'

I said, 'But, like Picasso, who is more three-dimensional than you, Fanny?' His expressive poor earthy clowns – his trick of movement.'

'Why, that's Fanny's greatest trick,' Broderick said. 'I'm not up in the arts, I go only as far as a $2.98 Hulga print, but which one of these Impressionists, as you call them, reminds you of Ina Claire?'

I told her, just as Seurat reduced the elaborate Impressionist technique to a series of shimmering witty circular dots, the stage glory of this technique was reserved for one woman – Miss Ina Claire. Seurat made seventy preparatory sketches before he painted *La Grande Jatte*. After tireless preparation and planning, his paintings were completed in a matter of hours with swift, practised strokes. He knew by heart every dot and where it belonged. The shimmering witty Miss Claire knew her dots as few do. And few had her chic.

Then I asked, 'Who was the greatest lover?'

And Broderick told us, 'Novelist George Moore once said, "No wonder Bernhardt could act of love – she *was* love."'

'And so, too,' I claimed, 'was the great Garbo. But unfortunately many of our glamourised motion-picture stars have only been stardusted with Hollywood-manufactured gilding. They swim the same current too long, continually repeating their canvases, and cease to tell anything new.'

'That's when they find themselves on the *Super Chief*, kid,' Fanny said, referring to Hollywood's favourite transport of choice between the west and east coasts.

'It's the test of time that counts,' said Helen. 'The public decides what it wants to buy.'

I said, 'How often have you heard people say, "What have they got that I haven't?"'

And Fanny finished with, 'They got stardust, kid. That's why their names are up there in lights today.'

At her height, Norma Talmadge was the number one box-office star. Her name was up in lights and she was one of the screen's most beautiful women. Fanny and Norma had made trips to Europe together. They had great respect for each other.

It was another evening at the beach house, when others weren't around, when Norma, Fanny and I got on the subject of women who trolloped their way to fame. We talked of an international beauty, and two who came directly out of 'houses' to star on the screen. One, a tragic blonde, was sexy, pretty and kind. I knew her before her stardom, in early musicals. The other, a brunette, was from south of the border, but with none of the fire or talent of wonderful Lupe Velez. She was well known on Vine Street before starring in a series of tasteless tales. Both died young.

Fanny told me of a 'house' in Palm Beach, Florida. Norma said that Joe – meaning her husband, Joseph Schenck – would always change the subject when they mentioned it. But one season when they were in Florida they got Sam Harris, the great stage producer, to point it out to them. It was near Bailey's Casino. Fanny said all the girls took the names of their favourite movie stars – among them, Pearl White, Mabel Normand, Mary Miles Minter and Theda Bara. Some of them took names from the New York stage.

Fanny said, 'There was one dame with brown hair and eyes, she called herself Norma Talmadge.'

Norma roared with laughter and said, 'That's all right, Orry, there was one named Fanny Brice.'

I asked her if Fanny looked like her.

'No, kid, she just looked like any other East Side broad.'

'Then fashion is not the only vogue that travels the world,' I told them, 'for at the same period, way down under, at the other end of the world, London trollops who had come out to Sydney were using the names of their favourite Gaiety Girls.'

And when I said I knew them all, Fanny's eyes lit up: 'What the hell would you be knowin' dames like that for, Orry?'

Making more coffee, she said, 'I gotta get a load of this. Tell me about Australia from the first.'

I told her, 'As you know, the word *aboriginal* means first.'

'No, I didn't know,' said Fanny.

I started to say, they were first on earth but Fanny only let me get as far as 'first on –'

She interrupted me. 'I know nothing about goin' on first – in vaudeville I always went on next to closing. But, stop talkin' in circles, Orry.'

Rosalind Russell
Auntie Mame

There's never been any in-between with me. It's got to be first class or steerage.

ROSALIND RUSSELL HAD MORE pent-up energy always ready to explode than anyone I knew. The moment an idea came to her she had to start on it at once. When she liked something it must stay the way it was, but when she was dissatisfied, it must be changed at once!

While being fitted for clothes to wear on a European vacation, she said, 'Do you realise, Kelly, I haven't had this bedroom done over in fifteen years?'

Surveying the room I came up from under her armpit where I was instructing the fitter to take another tuck, and said, 'Yes, I do.'

'Goodness,' said Roz, 'I didn't know it looked that tired.'

Two tucks later she was on the phone. She became Auntie Mame. Her secretary appeared. Her maid appeared. Her butler appeared. She gave instructions about getting samples of white carpet and white wallpaper and swatches of pink fabrics. I'd left the room and was at the bottom of the stairs when Mame saw to it that her voice trailed after me. 'I want samples of all shades of paint to blend with a large painting of pink carnations I'm going to buy, if a certain dressmaker isn't in too big a hurry to get out of here.'

In four leaps I was back up the stairs. I knew that *she* knew I had a large painting of pink carnations in my studio that would be perfect over her pink marble fireplace. When I came back into the bedroom, her secretary was making out a cheque, which Mame signed and handed to me. 'I hope this will keep you quiet,' she said, 'but it won't be quiet around here for the next three weeks. This project must be finished by the time Freddie returns. He's a very busy producer and I can't subject him to the confusion of decorators.'

A few mornings later, after Cobina Wright had given a dinner for the visiting Duke and Duchess of Windsor, I was painting the wallpaper in Mame's bedroom. She was watching me work.

The secretary entered. 'Miss Wright's secretary is on the phone. Would you like to order some photos taken at the dinner? She says there are three or four awfully good ones of the Duchess and you.'

Mame's eyes blinked and lit up as only hers could, as she said, 'Yes, it would be nice to have a picture of the Duchess.'

Then the secretary wanted to know if she wanted them in black and white or in colour. The coloured ones were twenty-five dollars apiece. Mame's eyes batted when she saw me reach for my pencil. I made a note in my little pad. She mumbled something like, 'Not for that book of yours, I hope.' I had already made a notation.

Rosalind was a real pro. I wanted to tell her what a joy it was to work for her. I myself am not prone to flattery, and I imagine I would go a lot farther in this business if I could praise people to their faces, but this always embarrasses me.

On one occasion I said to her, 'You, know, you're a pretty wonderful girl and you've been a wonderful wife. In fact, you've been a wonderful mother.'

A naughty Mame-ish gleam came into her eyes as she said, 'Yes, and I'm a hell of a lover.'

I think the most important thing of all is that Rosalind Russell is a truly religious girl. A good Catholic, but not, as Miss Barrymore would say, 'a professional Catholic'.

Cézanne painted some apples and a napkin and put new life into 'still life'. Soon every artist was painting apples and napkins. Roz Russell created Auntie Mame on Broadway, and soon every actress all over the world was playing Auntie Mame. Was it really Auntie Mame or Rosalind Russell? Those in the know claim 'one-third Mame and two-thirds very dry Roz'.

Originally Roz had wanted me to design the Broadway play *Mame*, but I was busy working on *Les Girls* at MGM. Travis Banton did the costumes for the Broadway show and was signed to do the *Auntie Mame* movie. When he died, I was asked to take over. I did all of the clothes and suggested ideas for the sets and coordinated the colour. I asked for credit

Rosalind Russell was the ultimate Mame. She owned that role on stage and film. And, like Auntie Mame, she was a joy to work with.

for the colour. I didn't get it. Again I was sabotaged somewhere along the production line at Warners. But then, the designers in Hollywood didn't even vote *Auntie Mame* as one of the top ten best-dressed pictures!

During early meetings before the filming of the picture, the different party scenes were discussed. When New York director Da Costa was asked if he had seen such-and-such a movie, he would smile and say, 'No, I seldom go to the movies.'

This stupid New York–California rivalry was dated, and should have gone out with high button shoes. Roz suggested Da Costa and I see some party sequences from other films. We did. After the lights came on, Da Costa shook his head and said, 'I wonder why Rosalind wanted me to see them? They're nothing like the party scenes in *Mame*.'

'You, know, you're a pretty wonderful girl'. A Mame-ish gleam came into her eyes: 'Yes, and I'm a hell of a lover'.

'Since you rarely go to the movies, maybe she thought it wouldn't do you any harm to see the work of men like Mankiewicz, Cukor, Stevens or Wyler,' I told him. 'Honey chile,' I continued, 'you can't go wrong looking at the work of men who've been making movies and studying their craft for as long as I've been sitting here on my pin cushion.'

With three stage hits behind him, which no one could deny, Morton Da Costa, first time out, strapped to the saddle by the help of old established technicians, galloped down the stretch to the winner's post in Hollywood with *Auntie Mame*.

Late in the filming of *Auntie Mame*, I received a phone call. The voice at the other end said, 'Last night I dined with Bill and Eddie Goetz and I saw there the most enchanting picture of five little Samoan boys. I would like to buy something similar.' There was a pause. 'By the way, do you know who this is?'

While the voice and its tone had a little bit of Britain's MacMillan, there was a big bit of that northern twang which Cary Grant was not about to lose.

It had been twenty years since he had called.

The conversation was very businesslike. He was making *Houseboat* at Paramount with Sophia Loren. Where was my studio? When could he see the paintings he wanted to buy? I gave him the address. Could he come that night? 'Yes,' I said, 'it's okay.'

Through the years we'd always nodded to one another, or said hello when we met at the fights or at a rare party, but that was all. We hadn't had any disagreement, we were simply worlds apart these days.

The meeting at my studio that night was strained on Cary's part, but certainly not on mine. He complimented me on my work and said he wanted about ten small paintings of mine for presents.

For the following few weeks, while he was finishing his picture, he came by two or three times a week. He told me about being hypnotised so that he didn't smoke or drink anymore. I imagine he believed wine to be non-alcoholic for he drank quite a bit of it at my studio. When he was in one of his more mellow moods, I found myself thinking sentimentally of the old days.

'Do you realise, Cary, the day those gangsters arrived at my "speak" in New York, they would have killed me?' I said. 'Thank Gawd you got back from the road and gave them that two hundred and fifty dollars.'

'Did you ever pay me back?' he blurted out before he realised what he'd said. I just looked at him for a few seconds, shaking my head.

'Don't you remember, Cary, in all those years, that was the only time you ever had any –'

He didn't let me finish to say 'money'. Immediately he became the diplomat, the Madison Avenue character he had been playing for so long. He strode across the room and examined a small yellow painting. 'Your yellow and golds are your best,' he said. 'You should paint in them all the time.' I think he remembered I'd paid him back that two hundred and fifty dollars and so many cents after my first two weeks in St Louis, and also got him three months' work.

He must have caught the look in my eyes because he didn't come around for a few days.

He was cutting *Indiscreet*, a picture he'd made abroad with Ingrid Bergman, out of Warners, with director Stanley Donen. I felt he was a bit magnanimous when he asked me to fall over at the thought of lunch with the Great Grant. I said, 'Okay.'

After lunch I asked him to drive over to Roz Russell's dressing room. After all, they had made many early pictures together, including *His Girl Friday*. Cary had been best man at Roz and Freddie's wedding, and when he'd separated from Barbara Hutton he'd gone to their house for comfort. In fact, he stayed with them for a while.

Naturally Roz was pleased to see him. Settling herself at the dressing table, she started to brush her hair, getting ready for her call. She talked to Cary in the mirror. I mentioned his beautiful Rolls-Royce outside. Cary remarked that he had another, just like it, in London. 'By the way, aren't you going to London?' he asked.

Roz said, 'Yes, I'm going over for ten days.'

'Why don't you use my Rolls?' Cary said.

This perked up Auntie Mame, and when Cary told her she could also use his chauffeur, her eyes lighted up: 'Oh, Cary dear, that will be wonderful!'

Whatever it was that always made him do it, I don't know. But he blurted out, 'I'll tell you what you do, Roz, when you arrive in London, call MCA, my agents. They will give you the rental fee and the cost of the chauffeur.'

Auntie Mame's powder puff bit the dust. Her head dropped discreetly. She seemed to bite her lip. She caught my eye. I coughed. There was an embarrassed pause. Then I said, 'I think, Mame, they're about ready for you on the set.'

The Rolls sped quietly down to Stage 17. The conversation was quiet. And the goodbye to Grant was even quieter. When we were alone, Roz said, 'We mustn't talk about this.' No one talks. That is the Hollywood slogan. With Rosalind Russell it was her matter of good home training. She could stand on her own. But in most instances, it's a case of never knowing when they may have to work together or need each other. This goes for producers, directors, stars, character actors, bit players and titbits.

One evening, just as I was about to dine, the phone rang. A Richard Gehman called. Could he come right over? He was doing a story on Cary Grant for *Good Housekeeping*. No, he couldn't – anyway, I was about to dine. Could he come after dinner? No, I would be busy during any story on Grant. As he was flying to London in two days' time and as I was busy, could he ask a few questions? When did I go to live with Grant? You mean, when did Grant come to live with me? He went on, but I didn't.

Through the years Cary always told me, 'Tell them nothing.' I don't know why. There was really never anything to hide; he had always lived a perfectly normal life. I did find out, though, that Grant was to give his approval of the story, which started out with, 'His former leading ladies – Katharine Hepburn, Rosalind Russell, Irene Dunne and Jean Arthur – now are cast, those of them who are still active, as middle-aged mothers, goofy aunts, or tortured spinsters . . .'

Anyone else would have pencilled that out, considering all four ladies were outstanding and distinguished artists.

It's difficult to get anyone in Hollywood – particularly established stars – to discuss other stars.

There are too many instances to write about where Cary's old friends had been disappointed in him. At an intimate party for Mary Martin at Ronald Reagan's home, Gracie Allen said she got only a nod from Cary across the drawing room, but Fred Astaire came and sat with her and had a long chat. And Mrs Randolph Scott told me that when Cary sold his half-interest to Randy of the Norma Talmadge beach house it was the splitting up of a ten-dollar bill that split up their friendship.

I wanted the closed-mouthed Roz to come out with a statement on Grant. Phoning her early one morning, I read her the quote from his story, which I thought most ungallant. When I finished reading I took a needle from my pin cushion and needled her with 'How does that strike my goofy Auntie Mame?'

'It strikes me,' Mame said, as I heard her over the phone calling for some coffee, 'that Cary never has had any social poise. He dare not be around people more than twelve minutes. He flits around, hiding from his own shadow, hoping nobody will notice, or that his shadow may expose the image he has created for himself. Yet, there's no one really like him – or you, for that matter – and at times I'm glad there aren't.'

Through the years Cary always told me,
'Tell them nothing.'

With Rosalind Russell between us, the gifted artist René Bouché and I sat in the open-air Greek Theatre. It was opening night. George Burns with his young guest star, Bobby Darrin, played to capacity audience.

In his intimate inimitable way, George Burns told the tales of his early days at the Myrtle Theatre in Brooklyn. Like his stories of my red dragons' tongues, he embroidered a bit, adding a few frills. Instead of Miss Edna St. Vincent Millay's door and candlelit windows as his 'centre door fancy', he had the starry heavens above Los Feliz hills. He needed no blankets for the night air. George's warmth came across the 'foots' like the funnies he so casually tossed at his audience.

Sitting directly in front of us was his Gracie, looking only a mite older than the first time I saw her on 47th Street – or Dream Street, as Damon Runyon tagged it.

As the finale began, a cloud floated down and clouded my eyes. Suddenly I was back on Dream Street; George Burns was singing 'Red Rose Rag', while Leo Beers pounded on my upright rented piano, and Jack Benny pounded his sides laughing. But no one laughed more than Gracie – George's Irish rose. Gracie was my next door neighbour. She had been educated in a San Francisco convent. She was very young.

And there were young tears. Through another friend, Blanche Merrill, a writer of vaudeville acts, I had met Bert Savoy ten days before he was struck dead by lightning. Savoy and Brennan rocked the Palace Theatre with laughter as no one had. It was Syme of *Variety* calling Blanche for an 'in memoriam' quote about Bert. She thought a moment and spoke into my wall telephone: 'He didn't know of that hasty call from the sky, but we found the man who made us laugh could suddenly make us cry.'

I thought of another evening: We had all begun to move up a bit – that is, with the exception of Cary Grant; he had just moved in. George was now doing his stuff, leaning over the baby grand piano in my Greenwich Village studio. Now Benny was on the floor, pounding the floor at George Burns' antics.

It's just as well – that is, for me – someone fouled up the taped Las Vegas ending George had planned to use. It was Gracie on tape answering George live: 'It's lonesome up here without you, Gracie.' And Gracie's recorded voice replying, 'You're never alone, George. I'm always right here beside you.' And I'm sure she will be – always, for that's the way it has been all through the years I have known them.

During that time I never had the slightest tiff with either of them. I treasured their friendship. They were a rare combination man-and-wife, on and off the boards. She was my first American friend. She was still wearing the same size dress as she did then. And Gracie's head size had never changed either.

As the finale ended, George stood on stage, taking more than Rena Arnold's 'three legitimate bows'. When he finally begged off, Roz Russell nudged me: 'Wake up, you old dressmaker, and help your Auntie Mamie into the warm coat you said she would need, but didn't.'

'I was only trying to warm you up a bit for Freddie's return,' I told Auntie Mame.

As we straddled the aisles, in back of us I heard a familiar laugh, a bit more tired, but unmistakable. It was Jack Benny and his Mary. I called out, 'A couple of those numbers bring back memories, eh, Jack?' Later I saw Mary Benny stepping into her Rolls-Royce. I thought of the evening – and the look on the frank honest face of Barbara Stanwyck when she told Mary,

'You are married to the most wonderful guy in the world, I hope you appreciate him. You're the luckiest gal in the world.'

Success has many relatives – in-laws, cousins, second cousins and wives. With just a few, it's luck. It all started way back with the magician – or was it the juggler's wife? In order to get free transportation and the Simmons bed the wife demanded, she was put into the act. She showed everything but talent. Usually she wore long sheer opera-length hose, showing lots of leg, bottom and bosom. Her acting consisted of handing and taking away something from her partner, but mainly taking more bows than she deserved. This 'writing off the wife bit' didn't stop with the magic man and the juggler. It was later to work magic with Uncle Sam's income tax. Some show business greats juggled their wives into their acts, but the 'wife bit' has not been without its yawns. Jack Benny had his Mary. Fred Allen had his Portland. And brilliant Steve Allen had the talented Audrey Meadow's sister, Jayne. And so it went, all the way down to the bottom of the heap. With Garry Moore, who had his humility – try and write that one off!

The hotel made famous onscreen by Some Like It Hot

For over a quarter of a century, in the fitting room, Hollywood stars had been treating me like a doctor – well, let's say a masseur. As I helped them dress or undress they often said, 'Kelly, don't bother to leave the room, just turn your back.' And there were those who didn't say 'Turn your back' and didn't bother to turn theirs. After thirty-odd years of turning and about-turning, you can see where Gypsy Rose Lee wouldn't look a whole lot different to me than Marjorie Main, of Ma Kettle fame, or even Marilyn Monroe.

Some Like It Hot was to star Marilyn Monroe, Tony Curtis and Jack Lemmon. It was to be produced and directed by Billy Wilder. I had long admired Miss Monroe's lovely face, her acting – but never her clothes. I did something I had never done before. I tested for the job. Armed with half a dozen lifelike sketches of Marilyn Monroe in the 1928 period, I descended on the wily Puck-faced Billy Wilder. Along with his famed biting wit I discovered he had great taste in almost everything, including women, for his wife Audrey was both beautiful and chic. Mr Wilder not only engaged me to dress Miss Monroe, but I was to make a couple of belles out of Tony Curtis and Jack Lemmon too.

I had been warned about Marilyn Monroe. She was difficult, she was always late, she was this and that. I have always felt if you give a star what is most becoming, even though the style may be new or foreign to her, with tact you can usually win out. Tact, that nice clean little four-letter word. What an important part it plays in the life of a dress designer.

At first I was fascinated with this girl, dusted with more stardust than anyone of her type since Jean Harlow. It's strange how the camera changes a person; I'd always thought her to be small, but in real life she was what you call a big girl – big in more places than one. In fact, I was shocked when I first met her, and so was the press, because they all mentioned her added avoirdupois.

Even though she was playing a tarty part, I had no intention of dressing her in the usual Hollywood conception of that role. I wanted her in black in the opening sequences. I explained to her about the great Madeleine Vionnet, my mentor, whose geometric bias cut allowed every line of the body to move. How much more flattering this slight ease is than the awful over-fitted look that made the average screen sexpot look like a stuffed sausage. Miss Monroe was all in accord.

For Some Like It Hot, director Billy Wilder not only engaged me to dress Miss Marilyn Monroe, but to make a couple of belles out of Tony Curtis and Jack Lemmon.

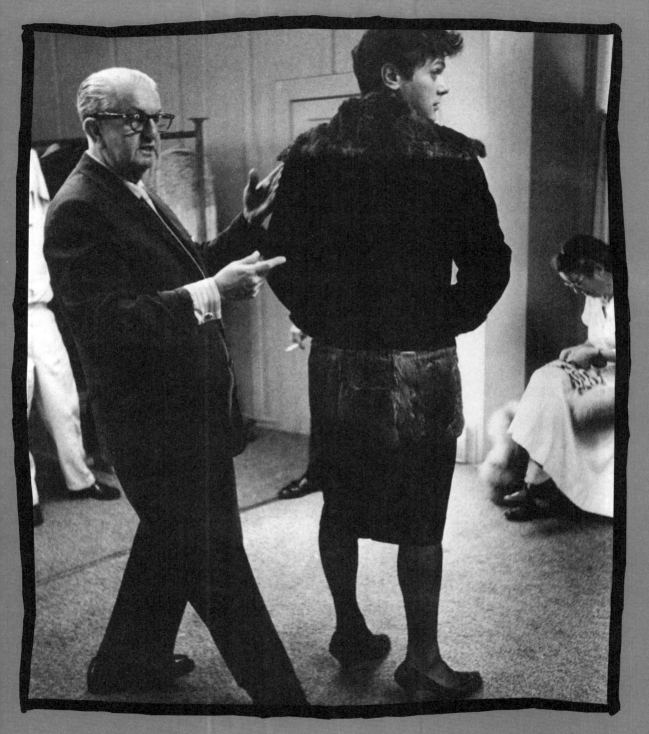

Making Tony Curtis into a lady for Some Like It Hot. It worked.
When Tony walked onto the set later, the crew gave him a wolf whistle.

Fitting Marilyn Monroe for that scene-stealing dress in Some Like It Hot. No one else could have done it justice.

My costume sketches for Tony Curtis and Marilyn Monroe in Some Like It Hot. My challenge was to transform Tony and Jack Lemmon into women. I thought they never looked lovelier.

Then I made my first mistake.

Tony Curtis and Jack Lemmon were to share scenes with her, dressed as women. I suggested we use a satin-back crepe. Shiny satin on her top shelf and dull crepe on her bottom. But that wasn't the way I put it to her. I was tactful. I explained she would be in the same scene with two men, and as men's bottoms are smaller than women's, on the screen, by comparison, Tony Curtis's rear would look infinitely smaller than hers. Kiddingly I said, 'We wouldn't want that to happen, or would we?' That was all, brother! She let me have it!

There was tension during the many fittings. Depending on her mood she was nice, not so nice, nasty.

We had a 2 pm call for what is known as a comparison test. Curtis and Lemmon were to be made up and dressed as women and photographed alongside Miss Monroe. Both the men, being men, weren't afraid to go all out in looking as much like women as they could. They kidded and were kidded by the crew. By 5 pm Mr Wilder, who is patience itself, got into his Rolls-Royce and drove home. Tony and Jack were good enough sports to wait around. Shortly after 5 pm the breathless Miss Monroe, with no apologies to either of her co-stars, appeared.

Tony got back into his high-heeled shoes and walked onto the set. The crew gave him a wolf whistle – something she was used to getting and liking. When one of them called out, 'Hi! Apple Cheeks,' Miss Monroe realised he wasn't referring to Tony's face. She dashed to her dressing room, took a look in her long mirror. This time she didn't look at her frontside, she looked at her backside. Every time she got a peek at Tony's dull black rear she'd dash back to her dressing-room mirror and look at her own shiny black rear. After two hours of breathlessly dashing back and forth, they finally got the comparison test.

The following day at noon everyone and everything connected with the picture, from the Mirisch brothers, who were to release it, down to Sydney Guilaroff's curling tongs and hairpins, were in the projection room. The tests were run. When the lights went on we all started to leave. I guess, by way of shaming the star whom he had directed before, Mr Wilder said in a very quiet voice in front of everybody, 'Marilyn, your call yesterday was for two, why did you arrive at five?'

She flushed immediately. Temper, not temperament, took over. She pointed her finger at me and started babbling, 'He said boys' arses are smaller than girls' arses and he said that Tony Curtis's arse was smaller than mine, and I told *that one*' – pointing at me – 'that some people like girls' arses and some people like – '

I didn't let her get any further with her bad taste, bad language and bad act. I hadn't been on the boards myself for nothing. I could be just as cornball as she. I went into *my* act.

'Just a moment, Miss Monroe,' I asked, 'are you pointing at me? As a child my mother told me one never points except at French pastry. "*That* one" I would say as I would point at the Napoleon.' The lesson on pointing over, I took up the subject of bottoms. I told her the only interest I had in that department was in trying to make her overly large one more attractive.

Paula Strasberg, Miss Monroe's $2500-a-week coach, hurriedly mumbled something about getting to work, as she escorted the crude Miss Monroe back to her dressing room. Mrs Strasberg had great influence with Miss Monroe, so I tried to talk to her. She explained that Marilyn had been hurt.

'She's been hurt!' I exclaimed. 'Everyone's been hurt in life – prop men, hairdressers, script girls. But they don't bring their wounded vanity to work with them. And dressmakers are lucky if they don't get at least two insults before lunch!'

It was a very bland look I got from Mrs Strasberg. I told her since Miss Monroe had bared more than her face to the whole world, she really ought to be nice to anyone who tried to help her.

I was to have one more example of her tantrums. In the train sequence she was to wear a black chiffon undergarment. Miss Monroe insisted on wearing nothing under the chiffon. Jack Lemmon, dressed as a girl, was to play a scene with her in an upper berth. When Billy Wilder tested her on the step ladder he turned to me: 'Are you kidding? We'll never get that past the censors.'

I added more lace where it was needed and sent the teddies to her dressing room. Then she sent for me. I got it again, only this time she went into a rage. Her lovely blush pink blued. For once I didn't open my mouth – she didn't give me a chance with her blankety blank blanks. I had hit her most vulnerable spot. For the first time I realised this thirty-three-year-old woman was a complete exhibitionist.

Later Billy Wilder covered her and her naked teddies with a black chiffon robe, and when the picture was released Marilyn Monroe was never seen with ninon over none-on.

The first draft of this book took just nine months. I was pleased when I thought I'd given birth to my baby on time.

It was eighteen months before I finished the final draft. No wonder two different publishers said I had two books. I decided to try for one. I engaged a young experienced writer to prune it. Instead, he grafted on so much of himself, little was left of me.

Recently I dined with the Jack Warners, just the three of us, as I so often do. Through the years I've learned Ann Warner is really my finest and closest friend. During the conversation, Miss Monroe's name came up. I said, 'I would rather go to Coney Island and open up a hot dog stand than dress that woman again.'

Jack Warner, twirling his cigar in the air, replied, 'Why go all the way to Coney Island, Kelly? You can open one up right here.'

Still, I don't think I'm quite ready for the hot dog stand, nor do I have to sing for my supper just yet. I've survived the New York hemstitcher's vicious rumour that I was unreliable, but there were long stretches when I wasn't offered a single picture. Still, I wouldn't accept anything that wasn't first class. There's never been any in-between with me. It's got to be first class or steerage. I preferred and stood in the unemployment line. I've made, spent, given away and enjoyed the million I made and have no regrets.

It will be four years this Thanksgiving since I gave up booze. Now I wake up bright and early, with a clear, fresh mind and with fresh ideas. I have more offers for pictures than I can accept.

I am now working on Gina Lollobrigida's clothes for *Lady L*. What a figure to dress, and what a charming, intelligent girl.

Henry Hathaway, the director, asked me to dress the model-turned-actress Capucine in the next John Wayne picture. I couldn't accept. Nor could I go to Rome for my dear friend of 'the perfect profile', Vivien Leigh, to do her picture. But I have promised to do a period picture when she comes to Hollywood. After *Lady L*, I begin Roz Russell's clothes for *Five Finger Exercise*.

This all sounds like the Tin Pan Alley composers who sit at the piano and say, 'And then I wrote . . .'

I tell this solely for the young designers: The reasons I am in demand is that I'm working harder than ever at my job and loving it. I am grateful to all the really nice people who have helped me.

EPILOGUE

Between life and death there is a big funhouse.

I AWOKE BEFORE DAWN one morning, filled with an unexplainable loneliness. Suddenly I wanted to be near the ocean. I drove down to a stretch of beach where Fanny's old house still stood.

The high tide had washed up many strange things from the bowels of the ocean. There was a shell exactly like the one I used to whisper my secrets into when I was a kid, on the beach in Australia.

Then I thought of many things. God made us the way he wanted – the way we are. I was sure I was meant to express my emotions and thoughts with my palette.

At least I've always had the ability to laugh at myself. I've loved and sinned, but I've lived up to at least a few things my mother taught me. To be unbiased, never to argue about politics or religion, and to be honest and truthful with myself and with my friends. My mother also told me I was put on this earth to multiply. If I have failed in this, I'll leave behind a seesaw of taste, canvasses that may be pleasant to one, unpleasant to another, just as things seem natural to one and unnatural to another. This is why I've lived elbow to elbow with the best and the worst.

With no more worries about the upkeep of a house, the servants and their problems, when not designing I feel I can honestly record a small part of what I've experienced now as I paint on double shift.

My one regret: that I can't borrow back some of my wasted hours as I multiply my painting to leave behind me.

Sitting there in the warm sand, watching the dark rise and fall of the ocean, yesterday's ghosts sifted through the sands and disappeared. Between life and death there is a big funhouse. I've never been afraid to gaze into those rounded mirrors which exaggerate my worst features. So many people run away from their distorted image. In *this* funhouse life is what you make of it. As you live, love, play and work, some are free, some not quite free, and others have no freedom at all.

I was told certain doors must not be opened; certain things are better left unsaid.

There are the wanted, the unwanted, the loved, the unloved, the sick, the insane, the lost, the homeless and the hungry. There are simple folk, too, content with little fun.

Two bottles are sold in this funhouse – one large, the other small. Booze and dope. You can't win with either. Too many people play too long, too hard and too often. Sometimes the innocent die young, others die at birth, and many die before birth. No one knows the answer. There are other natures, the creators of many arts, the King Davids, all the Caesars, the Michelangelos, the da Vincis, the Walt Whitmans – these people usually brilliant, sensitive, but always disliking their brazenly bold flaunting counterparts.

There are the hangers-on, the fetchers and carriers, those who sing for their supper. With them, everything and everybody is 'lovely'.

There are the robbers – those who steal the melodies, the words, the paintings of artists, superimposing their names over the signatures of the creators. They are the lowest of all thieves.

Life is a quilt that covers us as we sleep. The patterns are varied, rich and colourful, dull and drab; some are padded with the softest snow-white down, others torn thin and filthy. But there is one quilt that covers us all. It never varies, for we must all eventually pass through the long dark passage and exit from our funhouse into infinity.

As these thoughts passed through my mind, I sat doodling in the sand and gazing over the slate-blue Pacific. As the dawn curtain rose the last few seconds before the sun came up, I found myself thinking of my favourite poem I had recited as a child:

Breathes there the man with soul so dead
Who never to himself has said . . .

I looked down. I had written the next line in the sand:

This is my own, my native land.

At the end of those words was a smooth flat stone, similar to those I used to scuff the water with when I was a kid, on the beach in Kiama.

Picking it up, I heaved it with all my might.

'Look, Bijou,' I whispered, 'that one went all the way back to Australia.'

AFTERWORD

GILLIAN ARMSTRONG

WHEN PRODUCER DAMIEN PARER approached me with a documentary proposal, 'Gowns by Orry-Kelly', in June 2012, I was immediately hooked.

There was something completely compelling about this very talented, very outlandish, gay Australian rascal's journey in Hollywood.

And, yes, I had never heard of him either.

So who was Orry-Kelly? Slightly chunky, a lover of boxing and booze, he didn't look anything like the cliché costume designer. He was an outspoken rebel with a biting wit and he divided people, but he lived a life of artistic and personal integrity.

His was the journey of a talented artist, who helped create dreams, characters and stories in iconic movies that have survived the test of time. He won three Academy Awards for Costume, and was the designer behind classics like *Casablanca*; *42nd Street*; *Now, Voyager*; *Oklahoma!*; *Some Like It Hot*; *An American in Paris* and *Auntie Mame*.

His output, range and quality were outstanding. He designed 295 films, from the gritty Warner's gangster films like *Lady Killer* and *The Maltese Falcon* to the Busby Berkeley extravaganzas of *Wonder Bar* and *42nd Street*, working with actors like Kay Francis, Barbara Stanwyck, Humphrey Bogart and Ginger Rogers.

He headed Warner's costume department from 1932 to 1944. He formed a close collaboration with Bette Davis and helped create many of Bette's most outstanding films, from *Jezebel* to *Now, Voyager* and *Dark Victory*. He was still designing in the 1950s and 1960s for young Jane Fonda and Natalie Wood. He was nominated for many Academy Awards and won Oscars for *An American in Paris, Les Girls* and *Some Like It Hot* before his death in Los Angeles from liver cancer in 1964.

His costumes were the backbone of many great films and star's careers. He created clothes and wrote columns that affected women and dress worldwide, from Broken Hill to Tampa, Florida. He was known for bravery, class, understatement and style, which is why his designs have stood the test of time.

Yet very few people know that he was Australian, born in Kiama in 1897.

As there are very few still alive who knew Orry-Kelly well, our research for the documentary started with the discovery of letters to his close friends Marion Davies and Hedda Hopper, including a chapter from the rumoured 'lost memoir' he sent to the very ill Marion to read what he had said about her.

This confirmed that the precious Orry-Kelly memoir actually existed.

Our writer, Katherine Thomson, *had* to find it. So far we had a sense of Orry-Kelly's voice from 'our Hollywood star' style interviews with the Australian press on his return visits from the 1930s till late 1950s. But to track down his memoir with his real voice and real thoughts would be gold. So the hunt was on. For more than a year Katherine followed every possible lead, trawling through old newspapers and archives, consulting genealogists and costume historians and following up rumours from Kiama to Walgett to New York, but after a year of searching all we had found were dead ends.

Just when we were about to admit defeat, we had a breakthrough. I mentioned Orry in an interview on a Newcastle radio station and a friend of Orry's grand-niece contacted me, wondering if I'd be interested in meeting his niece who, by the way, had his memoir! She had been keeping Orry's memoir in a pillowslip in her laundry cupboard for her mother for over 30 years.

Finally, we'd struck gold! Orry's real voice, his wicked sense of humour, his real friends and enemies, and all his adventures. Finally we found out why he left Sydney, what happened in New York, what really goes on behind the scenes at the studio, and what our Aussie in in Hollywood *really* got up to.

The boy from the bush, as he called himself, had finally come alive!

It has been a challenge and a joy to try to bring Orry-Kelly's story to life and capture him with compassion and humour in our documentary, *Women He's Undressed*.

Here in this long-lost memoir, *Women I've Undressed*, is a priceless slice of Orry's extraordinary life in his own words.

Orry-Kelly lived a big, full life.

He had fun and he was a fighter.

I wish I had met him.

GLOSSARY

aigrettes: the tufted crest or head-plumes of the egret, used for adorning a headdress.

bachelor's button: an ornamental flower (also known as a cornflower) often pastel pink or purple in colour, worn as a boutonniere in a man's lapel.

B & B: a cocktail made of brandy and Benedictine liqueur, ideal as an after-dinner drink or nightcap.

B-girl: an attractive woman employed by a bar or nightclub to act as an escort for male customers, encouraging them to buy drinks.

blackjacked: to knock someone unconscious with a blackjack (a truncheon or club).

Black Maria: a slang term for a police van.

Black Velvet: a drink made of champagne and stout beer.

bluenose: a self-righteous moraliser.

borscht circuit: the performance circuit through the hotels and cabarets of the Jewish resort area in the Catskill region in Upstate New York.

broadside: a large sheet of paper on which announcements, ads or verse were printed for prominent display or framing.

buck and wing: a fast-paced, exuberant dance traditionally performed in clogs involving high kicks, shuffling and sliding.

butter-and-egg man: a big-spending, travelling businessman who likes to frequent nightclubs, an expression said to be coined by Prohibition era nightclub queen Texas Guinan.

centre-door fancy: part of a theatrical set often consisting of an ornamental arch and fine draperies.

cheapjacks: a peddler of cheap goods, an unscrupulous huckster.

chemin-de-fer: the original version of the card game baccarat, played at casinos.

chorines: a chorus girl.

clapper: a percussion instrument consisting of two long solid pieces of wood that are clapped together.

fair dinkum: Australian slang meaning true or genuine; someone who's a good sport.

grand tour: a traditional trip through Europe, considered a rite of passage, undertaken by mainly wealthy upper-class Europeans.

'hit the pave': to take up prostitution, to become a streetwalker.

kalsomine: an old cheap coating of powder mixed with water, applied with a broad brush to walls.

laced-mutton ladies: elaborately dressed, corseted prostitutes.

larrikin: Australian slang for a cheeky, coarse, unsophisticated lout.

Main Stem: another name for Broadway, the theatre district in Manhattan.

pak-a-pu: a Chinese lottery in which the tickets are sheets of paper filled with densely written characters.

pin money: a small amount of money provided for trivial expenses.

pipe-clay: to render a surface with a pale clay that is able to be polished to a high sheen.

salt cellar: the hollow above the collarbone. Spoken of Joan Blondell: 'The nape of her neck was salt cellar-less.'

sheilas: Australian slang for a woman.

shout: to buy a round of drinks.

sidecar: a cocktail traditionally made with cognac, orange liqueur and lemon juice.

single: a solo performance.

squatter: someone who settled on Crown land to farm livestock, especially sheep, at first without government permission but later with a lease or licence.

The Four Hundred: the social elite of New York City in the late 19th century; a term coined by socialite Samuel Ward McAllister, estimated as the number of people in the city who felt at ease in a ballroom or among high society.

tippet: a stole or narrow piece of clothing worn over the shoulders, often made of fur.

trull: a prostitute.

two-bob (hussies): a prostitute, so named because of her price of admission – two shillings or two bob.

two-up school: an illegal premise or street corner where gamblers gathered to play two-up, a game of chance involving the flipping of two coins. Players bet on whether the coins will be both heads or tails or 'odds'.

ORRY-KELLY FILMOGRAPHY

ACADEMY AWARDS FOR COSTUME DESIGN

1959 **Some Like It Hot**
1958 **Les Girls**
1951 **An American in Paris**
   (with Walter Plunkett and Irene Sharaff)

COSTUME DESIGNER (295 CREDITS)

1963 **Irma la Douce**
1963 **In the Cool of the Day**
1962 **Gypsy** (costumes designed by)
1962 **The Chapman Report**
1962 **Five Finger Exercise** (gowns: Miss Russell)
1962 **Sweet Bird of Youth** (costumes by)
1961 **A Majority of One**
1959 **Some Like It Hot**
1958 **Auntie Mame** (costumes designed by)
1958 **Too Much, Too Soon** (as Orry Kelly)
1957 **Les Girls**
1955 **Oklahoma!** (as Orry Kelly, costumes by)
1952 **Pat and Mike**
1951 **The Lady Says No**
1951 **An American in Paris** (costumes designed by)
1951 **Under the Gun**
1950 **Harvey** (as Orry Kelly, gowns)
1950 **South Sea Sinner**
1950 **Deported**
1950 **Colt .45** (uncredited)
1950 **One Way Street** (as Orry Kelly)
1950 **Woman in Hiding**
1949 **Undertow** (as Orry Kelly, gowns)
1949 **Once More, My Darling**
1949 **Johnny Stool Pigeon**
1949 **Take One False Step**
1949 **The Lady Gambles** (as Orry Kelly, gowns)
1948 **Family Honeymoon**
1948 **Rogues' Regiment**
1948 **Larceny**

1948 **For the Love of Mary**
1948 **One Touch of Venus** (gowns)
1948 **A Woman's Vengeance**
1947 **Mother Wore Tights**
1947 **Something in the Wind** (as Orry Kelly, gowns)
1947 **Ivy**
1947 **The Shocking Miss Pilgrim**
1946 **Temptation**
1946 **London Town**
1945 **The Dolly Sisters**
1945 **Conflict** (gowns)
1945 **The Corn Is Green**
1944 **Arsenic and Old Lace** (gowns)
1944 **Mr. Skeffington** (gowns)
1944 **The Adventures of Mark Twain**
1943 **Old Acquaintance** (gowns)
1943 **Princess O'Rourke** (gowns)
1943 **Watch on the Rhine** (gowns)
1943 **This Is the Army** (as Pvt. Orry-Kelly)
1943 **The Constant Nymph** (gowns)
1943 **Mission to Moscow** (gowns)
1943 **Edge of Darkness** (gowns)
1943 **The Hard Way** (gowns)
1942 **Casablanca** (gowns)
1942 **George Washington Slept Here** (gowns)
1942 **Now, Voyager** (gowns)
1942 **In This Our Life** (gowns)
1942 **Murder in the Big House** (uncredited)
1942 **Always in My Heart** (gowns)
1942 **Kings Row** (gowns)
1942 **Wild Bill Hickok Rides** (gowns)
1942 **The Man Who Came to Dinner** (gowns)
1941 **The Maltese Falcon** (gowns)
1941 **The Little Foxes** (costumes)
1941 **The Bride Came C.O.D.** (gowns)
1941 **Throwing a Party** (Short)
1941 **Million Dollar Baby** (gowns)
1941 **Affectionately Yours** (gowns)

1941 **The Great Lie** (gowns)
1941 **The Lady and the Lug** (Short) (gowns)
1941 **The Strawberry Blonde** (gowns)
1941 **Honeymoon for Three** (gowns)
1940 **The Letter** (gowns)
1940 **A Dispatch from Reuter's** (gowns)
1940 **No Time for Comedy** (gowns)
1940 **My Love Came Back** (gowns)
1940 **All This, and Heaven Too** (costumes)
1940 **The Sea Hawk** (costumes by)
1940 **‹Til We Meet Again** (gowns)
1940 **Virginia City** (uncredited)
1939 **On Your Toes**
1939 **The Private Lives of Elizabeth and Essex** (costumes by)
1939 **The Old Maid** (costumes by)
1939 **When Tomorrow Comes** (uncredited)
1939 **Indianapolis Speedway** (gowns)
1939 **Juarez** (costumes by)
1939 **Dark Victory** (gowns)
1939 **Women in the Wind** (gowns)
1939 **The Oklahoma Kid** (gowns)
1939 **Wings of the Navy** (gowns)
1939 **King of the Underworld** (gowns)
1938 **Comet Over Broadway** (gowns)
1938 **Angels with Dirty Faces** (gowns)
1938 **The Sisters** (gowns)
1938 **Secrets of an Actress** (gowns)
1938 **Four Daughters** (gowns)
1938 **Four's a Crowd** (gowns)
1938 **My Bill** (gowns)
1938 **Women Are Like That** (gowns)
1938 **Jezebel** (costumes by)
1937 **Tovarich** (gowns)
1937 **Hollywood Hotel** (gowns)
1937 **First Lady** (gowns)
1937 **It's Love I'm After** (gowns)
1937 **That Certain Woman** (gowns)
1937 **Confession** (gowns)
1937 **The Singing Marine** (gowns)
1937 **Ever Since Eve** (gowns)
1937 **Another Dawn** (gowns)
1937 **Kid Galahad** (gowns)
1937 **The Go Getter** (gowns)

1937 **Call It a Day** (gowns)
1937 **Marked Woman** (gowns)
1937 **The King and the Chorus Girl** (gowns)
1937 **Green Light** (gowns)
1937 **Stolen Holiday** (gowns)
1936 **Gold Diggers of 1937** (gowns)
1936 **Three Men on a Horse** (gowns)
1936 **Polo Joe** (gowns)
1936 **Here Comes Carter** (gowns)
1936 **Isle of Fury** (gowns)
1936 **Cain and Mabel** (gowns)
1936 **Give Me Your Heart** (gowns)
1936 **Stage Struck** (gowns)
1936 **China Clipper** (gowns)
1936 **Jailbreak** (gowns)
1936 **Satan Met a Lady** (gowns)
1936 **Public Enemy's Wife** (gowns)
1936 **The White Angel** (gowns)
1936 **Murder by an Aristocrat** (gowns)
1936 **Hearts Divided** (gowns)
1936 **The Golden Arrow** (gowns)
1936 **The Law in Her Hands** (gowns)
1936 **Sons o' Guns** (gowns)
1936 **Times Square Playboy** (gowns, uncredited)
1936 **I Married a Doctor** (gowns)
1936 **The Singing Kid** (gowns)
1936 **Snowed Under** (gowns)
1936 **Colleen** (gowns)
1936 **The Walking Dead** (gowns)
1936 **The Petrified Forest** (uncredited)
1936 **Freshman Love** (gowns)
1936 **Ceiling Zero** (uncredited)
1935 **Dangerous** (gowns)
1935 **The Widow from Monte Carlo** (gowns)
1935 **Broadway Hostess** (gowns)
1935 **Miss Pacific Fleet** (gowns)
1935 **Frisco Kid** (gowns)
1935 **Stars Over Broadway** (as Orry Kelly, gowns)
1935 **The Payoff** (gowns)
1935 **I Found Stella Parish** (gowns)
1935 **Personal Maid's Secret** (gowns)
1935 **Shipmates Forever** (gowns)
1935 **I Live for Love** (gowns)
1935 **The Goose and the Gander** (gowns)

1935 **Special Agent** (uncredited)
1935 **Little Big Shot** (uncredited)
1935 **Page Miss Glory** (gowns)
1935 **We're in the Money** (uncredited)
1935 **The Irish in Us** (gowns, uncredited)
1935 **Bright Lights** (gowns)
1935 **Broadway Gondolier** (gowns)
1935 **Going Highbrow** (gowns)
1935 **Stranded** (gowns)
1935 **Oil for the Lamps of China** (gowns)
1935 **The Girl from 10th Avenue** (gowns)
1935 **In Caliente** (gowns)
1935 **Go Into Your Dance** (gowns)
1935 **The Case of the Curious Bride** (gowns)
1935 **The Florentine Dagger** (gowns)
1935 **Traveling Saleslady** (gowns)
1935 **Gold Diggers of 1935** (gowns)
1935 **Living on Velvet** (gowns)
1935 **While the Patient Slept** (gowns)
1935 **Sweet Music**
1935 **The Woman in Red** (gowns)
1935 **Devil Dogs of the Air** (uncredited)
1935 **The Right to Live** (gowns)
1935 **Bordertown** (gowns)
1935 **Maybe It's Love** (gowns)
1935 **The White Cockatoo** (gowns)
1934 **Sweet Adeline** (gowns)
1934 **The Secret Bride** (gowns)
1934 **Murder in the Clouds** (gowns)
1934 **Babbitt** (gowns)
1934 **Flirtation Walk** (gowns)
1934 **I Am a Thief** (gowns by)
1934 **Gentlemen Are Born**
1934 **The Firebird** (gowns)
1934 **The St. Louis Kid** (gowns)
1934 **I Sell Anything** (gowns)
1934 **Kansas City Princess** (gowns)
1934 **Madame Du Barry** (gowns)
1934 **Happiness Ahead** (gowns)
1934 **Big Hearted Herbert** (gowns by)
1934 **A Lost Lady** (gowns)
1934 **The Case of the Howling Dog** (gowns)
1934 **British Agent** (gowns)
1934 **Desirable** (gowns)

1934 **The Dragon Murder Case** (gowns)
1934 **Dames** (gowns)
1934 **Housewife** (gowns)
1934 **The Personality Kid** (gowns)
1934 **Friends of Mr. Sweeney** (gowns)
1934 **Here Comes the Navy** (gowns)
1934 **Midnight Alibi** (gowns)
1934 **Side Streets** (gowns)
1934 **Return of the Terror**
1934 **The Circus Clown** (gowns)
1934 **Dr. Monica** (gowns)
1934 **Fog Over Frisco** (gowns)
1934 **The Key** (gowns)
1934 **The Merry Frinks** (gowns)
1934 **Smarty** (gowns)
1934 **He Was Her Man** (gowns)
1934 **Merry Wives of Reno** (gowns)
1934 **A Very Honorable Guy** (gowns)
1934 **Upperworld** (gowns)
1934 **Twenty Million Sweethearts** (gowns)
1934 **Harold Teen** (gowns)
1934 **Registered Nurse** (gowns)
1934 **A Modern Hero** (gowns)
1934 **Gambling Lady** (gowns)
1934 **Jimmy the Gent** (gowns)
1934 **Journal of a Crime** (gowns)
1934 **Heat Lightning** (gowns)
1934 **Wonder Bar** (gowns)
1934 **As the Earth Turns** (gowns)
1934 **Fashions of 1934** (gowns created and designed by)
1934 **Mandalay** (gowns)
1934 **Dark Hazard** (gowns)
1934 **I've Got Your Number** (gowns)
1934 **Bedside** (gowns)
1934 **Hi, Nellie!** (gowns)
1934 **Massacre**
1934 **Easy to Love** (gowns by)
1934 **The Big Shakedown** (gowns)
1933 **Convention City**
1933 **Lady Killer** (gowns)
1933 **The House on 56th Street** (gowns)
1933 **Son of a Sailor** (gowns)
1933 **Havana Widows** (gowns)

1933 **From Headquarters** (gowns)

1933 **Female** (gowns)

1933 **College Coach** (gowns)

1933 **The Kennel Murder Case** (as Orry Kelly, gowns)

1933 **Bureau of Missing Persons** (uncredited)

1933 **Goodbye Again** (gowns)

1933 **Captured!** (gowns)

1933 **Voltaire** (gowns)

1933 **Mary Stevens, M.D.** (gowns)

1933 **She Had to Say Yes** (gowns)

1933 **Baby Face** (gowns)

1933 **The Narrow Corner** (gowns)

1933 **The Mayor of Hell** (gowns)

1933 **Heroes for Sale** (gowns)

1933 **Private Detective 62** (gowns)

1933 **The Silk Express** (gowns)

1933 **The Life of Jimmy Dolan** (gowns by)

1933 **Gold Diggers of 1933** (gowns)

1933 **Ex-Lady** (gowns)

1933 **Lilly Turner** (gowns)

1933 **Picture Snatcher** (gowns)

1933 **Elmer, the Great** (gowns)

1933 **The Working Man** (gowns)

1933 **Central Airport** (gowns)

1933 **The Little Giant** (gowns)

1933 **The Mind Reader** (gowns)

1933 **The Keyhole** (gowns)

1933 **42nd Street** (gowns)

1933 **Girl Missing** (gowns)

1933 **Blondie Johnson** (gowns)

1933 **Grand Slam** (gowns)

1933 **Mystery of the Wax Museum** (gowns)

1933 **Ladies They Talk About** (gowns)

1933 **Hard to Handle** (gowns)

1933 **Parachute Jumper** (gowns)

1933 **Employees' Entrance** (gowns)

1933 **The King's Vacation** (gowns)

1932 **The Match King** (gowns)

1932 **Frisco Jenny** (gowns)

1932 **20,000 Years in Sing Sing** (gowns)

1932 **Lawyer Man** (gowns)

1932 **Central Park** (gowns)

1932 **Silver Dollar** (gowns)

1932 **You Said a Mouthful** (gowns)

1932 **I Am a Fugitive from a Chain Gang** (gowns)

1932 **They Call It Sin** (gowns)

1932 **Scarlet Dawn** (gowns)

1932 **Three on a Match** (gowns)

1932 **One Way Passage** (gowns)

1932 **The Crash** (gowns)

1932 **The Cabin in the Cotton** (gowns)

1932 **Tiger Shark** (gowns)

1932 **Life Begins** (gowns)

1932 **Two Against the World** (gowns)

1932 **Crooner**

1932 **Winner Take All** (uncredited)

1932 **The Rich Are Always with Us** (gowns, uncredited)

1932 **So Big!** (uncredited)

COSTUME AND WARDROBE DEPARTMENT (14 CREDITS)

1963 **Sunday in New York** (wardrobe)

1963 **In the Cool of the Day** (wardrobe designer: Jane Fonda)

1962 **Two for the Seesaw** (costumes: Miss MacLaine)

1962 **The Four Horsemen of the Apocalypse** (additional gowns: Miss Thulin)

1959 **Some Like It Hot** (gowns: Miss Monroe's)

1959 **The Hanging Tree** (wardrobe: Miss Schell)

1953 **I Confess** (wardrobe)

1952 **The Star** (gowns: Miss Davis)

1952 **Pat and Mike** (wardrobe: Katharine Hepburn)

1951 **Behave Yourself!** (gowns: Miss Winters)

1949 **Caught** (gowns: Miss Bel Geddes')

1948 **Berlin Express** (gowns: Miss Oberon - as Orry Kelly)

1947 **Night Song** (gowns: Miss Oberon - as Orry Kelly)

1946 **A Stolen Life** (wardrobe - as Orry Kelly)

1935 **'G' Men** (wardrobe - uncredited)

MISCELLANEOUS CREW (1 CREDIT)

1958 **Wonderful Town** (TV Movie) (clothes: Miss Russell)

SOURCES AND ACKNOWLEDGMENTS

Page ii: Kay Francis in *Mandalay* (1934), costumes by Orry-Kelly.

FOREWORD

Page xi: Bette Davis in *Now, Voyager* (1942), costumes by Orry-Kelly. Moviestore Collection/REX.

Page 3: (Top) Bette Davis in *Now, Voyager* (1942), costumes by Orry-Kelly. Moviestore Collection/REX. (Bottom) Nicole Kidman in *Australia* (2008). 20th Century Fox/REX.

INTRODUCTION

Page 4: Watercolour illustration of thread bobbin. Regina Jershova/Shutterstock.

CHAPTER ONE

Page 8: Costume sketch by Orry-Kelly. Courtesy Linda Goldberg.

Page 11: Orry George Kelly, Church of England Sunday School Concert, 1905. Courtesy Joan Fraser, The Kiama and District Historical Society.

Page 13: Young Orry in dinghy studio shot. Courtesy Sue Eggins, The Kiama and District Historical Society.

Page 14: Terralong Street, Kiama, NSW. Courtesy the Weston family.

Page 17: *That Tango Tea* sheet music, published by Pianola Co. Courtesy National Library of Australia.

Pages 18–19: Painting by Orry-Kelly. Courtesy Barbara Warner Howard. Photo: Anna Howard.

Page 21: Painting by Orry-Kelly. Courtesy Barbara Warner Howard. Photo: Anna Howard.

Page 23: 'The London Gaiety Girls: Their Arrival in New York' promotional poster. Courtesy of the US Library of Congress.

Page 27: Painting by Orry-Kelly. Courtesy Barbara Warner Howard. Photo: Anna Howard.

Page 30: Her Majesty's Theatre, Sydney, decorated and illuminated for the visit of the Prince of Wales and showing *Kissing Time*, 1920. Courtesy State Library of NSW.

CHAPTER TWO

Page 34: Painting by Orry-Kelly. Courtesy Barbara Warner Howard. Photo: Anna Howard.

Page 36: (Top) Chorus rehearses, c.1920s–1930s by Sam Hood. Courtesy State Library of NSW. (Bottom) Women's dressing room, Theatre Royal, Sydney, c.1930s by Sam Hood. Courtesy State Library of NSW.

Page 39: Painting by Orry-Kelly. Courtesy Barbara Warner Howard. Photo: Anna Howard.

Page 43: Painting by Orry-Kelly. Courtesy Barbara Warner Howard. Photo: Anna Howard.

Page 47: Poster for *A Kiss in a Taxi* (1927), featuring Bebe Daniels. Everett Collection/REX.

CHAPTER THREE

Page 52: 'An army of sly grog sellers, created by prohibition, vote no!' poster concerned with the Victorian licensing referendum of 29 March 1930. Courtesy State Library of NSW.

Page 57: Detail of painting by Orry-Kelly. Courtesy Barbara Warner Howard. Photo: Anna Howard.

Page 59: *Darlinghurst Nights and Morning Glories: Being 47 Strange Sights Observed from Eleventh Storeys . . .* Frank C. Johnson, 1933. Courtesy State Library of NSW.

Page 62: Painting by Orry-Kelly. Courtesy Barbara Warner Howard. Photo: Anna Howard.

CHAPTER FOUR

Page 68: Dolores del Rio in *In Caliente* (1935), costumes by Orry-Kelly. Everett Collection/REX.

Page 74: 'Times Square at Night, New York City' postcard. Colourbox.com.

Page 77: George Burns and Gracie Allen. Rohauer Collection/ITV/REX.

Page 83: Fanny Brice in *The Great Ziegfeld* (1936). Everett Collection/REX.

CHAPTER FIVE

Page 86: Kay Francis in *Mandalay* (1934), costumes by Orry-Kelly. Moviestore Collection/REX

Page 89: Archie Leach – later better known as Cary Grant, courtesy Muny Theatre.

Page 91: Cary Grant when he was still billed as Archie Leach. Tavin/Everett Collection/REX.

Page 92: 'Hello Sucker' poster for *The Night Rider* (1920), featuring Texas Guinan. Everett Collection/REX.

Page 94: New York nightclub entertainer Texas Guinan arrives in Miami for an engagement, 1925. Courtesy State Archives of Florida.

Page 97: A beaming Texas Guinan about to step into a paddy wagon. Bettmann Archive/CORBIS.

Page 103: Arrow dress shirts and collars advertisement. Courtesy Damien Parer.

CHAPTER SIX

Page 104: Playbill from the Ziegfeld Danse de Follies, New York, 1921. Note that the text refers to 'atop' the New Amsterdam Theatre; there were different shows performed upstairs and downstairs at the theatre. PhotoQuest/Getty Images.

Page 107: Fred and Adele Astaire dance together on the roof of the Savoy Hotel, 1923. Hulton-Deutsch Collection/CORBIS.

Page 109: 'The Great White Way, Broadway, New York City' postcard. GraphicaArtis/Bridgeman Images.

Page 111: Poster for *Wild, Wild Susan* (1925), featuring Bebe Daniels. Everett Collection/REX.

Page 112: Ricardo Cortez, Dolores del Rio, Al Jolson, Kay Francis and Dick Powell in *Wonder Bar* (1934), costumes by Orry-Kelly. Everett Collection/REX.

Page 115: Portrait of Belle Livingstone. Courtesy Billy Rose Theatre Division, New York Public Library.

Page 118: Costume sketch by Orry-Kelly. Courtesy Barbara Warner Howard. Photo: Anna Howard.

Page 121: 1626 Broadway, New York, Lindy's Restaurant. Courtesy the Museum of the City of New York.

Page 125: Poster for *It* (1927), featuring Clara Bow. CinemaPhoto/CORBIS.

CHAPTER SEVEN

Page 128: Barbara Stanwyck in *Baby Face* (1933), costumes by Orry-Kelly. Everett Collection/REX.

Page 131: Cary Grant and Mae West in *She Done Him Wrong* (1933). Moviestore Collection/REX.

Page 132: Mae West (seated) on trial, charged with producing an obscene play, being cheered up by Texas Guinan. Bettmann Archive CORBIS.

Page 135: *Boom Boom* sheet music. Courtesy The Shubert Archive.

Page 143: Four women line up and chug bottles of liquor in the 1920s to protest Prohibition. Kirn Vintage Stock/CORBIS.

Page 147: Cary Grant in his first feature film, *This Is the Night* (1932). Snap Stills/REX

CHAPTER EIGHT

Page 150: Bette Davis in *Ex-Lady* (1933), costumes by Orry-Kelly. Everett Collection/REX.

Page 153: 'Greetings from Reno, Nevada, the Biggest Little City in the World' postcard. Found Image Press/CORBIS.

Page 157: Lobby card for *A Reno Divorce* (1927), featuring Ralph Graves and Hedda Hopper. Everett Collection/REX.

Page 161: Hollywoodland – the original sign in Hollywood Hills, California. Everett Collection/REX.

Page 163: Poster for *Bordertown* (1935), featuring Bette Davis, costumes by Orry-Kelly. Everett Collection/REX.

Page 164: Interior of the Brown Derby restaurant, Hollywood, California. Courtesy Bison Archives.

Page 169: Comedians George Burns and Gracie Allen, c.1934. Pictorial Press Ltd/Alamy.

Page 171: Cary Grant in his first feature film, *This Is the Night* (1932). Snap Stills/REX.

Page 172: Hedda Hopper as a young actress, modelling a fur coat, 1929. Everett Collection/REX.

Page 175: Warner Brothers West Coast Studios, Sunset Boulevard, Hollywood, California. REX.

CHAPTER NINE

Page 176: Kay Francis in *Another Dawn* (1937), costumes by Orry-Kelly. Everett Collection/REX.

Page 179: Cary Grant and Randolph Scott by the pool in *Beefcake* (1933). Snap Stills/REX.

Page 183: Kay Francis in *I Found Stella Parish* (1935), costumes by Orry-Kelly. Courtesy Barbara Warner Howard. Photo: Anna Howard.

Page 184: Orry-Kelly talking wardrobe with Ruby Keeler (centre) for *Go Into Your Dance* (1935). Photofest Digital.

Page 186: Costume sketch by Orry-Kelly. Courtesy Linda Goldberg.

Page 189: Bette Davis wearing a 'Prince Albert' outfit designed for her by Orry-Kelly. John Springer Collection/CORBIS.

Page 190: Orry-Kelly dressing Kay Francis. Courtesy Barbara Warner Howard. Photo: Anna Howard.

Page 195: Painting by Orry-Kelly. Courtesy Barbara Warner Howard. Photo: Anna Howard.

CHAPTER TEN

Page 198: Bette Davis as an infatuated 'flapper' in *The Rich Are Always with Us* (1932), costumes by Orry-Kelly. Universal History Archive/Getty Images).

Page 201: Joan Blondell stuffs money in her stocking in the movie *Gold Diggers of 1933* (1933), costumes by Orry-Kelly. Underwood Archives/REX.

Page 205: Barbara Stanwyck in *Baby Face* (1933), costumes by Orry-Kelly. Snap Stills/REX.

Page 206: Film poster for *42nd Street* (1933), starring Ruby Keeler and Bebe Daniels, costumes by Orry-Kelly. Everett Collection/REX.

Page 209: Ginger Rogers as Fay Fortune, wearing a coin-cape costume, in a promotional portrait for *Gold Diggers of 1933* (1933), costumes by Orry-Kelly. Silver Screen Collection/Getty Images.

Page 210: Ruby Keeler and Dick Powell in *Gold Diggers of 1933* (1933), costumes by Orry-Kelly. Everett Collection/REX.

Page 213: Dolores del Rio in *In Caliente* (1935), costumes by Orry-Kelly. Everett Collection/REX.

Page 214: Barbara Stanwyck in *Gambling Lady* (1934), costumes by Orry-Kelly. Snap Stills/REX.

Page 215: Ginger Rogers in *Gold Diggers Gold Diggers of 1933* (1933), costumes by Orry-Kelly. Snap Stills/REX.

Page 217: Irene Dunne as Adeline Schmidt in *Sweet Adeline* (1934) costumes by Orry-Kelly. John Springer Collection/CORBIS.

Page 220: Window card for *The Maltese Falcon* (1941), featuring Humphrey Bogart and Mary Astor, costumes by Orry-Kelly. Everett Collection/REX.

Page 224: Gracie Allen on the catwalk being admired by Orry-Kelly, Edith Head, Howard Greer and partner George Burns c.1940s. Photofest Digital.

Page 227: Portrait of Ann Warner. Courtesy Barbara Warner Howard. Photo: Anna Howard.

Page 228: Autographed portrait of Marion Davies. Courtesy Barbara Warner Howard. Photo: Anna Howard.

CHAPTER ELEVEN

Page 234: Bette Davis in *Now, Voyager* (1942), costumes by Orry-Kelly. Warner Bros/The Kobal Collection.

Page 237: Bette Davis in *Now, Voyager* (1942), costumes by Orry-Kelly. Universal History Archive/UIG via Getty images.

Page 239: Ingrid Bergman in *Casablanca* (1942), wearing the famous and much-copied jumper dress, costumes by Orry-Kelly. Everett Collection/REX.

Page 241: Poster for *Casablanca* (1942), costumes by Orry-Kelly. Morris Everett Jr/Profiles/REX.

Page 245: Ann Sheridan and Monty Woolley in *The Man Who Came to Dinner* (1942), costumes by Orry-Kelly. Snap Stills/REX.

Page 246: Orry-Kelly talking wardrobe with Ann Sheridan for the film *City for Conquest* (1940). Everett Collection/REX.

Page 249: Rita Hayworth in *The Strawberry Blonde* (1941), costumes by Orry-Kelly. Everett Collection/REX.

Page 250: Bette Davis in *Jezebel* (1938), costumes by Orry-Kelly. Everett Collection/REX.

Page 253: Bette Davis with a smoking gun in *The Letter* (1940), costumes by Orry-Kelly. Universal History Archive/UIG/REX.

CHAPTER TWELVE

Page 254: Souvenir album for Irving Berlin's *This Is the Army* (1943), costumes by Orry-Kelly.

Page 258: 'Hollywood portfolio: sketches from Orry-Kelly's stylebook visualize autumn's mood and mode'. Courtesy Damien Parer.

Page 261: Handwritten note on Army Air Forces Technical Training Command letterhead. Courtesy the family's collection.

Page 263: Poster for *Arsenic and Old Lace* (1944), starring Cary Grant and Priscilla Lane, costumes by Orry-Kelly. Everett Collection/REX.

CHAPTER THIRTEEN

Page 264: Bette Davis playing the terminally ill Judith Traherne in *Dark Victory* (1939), costumes by Orry-Kelly. George Hurrell/John Kobal Foundation/Getty Images.

Page 267: Jane Wyman in an Orry-Kelly bathing suit in *Doughgirls* (1944), costumes by Orry-Kelly. Snap Stills/REX.

Page 269: The head of Warner Brothers, Jack Warner, astride a lion. Courtesy Barbara Warner Howard. Photo: Anna Howard.

Page 270: Betty Grable and Dan Dailey in *Mother Wore Tights* (1947), costumes by Orry-Kelly. Everett Collection/REX.

Page 273: Louella Parsons with Marilyn Monroe, 1953. Snap Stills/REX.

Page 274: Bette Davis on the set of *Dark Victory* (1939), costumes by Orry-Kelly. Hulton Archive/Sunset Boulevard/CORBIS.

Page 277: Orry-Kelly's mother and friend Eleanor aboard a ship. Courtesy Sue Eggins, The Kiama and District Historical Society.

Page 281: Orry-Kelly with his mother and friend Eleanor. Courtesy the family's collection.

CHAPTER FOURTEEN

Page 282: Jack Lemmon and Tony Curtis in *Some Like It Hot* (1959), costumes by Orry-Kelly. Everett Collection/REX.

Page 287: Postcard of the intersection of Hollywood Boulevard and Vine Street in Hollywood, California. Courtesy of the USC Digital Library.

Page 289: Bebe Daniels at a costume test for *42nd Street* (1933), costumes by Orry-Kelly. Everett Collection/REX.

Page 290: Verree Teasdale modelling an Orry-Kelly gown, 1934. Everett Collection/REX.

Page 295: Fashion Aces at West Coast Style Show, Los Angeles, California. Bettmann Archive/CORBIS.

Page 297: Signed photo of Fanny Brice. Courtesy Barbara Warner Howard. Photo: Anna Howard.

Page 300: Orry-Kelly's home in Hollywood. Courtesy the family's collection.

CHAPTER FIFTEEN

Page 302: Ava Gardner in *One Touch of Venus* (1948), costumes by Orry-Kelly. Everett Collection/REX.

Page 304: Orry-Kelly dressing Ava Gardner in *One Touch of Venus* (1948), costumes by Orry-Kelly. Photofest Digital.

Page 309: Hedda Hopper, Francis Lederer, Mary Astor, Don Ameche, Claudette Colbert, John Barrymore and Elaine Barrie in *Midnight* (1939). Everett Collection/REX

Page 310: Hedda Hopper testifying before a Federal Grand Jury in defence of actress Joan Barry in a paternity case involving Charlie Chaplin, 1944. Bettmann Archive/CORBIS.

CHAPTER SIXTEEN

Page 312: Costume sketch of evening gown by Orry-Kelly. Courtesy Barbara Warner Howard. Photo: Anna Howard.

Page 315: Costume sketch by Orry-Kelly. Courtesy Natasha Rubin.

Page 318: Costume sketch of orange dress by Orry-Kelly. Courtesy Barbara Warner Howard. Photo: Anna Howard.

CHAPTER SEVENTEEN

Page 322: Mitzi Gaynor, Kay Kendall, Taina Elg in *Les Girls* (1957), costumes by Orry-Kelly. Cineclassico/Alamy.

Page 325: Dolores del Rio in *Madame du Barry* (1934), costumes by Orry-Kelly. Everett Collection/REX.

Page 329: *Picture Show* magazine, featuring *Les Girls* (1957). Courtesy Damien Parer.

Page 332: Merle Oberon in *Affectionately Yours* (1941), costumes by Orry-Kelly. Snap Still/REX.

Page 337: Portrait of Kay Kendall from *Les Girls* (1957), costumes by Orry-Kelly. Everett Collection/REX.

Page 342–343: Costume sketches by Orry-Kelly. Courtesy Barbara Warner Howard. Photo: Anna Howard.

CHAPTER EIGHTEEN

Page 344: Marilyn Monroe in *Some Like It Hot* (1959), costumes by Orry-Kelly. Moviestore Collection/REX.

Page 348: Signed photo of Cole Porter. Courtesy Barbara Warner Howard. Photo: Anna Howard.

Page 351: Orry-Kelly seated at a table with actress Bebe Daniels. From the Core Collection biography files of the Margaret Herrick Library, Academy of Motion Picture Arts and Sciences.

Page 353: Errol Flynn in *The Private Lives of Elizabeth and Essex* (1939), costumes by Orry-Kelly. Moviestore Collection/REX.

Page 354: Lili Damita in *The Match King* (1932), costumes by Orry-Kelly. Imagno/Getty Images

Page 356: Ann Warner, Lili Damita, Marlene Dietrich, Jack Warner and Errol Flynn at the opening of Earl Carroll Theatre, 1948. Bettmann Archive/CORBIS.

Page 360: Verree Teasdale wearing gown designed by Orry-Kelly, 1934. Everett Collection/REX.

CHAPTER NINETEEN

Page 362: Natalie Wood in *Gypsy* (1962), costumes by Orry-Kelly. Pictorial Press Ltd/Alamy

Page 365: Publicity photo of stage star Ethel Barrymore in *Declasse*. Courtesy Producers Library.

Page 368: Portrait of Tallulah Bankhead. Moviestore Collection/REX.

Page 371: Bette Davis in *Now, Voyager* (1942), costumes by Orry-Kelly. Moviestore Collection/REX.

Page 372: Katherine Hepburn and Cary Grant in *Holiday* (1938). Moviestore Collection/REX.

Page 377: Fanny Brice as Baby Snooks. Moviestore Collection/REX.

Page 380: Fanny Brice and Constance Collier at a local Hollywood nightclub after a show, 1935. Bettmann Archive/CORBIS.

Page 385: Fanny Brice, Gracie Allen and George Burns goofing around on a tricycle at Franny Brice's birthday party, 1939. Michael Ochs/CORBIS.

CHAPTER TWENTY

Page 390: Rosalind Russell as Mame Dennis in *Auntie Mame* (1958), costumes by Orry-Kelly. Moviestore Collection/REX.

Page 393: Rosalind Russell posing in an Orry-Kelly gown from *Auntie Mame* (1958). Photofest Digital.

Page 399: Postcard from the Hotel del Coronado, featured in *Some Like It Hot* (1959). Collection of the Coronado Historical Association.

Page 401: Marilyn Monroe rehearsing on the train in a scene from *Some Like It Hot* (1959), costumes by Orry-Kelly. Moviestore Collection/REX.

Page 402–403: Orry-Kelly dressing Tony Curtis as a woman and Marilyn Monroe in 'that dress' for *Some Like It Hot* (1959), costumes by Orry-Kelly. Photofest Digital.

Page 404: Sketch of the girls – Tony Curtis and Jack Lemmon – by Orry-Kelly for *Some Like It Hot* (1959), costumes by Orry-Kelly. Courtesy Larry McQueen.

EPILOGUE

Page 408: Close-up of Orry-Kelly. From the Core Collection biography files of the Margaret Herrick Library, Academy of Motion Picture Arts and Sciences.

Page 411: Photo from Orry-Kelly's private collection. Courtesy Barbara Warner Howard. Photo: Anna Howard.

ABOUT THE AUTHOR

Orry George Kelly was born on 31 December 1897 in the small coastal town of Kiama in New South Wales, Australia.

His love of theatre, art and nightlife flourished when he was sent to Sydney at 17 for further study and during a brief stint working in a bank. In 1922 he moved to New York, with ambitions of becoming an actor.

In New York he met other aspiring artists Gracie Allen, George Burns and Jack Benny. He later befriended and shared digs with a young Englishman who was also dreaming of becoming an actor, Archibald Leach, later better known as Cary Grant. In between auditions, he eked out a living designing hand-blocked ties and shawls, then as a painter of murals for nightclubs, speakeasies and department stores. His mural work led to designing titles for silent movies, stage sets and costumes. Armed with sketches of his work, he moved to Hollywood in 1931 and became the head of the costume department at Warner Brothers from 1932 to 1944.

Orry-Kelly went on to become one of Hollywood's most successful and revered costume designers, creating iconic looks for classic films like *Casablanca*, *42nd Street*, *The Maltese Falcon*, *Oklahoma!*, *Some Like It Hot*, *Auntie Mame* and *An American in Paris*. He formed a close collaboration with Bette Davis and designed the costumes for many of her most outstanding films, from her Oscar-award-winning turn in *Jezebel* to *Now, Voyager* and *Dark Victory*.

In a career that spanned more than 30 years and 295 films, Orry-Kelly worked with all the big stars, from Bette Davis, Ingrid Bergman and Barbara Stanwyck to Marilyn Monroe and Jane Fonda. He was nominated for countless awards and won three Academy Awards for *An American in Paris* (1951), *Les Girls* (1958) and *Some Like It Hot* (1959). He created clothes and wrote columns that affected women and fashion worldwide.

Known to his friends as 'Jack', his circle of close friends included the legendary comic star Fanny Brice, Cole Porter and Ann Warner, wife of studio head Jack Warner.

Orry-Kelly died from liver cancer in Los Angeles in 1964. The pallbearers at his funeral were Cary Grant, Tony Curtis and directors Billy Wilder and George Cukor. The eulogy was read by Jack Warner.

THANK YOU

Team Orry at Random House would like to extend a special thank you to the people who helped us make Orry-Kelly's memoir, *Women I've Undressed*, possible.

First and foremost, we'd like to thank Orry-Kelly's Australian family for granting us the privilege of publishing his precious memoir, so carefully preserved in a pillow case for thirty years, and for their generous contribution towards the images we have used to illustrate Orry's fabulous life, both personal and public. We also owe thanks to the family's literary agent, Tara Wynne, of Curtis Brown, for entrusting us with such an extraordinary once-in-a-lifetime project, and for all her help and support throughout the creative process.

On that note, we have been blessed to have the most generous and creative collaborators in Damien Parer and Gillian Armstrong, the producer and director of the upcoming documentary film of Orry-Kelly's life, *Women He's Undressed*. If it wasn't for the tireless detective work of Gillian and her team, this priceless memoir would never have been unearthed. We are indebted to Damien and Gillian for their generosity in sharing so much information about the film and giving us access to so many of the wonderful images and sources they and their team discovered. We're also grateful to Damien for sharing images from his personal collection and to Gillian Armstrong and Barbara Warner Howard for allowing us access to a treasure trove of images and photographs Orry left to Barbara's mother and Orry's dear friend Ann Warner. A special thanks is also due to Naomi Hall for going above and beyond in helping us track down images, FrenchBaker for their assistance, and Anna Howard, the film's cinematographer who took many of the stills from the Orry-Kelly archive.

Many thanks also to Oscar-winning costume designer Catherine Martin for her wonderful Foreword, and the collectors and image agencies for helping us find Orry treasures, especially Simon Kain at ITN Source, Deborah Nadoolman Landis, Natasha Rubin, Linda Goldberg, Sue Eggins of the Kiama and District Historical Society, the State Library of NSW and the Margaret Herrick Library at the Academy of Motion Picture Arts and Sciences.

Last but not least, we owe an enormous debt to designer Christa Moffitt of Christabella Designs, for her exquisite work on the design of the cover and internals of *Women I've Undressed*. Her boundless creativity and her work ethic are legendary.

First published in Great Britain in 2016 by Allen & Unwin
First published in Australia in 2015 by Ebury Press
Copyright © Gosling Holdings Pty Ltd, 2015
Foreword © Catherine Martin, 2015
Afterword © Gillian Armstrong, 2015

Allen & Unwin
c/o Atlantic Books
Ormond House
26–27 Boswell Street
London WC1N 3JZ
Phone: 020 7269 1610
Fax: 020 7430 0916
Email: UK@allenandunwin.com
Web: www.allenandunwin.co.uk

A CIP catalogue record for this book is available from the British Library.

Hardback ISBN 978 1 76029 095 5

Design and typesetting by Christa Moffitt, Christabella Designs
Front jacket image: costume sketch for Bette Davis in *Bordertown* (1935) by Orry-Kelly.
Back jacket image: Marilyn Monroe wearing Orry-Kelly in *Some Like it Hot*. Moviestore Collection/REX.
Author photo from the Core Collection biography files of the Margaret Herrick Library,
Academy of Motion Picture Arts and Sciences.

Printed in China by Leo Paper Products.

10 9 8 7 6 5 4 3 2 1